"I didn't kill you because of the new rice seeds," says my host Tu Rang, former VC political officer.

New rice seeds. To me, they're one of the world's most powerful tools for peace. That's why I made the green revolution my profession.

We've just passed Duc Long. I remember friends being killed in a sampan north of this village, and Tu Rang must have ordered the ambush. I know I'm safe, but I never traveled this canal without an M-16.

I'd thought a lot about what my first return to Vietnam would be like. But I never imagined that my hosts would be local VC from those days—who would remember me.

I'm not the first American veteran to go back. But I may be the only one who has returned to an area as remote as Chuong Thien Province.

"Has any other American been here since the war?" I'd asked.

"No, you're the first foreigner—of any nationality—to return since 1975."

I can do it only because I work with rice.

A DRAGON LIVES FOREVER

War and Rice in Vietnam's Mekong Delta 1969—1991, and Beyond

Thomas R. Hargrove

IVY BOOKS • NEW YORK

Ivy Books
Published by Ballantine Books
Copyright © 1994 by Thomas R. Hargrove

Library of Congress Catalog Card Number: 93-94986

ISBN 0-8041-0672-X

Manufactured in the United States of America

First Edition: April 1994

10 9 8 7 6 5 4 3 2 1

Dragon:
An imaginary creature ... they usually breathe fire and are associated with water. Most dragons are symbols of evil, but in China, some are beneficient, and the dragon was the symbol of the emperor. Dragons are commonly associated with the gods, and in Christian symbolism they are seen as creatures of the devil. They often require human sacrifice.

—*Electronic Encyclopedia*

Come not between the dragon and his wrath.
—William Shakespeare, *King Lear*

The Mekong is one of the largest rivers in the world; it is 4,220 km (2,620 mi) long, springs from the Himalayas and flows through China, Burma, Laos, Kampuchea, and Thailand before crossing ... through the plains of South Vietnam. This portion of the river is called Cuu Long (Nine Dragons), a name inspired by the fact that the river flows into the East Sea through nine estuaries.

Hanoi was chosen as the capital of Vietnam by King Ly Nam De in 542. In 1010 ... King Ly Thai To officially renamed the capital Thang Long (Soaring Dragon). Legend has it that ... when King Ly Thai To arrived by boat from the former capital of Hoa Lu ... at a ferry on the Red River (Hanoi), a golden dragon came close to the regal boat, then soared into the sky. The king took this as a good omen, and decided to name the country's capital after the image of the soaring dragon. In 1831 ... Thang Long was renamed Hanoi.

—*Vietnam, My Homeland*

... the original gunships were modified World War II–vintage twin-engine C-47 Gooneybird cargo planes. Redesignated the AC-47, with the more elegant name Dragonship, they were known to ground soldiers as "Puffs" (from the song "Puff, the Magic Dragon") ...

—Harry G. Summers, Jr., *Vietnam War Almanac*

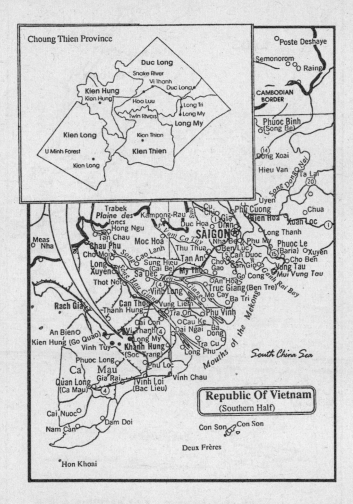

Choung Thien Province

Duc Long
Snake River
Vi Thanh
Kien Hung
Kien Hung
Hoa Luu
Duc Long
Long Tri
Twin Rivers
Long My
Kien Long
Long My
Kien Long
U Minh Forest
Kien Thien
Kien Thien
Kien Long

Poste Deshaye
Semonorom
Raing
CAMBODIAN
BORDER
Phuoc Binh
(Song Be)

Trabek
Plaine des
Joncs
Kampong-Rau
Hong Ngu
Tan Chau
Chau Phu
Cho Moi
Long
Xuyen
Sa Dec
Thot Not
Rach Gia
Thanh Hung
Can Tho
An Bien
Kien Hung (Go Quao)
Vinh Tuy
Phuoc Long
Ca
Mau
Quan Long
(Ca Mau)
Gia Rai
Cai Nuoc
Nam Can
Dam Doi

Dong Xoai
Hieu Van
Ta Lai
Uyen
Chua
Kampong-Rau
Cu
Cho
Gia
Duc Hoa
Dinh
Bien Hoa
Xuan Loc
Long Thanh
Moc Hoa
Cao Lanh
Thu Thua
Nha Be
Phu My
Phuoc Le
(Baria)
Xuyen
Sung Hieu
(Cai Be)
Tan An
Ben Luc
Can Duoc
Cho Ben
Vung Tau
My Tho
Cho
Gao
Go Cong
Mui Vung Tau
Vinh Long
An Hoa
Truc Giang (Ben Tre)
Vung Liem
Mo Cay
Ba Tri
Tra On
Phu Vinh
Cai Con
Cau Ke
Ba
Dong
Dai Ngai
Tra Cu
Long My
Khanh Hung
(Soc Trang)
Phu Loc
Vinh Chau
Vinh Loi
(Bac Lieu)

SAIGON

South China Sea
Mouths of the Mekong
Ganh Rai Bay

Republic Of Vietnam
(Southern Half)

Con Son
Con Son
Deux Frères
Hon Khoai

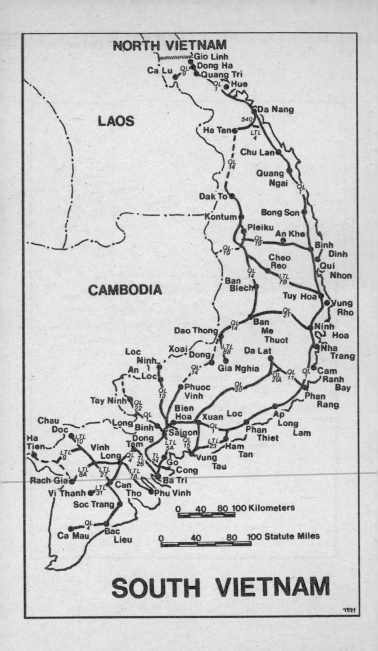

Transition 1

I'm stunned. I struggle for the right words, then simply ask, "Why didn't you kill me, Tu Rang?"

"Because you brought the new rice seeds, and our farmers needed them."

"But did you know I was an army officer?"

"Of course. Your civilian clothes didn't fool anyone."

The former Viet Cong and I look into each other's face, something we never did eighteen years ago. He's smiling, but he's hard—it shows. He's also telling the truth. I can sense it.

"I was less than a kilometer away whenever you traveled this canal in 1969," Tran Van Rang says. Today, Tu Rang is vice-chairman of the Vi Thanh People's Committee. But two decades ago, he was the Viet Cong political officer for this zone. I know that political officers held ultimate power in the Communist infrastructure—they gave orders to military commanders.

"You were entering *my* territory when you came here," Tu Rang continues. "The local farmers all supported the Revolutionary Forces, and reported on you. But intelligence officers were my main target."

This trip is getting heavy, I think as our sampan cuts north through the muddy waters of the Xa No Canal.

"I didn't kill you because of the new rice seeds."

New rice seeds. To me, they're one of the world's most powerful tools for peace. That's why I made the green revolution my profession.

But I learned about those seeds here, in the midst of car-

1

nage. Had there been no Vietnam War, rice wouldn't be my life. Now I must face a new reality; those rice seeds probably saved my life.

It's 4 June 1988, and we're in Hau Giang Province, one hundred and fifty miles south of Ho Chi Minh City. But to me, it's still 1969 and this is a terrible place called Chuong Thien Province.

Palm trees arch over the canal and thatch houses line each side. A green carpet of rice fields shimmers endlessly in both directions. The waterway is a kaleidoscope of color. That bothers me, but why?

The women rowing the sampans wear bright red, yellow, or blue blouses over black pants. The colors contrast beautifully against the cafe au lait waters of the canal and the shimmering palms and emerald rice. Then it hits me—*the colors*. The lower Mekong Delta is beautiful and peaceful—but I remember it as ugly, dangerous, and one of the most tragic places on earth.

We've just passed Duc Long. I remember friends being killed in a sampan north of this village, and Tu Rang must have ordered the ambush. I know I'm safe, but I never traveled this canal without an M-16.

I had thought a lot about my first return to Vietnam since the war ended. What would it be like? I never imagined that my hosts would be local VC from those days—who would remember me.

I'm not the first American veteran to go back. But I may be the only one who has returned to an area as remote as Chuong Thien Province.

"Has any other American been here since the war?" I'd asked earlier. My question was translated by Dr. Vo Tong Xuan, vice-president of the University of Can Tho. Xuan did his M.S. and Ph.D. work at the International Rice Research Institute in the Philippines. That's where I'd worked since 1973. We're old friends, and Xuan arranged this trip to show me rice production in the Mekong Delta today. Why did I ask to inspect rice in the old Chuong Thien Province?

"No, you're the first foreigner—of *any* nationality—to be in the lower Ca Mau Peninsula since 1975."

I can do it only because I work with rice.

CHAPTER I
The Diary I Never Wrote

Los Baños, Philippines, 1987

It was Saturday evening, 10 October 1987, in Los Baños, forty-five miles south of Manila, but I was back in the steaming Mekong Delta in the 1969 monsoon season.

My air-conditioned den was cluttered with ragged manuscripts, stained by paper clips and staples that had rusted with time. I had worked hard at my desk since noon, but I wasn't tired. Susan was visiting her mother in Texas, so I'd devote the weekend to the novel.

I had edited chapters with a soft-lead pencil all afternoon. Tomorrow morning, I'd give them to Cynthia, the Filipina secretary I had hired on off-hours, and pick up hard copy from edited manuscripts that she had captured on PC disk today.

How much text did I actually write in 1971 and 1972? I thought . . . four hundred pages? Six hundred? I hadn't counted pages, but thank God I'd drafted the book while Vietnam was still fresh. I couldn't do it now.

Characters swirled through my mind, and it was hard to distinguish among the real, the fiction, the ghosts. Lt. Dan Bridges worried me because I didn't want to be accused of writing about myself . . . either romanticizing or covering up what *I* did in Vietnam. Lieutenant Bridges was *not* Lieutenant Hargrove, but other characters were real: Ba Lien, the Vietnamese farmer who planted the first high-yielding rice varieties . . . Monique, beautiful and tragic, born of a mixed marriage in Vietnam but, in her mind, French . . . Khang, my teenage interpreter.

I'd created other names for composites of men and women

3

I knew in Chuong Thien Province. My God, that was seventeen years ago. But the fictional characters had grown more real than the flesh and blood from which I'd created them. I know Sgt. Joe Culver better tonight than I knew the *real* Joe—who was a little of every professional army sergeant I'd known. Nguyen Van Cam, the hate-filled village chief whose family the Viet Cong had assassinated, was a combination of many Vietnamese I knew. I don't like my synthesis of Norm Olsen and Frank Gillespie as Robert Cantwell. Norm and Frank were so different, but there isn't room in the novel for two strong civilians.

Why did I make Enrique, the Puerto Rican sergeant who once led a mutiny against my cooking, a Mexican? Maybe I should change him to the *real* Enrique.

I'd hit another frustrating gap in the story—something I wished I had written that winter of 1971. How do I move MAT 96, my fictional U.S. Army Mobile Advisory Team, out of the Vietnamese village of Nuoc Trong? I'd set the last half of the book in Pham Dong in Kien Hung District, an ethnically Cambodian region of Chuong Thien, but I never wrote a transition. Now I have to explain why the team leaves Nuoc Trong before finishing the new South Vietnamese outpost.

I stared at the computer screen, thinking deeply, fingers ready to capture memories, then modify and edit them. I don't want to create pure fiction, I'll base my book on things that *really* happened—not always to me, but to people I knew in Chuong Thien Province.

I thought . . . maybe I can use that big, straight-arrow lieutenant, the University of San Francisco graduate with the engraving on his silver bar—and how the colonel transferred his team to another village after the lieutenant actually kicked his village chief—his counterpart, whom he advised—from a jeep into the mud in front of the local Vietnamese troops. He thought the chief was queer, and was making a pass when the chief reached across the seat and grabbed his balls. How could the lieutenant . . . what was his name? . . . not know that ball grabbing was the way good ol' boys in the Ca Mau Peninsula showed camaraderie? Thinking about the incident made me laugh, softly and genuinely, but ironically. It really wasn't funny; the chief would have killed that lieutenant if the troops hadn't held him back and taken his rifle.

But what was engraved on his lieutenant's bar? And did the

higher brass give him any flak for wearing a bright silver bar instead of the black, camouflaged insignia that was regulation for Vietnam? I remember that his fiancée gave him the bar, inscribed "Our Father Who are in Heaven, hallowed be Thy name . . ." or was it "Yea, though I walk through the valley of the shadow of death . . ."? Anyway, maybe I could make that lieutenant kicking the village chief my reason for moving MAT 96 out of Nuoc Trong . . . but Sergeant Culver has to be the man who kicks him. I started punching keys.

"Hi, Dad! I'm home from the pool." Miles's interruption startled me. "And before you ask—yes, I've done my homework."

I hit "Escape-Save-Enter" on the keyboard, then turned to my fourteen-year-old. "Yeah? I'll believe it when I see it. Show me the homework."

"Dad, please . . . get off my case, will you? You'll see the homework in an hour, okay? Are you still working on that book? When will you finish it?"

Miles seemed eager to talk, not moody like so much of the time. I'd better talk to the kid. Since I started on the book again, I've felt almost resentful of anything, after work, that interferes with my writing. I have so little spare time to write. Then I thought—*save!* . . . no, I've already saved the last text.

"It's going okay, I guess, considering that I'm working with words I wrote three years before you were born." I talked with Miles like he was a man, which sometimes worked. What bothered me was that my two sons *would* be men . . . too soon.

"I have two main regrets, Miles. The first is that I didn't finish this book after I got out of the army, when I drafted it. I meant to, but things happened . . . difficult things and memories that made me put the manuscript on a closet shelf and leave it there . . . until last week.

"But my deepest regret is that I didn't keep a diary in Vietnam. Charley Scruggs, the editor of *Progressive Farmer* magazine, sent me a special letter just before I shipped out. He wrote that whatever happened, *I must* keep a diary. Charley's greatest regret was that he didn't record his experiences in World War II.

"But I was twenty-five back then, and knew I'd always remember the names of rivers and villages and people, Vietnamese phrases . . . and the powerful events. I was wrong, I've forgotten so much. I wrote a lot of it into my novel right after Nam, but a diary might have details as I saw them then."

"But, Dad, you *kept* a diary in Vietnam."

"No, Miles, I wrote only for the first week or ten days . . . then, like a fool, I quit writing." I paused. "Not because of emotional problems, like in the movies, but because I was too busy or too lazy to write down what was happening.

"If you're ever in a similar situation—and I pray to God you won't be—keep a diary."

"But, Dad . . ." Miles reached to a packed bookshelf and pulled out two black ledgers with red spines. "Remember, I asked if I could read these last year, and you said okay?"

"Yes, but I told you then, Miles, those ledgers cover only my first few days in Vietnam. I may have written eight or nine pages, no more."

"*Dad . . . I read your diary*, but we never discussed it. Dad, *look at this.*" Miles opened a ledger and flipped pages before me.

I was stunned. Those pages were crammed with words—in my handwriting. Miles handed me the first ledger.

I opened the inside cover and read. Thomas R. Hargrove 05421765, 1LT INF, MAC-V Advisory Team 73, IV CTZ, APO San Francisco 96215. Vi Thanh, Chuong Thien Province.

I skimmed the ledger pages—my entries were in different inks, but the handwriting was usually clear. I read names, places. Most entries were concise, with little emotion. I had recorded the deaths of friends factually, much like I'd described the "miracle rices" from the Philippines that were now so much a part of my life. Those pages were full of memories that flashed back as I read. The incidents were real, but until then I had never recorded them because, even when I drafted my book in 1971, I knew I had not written a diary.

But here were about three hundred pages . . . of diary.

"Look, Dad!" Miles interrupted my thoughts. "You even drew a map of an operation where some of your buddies got killed. *Dad, I know your writing. You wrote this diary, and you drew this map!*"

Miles turned to a sketch that I had drawn on 7 September 1969. My God, that's the "death trap," I thought. I stared at the LZ, the landing zone. The map was crude—but it showed the intersecting tree lines of Viet Cong positions. At the mouth of the trap were three huts that sheltered VC machine guns. That was down by the Snake River in Kien Hung District, where choppers dropped my fictional Lt. Dan Bridges—but I see here that his real name was Richard Carlile, how could I have forgotten that?—and the company of Cambodian troops into certain death. Along with Sgt. Joe Culver, and Sutton, the new lieutenant—now I know that he was 2d Lt. Stephen W. Young, from Collingswood, New Jersey.

The final chapter of my novel was based on how so many men died that day. Then I remembered that Carlile survived the trap. The bullet had lodged in his brain, and he was evacuated Stateside. Months later, he was still in a coma. But I'm sure he's dead now.

"Dad, how could you *not* remember writing all this?"

"I don't know . . ."

I gently turned to the first entry of the ledger:

1030 p.m. 19 June 1969. I'd never have believed it. Just left Travis AFB on a Braniff Military Air Transport flight. Stewardess comes over the intercom "Welcome to Braniff Airlines flight to Saigon, Vietnam, with en route stops in Honolulu and Clark Field, Philippines."

I then skimmed the second ledger and found my last entry in Vietnam:

19 May 70. Today is Buddha's birthday—more important, it's also Ho Chi Minh's birthday—VC mortared Vi Thanh last night—6 or 7 rounds hit 31st ARVN Regt. Also a plastic mine on one—

I hadn't finished the sentence.

The next diary entry was dated 22 June 1970 and was also written in Asia—but on a train from Bangkok to Chiang Mai, that ancient center of Buddhism:

Have been a civilian for 3 days. Maybe later I'll feel differently but right now I feel real contempt and resentment toward the Army. The whole situation is so tragic, I just feel disgusted and want to get away from it all. . . Vietnam is like a bad dream. My tour wasn't so bad and I didn't suffer much personally, but I saw so many who did.

Vietnam was so fresh, as I rode that train into the mountains
of northern Thailand, that I saw personal suffering, and watching others suffer, as very different states. They are, of course,
but time seems to blur the distinction. I read on.

I hope I can go back to Vi Thanh in 10 yrs and find a stable
government and no more war and a prospering economy,
and know that I had a little to do with it. But I'm not sure
that will be the case. Especially if Cambodia falls.
If VN goes, what will happen to all the people I knew and
worked with and helped in Chuong Thien Province?

Yeah, what happened to Khang? His brother headed the
Vietnamese side of *Phuong Hoang*—the Phoenix Program—in
Chuong Thien, the program to neutralize the Viet Cong infra-
structure. No, the end couldn't have been nice for my inter-
preter. What about Father Hoa, Monique, Captain Hong?
Those questions had haunted me since South Vietnam fell.

The month before I left was the worst of the year, in VC activity. Vi Thanh was mortared and rocketed 4 or 5 times,
plus mines ... hamlet, village chiefs assassinated. SFC
Walker, the medic at Long My ... and a fine man, stepped
on a mine and got a leg blown off. He died in the hospital
at Can Tho ... 1LT Steve Nabbin was with him and got a
back and arm full of shrapnel. Called in his own
Medevac—he never came back ... sent to Japan. Another
U.S. sgt, an advisor to ARVN's 31st Rgt of the 21st Div,
was killed ... set down on top of a VC Bn. But I didn't
know him.

"Dad ... what's wrong? You look like you've seen a
ghost."
I felt like I'd met my own ghost, but I couldn't explain that
to my son ... not then.
I read about walking among thousands of stark, white tombstones in a French military cemetery near the American air
base at Tan Son Nhut. The stones had been raked by machine-
gun fire, probably during the Viet Cong's furious 1968 Tet Offensive. Crosses were carved into most of the stones, but many
were marked by Muslim crescents. All bore the epitaph *Mort
pour la France* ... 1951 ... 1953 ... I looked up as a U.S.

Air Force F-4 Phantom streaked off on a mission, and a Medevac chopper barreled into the 3d Field Hospital with a load of wounded GIs. Being in that French cemetery brought back another memory ... I'd forgotten about the Viet Cong cemetery, its broken, lime-green tombstones marked with red stars. Where was that, Kien Thien District? Maybe the diary will tell me.

Something else bothered me about the diary, something strange. I skimmed the ledgers. Then I realized—except for the "death trap," little of what I had written in the diary was in my novel. I remembered a moody Sunday afternoon a few years before when I took my manuscript off the closet shelf and skimmed it and wondered why I'd chosen certain events, not always the most dramatic, to fictionalize. Why didn't I write about calling that air strike on a U.S. Navy PBR boat, dropped somehow into a rice field from a Skycrane chopper? Or about the official Viet Cong policy on the "miracle rice"? I'm probably the only living American who knows that, and I know only because I asked during the interrogation of that VC political officer who defected.

It's like something drove me to write first into my novel the memories that were vivid back then, but I didn't record in my diary—the diary I never wrote. How can I explain that?

This diary will open windows, I realized. Some of those windows have been shut for a long time—and I must have closed them purposely, but at a subconscious level. I'll open those windows—but I must open them carefully.

Later, I took a long walk in the monsoon drizzle, through the palm trees and bougainvillea around my home, still clutching my diaries. Then I returned to my computer.

CHAPTER II
The Letter, the Diary, the Novel

Los Baños, 10 October 1987. Vi Thanh, May 1969

Finding the diary shook me. An hour later I was still stunned. Hargrove, did you *really forget* writing three hundred pages of diary? I thought deeply. Yeah, I really forgot, and that's scary.

How? I don't know.

But you set this evening aside to edit the novel, Hargrove, so do it. I stared at the ragged manuscripts, then at my computer screen, but I kept looking at those two black-and-red ledgers. I couldn't edit, or write.

That damned letter started this, only a week ago. It was from a professor of English literature at a private college in Redlands, California. Bruce McAllister had a strange request— for information on the role that *rice* played in the Vietnam War. Why would he want that?

Questions like: What rice varieties did farmers plant in North and South Vietnam in the late 1960s? Did they grow deepwater rice along the Red River? In the Mekong Delta?

I'm head of communication and publications at the International Rice Research Institute (IRRI), so his letter landed on my desk.

McAllister was writing a novel, *Dream Baby*, "set in Vietnam during the war years." A novel? He had *lots* of questions—specific questions—about angles to tie rice and the war.

Is this guy writing about the *pacification program*? I skimmed the rest of his letter. Probably not. McAllister asked about IR8, the IRRI rice variety that revolutionized Asian agriculture, but he seemed especially interested in North Vietnam: Did farmers in the Red River Delta grow IR8 in the early 1970s? What types of rice would Montagnards, or hill tribesmen, grow around Dien Bien Phu, the valley in North Vietnam where the French made their last, tragic stand in 1954?

His book must be about Lurps, long-range reconnaisance patrols, or maybe the Green Berets. The theme is probably clandestine operations—over the fence and into the North.

But why all those questions about the IRRI rice seeds? Could McAllister be onto the war *I knew*? Almost nothing—certainly, no novel—has been published about *that* war—not yet, anyway. My book comes closest, but it's still sitting on that closet shelf.

I sensed that the novelist was not a Vietnam veteran, and that was a relief. Now, how do I answer his letter? Can I send him an IRRI publications list and ignore the questions? No, I can't do that, he's writing a Vietnam novel. Besides, McAllister wrote to IRRI at the suggestion of Dr. Walter Falcon of the Food Research Institute at Stanford University. Wally is a friend of IRRI. I'll never finish the novel anyway.

I started answering the letter on Saturday afternoon, 3 October, and wrote for two hours. On Sunday, I spent six more hours at my home computer, giving McAllister more information about rice and the war than he could possibly use.

Monday morning brought me back to the pressure and excitement of work at IRRI. My in-box was filled with messages that arrived over the weekend: telexes, electronic mail, and letters from across Asia, Africa, Latin America. I gave my disk with the McAllister letter to Elma Banilbo, my secretary, and asked her to output it on the laser printer when she had time. Elma handed me twelve single-spaced pages that afternoon:

Dear Mr. McAllister:
Your letter almost frightened me. I knew I could spend hours or days answering your questions about rice, the world's most important and fascinating crop; and its role in that awesome experience, the Vietnam War.

Maybe I should explain. In 1969–70, I was a U.S. Army first lieutenant assigned to MAC-V [Military Assistance Command-Vietnam] Advisory Team 73 in what was then called Chuong Thien Province, almost at the southern tip of

the Mekong Delta. We were advisers to the Vietnamese
military and government under CORDS, or Civil Oper-
ations/Revolutionary Development Support.

Chuong Thien was an awful place, especially for a dryland cotton farmer from West Texas. The average elevation
was less than 2 feet, and 97 percent of its land was covered
by water—rice fields or swamp—during the six-month monsoon season.

It was also a Viet Cong stronghold. One month, the CIA
and U.S. military classified Chuong Thien as Vietnam's
least-secure province. Putting it another way, we were the
Viet Cong's most *securely held* province.

A dozen U.S. advisers were killed in Chuong Thien that
year. Five were ambushed in sampans, our only transport
along the canals and rivers during the monsoon season. *No
one* survived a sampan ambush.

Those casualties don't sound high, but only 160 Americans
were stationed in Chuong Thien, and only 30 or 40 advisers
worked outside the small Army compound at provincial HQ
in Vi Thanh. If Chuong Thien were a typical province, we'd
have had only 7,000—instead of 550,000—U.S. troops in
Vietnam in 1969.

But our largest losses were to hepatitis, the A strain,
spread by filth and bad water or food. Most hepatitis in a
regular army unit in the Nam of 1969 was strain B, spread
by needles.

The international media seldom mentioned Chuong Thien,
because Vietnamese mostly slaughtered Vietnamese down
there. No "regular" U.S. Army or Marine units ever fought
that far south. The only Americans were advisers to the
South Vietnamese. Most were in the "pacification
program"—winning hearts and minds in the countryside . . . or at least, denying the VC use of those symbolic
organs.

For us, it was a different kind of war, because hearts,
minds, and blood mingled freely in Chuong Thien.

I was an Infantry officer with B.S. and M.S. degrees in
both agricultural science and journalism. That was a rare
background in those days when most educated men found
ways to avoid an unpopular war.

Rice was the lifeblood of the Mekong Delta and, in a
sense, what the war was all about. Seventy percent of

Chuong Thien's population was rice farmers. Their support was crucial to "Vietnamization," the U.S. strategy for getting out of the quagmire. Generating popular support for GVN, the South Vietnamese Government, would allow American forces to transfer combat responsibility to ARVN, the Army of the Republic of Vietnam.

The legendary John Paul Vann ran the war in the Mekong Delta. Vann reviewed my records, saw my farm and educational background, and assigned me to Chuong Thien, the only province in the Mekong Delta without an agricultural adviser. The word was, none would go there.

IRRI had released IR8, the high-yielding variety that launched the Green Revolution in Asian agriculture, in late 1966. It played a significant—but almost undocumented—role in the Vietnam War.

President Lyndon B. Johnson had visited IRRI, accompanied by Philippine President Ferdinand Marcos, in October 1966, just before flying to Cam Ranh Bay "to visit our boys over there." LBJ appreciated farmers, and went into the IRRI experimental fields to see, first-hand, IR8. He pressured the U.S. Agency for International Development to promote the hardy variety in Vietnam.

Meanwhile, the first IR8 seeds were smuggled into Vietnam in 1967 by my old friend José Ona, a Filipino agronomist who had done his M.S. research at IRRI and later became a USAID rice specialist for the Delta. A friend at IRRI had stolen those seeds from IRRI experimental plots.

Ona had the IR8 seeds planted at a *hoi chanh* (VC defector) center in Vinh Long Province. Ironically, turncoat Viet Cong grew the first IR8 crop in Vietnam.

Joe then set up demonstration plots in each province of the Mekong Delta . . . and the seeds spread. Farmers had planted IR8 on almost 1,000 hectares (about 4 square miles) in Chuong Thien when I arrived in July 1969.

I could spot the semidwarf variety easily from choppers because it looked like a crew cut. IR8 had short, stiff stems that held it erect, while the tall traditional varieties fell over and lay flat. Thus, IR8 could convert nutrients to heavy heads of grain, and hold them upright.

That genetic trait made IR8 outyield any rice that tropical Asia had ever known. Farmers started harvesting 5 or 6 tons

per hectare from fields where production had stagnated at 1
or 1.5 tons for centuries.

The Western press called IR8 the "miracle rice." Its official name in Vietnam was *Lua Than Nong*, or "Rice of the
Farming God." But Vietnamese farmers quickly dubbed IR8
Lua Honda—because one good crop bought a new motor-
bike.

I brought IR8 seeds to farmers across Chuong Thien, a
province torn brutally by the war, to farmers who suffered as
much as any people I have ever known. We traveled mostly
by sampan on those brown-water canals and rivers with
Vietnamese agricultural cadre and soldiers. The new rice
seeds were the only good thing I saw happen there.

To me, new seeds now offer the world a chance for peace.
Maybe that's why rice improvement became my profession
soon after I left Vietnam.

But I learned about those seeds in a setting of death. Rice
became my life in Chuong Thien Province.

Information is scarce about how IR8 and other IRRI varieties spread in North Vietnam. I've read that in 1968 or
1969, an Eastern European vessel—I believe it was Polish—
purchased a shipload of IR8 at Dhaka (then in East Pakistan) and quietly off-loaded the seeds at Haiphong, the main
NVN port.

Farmers in NVN's Red River Delta probably grew IR8 by
the early 1970s—but they weren't told that the new seeds
were bred at an institute then funded entirely by the Ford
and Rockefeller Foundations, spawned by capitalism.

IR8 was called *Nong Nghiep* 8, or "Agriculture 8," in the
North.

About the mountains around Dien Bien Phu. Even today,
farmers plant traditional upland or dryland rice varieties of
the "bulu" type, and grow them like wheat or corn. The
bulus have long, beautiful panicles of heavy grain, and can
tolerate drought. But they yield no more than 1 ton per hectare. Montagnards grow hundreds of varieties for special pur-
poses. Some are sticky, some are aromatic, some are grown
only for candies or rice wine. Farmers harvest bulu rices
panicle-by-panicle with small *ani-ani* knives.

Deepwater rice is far more common in the Mekong than
in the Red River Delta. A DWR plant can elongate to 18
feet with rising floodwater, and grow in water as deep as 12

feet. Farmers in SVN sometimes harvest DWR from boats. The DWRs sprout roots not only at the base, but also on their stem nodes, to absorb nutrients from silt in the water.

During floods, a farmer's DWR crop sometimes uproots and floats downriver—for another farmer to harvest.

An angle you might use, if you write about DWR, is that An Giang, the heart of the DWR region, was SVN's most secure province. Why? An Giang was the religious center of the *Hoa Hao* sect of Buddhism. In the 1950s the Viet Minh murdered the HH founder and spiritual leader. Every HH swore vengeance against the Communists. The HH hated the VC, and so became our most reliable troops.

The HH probably practiced ceremonial cannibalism. I never witnessed it, but other U.S. advisers and VN counterparts swore they attended HH ceremonies where troops ate pieces of the livers of slain VC, usually the night before an operation.

The HH also used marijuana in religious ceremonies.

In 1986 I read that today's VN Army was fighting bandits in An Giang Province. Those "bandits," I suspect, were HH who still refused to accept Communist control.

I wrote pages more about rice and the war. But somehow the letter ended with thoughts on the *literature* of war.

Your book intrigues me because I read almost every new book, especially fiction, published on the VN war. I'm waiting for the "great VN war novel," but haven't found it yet. The best was one of the first: *Fields of Fire* by James Webb who, in June of 1987, became U.S. Secretary of the Navy at age 41. I also greatly admire Philip Caputo's *A Rumor of War* and, even more, *Del Corso's Gallery*.

But have any of those books even been considered for a Pulitzer Prize?[1] Vietnam has not yet produced literature like *The Red Badge of Courage* or *All Quiet on the Western Front* or *A Farewell to Arms* or *From Here to Eternity* or *The Winds of War*.

---

[1] Two years later, the 1989 Pulitzer Prize for nonfiction was awarded to *A Bright Shining Lie: John Paul Vann and America in Vietnam*. Veteran war correspondent Neil Sheehan authored the biography of the man who assigned me to Chuong Thien Province.

An excellent high school English teacher back in West Texas, Mrs. Eunis Yantiz, taught that all great literature is based on one, or a combination of, four themes: Man Against Nature, Man Against Man, Man Against God, Man Against Himself.

The main theme of the great VN novel *must be* "Man Against Himself."

World War I novels—the best, I think—used that theme. But most WWII literature was "Man Against Man"—WWII was much "cleaner and more moral" then WWI or Vietnam.

Why didn't Korea produce any "great" war novels? Korea had all the essential elements.

Back to VN. I assume, from your letter, that you did not serve in Nam. I can tell, within the first three pages of each new novel, if the author is a veteran—soldiers' slang, the language of radio transmissions, details about weapons and ammo and artillery—but more than that, *the sense of being there*.

You should work closely with VN veterans to capture that sense.

Last, I do not consider this long response to your request for information about rice in Vietnam an imposition, because I *wanted* to write it. I should record what I know about rice in that war while it's still in my memory. Maybe this letter will be the start of an article—but where would I publish it?

Incidentally, I have about 500 manuscript pages, written in the early 1970s, of an unfinished novel about a lieutenant on an advisory team in the Mekong Delta in 1969–70.

Maybe I should force myself to finish that novel . . .

I signed and was about to mail the letter when I thought: Hargrove, do you *really* want to send this? You wrote this letter for *yourself*, not McAllister. My own Vietnam novel doesn't focus on rice, but the IRRI seeds are part of it. Some events described in this letter are also in *my* book. Others could be.

That night, I took the stack of old novel manuscripts from the closet shelf. I knew that reading the scrambled chapters was a serious move, because I remembered Ames, Iowa, in the spring of 1977. Thank God I found the strength to push that door shut before Chuong Thien destroyed me.

So why am I with her again? I left Chuong Thien for good

that terrible black spring, and swore I'd never take her back . . . didn't I? But I left her other times, too . . . 1970 . . . again in '72 . . . I erased the thought, and continued reading.

But I'm an editor. I had to take a pencil and rewrite copy as I read. That's intuition.

Late that night, I edited my letter to the novelist. Professional ethics demanded that I leave in all technical and historic details about rice and Vietnam. *But not my own story.* I slashed everything personal from the letter, harshly, but with caution.

I reedited on Tuesday night, and finally mailed the mutilated letter—now half the length of the original version—to McAllister on Wednesday.

That afternoon, I hired Cynthia to rekey those torn and faded chapters in Microsoft Word.

I spent the next three nights doing what, when my head finally cleared in 1977, I'd sworn never to do again. I threw myself back into Chuong Thien Province.

I worked on the novel past midnight every evening, barely taking time to eat the dinners that Diding, our maid, brought to my den on a tray. This time, *I* was in control of Vietnam, not vice versa. I was running strong, and I *would* finish the novel.

Then tonight I find that diary . . . *what's going on here?*

I set the diary aside and shuffled through my novel until I found the crisp, laser-printed chapter 1 that Cynthia had given me that morning. But I flipped to the back of the file, to the original document, scarred by half a dozen edits in pencil and fading inks. Most pages were held together by yellowed, brittle Scotch tape.

Back in 1971 I wrote my first draft like two book ends . . . I don't know why. I first wrote chapter 1, where Lt. Dan Bridges arrives in Vi Thanh. That was partly me, back in 1969 . . . but it wasn't *really* me. Next I wrote "The Final Chapter"—that's the title I gave it. There, eight months later, Bridges and a new second lieutenant and Sergeant Culver die on an operation in the "death trap." That was 1st Lt. Richard Carlile and 2d Lt. Stephen Young and a sergeant . . . but I didn't know that until tonight.

Then I wrote about thirty more stand-alone episodes as fast as I could in those days of strike-on type. I called them "chapters," but most were only fictionalized slices of life and death in Chuong Thien. I didn't try to keep events in sequence; I wrote whatever came to my head.

I would capture vivid memories and combine them with imagination to create scenes. I could easily edit those chapters, later, into a war novel that flowed. *That's what I thought, in 1971.*

I read chapter 1. The first few pages bothered me, but *why?* Partly because it didn't begin quite that way. My own story, I mean. *But the book's not about me*, it's fiction, just set in a *very real place* . . . one of the saddest places on earth. Yeah, Chuong Thien was real . . . as real as she lurks in my memory.

I couldn't know, as I read that intense evening, that I'd return to Chuong Thien Province within the year.

Chapter 1

She gazed at the palm trees that arched across a sluggish canal, then turned from the window and pecked at a manual typewriter. Outside, the sun reflected fiercely off the muddy waters, and heat waves distorted a sampan floating down the timeless waterway. May of 1969 was hot and miserable, but June would bring the cooling monsoon rains.

A U.S. Army jeep braked in front of the stucco building, stirring up fine black dust. The provincial headquarters was a blend of East and West. Its high ceiling and green shutters were a legacy of the French, but the pagoda roof of red tile came from an earlier period of Chinese colonialism.

She watched the lieutenant swing a long leg over the side of the jeep, then pull out an M-16 rifle, a bandolier of clips, and an olive duffel bag.

The young officer slung the rifle and bandolier over his right shoulder, then hoisted the duffel bag to his left. His tropical fatigues were unfaded, and his jungle boots were dull black. His tan was light and pleasant, left by good times under a friendly sun—not the leathery tan of men who have baked in the tropics. She knew he was fresh from the States.

"Thanks for the lift, Sergeant. Which way?"

"That office where the girl's sitting. Ask for Robert Cantwell. He's a civilian, Foreign Service type. But he's second in command, just under the colonel, and the colonel's out in the boonies."

"Okay, Sarge. See you around."

"Lieutenant?"

"Yes?"

"I forgot to tell you, sir. Welcome to Chuong Thien Province, the asshole of the Mekong Delta," the sergeant said flatly.

"Thanks. To me, Chuong Thien sounds like a brand of instant Chinese food." The lieutenant instinctively touched the brim of his new jungle hat, expecting to return a casual salute. But the sergeant wheeled the jeep away in another dust cloud.

Then he realized. I'm a long way from Saigon and Can Tho. You don't salute this deep in the Mekong Delta. That could mark an officer for assassination.

He walked into the hybrid building, dropped his gear, and leaned his rifle against a wall.

She looked up from behind the typewriter and read the fresh white stencil on the duffel bag: DANIEL C. BRIDGES 06467479 ILT INF.

The secretary scared Dan a little . . . girls like that usually did.

"Uh . . . *chau co* . . ."

"Yes?"

"You speak English?"

"A little. May I help you?"

"Yes, I'm Lieutenant Daniel Bridges. I just arrived. I'm to report to someone called Mr. Cantwell." He added, "A *Robert* Cantwell."

"Mr. Cantwell is deputy senior adviser for Chuong Thien Province, sir," she said, as if Dan should have known. "But right now he is gone only for a little while. You please sit down, and he will be back in maybe just a minute."

Dan stretched his legs in front of the metal folding chair. Then he thought, took off the slouchy jungle hat, rolled the brim and wrapped it with the chin string, and stuffed it into a side pocket. He wiped sweat and black dust from his face with a GI-issue handkerchief. Christ, this humidity is awful, Dan thought. The Delta is hotter than South Texas, but I'd better get used to it. I've got eleven months and twenty-one days to go.

Dan pulled a paperback from a side pocket of his fatigue jacket. Page 32, and he'd been reading for a week. He tried to concentrate on *The Quiet American*, a thinly disguised novel by Graham Greene that was *really* about Col. Edward Lansdale, a legendary U.S. adviser in the Philippines, then

Vietnam—legendary, at least, to those who had studied guerrilla war.

But he couldn't read. Too much frustration and anticipation since leaving San Francisco, then landing at Tan Son Nhut Air Base and that long journey of forms, equipment issue, and briefings from Saigon down to Can Tho, and now to this God-forsaken village in the Ca Mau Peninsula. Dan read one paragraph, another . . . then realized that he didn't remember what he'd just read. He dog-eared the page and stuffed the book back into his pocket.

Pretty girl, he thought. But she doesn't look like the Vietnamese girls I saw in Saigon and Can Tho. There's something about her . . . she's got one hell of a body.

The young woman's jet-black hair fell straight down both sides of her neck and rested across full breasts. She wore a brilliant yellow *ao dai*, the traditional Vietnamese dress: high-necked but formfitted, with long, tight sleeves. At the waist, two panels fell front and back over white satin pants, forming side slits to her sandals.

The dress is like a Chinese slit skirt, Dan thought. Vietnamese women look like butterflies in the *ao dai* . . . but how would an American girl look in one? That thought took him back to Janice . . . tall, funny Janice, also pretty, although she doesn't think so, with freckles and sandy hair to her shoulders. For a long moment, Dan and Janice were back at the lake in Texas, a week before leaving. Then they were at Hobby Field in Dallas, waiting for the United Airlines flight to San Francisco . . . then the scene at the airport, just before boarding. Thank God, I won't go through that again. Janice is wonderful, and I love her, and leaving was hard. But *did it have to be like that?*

The Pipeline took Dan to Travis Air Force Base and lines, forms, more depressing lines that led slowly to a DC-8 military charter, with cheerful American stewardesses in Braniff uniforms to fly them to war. Most of the plane's contracted cargo was eighteen-year-old draftees, the first airplane ride for many, but Dan was surprised to see a few female civilians and children, dependents of U.S. embassy officials in Saigon or Da Nang.

The DC-8 took off in darkness, flew over black Pacific waters for four hours, then stopped at Honolulu International Airport. Servicemen lined the bar, three bodies deep. The soldiers reboarded the Braniff flight an hour later and flew sixteen more hours through the night.

As the smoke-filled plane left Hawaii further behind, the rumors grew wilder and spread faster. A petty officer in the row behind Dan had drunk from a hidden pint of Old Crow since leaving Travis. He tapped Dan's shoulder and confided "Lieutenant, you should know this. I got it straight from a sergeant coming home from Nam when we refueled in Honolulu. All hell's busted loose over there. This bird is settin' down at Clark Field in the Philippines so we can draw full battle gear. We're gonna have to fight Charley off the runway in Saigon."

Why did they fly us to Vietnam in darkness, in that eerie, twenty-hour extension of the night? The unthinking Green Machine . . . the Pipeline.

Dan shifted mental scenes to a blanket in the sand by that lake. Blondish hair blocked the Texas sun as Janice pressed hungrily against him. He reached behind her back and untied her halter top—

"Excuse me, please, Lieutenant."

The secretary's interruption wrenched Dan from that afternoon.

"Where is your home in America?"

"My home? Texas. Do you know where Texas is?"

"*Of course* I know Texas, Lieutenant. Cowboys. Dallas, where President John F. Kennedy died. Then came President Lyndon B. Johnson. *Everyone* knows Texas."

"Yeah. I guess so. You described it, all right."

"Do you have a family in Texas?"

"A family? Yes. Well . . . no . . . I have a father, mother, two brothers." Then Dan added, "No wife."

It's her eyes, he thought. No Vietnamese girl has big, brown eyes like that. Her eyes make her different.

Dan fumbled for something to say, anything to keep the conversation going.

"Do you live here?" What a stupid goddamn question, he thought. Like, you think maybe she's a tourist?

"I'm Dan to my friends. Please don't call me 'Lieutenant.' What's your name?"

"My name is Monique Chantrel," the girl said proudly.

"Monique? That's not a Vietnamese name."

"I am not Vietnamese, Lieutenant Dan. I am French."

"Just Dan, please. Hey, I was in France last year, for a week ... traveling through Europe after grad school. I had some time—and very little money—to spend before reporting to the army. I loved France. The cathedrals, and history, and the food and wine. What part of France are you from?"

"I have not yet been to France, Lieutenant Bridges. But I am French. Do you perhaps speak French? The language is beautiful, and we can talk so much better."

"Just Dan. No. Sorry, but I only speak English ... and fair Spanish, and I've studied Vietnamese ... but do you mean, you're not a Vietnamese?"

"Excuse me, Lieutenant Bridges, here now is Mr. Cantwell."

It was 10 October 1987 again. I thought about the CORDS building in Vi Thanh, and Monique—the most real, and the most fictional, of my characters.

Her father was a French soldier who married in Vi Thanh, opened a motor repair shop, and never returned to France. He died a few months before I arrived.

Monique carried that hybrid beauty of a union of East and West. She was voluptuous, and vain, and just a little overweight. Monique's skin was golden and her eyes were large and brown, with a hint of a slant that made her more exotic. Her *ao dais* were brilliant yellow, red, pink, or sometimes, psychedelic. She spoke Vietnamese, of course, but considered French her native tongue. Monique knew she was meant for something better than backwater Vi Thanh.

I made the Monique of my fiction the lover of Lt. Dan Bridges. She suffered enough from the war, but I learned, in 1972, that the *real* Monique also had a tragic story.

CHAPTER III
Let Slip the Dogs *or* Next Stop Is Vietnam

10 October 1987, Los Baños, Philippines. En route to Chuong Thien Province, June, 1969

> Cry "Havoc!" and let slip the dogs of war.
> —William Shakespeare, *Julius Caesar*

> It is required of a man that he should share the actions and passions of his time at peril of being judged not to have lived.
> —Justice Oliver Wendell Holmes, Jr.

I set chapter 1 of my novel aside, and turned back to 19 June 1969 in the diary. My actual flight to Vietnam was pretty much like in the novel, but the fiction didn't capture its absurdity.

Flying to war in darkness . . . that's my strongest memory. Why didn't some military psychologist figure out that sending troops to Vietnam in the black of an extended twenty-hour night was bad psychology?

No wonder the rumor spread through the plane . . . the Viet Cong have taken Saigon . . . we'll have to fight Charley off the runway at Tan Son Nhut.

More absurd, we flew in a chartered, baby-blue DC-8. The wholesome Braniff stewardesses didn't serve cocktails, but otherwise it was like any international flight. Except for the two hundred and fifty passengers.

They were mostly eighteen- and nineteen-year-old kids,

draftees who had never stayed in a hotel, never had a bank account, and made their first air flights courtesy of the army or Marine Corps. Before The Notice came, these kids pumped gas or sold dope or fixed refrigerators. The Pipeline sucked in the poor, the uneducated, the blacks and chicanos, the white trash from the South . . . The Great American Unwashed. Kids who could never get college deferments and weren't savvy enough to beat the draft.

It was ironic because to me, the war really began with the "beautiful people" in Camelot . . . those ringing words at President John F. Kennedy's 1962 inauguration:

> Let every nation know, whether it wishes us well or ill, that we shall pay any price, bear any burden, meet any hardship, support any friend, oppose any foe to assure the survival and the success of liberty.

Yeah, the children of Camelot committed us to war, but the realities of Indochina soon soured their idealism. Camelot set the Pipeline into motion, but the beautiful people didn't go into it. That job was left to the kids on my plane, and few had even *heard* of Camelot.

To me, that class discrimination was the most immoral part of America's role in the Vietnam war.

The irreverent lyrics of Country Joe and the Fish droned through my mind as the DC-8 flew through darkness:

> *And it's one, two, three,*
> *What are we fighting for?*
> *Don't ask me, I don't give a damn*
> *Next stop is VietNam;*
> *Now it's five, six, seven,*
> *Open up the pearly gates*
> *There ain't no time to wonder why,*
> *Whoopie—we're all gonna die.*

Did I resent that message? No, Country Joe's lyrics were catchy and captured the spirit of the time. It was 1969, and we were flying through the night on a DC-8 to a war that America couldn't win but wouldn't concede.

Susan and I had spent our last night together in the St. Francis Hotel in San Francisco. The newest issue of *Time* was on the stands as we checked out that same morning. The cover photo showed the first of twenty-five thousand U.S. 9th Infantry troops loading onto C-47s, leaving the Mekong Delta. The headline was COMING HOME. U.S. strength had peaked, with five hundred and fifty thousand troops in Vietnam—but I was going in as America was pulling out. Another one hundred seventy-five thousand troops would come home over the next year.

I read the second diary entry I'd written on that plane:

> Susan rode with me on the bus to Travis AFB and left 30 minutes before my flight. She was brave, and I appreciated it. I don't know what the next year will bring. But it will surely be different and interesting.

I felt almost guilty, writing that. I knew I shouldn't be excited about going to a lost war. But Vietnam was shaping my generation. Something in my psyche said, "Hargrove, you'll always regret it if you don't go."

I was young enough, that night, to know I wouldn't die in Vietnam. A few months later, I simply ignored that possibility.

I hadn't volunteered for Vietnam, but Susan would never really believe that. Most second lieutenants got orders soon after Infantry Officers School, but mine didn't come. I was prepared to sit out my two-year tour at Fort Bragg when that inch-thick sheaf of orders arrived. I acted depressed, but was secretly relieved. The cryptic text was hard to understand, but two phrases stood clear: *Republic of Vietnam* and *MAC-V.*

MAC-V meant Military Assistance Command-Vietnam. So I'd be an adviser to the South Vietnamese somewhere, doing something. That's all I knew.

The orders surprised me, because I was in some far-out stuff at the John F. Kennedy Center for Special Warfare, the Green Beret headquarters.

In fact, I didn't think I *could* go to Vietnam, even if I volunteered—not after getting the Top Secret clearance and moving into PolWar.

Langley, Virginia, obviously called the shots for the new political warfare program—to build a political officer structure, like that of the Communists, into the South Vietnamese Army. But the Agency must have pulled the plug on PolWar, because I was now flying into the night. I wrote in my diary:

Susan and I left Rotan a little more than a week ago . . .
Mother insists on sending me chili peppers, Tabasco sauce,
etc., while I am gone.

4 A.M. (S.F. time)
Landed at Honolulu Intl Airport for an hour layover. Sent
postcards home and had a couple of beers. The bar was
three deep with servicemen going to and returning from
Vietnam.

1110 A.M. (S.F. time)
We are 3 hours out of Clark Field, Philippines. . . . The last
few months have been hectic. Travelling from Ft. Gordon,
Ga. to Texas, then S.F. in an unairconditioned car loaded
with pets, a wife, and God knows what else . . . going to
war isn't what it used to be. I wish for the Roman days,
when you'd gather your legions, head 'em up, and move
'em out. But it probably wasn't that simple back then either.

After Fort Bragg, the army had sent me to Civil Affairs
School at Fort Gordon for six weeks. That time was idyllic.
We paid far more rent than a lieutenant could afford for a two-
bedroom plank house with peeling red paint. The shack was
isolated, deep in the cool Georgia pines, but we didn't select it
for its rustic intimacy. It was the only place available near the
army town in those peak war years.

Our closest neighbors were a friendly hillbilly couple, three
hundred yards down the road, who first thought that Daphne
was a monkey because they'd never seen a Siamese cat. They
kept some coon dogs and couldn't understand how anyone
could love a dog as worthless as Bacchus, Susan's miniature
dachshund.

Fort Gordon was the ideal army post. Where else would you
stir up coveys of quail, walking from the parking lot to the officers club? Classes ran from 7:00 A.M. to 3:00 P.M. After that,
Susan and I packed gear and pets and went fishing on peaceful
green lakes, then maybe stopped in Augusta for catfish or barbecue. We didn't try to save money, we lived like there'd be
no tomorrow. We knew, too well, that we might not have one.

My civil affairs class was mostly lieutenants serving two-
year tours. Our backgrounds were varied, but we shared two

things in common: orders to Vietnam, and a laid-back attitude toward the army. "What can they do? Send me to Nam?"

Those days ended quickly. Susan and Bacchus and Daphne and I were soon driving across America in a cramped 1964 Corvair. I had ten days' leave to visit Mother and Daddy, and move Susan to the West Coast. Her parents were returning to Iran, but wanted to keep their San Francisco flat, so Susan and Linda Lanning would live there for the next year. Lee Lanning, whose friendship spanned high-school days in Fisher County, then Texas A&M and Fort Bragg, had left for Nam two months earlier. Our wives had met, then became friends at Bragg.

Our zoo stopped in West Texas, but only for three days. My folks had just moved from the old home place, eleven miles west of Rotan, to a new house on the paved Farm-to-Market Road 282, only seven miles from that town of two thousand. The new house was nicer, but it wasn't really home. I missed the road along turnrows of cotton fields, and the dry creekbeds and lonely canyons I'd wandered or ridden by horseback as a boy.

Mother and Daddy didn't understand why America was *in* Vietnam, but accepted that a man had to do his duty . . . whatever that was. I couldn't explain it very well myself, so we didn't talk much about the war.

Susan and I drove back from Rotan at sundown on our last day in Texas. Daddy stood alone in the yard, and looked a lot older than when we'd left. I sensed he had something bad to tell me. I was right. A passing car had hit and killed Bacchus.

Susan ran into the house, crying. I told Daddy no, I didn't need help. I wrapped the dachshund in a cottonseed sack and laid him in the back of our Corvair. Susan returned with Bacchus's blanket and some of his rubber toys, so I put them in the sack too. I found a shovel in the tractor shed, then remembered how hard that red clay could be. I threw in a grubbing hoe, and drove west to the home place.

I was awfully upset, but it was more concern for Susan than grief for a dog. You'd have to know Susan to understand . . . how she loves animals and how they love her. Bacchus had been her friend and supporter since that Saturday afternoon when I brought the puppy, in a paper sack, to the Fort Bragg quarters we called home. Lee Lanning spent hours trying to teach the dog army Ranger techniques to rappel over an ironing board, but all Bacchus learned was how to lick his postage stamps. Michael Arnovitz, one of the few soldiers who knew that *Bacchus* was the Roman god of wine, plied the dog with drinks.

I didn't pray after I covered Bacchus with West Texas red dirt. I cursed God or fate, or whatever force could be so cruel to Susan as I was leaving for Vietnam.

Mother was watering her new lawn when I got back. Fresh water was a luxury at the old place; we paid to have it trucked in. But my folks built the new house over a pipeline with inexhaustible water.

"When times get really bad, I shut them out by turning on a hose and watching the water run," Mother said. Only a woman who'd always lived on dryland Texas farms without piped water would react like that.

Years later, Lee Lanning and I drank beer by a dry stream bed with a presumptuous name: the Salt Fork of the Brazos River, which ran through Fisher County, Texas. Lee told me how he'd learned of Bacchus's death through a letter from Linda. He was in the field, surrounded by dead and wounded GIs from his own platoon. "I'd learned to live with that," Lee said, "but I cried when I read about Bacchus."

Looking back, the death of a dog makes me realize how callous we became, so quickly. I never cried over deaths, Vietnamese or American, in Chuong Thien Province. One in seven of my Texas A&M class who took an army commission was killed in Indochina . . . I didn't cry for them, either. When the *Army Times* reached Vi Thanh, I first skimmed its DEATHS list, searching for fellow officers or NCOs I'd served with at Texas A&M, Fort Benning, Fort Bragg, Fort Gordon. Names were there, far too often.

Why? Did those men die for *anything*? I never let myself think that way. I couldn't, not back then.

Yet Lee Lanning and I cried over a damned, worthless dachshund.

The first time I let myself cry for my friends was in the spring of 1977. I should have done it years earlier . . . but by then, it was too late to stop what would happen.

Two days later, Susan and I drove across the baking Mojave Desert. The Corvair was a little less crowded with Bacchus gone, but not more comfortable. We were talking about what Susan would do while I was in Nam. I thought she should finish her college degree, but she wanted to work. That's when I saw the blinking red light of the Arizona Highway Patrol.

"I clocked you at seventy-eight miles an hour in a seventy-mile zone," the patrolman said. "What's your hurry?"

I was now counting each dollar, and wishing we'd been more frugal in Georgia. I did *not* want a speeding ticket.

Patriotism might work with an Arizona cop, I thought. "I'm in the army, orders to Nam. I ship out from Travis Air Force Base in three days. That's why I was speeding . . . sir."

"Good luck over there," the cop said as he wrote a ten dollar ticket. "If you don't have time to see the judge in Quartzite, you can mail a check from Vietnam."

We were on California's Highway 101 at noon the next day, anxious to get to San Francisco, where we'd spend my last day Stateside moving Susan into her parents' flat. I was looking for a truck stop that offered a quick, cheap lunch. I saw a green-and-white freeway sign: SALINAS: NEXT EXIT.

Go for it, Hargrove, I thought. This is your last chance. I wheeled off the interstate.

"What are you doing?"

"Something I've always wanted to do," I said. "We're going to find John Steinbeck!" I had always admired the author of *The Grapes of Wrath* and so many other classic American novels, many set in Salinas. The 1962 Nobel laureate for literature had died in late 1968, but I hoped that memories of Steinbeck lingered in his home town.

Susan had met Steinbeck and his crew-cut son in a London hotel years before. The younger Steinbeck would later write *In Touch*, a Vietnam-war saga about a year spent smoking dope.

Susan remembered the day I'd detoured through Sauk Centre, Minnesota, to search *Main Street* for Sinclair Lewis. I wouldn't find Steinbeck either, but what the hell? I was headed for Nam, and she was destined for the life of a waiting wife. Susan rolled her eyes, then shrugged.

"All right, go find Steinbeck. But let's try to get to San Francisco before dark, okay?"

We stopped at a drugstore-bookstore in downtown Salinas.

"I'm looking for someone who used to live near Salinas," I told a bored twenty-year-old clerk at the sales counter. "Did you know John Steinbeck?"

The clerk popped her gum and said, "I never heard of a *John* Steinbeck. But there's a buncha' Steinbecks around here."

We pulled up beside the "regular" pump of a run-down Shell station at the end of the street. The gas attendant had three-days' growth of scraggly white beard—the type of man Steinbeck might write about. "Did you know John Steinbeck?" I asked as he filled the Corvair.

"I don't know *nobody* in this town. I got here two months ago, and I'm headed for Oregon as soon as I can put some money together." He scratched through greasy overalls and spat tobacco juice.

I knew I wouldn't find Steinbeck in Salinas. Great writers are never appreciated in their home towns.

"Let's hit the road," I said. But still, we had to eat.

Ahead was a restaurant with a battered neon sign: SUPPER CLUB. It looked expensive, but I pulled up.

The restaurant was dark, but once our eyes adjusted, we could tell that it was the best in Salinas . . . in 1938. Booths of torn red leather circled black formica tables, each lit by a flickering candle in a stained red-glass holder.

We skimmed prices on the menu, and ordered hamburgers. I went to the bar.

The bartender wore a white shirt and a red bow tie, and was rolling dice with a tired-looking elderly couple who sipped noontime martinis. I ordered two bottles of Coors and thought: Why not try one last time?

"I'm looking for an old friend from Salinas."

"I've lived around here all my life, son. Who?"

"John Steinbeck."

"I'll be damned! *Did you know John?*"

"Sort of . . . I've read everything he wrote."

"Young man, this was *John*'s bar. Why, John used to sit right here and drink till we'd almost have to carry him home!"

We listened to Steinbeck stories for two hours, rolling dice for drinks with the old couple, and drinking too much Coors. But I was pleased when we pulled back onto Highway 101. I had found John Steinbeck.

We stayed in the St. Francis Hotel that night. Because Susan had been raised in Kuwait, we chose Omar Khayyam's, one of San Francisco's finest Middle Eastern restaurants, for our last dinner. The owner, George Mardikian, stopped by our table. He was an Armenian refugee who had fled to America for religious and political freedom. Susan told Mardikian that I'd ship out to Vietnam the next day. He gave her a jar of his special rose-petal jam and a copy of his book *Song of America.* Mardikian had made us both feel good—almost patriotic—so I wrote a thank-you letter on the baby-blue Braniff.

That morning, on 19 June, Susan and I had checked out of the St. Francis Hotel and driven to The Presidio, the old Spanish fort, now a U.S. Army post, in the heart of San Francisco. There we learned that wives or girlfriends could go with their men on the military bus to Travis Air Force Base. My ticket was free, but I paid for Susan's.

The bus was packed with scared GIs. We boarded, and found that Susan's seat was across the aisle and two rows back from mine. Typical military screwup, but no problem, I thought.

"Excuse me," I said to an air force enlisted man seated by Susan. "This is my wife, and I'm on the same flight to Vietnam that you're on. Could we trade seats, so we can talk on the way to Travis?"

The teenage airman saw my gold lieutenant's bar, hesitated, then glared. "No, sir, this is *my* seat." I knew the kid was scared, and frustrated, and this was his first chance to tell an officer to go to hell without paying the price. Still, I wanted to slug the wimp.

A master sergeant beside me saw what was going on, and traded seats with Susan.

Travis was a madhouse. Travis was dozens of depressing lines of GIs in bad-fitting khakis lugging olive-drab duffel bags. Travis was loudspeakers blaring flights that left every thirty minutes for Da Nang or Cam Ranh Bay or Tan Son Nhut. My flight was finally announced. It was delayed.

Susan and I thought that was good news, but it wasn't. We walked to the officers club and made small talk while nursing drinks for two long hours. We had nothing left to talk about, and it would have been better for us both if I were on that plane, and Susan on the bus back to San Francisco.

We finally returned to the terminal. Susan took a gold Allah charm from her bracelet and strung it onto my dog-tag chain. I hugged her and said something like "Cheer up! I love you, and I'll see you in six months on R & R in Hawaii. Take care of yourself, and write. I've gotta go now."

Susan nodded and disappeared as I joined the khaki line.

I started my diary right after takeoff. Tonight, eighteen years later, I turn back to it:

A Naval petty officer is sitting in the row behind me. He keeps nipping at a pint of booze. Next to him is an ARVN sergeant:

"How many kids you got, buddy?"

"Six, I have six childrens."

"Goddamn, you don't get much sleep, do you?" (laughs) Puzzled look on VN sgt's face.

"You know—you have six kids. You must stay busy at night, huh?" (laughs)

"Oh." VN sgt laughs politely.

"You got any sisters or cousins in Saigon? Good-looking females?"

"Yes . . . I have fambly in Saigon."

"Good! I'll look 'em up when I get there!"

The VN sgt smiles, nods politely. He doesn't understand the conversation. And on it goes. We seem to be so different, so distant, and have so little understanding of the culture of the people with whom we are fighting.

21 June 69. Saigon—MAC-V HQ
Arrived at Clark Field in the Philippines at sunup after flying 20 hours in the dark.

I was promoted from 2LT to 1LT on 20 June—a day I never saw. We left on 19 June, flew in darkness across the international dateline, and landed in Saigon at around 10 a.m. VN time on 21 June.

I was surprised—but shouldn't have been—as we approached Tan Son Nhut Air Base. Down below were almost perfectly round holes, filled with water—bomb craters—right to the edge of the runway. Also, buildings destroyed in battle.

We were on a bus, windows covered by steel-mesh grills, within fifteen minutes of landing.

A description of the personal fear one feels as the plane lands and you walk into a war zone seems mandatory in Vietnam stories. But I wasn't afraid; I was excited as we taxied down the Tan Son Nhut runway outside of Saigon. I hoped to see the *Pearl of the Orient*, the city I had read so much about, before whatever lay ahead.

Most of the army troops on the plane went to the 90th Replacement Depot at Long Binh. But a dozen of us—mostly lieutenants and captains—were to be advisers, so we were bussed to "Pentagon East," the white, air-conditioned MAC-V headquarters complex near Tan Son Nhut.

We signed in at MAC-V and were assigned barrack bunks. Everyone else headed for bed or the bar, but I scrounged a cab and went to Saigon.

I spent the next day filling out forms, drawing equipment, and being briefed. One lecture was on the *ear-lopping syndrome.* I wrote in my diary:

"Don't take bodily appendages as war souvenirs, and if you do, don't send them home through APO [the Armed Forces Postal Office]. The price is 2 years in military prison at Ft. Leavenworth, plus a dishonorable discharge. Still, it continues . . ."

An officer could choose his personal weapon: an M-16 or a .45. As a Texas farm boy, I'd been raised with rifles, but was inept with the heavy automatic pistol. I took the M-16.

The MAC-V PIO, or public information officer, a major, learned that the Pipeline had brought a fairly experienced journalist among the new group of officers destined to be military advisers. He interviewed me, then offered an assignment in his shop. I had already realized, when pressured to take a PIO assignment at Fort Bragg, that my M.S. degree in agricultural journalism almost guaranteed that I'd never lead a rifle platoon.

I thought about it. A year in Saigon might be a lot more fun—and far safer—than wherever I'd end up. But communication would be my business after the army, so I turned down the PIO job. I wanted to see the war.

I had little to do but wait for orders for the next four days. I played tourist, mainly to see Saigon, but also because I knew that work would be found for a visible lieutenant who hung around MAC-V with time on his hands.

I found the Orient's Pearl a bit tarnished. On 22 June I wrote:

Saigon—I can't quite describe it. A city in its death throes—or Camus's Oran in *The Plague.* We may not be here tomorrow, so raise hell now. Citroen taxis, pedicabs, buses, bicycles, motorbikes—weaving in and out at breakneck speed ... bright neon lights and rock 'n' roll from the bars. Sandbagged bunkers on the corners, where M-60 machineguns stare at you. Drunken soldiers in from the bush, staggering down Tu Do Street with quarts of Jim Beam sticking from the pockets of their jungle fatigues. Dope peddlers, kids begging, trying to sell everything from hot watches to their sisters. The windows of restaurants and Army buses have wrought-iron screens to prevent terrorists from tossing in bombs or grenades. Even in bright, neon-lit streets, you hear sporadic H&I [harassment and interdiction] artillery—fired along trails the VC might use, or on VC rally points. Rumors, rumors ... the best rumor (or is it true?) is of a babe who cruises Saigon on the back of her boyfriend's Honda until she sees an American—preferably an officer—standing alone, then draws a .45 from her blouse, and blasts him away.

During those restless days, I visited the Saigon pet market, the botanical gardens and zoo, and the Xa Loi Pagoda, where Buddhist monks had cremated themselves in protest of the Diem government. I called them *self-immolating monks* in my diary.

I dined Cantonese style at the My Canh floating restaurant on the Saigon River where, half a decade earlier, a terrorist bomb had blown away a group of U.S. advisers—marking the beginning of a war for folks back home. And I listened to Filipina singers over twenty-five-cent drinks and T-bone steak at the officers club on the roof of the Rex Hotel, then the Rex BOQ, or bachelor officers' quarters.

How did I know where to go? Through color brochures from the Saigon Tourist Information Office.

I received my first orders on 24 June, and wrote in my diary:

IV Corps, CORDS ... the Mekong Delta, which is 95% under water during the monsoon season. CORDS stands for Civil Operations/Revolutionary Development Support. And that could mean almost anything.

On 26 June I flew south to Can Tho on a C-7 Caribou flown by the Royal Thai Air Force. The Caribou was logical. Like the DC-3 (the civilian version of the C-47), it was a war-horse of Vietnam. A Caribou could take off from short, bad runways, and its giant rear door let men kick cargo out fast. But I'll never know why the Thais were flying deep into the Mekong Delta. That was the only Thai plane I saw over the next year.

I reported to MAC-V's Eakin Compound, named after a U.S. Army captain, an adviser who'd been killed near Can Tho. I drew a bedbug-infested bunk and waited, again with little to do, for my final assignment. I killed time by tagging along on interesting missions. I went south to Thanh Duc village with a PsyOps, or psychological operations, team filming a TV documentary on "Land to the Tiller," Saigon's new land-reform program.

The next day I visited a *Hoa Hao* Buddhist temple on Ca La Island in the Bassac River, one of the Mekong's nine branches. The *Hoa Hao* were known for their fanatical hatred of the Communists, and willingness to die fighting them. But while sipping tea with a maroon-clad *bonze*, or monk, I learned that the hostility was based on religious vengeance, not politics.

The Viet Minh, the equivalent of the Viet Cong during the French Indochina War, had brutally murdered their leader. The *Hoa Hao* didn't fight *for* South Vietnam, they fought *against* the VC.

That was my introduction to the role of religion in the war—and the beginning of the end of any naive beliefs in the *gentle Buddhist.*

The PIO for MAC-V IV Corps called me in. Like the PIO in Saigon, he offered me a job working with the press. I didn't take it, because I wanted to get closer to the action.

I bought the 27 June issue of *Life* magazine in the Can Tho PX. It featured photos of the 241 U.S. servicemen killed in Vietnam the week before. The article's title was excerpted from a soldier's letter, an infantryman who'd fought on Hamburger Hill a month before:

You may not be able to read this. I am writing in a hurry. I see death coming up the hill.

I knew about the battle for Hamburger Hill, of course. But I didn't know that my Texas Aggie buddy Lee Sanders had led the company that made first contact with North Vietnamese regulars there, a company that took 100 percent casualties and ceased to exist, before its few remaining troops fought to the hill's crest. Nor did I know that Sanders was lying in San Antonio, hit badly, and starting treatment that would last a year.

I just knew that those 241 photos, mostly of teenagers, scared me.

On 30 June, I met a lieutenant I'd known at Fort Bragg, who was now a MAC-V propaganda officer. I wrote his comments on the U.S. pullout in my diary:

"Look, we all know the South Vietnamese Army isn't ready to take over the war. Any honest ARVN officer will tell you that. But we're leaving, and must explain it. So right or wrong, our propaganda line is that ARVN has strengthened so much, there's no more need for U.S. troops. That's what we have to do."

I tried to learn about Mekong Delta politics, and wrote:

A local province chief was just replaced because the Anti-Corruption Committee charged that Chinese money lenders gave him huge bribes not to start Credit Unions. Then other members accused the head of the Anti-Corruption Committee of corruption. That's not so bad, because the Anti-Corruption head who charged the Province Chief with corruption disappeared & hasn't been heard of since . . . I will go batty if I don't get my assignment soon.

I woke at dawn on 2 July 1969, grabbed a pen, and scribbled the text of a dream before it vaporized. Later, I sent a copy to Susan. It scared her at first:

The Ultimate Enemy

It was quiet and still and we were lying in our bunks in the humid Delta night when they attacked. We fought with poison sprays and with our bare hands, but that only infuriated our enemy. We couldn't stop them. The moans of the men they had reached drifted across the infested compound. If we could only hold out till daylight . . .

It seemed like a thousand years, but the tropical sun finally began to climb across the horizon. The enemy retreated without a sound, burrowed back where they came from.

But we knew they had not given up, that they would return with the first cover of darkness. Another night of fighting, of pain would follow, and we would never defeat this determined enemy.

Because that's the way it is, with bedbugs.

That day John Paul Vann reviewed my records and assigned me to MAC-V Advisory Team 73 in Vi Thanh, Chuong Thien Province.

I'd heard stories about Chuong Thien. All were bad. It was consistently rated the second or third of Vietnam's forty-four provinces in VC control. It was also one of Vietnam's only provinces without a USAID, or U.S. Agency for International Development, agricultural adviser. The word was, no agricultural expert with any sense would go there. But I was army, not USAID. I'd oversee everything concerning agriculture or land reform in Chuong Thien, plus the routine duties of a lieutenant on a provincial advisory team.

Later that day, I recorded:

Some typical comments about Chuong Thien. Sitting at a mess hall table talking to an American Lt, adviser to an ARVN Ranger Recon unit:
   "Have you been in Chuong Thien?"
   "Yeah, I was down there last week."
   "How was it?"
   "Beaucoup VC. We killed 140."
Others just shake their heads. The most optimistic comment so far was from a VN interpreter who said "Chuong Thien, Sir, should be *very interesting*."
Anyway, Chuong Thien is considered a VC province. Three of its 5 districts can be reached only by air, according to a MAC-V briefing paper. Roads and canals are mostly VC-controlled; there are only 5 tractors in its 23,000 hectares. Chuong Thien's eastern edge is the famous U Minh Forest, strong Charley country since time began.

I wrote, on 3 July:

Chuong Thien Province can't be as bad as they say. An ag

adviser (a Texas Aggie) said he doesn't usually carry a weapon. "But I always carry a concealed pistol in Chuong Thien—and you should too." Other advice: Be back in Vi Thanh by 5 p.m. ("Almost everyone I know who has gotten into trouble was out after 5.") Carry a carbine in your jeep. And so on. The VN woman at the laundry asks where I will go. "Chuong Thien." "Oh, Sir . . . *beaucoup* VC in Chuong Thien, too many VC."

On 4 July, I met Major Hoass, a West Point graduate who'd been in PsyOps courses I had taught at Fort Bragg. He was intelligent, articulate, well read, and above all, dynamic. My concept of the ideal infantry officer. And he offered me a job, as a company-grade adviser with the Vietnamese 414th Ranger Battalion.

"But I'm assigned to MAC-V/CORDS, in Chuong Thien."

"I can fix it," Major Hoass said. "Come with me, Tom. We'll live in the field with our Rangers, kicking the hell out of the 237th VC Battalion."

I eyed Major Hoass's black beret and the black-panther shoulder patch on his camouflaged tiger fatigues. I felt proud that this real soldier wanted to take me with him. Part of me wanted to go . . . but I didn't.

What would my Vietnam tour have been like if I'd joined Major Hoass? Would I be alive today?

Maybe. But I wouldn't be with the International Rice Research Institute. I have no regrets, but I'll always wonder what I missed by not going with the Vietnamese Rangers.

That afternoon I went to Special Forces Camp C-4 at the Can Tho airfield. I wanted a pistol, and everyone knew that Green Berets sold weapons.

The walls of C-4's Alamo Lounge were lined with Viet Cong flags, AK-47s, North Vietnamese Army pith helmets with red stars, Chicom or Chinese Communist SKS rifles, crossbows—an arsenal of captured enemy weapons and equipment.

I ordered a beer, and twenty minutes later paid a Green Beret sergeant eighty-five dollars for a Colt Cobra .38 Special with aluminum frame and a two-inch barrel. The sergeant's profit was obviously eighty-five dollars, and I was glad to pay it. I later learned that the CIA had shipped in thousands of the snub-nosed revolvers for its operatives.

On 5 July, I caught a U.S. Air Force Caribou south. We flew about forty miles, then circled a V-shaped village wedged between two intersecting canals. The countryside looked like a lake; flooded rice fields stretched as far as one could see. The monotony of brown water was broken only by rice paddy dikes and lines of coconut palms along the canals.

We descended steeply to avoid ground fire, but I didn't know that was why. The C-7 set down at an air strip—the only one in Chuong Thien that could land fixed-wing aircraft—half a mile outside the village, and raised its tailgate. I grabbed my gear and walked across pierced steel planking (psp), designed for temporary runways in World War II.

Ahead was an open shed of hollow concrete blocks with a tin roof and a pole that flew a limp yellow flag with horizontal red stripes: the flag of the Republic of Vietnam. A sign across the shed's front read *Phi Truong Vi Thanh*. The words were flanked by painted South Vietnamese flags.

A light observation chopper, called a "Loach," and two Cobra gunships were airborne and circling as lines of skinny Vietnamese soldiers in combat gear loaded into a "stick" of five "slicks"—troop-carrying Hueys armed only with 7.62 mm door guns—whose blades never stopped. One soldier had strapped a live duck to his web gear at the back.

A black American sergeant cursed through a bullhorn as he waved Asian troops onto choppers.

"Get the fuck off this runway! Now!" he yelled at three children clinging to an old woman wearing a cone-shaped straw hat and black pajamas. "I'll call you when there's a ride to Kien Long. You motherfuckin' gooks got *shit* for brains!"

The soldiers continued loading. The woman stood on the runway, not understanding a word the sergeant shouted.

"You look like a FNG!" I turned to a sergeant at the wheel of a U.S. Army jeep. "Want a ride to Vi Thanh, sir?"

"Sure, could you drop me off at CORDS headquarters—wherever that is?" Maybe I should have resented the sergeant's calling me a *fucking new guy* . . . but I was one. I threw my gear into the jeep. The road was mire, but the ride was bone jarring.

I flipped through the next couple of months of diary entries, and realized how quickly I'd learned. I read a typical entry:

9 August 1969. Vi Thanh.

Am on TOC [tactical operations center] duty again. Quiet night—a couple of VC contacts and 2 VC KIAs. The past week, according to tonight's S-2 [intelligence] briefing, was one of the year's calmest, partly because most VC, like the other farmers, are busy transplanting rice. S-2 also says the four VC battalions that now operate in Chuong Thien are training and resupplying.

North Vietnamese units have entered the Ca Mau Peninsula for the first time and are in the U-Minh Forest in western Chuong Thien. There was a good fight at Rach Gia last week; about 70 NVA were KIA.

Later. Just got a call from D-TOC [division TOC, 21st ARVN at Bach Lieu]. Spotted a VC unit in Kien Long District, southern Chuong Thien. I contacted VNTOC, my counterpart. Brought artillery on Charley immediately. Nothing else much has happened.

I found out today that Ming thought I would buy the pigs for the farmer demonstration project with CORDS funds—and I understood *he* had the funds available . . .

10 August, 0710h

Still on TOC, will be relieved at 0800h. Last night 4 civilians were seriously wounded at Kien Thien. I requested a Medevac, but a pickup of wounded VN requires a parallel request from the VN side. When the VN finally paralleled, 20 min later, 1 civilian had died. Shell fragment wounds.

Now I remember that I wrote a lot—letters and diary—during slow times when I pulled TOC duty. I hated TOC. An American adviser, with a Vietnamese counterpart, had to stay up all night, monitoring radio traffic and running the war in Chuong Thien.

Duties were routine, like calling 155mm artillery when Charley hit a South Vietnamese outpost, and he always did. But the American TOC officer didn't call the fire directly, a Vietnamese had to radio the final artillery request and coordinates. After all, we were *advisers*.

But not all artillery was outgoing. Vi Thanh was a constant target for VC shelling.

An entry made the night of 12 September 1969 catches my eye, and I'm sitting under a mosquito net on a hard teakwood bed in the hootch of the Dinh Ahn village chief, in the ethnic

Cambodian district of Kien Hung. Sleep is impossible. The heat is stifling because the chief has locked all windows and doors tight. Soldiers brought five giant fruit bats for dinner, but Capt. Bud Shields and I settled for fish and rice. There's a dog-fight at the foot of my bed, and pigs are grunting across the room. That's when I record what seems a significant event:

Vi Thanh was not mortared last night.

The TOC officer also called Medevacs to bring the maimed to Vi Thanh, if they were Vietnamese, and they usually were. We'd occasionally call a *Dustoff*, the same choppers except the Dustoff code told the crew they were to pick up an American. It made a big difference. My mind drifted and I was riding out of some backwater village . . . I'd hitched a ride on a ghastly Medevac stacked with wounded Vietnamese and corpses. The pilot is shouting in a Southwestern drawl, above the *whomp-whomp* roar as we lift off, "We'll bust our ass for a Uniform Sierra. No sir, we're not gonna leave any U.S. casualty behind if we can help it. But it pisses Ol' Gene Autry off to risk our necks for these fuckin' gooks!"

The TOC officer usually arranged a K-Bar—two gunships and five slicks—for the next day's operation. No choppers were stationed in Chuong Thien, so we called those birds by land line, or *lima-lima*, from Soc Trang or Bac Lien or Can Tho. One hectic night, I forgot to encode the coordinates by KAK wheel, and sent them in the clear. The colonel canceled the operation and chewed my ass. I deserved it, of course. Any fool assumed that the VC had tapped our line.

But the TOC duty I hated most was calling *Arc Light*, the code for B-52 strikes. The 52s flew from Guam, Okinawa, or Thailand. Targets were radioed as they approached Vietnam at thirty thousand feet. The VC couldn't see or hear the planes until the sticks of five-hundred-pound bombs hit. Each bomb gouged a crater the size of an Olympic swimming pool. If you plotted a B-52 run wrong, you blew away all friendlies within four hundred—or was it six hundred?—meters from the target. We never had the information to call an Arc Light with that precision. Besides, was there a target in Chuong Thien half a kilometer from civilians? But a lieutenant didn't argue . . .

Snap out of it, Hargrove! This is 1987, in the Philippines.

Don't let yourself drift too far ... you know how dangerous that can be.

I looked at my watch for the first time in hours. It was 3:00 A.M. I shut the computer down and took my diary upstairs to the bedroom. I drifted off to sleep two hours later.

Transition 2

Chuong Thien Province, 1988

I feel like I'm returning to an old lover, years after breaking off a tragic affair ... and I should know better.

I've always thought of Vietnam, and especially Chuong Thien Province, as female. An older woman, seductive and mysterious—but angry, hurt, and dangerous because so many men have abused her. I left Chuong Thien, and the army that brought me to her, in June of 1970. Is returning a mistake, letting rice bring me back to where it began?

I had returned to Chuong Thien once before, of course. That was in the fall of 1972. It was the most depressing and guilt-filled experience of my life. My Vietnamese friends were amazed—why would an American, who had survived a year in this miserable place, come back? But *I* left the next day. The Vietnamese couldn't escape her.

Why did I go back that time? I don't know, *it was something I had to do*. Why am I back now?

Just six months after that return in 1972, I joined IRRI, the source of those rice seeds that had impressed me so deeply. My family and I have lived in the Philippines for fifteen years, and my IRRI work sends me to dozens of countries. I could have returned to Vietnam years ago, but kept putting it off. Too many memories that I wasn't sure I could handle.

The sampan docks at the Thanh Binh Agricultural Cooperative. We're met by its manager, Mr. Bien, and a delegation of
rice farmers. I soon learn that Bien, like my host Tran Van
Rang, had been a local VC political officer.

I remember this hamlet. We used it as a temporary base to
redistribute to farmers two- and three-hectare plots of land
from an expropriated French plantation.

But I also remember the day a Vietnamese sergeant and I
canceled a sampan trip to Thanh Binh because the land reform
cadre didn't show up. Later, I was glad they didn't. Should I
ask about the men who died here that day? Probably not.

I'd written in my diary on 19 August 1969:

Yesterday morning 1LT Donoway and Sgt. Ard and their
VN interpreter, all of MAT 54, were killed from ambush
while riding by sampan down a canal about 6 miles north of
Vi Thanh. The Lt's body was riddled with bullets. Neither
the sampan nor their weapons were ever found. Maybe they
sank in the canal; maybe Charley took them.

And something strange happened to me. Sgt. Minh, 2 Land
Reform cadre, and I drove to Duc Long village. We were to
meet another LR cadre and go by sampan up the canal. We
heard nothing about the 2 Americans and 1 VN being killed.

I had described how the Vietnamese had left the rendezvous
point before we arrived, and I was "damned mad and disgusted" at having to cancel the trip . . . until I learned about
the ambush.

Now, in 1988, a Thanh Binh farmer explains how rice farming has changed as we sip tea under portraits of Ho Chi Minh,
Marx, and Lenin. *Bac* Ho, or "Uncle Ho," seems natural here
in rural Vietnam. The other two don't.

"Before IR8, a ton and a half per hectare was a good rice
crop, and we harvested once a year. IR8 gave us four or five
tons. But that's only average today."

These farmers now grow two crops a year of a newer IRRI
variety, IR13240, and harvest five to six tons per hectare from
each crop. IR13240 is the most popular rice in the Mekong
Delta because IRRI scientists bred into its seeds the genetic
ability to yield well, mature early, and resist most insects and
diseases.

We walk through the fields. The rice is excellent—and this is *not* a showplace for foreigners.

Back in the village, farmers chop open fresh coconuts with machetes. I'm hot and dry, and I drink the water of two coconuts from the shell.

Now we'll head south to find Ba Lien, the old farmer who befriended me so long ago. But at the Thanh Binh dock, I decide that I *must* ask.

"Do you remember, *Ong* Bien, when the Viet Cong ambushed two American advisers and their interpreter in a sampan near here in 1969? I think it was north of Thanh Binh."

"No," Bien says softly. "They died *there*, across the canal." A cemetery for *Mat Trang*, the National Liberation Front, has since been placed over the ambush site. He points to a concrete monument, topped by a yellow star against a red background. His words are sure, and I don't argue. Bien was the political officer, so I know he ordered the ambush. He remembers, too.

Chapter IV
Truth and Invention

Los Baños, February, 1988

> A writer's job is to tell the truth.
> His standard of fidelity to the
> truth should be so high that his
> invention, out of his experience,
> should produce a truer account
> than anything factual can be.
> For facts can be observed badly; but
> when a good writer is creating something,

> he has time and scope
> to make it an absolute truth.
>   —Ernest Hemingway, *Men at War*

My favorite time in the Philippines is the two months after Christmas. Half a year of monsoon rain has ended, but the dry season heat isn't stifling . . . not yet. The skies are clear, and the days are balmy. The jungle turns so green, it looks blue.

It was late February 1988. The Hargrove family had dinner on the veranda of our home on Mount Makiling's wildly tropical slope. The garden flamed with birds of paradise, hibiscus, and tropical lilies, softened by a dozen varieties of orchids, ferns, anthuriums, and tiny African violets growing in the shade. Mahogany trees and MacArthur palms canopy our porch, and rain forest grows to the back fence.

At dusk, the jungle burst with the primeval call of millions of crickets. The insects start their electric song simultaneously, to a millisecond, but so softly you don't notice unless you're listening. Yet if you tried to escape that penetrating Asian rhapsody, you couldn't.

Vietnam films are made in that rain forest because it's the closest one to Manila. I watched part of *Hamburger Hill* being shot on Mount Makiling. *Platoon* and *Apocalypse Now* were both filmed nearby.

But I knew the forest would go soon. Mount Makiling is somewhat protected from the loggers that have denuded most Philippine forests, but slash-and-burn farmers were moving in to clear plots of land and grow upland rice and cassava. What choice do the squatter families have? The Philippines has no more land suited for farming, and population is increasing by 3 percent yearly.

Susan and I talked until Diding came to clear the dishes. But books don't write themselves, so I went to the den and booted my computer. Susan went to the bedroom to read.

Fifteen years at IRRI was tough for Susan, and I knew it. It was a great life when the kids were young, but they were now fourteen and fifteen, and growing up fast. IRRI was still exciting for me—prestige, travel, good facilities, an excellent support staff. Plus the satisfaction of knowing that rice feeds a third of humanity, and 800 million people, mostly in Asia, are alive today, thanks to the new rice technology. That's about one of every seven people on earth.

But Philippine law prohibits IRRI from hiring spouses, so Susan didn't share my fulfillment of meaningful work.

Isolation is another problem. The only international community in Los Baños is IRRI itself, so the Institute dominates our social, as well as professional, lives. Making friends in Manila doesn't work. No one's dinner party is worth spending three or four hours in a car.

It was time for a change, but I had a problem—one that many would envy. I already held what I considered the world's best job in my profession, communication for global agricultural development. Moving to any other international agency would be a step down, professionally. U.S. universities had offered me positions, but I had learned how agonizingly dull that could be when I joined Iowa State University after Vietnam.

Only one thing, other than IRRI, appealed to me. Writing. Maybe my book will somehow lead to a new way of life. If I could make a little money, not a fortune, just enough to free me from bondage to a monthly paycheck for a year, we might move back to our place in Texas, and I'd still go to work every morning . . . on my computer, writing my next book. But I don't dare think of that until I've finished the novel . . .

My Vietnam fiction went well at first. At least, for a few weeks after I got that letter from Bruce McAllister. I had edited 1971 and 1972 drafts heavily before and after dinner each night and on Sunday afternoons. The chapters I liked best had gone through half a dozen edits. Some were good, and the plot was . . . well, better than most Vietnam novels. I knew, I had read them all.

Now I wanted, desperately, to wrap up the novel while this new interest in Vietnam was high. But I couldn't create the honest and realistic scenes that I needed to blend those fragmented chapters into a book. I *could* have . . . but I can't change what I didn't write in 1971.

Maybe my mind set up a blocking mechanism after that black spring of 1977 . . .

Two hours of struggle with Vietnam after an intense day at IRRI exhausted me, so I shut the computer down and went upstairs. I showered, then sat on the bed and talked with Susan about Miles and Tom G . . . her day . . . bits of gossip about the sixty families from a dozen nations who are our neighbors on the IRRI housing compound.

Susan asked about the novel; her question surprised me, because she hadn't read a word of it. That may seem strange, but I understood. Susan carries her own scars from Vietnam, and worse wounds from its aftermath. But she had recently commented that she felt we'd leave IRRI soon after I finished the book. Maybe that explained her interest.

I said I hadn't written about . . . whatever it was.

"What about the Texas Aggies? Did you write how you were so gung ho, and afraid the war would end before you got there—when everyone with any sense was trying to *stay out of* Vietnam?"

"I didn't mention Texas A&M. My character is a Texan—it's easier to write in little details, that way—but he graduated from Texas Tech."

"But you *did* bring in Fort Benning and that jackass colonel who welcomed your infantry class—and *us Little Army Wivies*—with that awful speech about 'I never went to no university, but I belong to the world's greatest fraternity, 'cause I'm a graduate of the United States Army Infantry Officers School'?"

"No. Dan Bridges is infantry, but I didn't write about Benning."

"What about Fort Bragg, and that unbelievable PsyOps company? That awful statue of a Green Beret that John Wayne left us? And the Special Forces chapel with the stained-glass windows showing Green Beret troops bandaging little children for God, and throwing grenades into tunnels?"

Typical Susan. Witty but caustic . . . tonight, she's pushing too hard.

"My character was never at Bragg."

"Did you write about your problems *after* Vietnam?"

"Damn it, Susan, I'm writing a *novel*, not an autobiography. My character dies on an operation on the Snake River—but *I didn't*. Everything in my book happened to people I knew, *but it's fiction*. The setting is Chuong Thien Province in 1969, yes, but the book is *not* about me."

"Okay . . . but I bet your own Vietnam story is more interesting than whatever you're writing. Frankly, I don't think you're happy with the novel. I feel you should start over, and write nonfiction. Begin the book in West Texas, or in the Corps at Texas A&M about the time that Kennedy died. The story might flow, because *it happened to you*."

Susan's unsolicited advice irritated me, so I went back to the den to work on my fiction.

A few weeks earlier, I'd received quite a surprise—a letter from New York with the return address: Owen Lock, editor in chief, Random House/Del Rey Books.

I hadn't met Lock, but I certainly knew who he was. Lock had commissioned Lee Lanning's two Vietnam books. The first, *The Only War We Had*, had hit the market three months ago. I was proud to see Lee's nonfiction account of *his* war on shelves of airport bookstores in Bangkok, Amsterdam, Hong Kong. *But where was my book?*

Lee had introduced me by letter, and Lock agreed to review sample chapters of my novel. I had sent him what I considered my better writing, and threw in the "Prologue"—my account of finding the diary.

Maybe this is the break, I thought, ripping the envelope.

Lock's letter was short but personal:

I've just read your piece on the diary you didn't write. Excellent. I look forward to the novel. Would it be possible to see a copy of the diary? As you know, we *do* publish nonfiction.

Lock's note excited but depressed me. I'm trying to sell my novel, but Random House is more interested in that damned *diary*? Lock doesn't understand. I never led a platoon, I wasn't wounded or captured, I didn't kill anyone. Not really, not with a rifle.

Finding that diary was one of the most incredible experiences of my life, and I had hoped it would help me finish the novel. After the initial shock, I thought . . . maybe those two black ledgers hold some bad scenes that will explain why I erased them from my memory . . . something I can rewrite as fiction to move the novel forward.

I was disappointed. My diary was *not* a great war chronicle. The text was clipped, unemotional. I wrote mostly about dull agricultural and land reform projects I supervised, mixed with matter-of-fact loggings of the violence that surrounded us.

If only I could go back to 1969–70 and rewrite that diary, knowing that two decades later I'd use what I saw, thought, felt in a book. But I can't change the diary, it's *not honest*.

I'd paid an IRRI secretary to transcribe the diary in

Microsoft Word, then loaded it on my computer's hard disk. I could easily have sent Lock a printout, but didn't—there was no book in those red-spined ledgers.

No, my 1971 fiction describes the war deep in the Mekong Delta far better.

I sorted my stack of novel manuscripts until I finally found it, the second chapter I had drafted in 1970. But I didn't title it chapter 2; it was "The Final chapter." I had created Lt. Dan Bridges and Monique in chapter 1, then jumped to the end of the book, where Chuong Thien Province destroyed them, along with Sgt. Joe Culver and 2d Lt. Monroe Sutton.

Why did I write that way? It wasn't logical.

Maybe I wasn't either, seventeen years ago . . .

CHAPTER V
The Final Chapter

Los Baños, Philippines, 1988. Chuong Thien Province, 1969

Los Baños, 1988. The Final Chapter was fiction, but based on a real operation in Kien Hung District of Chuong Thien Province in 1969. But I wasn't on that operation, it was lieutenants Carlile and Young and a sergeant whose name I didn't record in my diary, and forgot long ago. It was near the muddy Cai Lon River. We American advisers called it the "Snake River," because it twisted and contorted on its way to the Gulf of Siam.

I skimmed the 1971 manuscript. Would I have written differently about the day Mobile Advisory Team 54—the "hard-luck" MAT team—was trapped, and so many men died, if I'd known I had a diary for reference?

The Final Chapter

The UH-1s cut through the morning haze like a formation of angry giant insects, swung their whirling tails, and set down in the clearing outside of Pham Dong. The Hueys's rotor blades never stopped as lines of Cambodian troops loaded. To Lt. Dan Bridges, they looked like green rows of huge American steel helmets with dark skinny guys under each dome, not soldiers.

"Why the hell ain't *Trung Uy* Tu here?" Sgt. Joe Culver said again, as the ethnic-Cambodian 411th Regional Force Company filed onto the troop-carrying choppers. "Tu's the company commander, that's *his* troops loadin' onto them slicks!"

"The lieutenant knows he should be here," Dan snapped back.

A frail second lieutenant stepped up to Dan and saluted. *Thieu Uy* Sarun, XO of the 411th RF Company, spoke in Khmer.

"The lieutenant say 'cuse me please, but *Trung Uy* Tu is very sick," Thua, Dan's new interpreter, translated. "Lieutenant Sarun will command op'ration today."

"Sick? Lieutenant Tu was okay yesterday."

"Yes, but he become very hot this morning, have high feber. So sick."

Dan winced. No, don't think like one of *them*.

"Okay, tell *Thieu Uy* Sarun to move 'em out."

The lieutenant grinned and barked an order. A Cambodian sergeant scurried from chopper to chopper, counting and marking on a clipboard.

Sergeant Culver motioned Dan aside. "You look worried, Lieutenant."

"Sorry, I didn't know it showed. It's just . . . a lot of things."

"This operation?"

Dan locked Culver's eyes. "I don't like it, Joe. Everything in my life seems fucked up, and now the *trung uy* doesn't show and—"

"You're gettin' superstitious as a gook, Lieutenant," Culver tugged at his walrus moustache. "You're thinkin' about Lieutenant Tu's rabbit-ass story about his dead kid's ghost,

the boy he claims warns him when an operation will go bad
. . . ain't you?"

"No, not that—I'm just fed up with this shit, Joe. We're advisers, but we won't advise. We're going on this sweep to call for American air strikes and firepower and Medevacs if the Cambodes get into trouble.

"And what if we *do* kick ass today? The slicks will pick us up at the Snake River and we'll ride back to Pham Dong. Charley moves back into the Old Frenchman's Plantation tomorrow, and Major Nghia keeps robbing the district blind."

"There's nothin' wrong with being nervous, Lieutenant," Culver said. "Tight-puckered assholes ought'a be government issue for a little hot walk in the sun, like today."

Dan shrugged. "You're right, Joe. It's always like this before we go out, I guess."

Culver slapped Dan's back. "Just think, Lieutenant. Next week you and that Texas gal'll be on R & R, layin' on Waikiki beach . . . or somewhere."

"Or somewhere." That broke the tension and Dan laughed a little, then turned back toward the choppers.

But it *won't* be that way, Dan thought. How can I let Janice fly to Hawaii, then tell her I've gone ape-shit over a half-French, half-Vietnamese girl? Monique is the only good thing I've seen here . . . now she's pregnant, and I don't know what to do. God, I leave in three days. Can I cable Janice to stay home, that the army has cancelled my R & R? Whatever I do will be wrong.

Think about that tonight, Dan. This morning, think about the operation. But he knew it wouldn't work.

Second Lieutenant Monroe Sutton watched, trying to look calm before his first operation. He wondered what his new commander and the sergeant were discussing.

"Joe . . . watch Sutton close, okay?"

Culver grinned. "I've took care of many a green lieutenant in my time, sir. I'll keep an eye on this one. He'll be okay." Then, for no reason, the sergeant added, "We'll *all* be okay."

Culver's worried too, Dan thought. We both know these troops aren't prepared. Only a few soldiers carried grenades on their shoulder harnesses. Most didn't carry even their *basic load* of ammunition. The bandoliers are heavy, and chances are they won't need the ammo anyway. No one expects more than a sniper or two.

I can't do much now, but Culver and I have to pressure *Trung Uy* Tu to make his troops carry a full load of ammo on the next operation.

Los Baños, 1988. I remember going to the tactical operations center all through that drizzling monsoon day to monitor the radio, hoping we'd somehow rescue lieutenants Carlile and Young before they died by the Snake River.

I'd better check what I wrote about that operation in my diary, I thought.

I opened the subdirectory *Diary* on my computer's hard disk, hit "word search," and entered *death trap*.

MS Word is efficient. The words appeared in seconds, highlighted on the screen:

The choppers set down in a *death trap*. It looked like this:

My computer program didn't have graphics, so I checked the entry date, then looked up 7 Sep 69 in my red-spined diary. I found the sketch Miles showed me three months before, the night I found the diary I'd forgotten. VC machine guns on all three sides of the V-shaped landing zone . . .

I turned back to the computer and scrolled to my first entry about that operation:

6 Sep 69. The VC have proposed a ceasefire 8–10 Sept, observing the death of Ho Chi Minh. But I doubt they'll respect it, they're doing all the damage they can now.

Charley was bad in Kien Hung District today. One U.S. KIA and God knows how many VN KIA . . . 3 U.S. chopper crewmen shot up and evacuated to Can Tho. Medevacs are flying wounded VN into the Vi Thanh hospital.

I spent this morning at the Vi Thanh air strip with 3 VN cadre trying to hitch a chopper ride to Kien Long District where planthoppers are devouring the IR8 rice crop. We couldn't get there because of the trouble in Kien Hung. Kien Hung and Kien Long Districts are in bad shape. So is Kien Thien. I was at Khang's home [Khang was my interpreter] tonight. He and Bac and Oahn say the VC have cut off Kien Thien HQ on 3 sides. I planned to stay in Kien Long till Monday.

But the VN have word that Charley and/or the NVA plan to wipe out Kien Long. They aren't just cautious, they are emphatic and say going to KL now could be suicide. They have a lot better intelligence than us Americans. I didn't listen on 19 Aug when the VN warned to stay off the Xa No Canal from Vi Thanh to Thanh Binh . . . and 1 LT Donoway and Sgt. Ard of MAT 54 were ambushed and killed on that strip of water.

7 Sept. We were mortared again last night, about midnight. The fight is bad along the Snake River in Kien Hung, about 8 miles from here. Lt. Donoway's replacement on MAT 54, 2LT Young, was KIA yesterday. Three other U.S. advisers were wounded, including 1LT Carlile, who I had visited the day before at Duc Long. It took the choppers 9 hours to get Carlile out.

I turned back to The Final Chapter:

Dan watched Sutton rub the gold second lieutenant's bar pinned to his collar. Should I make him wear the camouflaged bar of black cloth required in Vietnam? But Sutton's wife had sent that gold bar, engraved "Yea though I walk through the valley of the shadow of death . . ." He promised to wear the bar in Vietnam, so I let him . . .

Why does having someone on the team who puts so much faith in God worry me? Maybe it's because *we* make the decisions, and we'll need more than spiritual help if we get into deep shit today. But we won't.

The Cambodian militia, five in a row, now dangled their feet from both open sides of the Hueys, ready to jump when the choppers touch the LZ, the landing zone—or before. You'd think a string of troops would fall out, Dan thought, but each man holds the next. No way could they shake loose, not even when the choppers bank way over.

Dan, second lieutenant Sutton, and *Thieu Uy* Sarun took canvas seats behind the RF troops in the lead slick. The Vietnamese lieutenant was smiling but Dan knew that a smile in Vietnam often masks fear, embarrassment, or defeat.

Thua sat in the gun well by the American door gunner. Sergeant Culver climbed in last and squatted, leaning against the pilot's seat. He unhooked the handset of the PRC-25 on his back and handed it to Dan.

"Viking Six, Viking Five, this is Viking Mobile, over."

"Viking Six here," Maj. Clyde Bommel answered from the C & C, or Command & Control chopper. Bommel was S-3, operations officer, for Advisory Team 73, Chuong Thien Province. He and his counterpart, *Tu Tau*, or Major Nghia, the Kien Hung District Chief, were already in the air. They'd direct the operation from a two-thousand-feet orbit above the LZ.

"This is Viking Five." That was Sp.4 Bob Saunders from home base at Pham Dong, the team hut of MAT 96.

That dopehead had better stay straight while he's on the radio, Dan thought. He probably will, he's scared shitless of Joe Culver, and I told that redneck sergeant to handle it his own way if we even *suspect* Saunders of smoking grass on duty again.

"Viking Six, Five, we're lifting, over."

"Keep us posted, Mobile. Out."

Sergeant Culver hooked the handset back on his shoulder harness. The radio gave him a feeling of security. This Prick-25 puts us in communication with Pham Dong, Vi Thanh, the C & C ship, he thought. To *help*, if we need it.

Dan caught Lieutenant Sutton's eyes and nodded, like saying "It'll be okay." Sutton can't know how scared I am, he thought. Thank God we have Culver, and let's pray the LZ's not hot. How will Sutton act if it's hot? Dan looked at his watch. We may know in five minutes.

Dan thought about Major Nghia. That's the son of a bitch who should be on the ground today. Maybe Charley would shoot his corrupt ass off.

Then Monique wrenched back to the forefront of Dan's mind. She's so goddamned . . . *tragic*, that's the only word to describe her, she symbolizes Vietnam. The immense tragedy began thirty years ago, and when will it end? In four months, because I'm through with Vietnam 114 days after

R & R. A separate peace, that's what Hemingway called it
. . . but will it be? What about Monique?

Dan touched Sutton's shoulder.

"Stick close to Culver and me!" he shouted to his new
XO. "But not too close. Don't bunch up. Move behind an
RF troop when you can. *Step where the Cambodes step, you
hear?* Let *them* hit any booby traps."

I don't mean it that way, Dan thought. But if anyone dies
for Vietnam today, it should be a *Vietnamese*, not one of us.
Then he thought . . . *these* troops aren't even Vietnamese,
not really. They're *Cambodians*, and have no loyalty to
GVN. Why should they? The Vietnamese despise them. The
Cambodes will gladly kill VC today . . . but only because
they're *Vietnamese*. They don't give a damn if the dead are
Communist or GVN.

And why the fuck isn't Lieutenant Tu here? The rational
side of Dan's mind said: Culver's right, it's only a ghost
story, the kind the Cambodes tell all the time. Don't think
like one of *them*.

Los Baños, 1988. The ghost story . . . I opened a filing cab-
inet and found the article I'd written in Iowa that icy winter of
1971. I should have ended that story more dramatically—but I
wouldn't contaminate what *really* happened with fiction.
Maybe that's why it never sold:

AT YOUR USUAL RATE

A Medal for the
Cambodian Lieutenant's Dead Son

Tom Hargrove

Can a U.S. Army officer award a medal to a *ghost*? I don't
think so, especially a medal for valor to the spirit of a Cambodian child who died five years ago.

But that's what I was asked to do in that strange war deep
in the Mekong Delta, where the only American soldiers are
advisers. It was in the spring of 1970 in Chuong Thien
Province, 150 miles south of Saigon.

We'd flown to Kien Long District that morning by the
swing ship, a Huey UH-1 that delivered mail and supplies to

district teams and MATs—remote four- and five-man mobile advisory teams. We then went south by sampan, the only transport available.

I was traveling with Nguyen Van Duc, chief of Chuong Thien's Land to the Tiller, or land reform program, and Khang, my sixteen-year-old interpreter who knew about two hundred English words.

Land reform, the redistribution of huge rice plantations once owned by French and Chinese landlords, is one of the most powerful weapons in the pacification program, Saigon's countryside war for "hearts and minds."

Trung Uy Tu, commander of the 411th Regional Force Company, had pushed the main-force Viet Cong from this area three weeks before, and was now building a triangular outpost. When the area was reasonably pacified, the 411th would push west and start a new outpost. It's part of pacification . . . the *oil slick strategy*.

Our land reform teams followed the troops a few weeks later to distribute titles to 2.5 hectares, or 6 acres, of rice land to farmers.

Most were former tenants of the Old Frenchman's Plantation, claiming land their families had worked for decades. Others were settlers who wanted land badly enough to move here and build new palm-thatch huts around the new outpost.

This part of Kien Long was one of the few pockets of Cambodians remaining in the Delta. Both the farmers and the soldiers spoke Khmer, not Vietnamese, and identified with Phnom Penh, not Saigon. The mighty Khmer Empire ruled the Mekong Delta until two centuries ago when the aggressive Vietnamese pushed down from the north, exterminating or driving the Cambodians away.

Trung Uy Tu was the largest Indochinese I had ever met—taller than I, and I stand six feet one. The first lieutenant had commanded this unit of Cambodian cannon fodder for almost a decade. Tu would be a major, maybe a colonel, if he were a *true*—that means ethnic—Vietnamese.

Soldiers strung concertina barbed wire around raw earthen berms of the outpost as Tu's batman poured toasts of *baxide*, homemade rice whiskey.

Lunch was roast duck with side dishes of coagulated duck's blood, rice-fattened field rats (the Vietnamese call the delicacy *chuot dong*); mudfish; saucers of *nuoc mam*, the fermented fish sauce that most Americans hate, slices of red pepper, and rice. The batman respectfully offered me, the *co van My* or American adviser, the choicest morsel. I pretended to appreciate it.

Bone-white eyes stared blindly, but I broke the duck's skull with my knife, picked up the head with chopsticks, and ate the brains. One changes over here, I thought. This isn't so bad, and neither are the rats.

Lieutenant Tu spoke hesitantly in Khmer. A Cambodian sergeant translated to Vietnamese, then Khang spoke in broken English.

"*Trung Uy* Tu ask please you help him get medal for his son."

"I didn't know the *trung uy* had a son. Is he a soldier?"

Khang translated, then answered "Oh, no, *Trung Uy* Tom. His son cannot be *real* soljer because he only seb'en year old—six, American age."

"Then why should he get a medal?"

"'Cause he help Cambode soljers too much, tell them where VC hide, warn them before VC ambush. He is numba-one boy."

A medal for a seven-year-old ... I kept my face stoic, like an Asian would.

"Ask *Trung Uy* Tu if I can meet his son."

Khang translated.

"You *cannot* meet—the boy is dead in 1964. *Trung Uy* Tu wants medal for ... the *spirit* of his son. Mebbe so you call it the *ghos'*."

"For the *ghost* of a seven-year-old who died five years ago? Are you joking?"

"*Of course* I don' joke."

"You'd better ask *Trung Uy* Tu to explain."

Lieutenant Tu's batman poured more *baxide*, but I turned my glass mouth down. A few heavy raindrops raised puffs of dust like tiny artillery shells. The fluffy clouds that sailed overhead were darkening each day, announcing that another monsoon season would soon begin.

A few days before, the saffron-robed *Sai* Ngoc, a Cambodian monk who spoke English, had used the timeless cycle of monsoon rains to explain Buddhism's endless circle of life, death, and rebirth in the quest for Nirvana.

The old monk and I were sitting before a gold-leafed

Buddha in the Cambodian *wat*, or temple, at Kien Hung. I'd
left my rifle and radio—and even my boots—at the entrance. I didn't like it, but you couldn't approach that serene
Buddha carrying an M-16 and a Prick-25. Besides, I felt
fairly safe with the Cambodians, and *Sai* Ngoc assured me
that not even the VC would violate the sanctity of the monastery.

"How can you speak of this 'Nirvana,' a state of peace
and harmony with the universe?" I had asked. "There is no
peace in Chuong Thien Province. And *your* people—the
Cambodians—suffer more than any I've known."

"The Lord Buddha taught us that life *is* suffering," *Sai*
Ngoc replied. "But He also taught that we humans *cause* the
suffering by our passions, our greed for material things that
mean nothing and satisfy the body, not the spirit. To end the
suffering, we must remove ourselves from passion and
greed, we must be humble and selfless."

"Will you enter Nirvana one day?"

"Perhaps, after many more cycles of birth and death."

"Does Nirvana last forever?"

"The way you use that word! *Forever* means nothing to
us. I cannot say that Nirvana lasts forever—or even for one
second—because our time does not go from the past to the
future, but repeats, endlessly." The monk shook his head.

"You Westerners think time runs in a straight line. It's
something finite, limited . . . a commodity that you have
only so much of, like . . ." He pulled some piastres from beneath his robe. "Like a roll of money. Each day you spend
one bill, another day of your life." The monk dropped notes,
one-by-one, on the rattan mat.

"Until it runs out. Once your life on earth is spent, you
will never have it again."

Communist soldiers can never defeat America, the monk
explained. But the Asian concept of *time* will break our
commitment to Vietnam—just as time, not the Viet Minh,
defeated France.

"American leaders are desperate to win the war as fast as
possible. Supporting a long and unpopular struggle, with
many deaths, in faraway Asia is political suicide. But *your
enemy's strategy* is to make the war last as long as possible,
to use *time* as the *ultimate weapon*."

Khang interrupted my thoughts, bringing me back to Kien Long. "*Trung Uy* Tu wants to tell you 'bout his son."

The 411th RF was fighting near Tuy Luu when the lieutenant learned of his son's death, Khang explained. Contact was heavy and frequent, so it was several weeks before he could return home. The next year, the lieutenant's wife also died.

"*Trung Uy* Tu had dream while in field two years later. He see his boy so clear, hear him say not have secur'ty there, VC shoot mortars soon.

"*Trung Uy* Tu wake up, but he think only a dream, then . . . *boom, boom* . . . beaucoup mortars fall on his men, kill too many.

"After that, the ghos' always stay with the *trung uy*, warn him many times 'bout VC."

The lieutenant nodded, then Khang continued.

"Right here, just last week, his son tell *Trung Uy* Tu to *di-di mau*. He run fast to bunker, and Chicom B-40 rocket hit right where he was sleep." The lieutenant gripped Khang's sleeve, and spoke again.

"Now, the ghos' comes to the *trung uy* ever' night, tell him he want GVN medal, same-same brave soljer, because he is numba' one troop too, help kill so many VC."

"Requests for medals should go to the province chief," I said. "Not me."

"*Trung Uy* Tu already ask, but Mr. Province Chief don' like Cambode off'cer so much, and nothing happen. So please you ask Mr. Province Chief for medal. Mebbe so he listen to you, an American off'cer, for chure."

"Do you believe that story, Khang?"

"Oh, yes sir. Cambode men know many thing that other men don' understand."

I knew that the Cambodians' reputation for sorcery and supernatural powers makes the Vietnamese contempt a fearful one. They won't openly scorn someone who might place a curse on their homes, or disrupt harmony with the spirit world.

"Khang, getting medals for the ghosts of dead children *is* a little out of my line . . . I've never *done* anything like that before." I searched for words that would get me out of this gracefully.

"I agree, the kid *should* have a medal but—"

"You will help him? Oh, you are so good, *Trung Uy* Tom!" Khang spoke in Vietnamese and the Cambodian lieutenant pumped my hand and refilled our glasses.

"The *trung uy* is very happy to you, he say t'ank you *beaucoup!*"

I drank another reluctant *baxide* toast with Lieutenant Tu, then wandered around the outpost. I balanced carefully and crossed the bamboo footbridge over the dry moat that monsoon rains would soon fill. A path twisted through the concertina perimeter toward an abandoned cemetery.

Then I saw that the mounds of clay weren't graves, they were eroded bomb shelters of mud, a part of every rural Vietnamese home. The bunkers and scattered pieces of pottery water jars were all that remained of a village that stood along this canal—a year, five years, fifteen years ago?

It was time to start back to Kien Long. The canal was dangerous by day, deadly at night.

"*Trung Uy* Tu invite that we drink *chi* before we go," Khang said. I sat back down for the inescapable pyrex glasses of green tea, and sugary French pastries.

Lieutenant Tu spoke softly as a soldier cranked our sampan's motor with a greasy cotton rope.

"The *trung uy* say for chure you will talk to Mr. Province Chief about the medal?"

"Yes, when I return to Vi Thanh."

But I didn't. Colonel Le Vasseur, the province senior adviser, already thought I'd gone a bit native. Requesting a medal for the ghost of a dead kid would convince him I'd gone off the deep end.

I went up to Saigon two weeks later. My tour was almost over, and I'd requested discharge from the army in Vietnam instead of returning to the States. That meant red tape, paperwork, and a lot of explaining. The request was legal, but no one considered it rational.

First Lieutenant Chauvin Wilkinson met my Air America flight back in Vi Thanh.

"Any excitement while I was gone?" I asked as the Louisianan wrestled the jeep through the mire. The monsoon rain poured down in sheets.

"It's been pretty quiet, except for the 411th RF Company."

"The Cambodian unit that opened the new outpost in Kien Long? What happened?"

"A VC battalion overran the outpost. Seventy-five percent of the 411th was killed or captured."

I told Chauvin about *Trung Uy* Tu, the ghost, and the medal.

"Looks like the kid didn't come through this time," I said. "What about Lieutenant Tu?"

"People were talking about that. Tu wasn't even *at* the outpost, he was in Vi Thanh checking on supplies. Tu left his XO in command, and *he* was killed when the fight began."

I thought about Lieutenant Tu, and the ghost who protected him. No, it's only a story, the kind these people tell all the time. Don't think like one of *them*.

-end-

I'll have to rewrite this as an earlier chapter to explain why Lieutenant Tu doesn't show up for the operation, I thought that night in 1988. It might be easier to edit *Trung Uy* Tu and his ghost from the novel. But if I write the story as fiction, I can embellish it, add drama, some of the exoticism I felt around the Cambodians . . . I turned back to The Final Chapter.

The chopper dropped lower. Not long now.

Below, Dan saw miles of shimmering rice fields, intersected by paddy dikes and canals. A broken archway, blown apart two decades before, came into view—the entrance to the Old Frenchman's Plantation. Dan had walked through the ruins on an earlier operation. Only the foundation of the mansion remained. A lone ming tree, in what had been a courtyard, was a poignant memorial to the Frenchman who once ruled a small empire

The choppers approached a marshy area of reeds, water, and worn dikes from rice fields that farmers had given up long ago. Ahead was a V where tree lines along two canals intersect—the landing zone. The 411th RF would insert—the abandoned rice field between the two canals, sweep east through the tree line, then cross the Old Frenchman's Plantation for pickup by the Snake River.

Dan watched two Huey Cobra gunships work thirty feet

above the tree lines as the slicks circled the LZ. Each attack chopper carried racks of seventy-six 2.75-inch rockets and two Vulcan Gatling machineguns that fired six thousand 7.62 rounds per minute. They spewed the canal banks with death, but took no return fire.

Major Bommel and *Tu Tau* Nghia were circling the LZ in a light observation helicopter—a LOH or Loach. They could abort the operation if the LZ looked hot. Send the K-Bar back and dismiss the troops. Or they could call it a go. Major Nghia, as the Vietnamese C & C, had the final say, but Bommel knew that *he* would ultimately call the shots.

I've had bad luck lately, Major Bommel thought. Maybe aborting that last operation was a screw-up—the colonel sure as hell thought so, and there was hell to pay. But it could have been a trap and maybe I saved some American lives. I'm not going to abort *today*'s sweep unless I damn well *have* to.

Pushing the Vietnamese officers into real Indian country is tough enough. It's harder to force them to make contact, to kill VC. I want this operation to go smoothly, but I also want to *get some*. We haven't got many lately . . .

Major Bommel scanned the LZ, two thousand feet below, then turned to his counterpart. *Tu Tau* Nghia nodded. Bommel spoke into the helmet microphone on the same frequency to Viking, the slicks, and to Outlaw, the Cobra gunships.

"This is Viking Six. Looks clear. Proceed. Out."

Dan yelled, "Get ready!" to Sutton on the lead slick, forcing a grin and raising a thumb. Dan's hand was shaking, so he used it to unsnap his seat belt. His throat was a tight knot.

Thieu Uy Sarun was releasing his own seat belt. He's even scareder than me, Sergeant Culver thought. I love to see that little fucker scared.

Major Bommel watched the slicks descend into the LZ. Then the lead chopper banked to the left, and climbed steeply. The other slicks followed.

"Viking Six, Viking Mobile! The canal bank looks disturbed along the southwest tree line," Outlaw Six, the command Cobra, broke in. "I don't like it. Over."

"Six here," Bommel answered. "I see no sign of enemy activity. Did you see troops? Over."

"No troops, but I'm worried. I'll stand by for your decision."

Abort this mission, and we'll never push the gooks back in, Bommel thought. Of course Major Nghia could stop the operation, instead of me . . . but he won't. He'd lose face. Besides, Nghia is Vietnamese, and those are *Cambodian* troops. He doesn't give a rat's ass about them.

Major Clyde Bommel wished he could be anywhere—anywhere—except sitting in that C & C seat.

What should I do now?

An eighteen-year-old pilot thought he saw a VC trap on the last operation, and panicked. I aborted, and caught shit for it. But what if Charley *is* down there?

That might be okay, too. We haven't made contact in a week, our body count is down. Shit, I've got to decide—fast!

"Viking Six, what are your orders? Over."

Major Bommel's decision was the easier alternative. "This is Viking Six. Outlaw Six, hose the tree lines again. Viking Mobile, if no return fire—*Charlie Mike*, continue mission, over."

"This is Outlaw Six. Roger that. Out."

"Viking Mobile here," Dan acknowledged. "Wilco. Out."

Los Baños, 1988. I turned back to my diary:

Some bad screw-ups in yesterday's operation are coming to light. Maj. Johnson was at Lloyd's room tonight to "discuss" it—but really, to cover his ass. The RF troops thought it would be a nice walk through the rice fields with no contact. They were not prepared. Some had only one clip of ammo. The VN "back seat" was a green Lt.

The choppers spotted Charley while heading into the LZ. But the back seat said those troops were friendlies, and wouldn't authorize them to fire. The choppers set down in a death trap. . . . Estimates on the VC force run from a heavy weapons company to a battalion. Lt. Carlile was hit bad in the head on the LZ and the US sgt with him went into shock. We took six US casualties, plus God knows how many VN, trying to get them out.

Now Maj. Johnson is sweating for allowing this to happen. He's laying a cover story in case there's an investigation— but he overplayed his hand, talking far too much and getting in deeper. I feel sorry for him, but I guess that's war.

So it was a Vietnamese officer in Bird Dog—the single-engined Cessna that flew FAC, or forward air control, who said there were no Viet Cong on the LZ that day. Lieutenant Bugansky was the Bird Dog pilot. He owned Rat Dog, a mongrel who could kill rats almost his size. Bugansky was awarded a Distinguished Flying Cross for flying Bird Dog day and night, directing air strikes during the thirty-six hours the men were trapped. Still, Major Johnson and his Vietnamese counterpart in the C & C ship could have aborted the operation.

So who's to blame?

Does it matter, after all these years?

I turned back to The Final Chapter . . .

Thieu Uy Sarun shouted to Thua in Khmer when the lead slick climbed. Lieutenant Sutton looked scared, but didn't know what was wrong. Maybe the major will abort the mission, Dan thought.

The slicks circled the LZ at fifteen hundred feet as the Cobras raked the tree lines again with machine-gun fire and rockets. Then the UH-1s headed back into the LZ.

Sergeant Culver watched the open field where they would insert in a few seconds. It don't look right to me, Culver thought, but I've gone into worse shit.

The roar was deafening as the door gunners on each slick pumped streams of 7.62mm bullets into the tree line. Dan braced for return fire . . . but it didn't come.

The LZ's not hot, Dan thought as the ground approached. Thank God, it's not hot.

The choppers hovered, door gunners firing madly. Culver pushed to the door, and leaped into the mud. The Cambodian troops followed, and sloshed through the mire toward the canal and tree line.

"Sutton! Go!" Dan slapped the lieutenant's back.

The lead chopper tipped its nose forward and skimmed the ground. Sergeant Culver's radio antenna whipped in the rotor blast as the slicks left the LZ.

It didn't begin suddenly, it was more like a continuous roar. The roar of the choppers and their guns faded, and a terrifying new sound took over. Dan first thought it was the RF troops firing, then . . .

Two green-clad Cambodians folded into the mud! One thrashed, clutching at his throat. The other lay face down, motionless, in a pool of gushing blood. An explosion rocked the ground behind Bridges.

Dan saw a ridge. Cover. A shallow canal, bordered by three-foot-high dikes, about fifty feet ahead.

Got to keep movin' and hang onto the radio, Sergeant Culver thought. Are you fuckin' crazy? There's no way I'd turn loose of this sweet Prick-25. But we gotta get the fuck outa here—fast!

He dived into a low spot and clutched the mike.

"This is Viking Mobile. We're drawin' heavy fire from—" A bullet cracked by. That's too damn close, he thought. That bullet didn't zing; it *cracked*.

"From about fifty VC, that's five-zero Victor Charlies. Heavy automatic-weapon fire and B-40 rockets from the two canals to our east, and other fire behind us. It's a trap! Request immediate evacuation. Over."

Two explosions to his left threw up geysers of water and mud. A Cambodian rifleman crumpled.

Holy shit, *two rocket launchers*! We're fucked ducks. Those slicks can't get back in here. I gotta do something!

Ahead, he saw the canal. Shallow, but it's cover. The sergeant didn't think the words, he felt them, and sprang forward.

Lieutenant Sutton was hugging the near side of the canal dike. How did *he* get there? Sergeant Culver thought. Don't he know Charley's *behind* us, too?

Where's Bridges? We've got to get to that canal. He looked over his shoulder as he ran, saw Dan, and shouted. "Lieut—"

The rocket exploded at Culver's feet. He never felt the hot shrapnel that shredded his left leg and tore into his groin and belly. He only saw sky and ground, silently tipping, turning. It was peaceful, and SFC Joseph Culver was dead when his body hit the ground.

Lieutenant Sutton was watching, urging Culver forward when the sergeant disappeared in the explosion, then reemerged, sprawled in the mud. Sutton whimpered, then a body hurled itself on him. He screamed!

"Goddamn, Sutton, get hold of yourself!" Dan yelled, pulling the new lieutenant over the dike by his web gear.

"Oh, God, Dan, God, dear Lord Jesus, look at Culver," he sobbed, praying, not cursing. He rose to point at the dead sergeant.

"Shut the fuck *up*, Sutton!" Dan yelled, pulling him back into the shallow brown water. "And *keep your fucking head down*! We're dead if we don't get our shit together!"

Sutton reached deep inside and somehow took hold of his mind.

Culver's gone, I've lost the best friend I ever had, Dan thought. But I've got to stay calm. Don't panic like Sutton. Not till we're out of this shit. I can think about Culver tomorrow, I can think about Monique tomorrow, I can go crazy tomorrow. But not today.

You're handling yourself fine, Dan thought. Keep it up. The other internal voice spat back: You dumb son of a bitch, we're screwed! Culver's gone, the radio's with him, out in that VC free-fire zone, and where's Lieutenant Sarun?

Dan checked the muzzle of his M-16. It was clear. He wiped mud from the rifle's action with an olive army-issue handkerchief, then handed the cloth to Sutton.

Dan peered over the dike. Culver and the PRC-25 lay among half a dozen broken Cambodian bodies. Dan scanned his own position, and could see only a few huddled RFs. A soldier raised his M-16 and fired blindly, his head buried behind the dike. The noise was maddening, the staccato of AK-47s and the *zing* of ricocheting bullets, explosions, scattered bursts of the Cambodians' return fire.

Sutton *has got to* calm down. Me, too. We've gotta get out of here. Alive. *But it's a little late for Culver*, Dan's antagonistic voice answered. How the fuck did we get into this mess? Better worry about getting *out*, my friend, that inner voice replied.

But there's *no way* out of this trap. With Culver and the radio, maybe we'd have had a chance.

"Have you seen *Thieu Uy* Sarun?" Sutton shook his head.

The firing died down and Dan tried to picture the terrain, hoping for an escape. I *know* what the map will show, he thought, but pulled the waterproof case from his side pocket.

The map was folded to show the LZ, marked in red wax pen. Dan studied it desperately.

VC bunkers on both canals that intersect in front of us. Machine guns behind us. How the hell did Charley know we were coming, that we'd insert here? *Insert's the word*, isn't it? We're fucked. God in heaven, we're fucked this time.

Dan shook those thoughts away. "We'll get out, Sutton. I'll find Lieutenant Sarun. He has another radio, I can change his frequency and call an air strike."

Sutton shook his head, and pointed toward the half-dozen muddy bodies lying in the rice field. A smashed radio lay beside a Cambodian who was using his left hand to press a bandage to stop the blood flowing from his right shoulder.

Oh, Jesus Christ, no! That's the *thieu uy*'s radio man, and his radio is shot to hell. That means our only radio is strapped to Culver's back.

You fucking goddamn army, you got us into this shit, now get us out!

Cut that out, the voice of reason regained control. We don't have a chance if you panic.

Then Dan heard the most welcome sound of his life.

"Sutton, it's the major! It's Major Bommel in the C & C ship, coming to take us out! Look at that Loach! It's wonderful!"

What about the Cambodians? Sutton and I will overload the light chopper. Can we leave the Cambodians trapped?

You bet your sweet ass I'll ride that Loach out of here! Why should *I* die when I can escape? I'm sorry the Cambodes that are still alive don't have a chance, but I'm going back to Monique.

"Come on, come in. Be careful, but get us out of here," he whispered hoarsely to the chopper. "Please, God, help that beautiful Loach make it."

Major Bommel had watched the two gunships' deadly firing passes. He wiped sweat away as the Cambodians and their American advisers leaped from the slicks and headed to the tree line.

Then came what Major Bommel feared most. One, then another tiny green soldier fell . . . puffs of smoke—rockets—hurled more to the ground.

The gooks set a trap! They knew we were coming, and now three Americans are caught down there! Major

Bommel felt sick, terribly sick. It's my fault, why did I do it? The Cobra pilot wanted to abort the operation, but I couldn't. I *had* to put them in. Why? Whywhywhy?

"Viking Mobile, this is Viking Six," Bommel tried to contact Bridges or Culver. "Do you read me? Come in Viking Mobile, this is Six, come in Mobile. Over."

No answer.

Then Major Bommel saw the mud-smeared body with the radio strapped to its back.

That's Sergeant Culver, so I've already got one American killed today. No, Culver may still be alive. Where are the two lieutenants?

There, pinned down in the lateral canal. Maybe we can save them. We've *got* to get them out. Maybe the gunships can blast those VC bastards out of that tree line. But they must be dug in deep.

Major Bommel pushed the talk button.

"Outlaw Six, this Viking Six."

"This is Outlaw Six. Go." The Cobra pilot didn't try to hide his anger.

"Outlaw, we've got three Uniform Sierras trapped down there. One is wounded or dead. Lay heavy cover fire so I can go down for those Americans!"

The Cobras hovered, fired rockets, then swept the tree line.

Dan watched the two gunships work the canals. Look at that fucking firepower! Fantastic! If Charley sticks his head up, those Cobras will blow him away!

The LOH pilot nodded, and pushed the chopper toward the V between the two canals. Maybe we'll get them out. Maybe we'll get out too, Major Bommel thought.

"Come in, please come, Major!" Dan shouted as the Loach grew bigger. "He's going to make it, Sutton! We're going home!"

The LOH pilot and copilot were pushing the chopper down. God, help guide that beautiful Loach in . . .

"No!" Dan's hands clenched.

Round holes stitched the LOH's Plexiglas bubble, and the chopper shuddered. Dan's right fist flew to cover his mouth as the chopper shook, then paused in the air. The LOH banked sharply, then climbed away.

"What happened, Dan? That chopper's *got* to take us out

of here—or we'll die! Dan! Where's he going? Bring him back."

The chopper became a speck in the sky, then disappeared.

Los Baños, 1988. I'm glad I wrote that into the novel because, no matter who screwed up, Major Johnson *did* try his damndest to rescue Carlile and Young and the sergeant that day. But they had to turn back; flying through that withering firepower was suicide.

We don't have a chance now, Dan thought. No, don't give up. We're trapped, but we can hold out in this little canal until Vi Thanh sends more troops in. Could the VC attack from those bunkers? No, not until dark. The Cobras would slaughter them.

The two gunships still circled, but Dan knew they wouldn't waste their dwindling firepower on the elusive VC bunkers. They *have* to keep enough ordnance to hold off the VC if they cross the open field.

A machine gun fired a short burst, and Dan saw muzzle flashes. My God, the Viet Cong bunkers aren't even *in* the tree line, they're camouflaged in front of it! The Cobras are useless unless they know that.

If I had the radio, I could direct the Cobras, I could call 155 artillery on the bunkers from Vi Thanh . . . why didn't the major call us some artillery?

Then Dan thought. Why haven't the VC mortared us? No . . . don't even *think* about that. They don't have mortars, or they'd be using them. One good tube could drop rounds in our hip pockets.

We're fucked if we're still here when it gets dark. The VC'll swarm out of that tree line, sure as hell. Then Dan thought about Puff, the customized C-47 cargo planes that helped units in trouble at night with an inexhaustible supply of parachute flares plus Vulcan Gatlings, rockets, grenade launchers, and laser to mark targets for fighter planes or bombers. A Dragonship had better be here when the sun goes down.

Sutton was rubbing the engraved bar on his collar like a rosary, feeling the minute passage from Psalms etched into the brass: "The Lord is my Shepherd; I shall not want. He maketh me to lie down in green pastures. He leadeth me beside the still waters . . ."

"Sutton, we've *got* to know how many men we still have," Dan said. "Crawl along the dike to the right, and I'll go left. Count heads. Make the troops dig in. I don't think we'll have a ground attack before dark, but Charley could mortar us any minute."

"Okay, Dan. Should the troops return fire?"

"No, we don't have enough ammo." Dan remembered the soldiers who didn't bring their required load of ammunition. Don't get pissed off now, that won't help. He erased the temper flash, then just felt frightened. "Have them dig fighting positions."

"Dan . . . ," Sutton tried to grin. "Don't worry about me. I'm scared, but I've prayed to our Savior, and I know He'll bring us out of here."

Sutton turned on his belly and crawled to the right. Sporadic shots rang out, but the LZ was quieter.

Dan inched along the dike to the left. Three riflemen were huddled.

"Trung Uy!" A sergeant in his fifties placed his hands together in a traditional Buddhist welcome that seemed out of place here. "Okay Sa-lem *Trung Uy?*" He offered a crumpled pack of cigarettes.

"No Salem, papa-san," Dan said, and wondered what happened to Thua . . . he needed an interpreter to ask about Lieutenant Sarun.

"Di dau Thieu Uy Sarun?" Dan hoped the Cambodian would understand his pidgin Vietnamese.

"Het roi." The sergeant drew a forefinger across his throat and pointed to a body caked with black blood by the dike.

So Lieutenant Sarun is *het roi* . . . dead, too, like his radio man.

"VC numba' ten, *Trung Uy?*" The Cambodian cupped his hands to light a cigarette.

"Yeah, papa-san. VC number ten thou'. *So spread out*, for Christ's sake." Dan motioned the Cambodian soldiers apart.

"Over there, papa-san." The old man nodded, grabbed his rifle by the muzzle, and crawled to his new position. "Now *dig in*," Dan simulated digging.

"Maybe-so pretty soon *beaucoup* boom-boom!" he added,

imitating mortar explosions. Papa-san dug patiently into the mud with a bayonet.

Dan positioned the other two soldiers. One had lost his rifle, but Dan made him dig in anyway. He crawled further along the dike and found five troops huddled like sheep. He motioned and shouted "Spread out!" The soldiers stared but didn't move. Dan turned and crawled back toward Sutton.

Things could still be worse.

Dan reached the spot where Sutton and he had lain before.

No Sutton.

I'd better find him, he may be in trouble. Dan crawled to the right, the direction Sutton had gone.

Reeds blocked the canal ahead of Dan. He cradled his rifle and pushed ahead.

He stopped. A mud-caked boot stuck from the reeds in front of his face—an American boot. Dan stared at the foot for several long seconds, then eased forward.

Sutton lay sprawled flat, his arms outstretched like he was praying. Dan turned the body over. Flesh, bone, and teeth were torn from Sutton's face, but his eyes were open.

"Sutton, no!" Dan whispered. "I'm sorry, Sutton. I shouldn't have left you, you don't belong here. I didn't even know you, Sutton. None of us did."

Bile flooded Dan's mouth, and his stomach contracted. He vomited into the mud, inches from his face. He continued to retch and pressed his face against the cool mud. Then he backed through the reeds.

Sutton's gold bar, Dan remembered. I have to return it to his wife. He crawled back to the body, trying to avoid Sutton's eyes. But he couldn't unpin the gold bar from the dead lieutenant's collar; his fingers were slippery; there was too much blood. He grasped the collar with his left hand, sawed at the cloth with his bayonet, then backed out again.

Why did you let it happen, God? Why did any of this happen?

Once Dan left the reeds, he rolled onto his back. I should have closed Sutton's eyes, you're supposed to do that ... but what does it matter? Dan felt the engraving on the bar, and wiped blood away to read its message: "Yea, though I walk through the valley of the shadow of death, I will fear no evil, for thou art with me; thy rod and thy staff they comfort me . . ."

No one is with *me* now, Dan thought, putting the piece of collar with its gold bar into the front pocket of his fatigue jacket. I'm alone and helpless, and I fear a hell of a lot of evil. I could pray for God's deliverance—but that didn't help Sutton.

Where's my Buddha! He reached for his dog tags, then groped along the chain. No, I took it off two days ago . . . Dan's mind flashed back to that lost weekend of smoking pot with the bar girl in Can Tho . . . her warning when he promised to wear the ivory Buddha on his dog-tag chain . . . "I'm not chure. American's promise not always so true. But I pray so much you wear the Buddha, 'cause I'm 'fraid something bad happen if you don't."

Now, even the Buddha's gone.

That radio is my only chance! I could direct artillery with the radio, I could call choppers to get us the fuck out of here! No, this three feet of mud dike is all that's keeping me alive, and I want to live! But now there's just me and a dozen Cambodes and the VC have us by the balls and they'll overrun us when it gets dark, or they'll bring in a mortar and blow us away like rats. I could direct the Cobras with a radio. A couple of 2.75 rockets into their firing slits would fix those bunkers! But first I've got to have that radio! It's the most important thing in the world.

Don't panic, Dan. Keep your head. He looked over the dike. The radio antenna rose above Sergeant Culver's body.

Panic, hell! *Without that radio I'll die!* I've never thought clearer.

Dan sprang over the dike into the mire.

I'm going to make it, I *have* to make it, Dan thought, dreading the bullets he knew would come. No one fired. The radio loomed bigger as Dan ran toward Culver. Almost there. Thank God, I'll make it.

Dan's legs quit and he plunged head-first across Culver, then rolled back behind the corpse.

What happened to my goddamn legs? Dan reached and drew his hand back. It was sticky with hot blood. He looked down. A piece of white bone jutted starkly from his left thigh.

So this is how it ends, Dan thought. It's not fair. I didn't want it like this. Monique, what will happen to her? Janice? I've fucked up my life, but I don't want it to end now, and I know it will. I haven't even fired my rifle today. I've never *seen* those people who shot me. But now I'm going to die in this rice field.

No, I'm still alive! The radio. I came over that dike to get the radio and here it is!

He rolled onto his side. Funny, the leg doesn't hurt. Dan pulled at Culver's stiffening body and felt along the shoulder harness until he found the handset. He unhooked the mike, but it wouldn't reach him. Dan yanked the radio, but Culver's harness held it. He tried to lift the dead man's arms back to slip the radio off. The arms wouldn't move.

Dan unsheathed his bayonet and slashed the canvas. The radio slipped off.

Mud splashed in front of Dan, but he didn't hear the bullets. He set the radio as a shield between his head and the tree line, and clutched the handset.

Nothing. It's dead!

Push the talk button, Dan thought. A rush came through the receiver. It works! Now they'll know I'm alive!

"Hello, hello, anybody! Who's monitoring?" he shouted into the receiver, forgetting radio procedure. "This is Bridges. This is Viking Mobile, is someone out there?"

At the MAT 96 team hut in Nuoc Trong, Sp.4 Bob Saunders monitored the empty frequency, still hoping for a transmission. He'd called an air strike, and a Vietnamese infantry company was loading onto a K-Bar of five Hueys to land behind the tree line. Two Medevacs and more Cobras should reach the LZ in a few minutes.

Bob heard the metallic voice and clutched the mike.

"Viking Mobile, this is Viking Five. Don't yell into the radio, I can't read you. Say again. Are you okay? Say again!"

The voice came back, but weaker.

"Saunders, this is bad. You've got to get some choppers to take me out, do you hear? If I don't get out soon, Saunders, I'm dead, so you've got—"

The transmission ended.

"Viking Mobile, Viking Mobile, come in Viking Mobile, come in Mobile. Over!"

Bob repeated his transmission frantically, but no one answered.

-end-

Los Baños, 1988. I remember that Second Lieutenant Young was killed on the LZ, and First Lieutenant Carlile lay wounded and exposed in the mud. The Viet Cong were shooting at the bodies, so Carlile set the PRC-25 as a shield for his head. But an AK-47 bullet pierced the radio, and lodged in Carlile's skull. The VC thought he was dead, and shifted their fire.

Yeah, the actual operation was pretty much like I fictionalized it. Except that Richard Carlile never tried to leave his troops; nor would he have.

Months later, I heard that Carlile was still in a coma. Did he pull through? Maybe I wrote something about that.

I scrolled my diary on the screen . . . entries of death and terrorism before and during those three days of "cease-fire" for Ho Chi Minh's death. The VC kidnapped our head security guard on 5 September as we impotently watched houses in Vi Thanh burn. Norm Olsen and I almost walked into a firefight north of Long Tri. We'd gone there by sampan to inspect Agent Orange damage. Operation RANCH HAND hit the wrong target, and sprayed the defoliant on a friendly area with one of the finest IR8 rice crops in Chuong Thien . . . the VC killed the wife and baby of one of my agricultural cadre. I found another note on the death trap:

10 September 1969. Results from Saturday's operation in Kien Hung: 16 VN KIA, 1 US KIA, 5 US WIA [wounded in action]. As Lt. Carlile lay in the open paddy after being hit bad, VC snipers shot him 5 more times to make sure he was dead. But he wasn't. . . . Charley slipped away when it got dark.

Then I found an 11 September 1969 entry:

I went to the memorial service of 2LT Stephen W. Young of MAT 54 this morning. KIA on Saturday. Shot in the head as they left the choppers in the VC trap. The service was ironic because Young had been in Chuong Thien only 2 wks, and few men really knew him. The chaplain flew in from Can

Tho for the service. He started by recalling that Young had attended the service he'd given for 1LT Donoway on his first day in Chuong Thien. Young then replaced Donoway on MAT 54. Two weeks later, the chaplain is holding Young's service in the MAC-V messhall. Young was from Collingswood, New Jersey.

The chaplain replaced a red-checkered plastic tablecloth with white linen for the service, and symbolically set a steel helmet, a pair of jungle boots, and an M-16 rifle before a metal cross.

My next entry about the Snake River operation was on 12 September. It seemed funny at the time:

Still trying to get to Kien Hung. Long, an ARVN interpreter that TOC assigned to me a few weeks ago, is there now. I worked Long pretty hard, and he was used to hanging around TOC and not doing much. So Long requested another assignment. Now here is what's funny. They sent Long to MAT 54, whose last two interpreters, along with its last two US Lts, have been killed over the past 3 wks.

On 27 September I recorded:

Met 1LT Briggs today at the outpost just outside of Hoa Luu. First name is Rob. Seems like a real nice fellow . . . but he's MAT 54's third team leader in a little more than a month.

Transition 3

Chuong Thien Province, 1988

Ba Lien is still alive, and we're going to his farm. He was the first in Chuong Thien to grow IR8, but the old farmer means more than that. To me, he's a link to the past, a positive one. I learned about rice through Ba Lien.

I'm pretty sure Ba Lien will be the only old friend I'll find. Anyone who served Saigon or the Americans must be gone now.

Learning that Ba Lien is still alive didn't really surprise me. He's the epitome of a tough peasant farmer, so close to the land, he's part of it. Those kind always survive . . . at least, a few do.

I'm glad we're traveling by sampan, not road. The true highways of the Mekong Delta are its canals and rivers.

I scan the banks of the Xa No Canal intensely as we weave among sampans and wooden cargo boats. Before, I'd have been watching for Viet Cong ambush sites, but now I look for changes. Women exchange snatches of gossip as sampans pass one another. Naked children laugh as they dive into the canal waters from the steel remnants of a shot-up South Vietnamese Navy patrol boat.

The Vietnamese still paint twin eyes on the bows of their sampans to watch for evil water spirits. But in 1969, most sampans had motors. Today, almost all are driven by oars. Gasoline is scarce and expensive.

The people seem even poorer than during the war, but happier . . . at least, here in the countryside.

I was never sure about Ba Lien's politics. I doubt that he

had any. IR8 was the bond of our friendship. Ba Lien was the most respected farmer in the region, so Joe Ona and I tested and demonstrated the IRRI varieties on his farm. I felt not only welcome but, rarer in those days, *safe* at that farm, even though the area ranged from dangerous to suicidal for Americans. Khang, my interpreter, and I shared dozens of simple meals with Ba Lien and his family. It was mostly rice and fish or pork, but sometimes dog or snake or roasted field rats.

I believe Tran Van Rang's claim to have ordered me not killed in 1969. But something bothers me. I know that, at first, the Viet Cong saw the new rice seeds as a threat.

I know because Vietnamese troops brought in an unusual *hoi chanh*, or VC defector, in April 1970. He claimed to be a political officer, like Tu Rang—and those guys *never* gave up. He could have been a double agent and the South Vietnamese Army had him, so we doubted he'd live long. I cabled Capt. Doug Lovejoy, a friend from previous duty at the John F. Kennedy Center for Special Warfare—the Green Beret headquarters. Doug was S-2, or intelligence officer, for the 2d PsyOps Group. When he learned we had a *political officer*, Doug caught the first Air America flight to Can Tho, then hitched a ride south on a Huey to Vi Thanh.

I was at the defector's interrogation. That word sounds ominous, but it was just a questioning session, nothing nasty. The defector talked a lot, but I asked only one question: What is the official VC policy on IR8?

The *hoi chanh*'s answer confirmed intelligence reports. Until a few months before, VC propagandists were ordered to spread rumors that IR8 was a plot of the U.S. imperialists to spread leprosy and sterility.

But a new directive had just arrived from COSVN, the Central Office for South Vietnam—the VC headquarters in Cambodia. Propagandists were now to learn the IR8 technology, the turncoat VC said, and bring seeds to "liberated" areas.

I ask Tu Rang about the early VC campaign against IR8; he claims not to remember it. Political officers aren't known for admitting that *Mat Trang*, "The Front," made mistakes.

Of course, Tu Rang had been a rice farmer, so he may have ignored the first order.

But what a tribute to the new rice seeds—a weapon of both sides in the battle for hearts and minds.

Within two years after Ba Lien planted the first "Honda

Rice," it had spread to most of Chuong Thien's rice land . . . land that was scarred by bomb and artillery craters. That's what makes it tough to come to a personal peace with Vietnam. In my other role, as an army officer, I called a lot of the explosives that left those scars. The bombs and artillery also wasted farmers who were grateful for the IRRI seeds. Of course, many supported the VC, or clandestinely fought with them. War and peace. Working with both was hard.

"How many Vietnamese died in Chuong Thien during the war?" I ask Tu Rang. Dr. Vo Tong Xuan translates.

"We don't have such statistics," Tu Rang replies.

"It must have been thousands and thousands."

Tu Rang shakes his head. "No, it was tens and tens of thousands."

He's right, of course. I remember the steady flow, day and night, of wounded and dying through the dismal hospital in Vi Thanh. And I saw only a fraction of the soldiers and civilians that died in Chuong Thien's swamps and rice fields or in the U Minh, the "Forest of Darkness" on our western boundary.

"The fighting was terrible in 1972," Tu Rang says. That was the year I returned. "B-52s flattened this section of the canal. But Ba Lien was lucky. His home survived the bombing. Will you recognize it?"

The palm-thatch houses along the canal all look alike.

"I thought I'd never forget . . . but it's been eighteen years." I wonder if I'll even recognize Ba Lien.

Chapter VI
The Velvet Glove

October 1987. On Thai International, from Manila to Seoul

> The velvet glove that cloaks the iron
> fist of American imperialism.
> —Viet Cong propaganda description
>   of the U.S. pacification program, late 1960s

> The iron fist in a velvet glove.
> —Thomas Carlyle, referring to King
>   Charles V, around 1830

"Oh! *I'm sorry!*" The tap on my shoulder made me jump. I'm sorry, too, that I scared the Thai International stewardess. That happens if you disturb me when I'm thinking hard. It's worse . . . much worse . . . when my mind is back in Vietnam. I wish I could change that.

"Didn't you hear the captain?" the stewardess said. "Please fasten your seat belt. We're about to enter turbulent weather."

It was 19 October 1987 . . . only nine days after I found my diary. Susan was still in Texas, so I welcomed the unexpected memo from Dr. M. S. Swaminathan, IRRI director general, asking me to fly from IRRI's research center in the Philippines to Washington, D.C., for the annual meeting of donors and directors of thirteen International Agricultural Research Centers. All were patterned after IRRI.

My job would be to help run a press conference to explain the International Centers to the American public, and help write proposals for more funds for rice research.

Those thirty hours of flying over Pacific waters and waiting in airports in Seoul, San Francisco, and Detroit were always boring. But I'd make some of the hours go faster on this trip by editing the novel. As the 747 lifted off from Ninoy Aquino International Airport, renamed for the Filipino reformist who President Ferdinand Marcos allegedly ordered shot down on its tarmac in 1983, I started on my sixth draft of chapter 2:

Chapter 2

Dan watched another world float by, straight down from the Huey's open door. The chopper's whomping roar masked the sounds of a land both strange and, somehow, vaguely familiar.

White smoke columns rose from dry fields as farmers burned rice straw to prepare for the monsoon rains and the next planting. The countryside was cut by straight canals laden with silt and the color of strong coffee and rich cream. Water buffalo wallowed in mud by a river.

The chopper flew over a village of thatch huts on a canal bank. From its center rose a white, fairy-tale temple, with spires flowing gracefully from its eaves. A swampy area outside the village was pocked by water-filled bomb craters, like a moonscape.

A sluggish river meandered, snakelike, toward the Gulf of Siam. It contorted into a series of *S*'s. Dark mangrove swamp covered the land between its loops.

The toy boats and sampans on that river are straight from "Terry and the Pirates," Dan thought. But these boats have long, shrimp-tailed motors, not patched sails. Trails of white foam frothed behind the boats for a second, then disappeared. Where are they going? Imagine life on one of those boats, up and down that timeless river.

Dan felt a hand on his shoulder. A few blond whiskers sprouted above the pudgy door gunner's lip. *This kid should be home worrying about high school graduation, or tinkering with an old car—not here.*

The gunner pointed to balls of gray smoke rising above the mangrove banks of a tributary off the river. Another puff appeared, then Dan realized. That's *artillery.* God, men are being shelled down there, dying as we drift by like it's nothing. It's . . . *irreverent.*

The chopper continued on its compass azimuth west. This

is absurd, Dan thought. I'm going to a funny-sounding village called Nuoc Trong, so small it isn't even one of those little dots you look at on *National Geographic* maps and wonder what it would be like to visit. But I'll *live* in that village, an adviser to a remote Asian militia unit fighting a lost war. That's straight from Kipling. Can I make it in that brutal picture book down there?

Maybe this trip is a dream—I'll wake up in Janice's apartment back in Austin. We'll be snuggled on those big feather pillows, and Janice will have that musky woman-smell like always when we've made love. No, this is for real. Insane, but real.

Another shell puffed along the river. It seems magic—like a genie waving a wand and "puff," a dragon appears . . . or someone is sprinkled with stardust . . . then disappears in smoke. How does it feel, under those white clouds? What does it smell like? Dan thought of the sharp smell of cordite—exciting, when shooting at white-winged doves on September afternoons in the Rio Grande valley, but frightening in infantry exercises at Fort Benning.

The chopper flew on. The distant battle moved silently out of sight. It was no longer happening.

Dan shifted his thoughts to yesterday in Vi Thanh . . .

Vi Thanh . . . maybe the most backwater provincial capital in Vietnam, I thought on the plane to Washington, D.C. in 1987. Vi Thanh was a village, really, with only five thousand residents. That's a lot smaller than a U.S. town of five thousand.

Vi Thanh had a couple of bad restaurants, a few shops that sold only essentials, and a spartan hospital run by a Korean surgeon. We called him "Whiskey-Drinking Dr. Chee," and his main business was cutting out shrapnel and sewing up wounds. Business was good.

That hospital: my strongest memory of Vi Thanh, one that the opening scene of "*M*A*S*H*" on TV always brings back.

The village was headquarters for the 31st Regiment of the 21st Division of ARVN, the Army of the Republic of Vietnam. About sixty Americans also lived in Vi Thanh, in three heavily armed compounds. One was for my U.S. Army unit, MAC-V Advisory Team 73. But I lived in prefabricated quarters of the adjacent CORDS compound. CORDS was the joint military-civilian "pacification command": Civil Operations/Revolutionary Development Support.

The third compound, OSA, was over by the police station. The most comfortable, and secure, place in Vi Thanh, OSA housed only three Americans—two civilians and a navy SEAL. But the OSA compound was protected by thick concrete walls topped by concertina barbed wire and fourteen Nungs, ethnic-Chinese mercenaries hired as guards because they had few loyalties to Vietnamese of either side.

The three OSA boys had a dozen vehicles—new four-wheel-drive Ford Broncos, not army jeeps or battered Scouts like the rest of us. OSA had a projection room where the latest American movies, delivered daily on special Air America flights restricted to OSA passengers and supplies, were shown nightly. I enjoyed the movies, but went only when invited. You didn't just drop in on the *Office for the Special Assistant to the U.S. Ambassador.* Every province in South Vietnam had a similar compound—often called the "Embassy House," because the name implied direct contact with the U.S. ambassador.

OSA would be called *CIA* anywhere but in Vietnam.

Chuong Thien was probably the only province in South Vietnam without a single bar for GIs, except for our little MAC-V club that was usually out of beer. It's only brothel was a dingy hotel that provided women for ARVN soldiers. The scarcity of fleshpots didn't reflect morality, it was because Vi Thanh was off-limits to American soldiers unless they had a good reason to go there. Partying didn't qualify. Except to go on R & R, some support troops like radio operators, mechanics, and cooks never left the MAC-V compound for their one-year tours of duty.

I worked with the Vietnamese and, as an officer and adviser, traveled across the province. In Vi Thanh, I came and went as I pleased. I was with Vietnamese friends and counterparts several nights a week.

As the Thai 747 droned toward America, I opened my diary, and read what I'd written on my second day in Vi Thanh:

6 July 69. The CORDS compound is surrounded by a chain-link fence with a perimeter of concertina barbwire, and lots of bunkers. The men here say things have been quiet; the VC haven't mortared or rocketed for the past 2 weeks.

There's a field ration mess at MAC-V, plus a small club that serves soft drinks and beer (when they have it), but no officers mess or officers club. Another hut is called a PX because it sells cigarettes and whiskey and cans of Spam and Vienna sausages and boot polish. It's open from 5 to 6 each evening.

Vietnamese soldiers shoot at anything that moves after dark, and artillery fires H&I rounds all night. About 1 a.m. I woke to two short bursts of AW [automatic weapon] fire right outside the compound. Still don't know what it was. Probably an edgy guard, or was it VC infiltration?

Rice production is low in Chuong Thien Province, but Norm Olsen doesn't think local farmers are so far behind. So a lot of rice must be going somewhere, to Charley, for instance. The average rice yield is reported as 1.9 tons per hectare, but it's *really* well over 2 tons. Charley takes his cut before the rice goes to market.

MAC-V rates Chuong Thien the second least secure of Vietnam's 44 provinces. During the 1968 Tet Offensive, the VC regained control of CT up to the fences of MAC-V and CORDS. S-2 [Intelligence] anticipates a VC offensive this month.

This province is low-priority for the pacification program. Top priority goes to the provinces around Saigon and up in I Corps by the DMZ [Demilitarized Zone].

Chuong Thien is, truly, at the end of the line.

The southwestern corner of Chuong Thien is a garden spot—the infamous U-Minh Forest, probably Charley's strongest and best-held region in all VN.

Lloyd Craig is in the room next to me. He's a former police officer from Milwaukee, and seems to know what he's doing.

Lloyd says there is very little major crime in Chuong Thien—because the police blame anything complicated on

Charley: murder, theft, juvenile delinquency, etc. A man and a woman were killed by a claymore mine last week at the *Hoi Chanh* [former VC who had defected to GVN, or Government of Vietnam] Center. It was classified a VC reprisal attack but was, actually, murder—an *eternal triangle* affair: two men and one woman. But it's easier for VN Govt officials to call it terrorism.

7 July. Met Mr. Ming, the Agr. Service Chief and my counterpart, today. VC land mine blew up a commercial bus about 7 or 8 miles from here today. Killed 4, wounded 10. A *plastique* bomb blew up a movie theater yesterday, and VC threw hand grenades into movie theaters and restaurants in Bac Lieu and Soc Trang. Selective terrorism, to show that GVN can't protect the public. Especially effective now, because ARVN has been pushing Charley pretty hard. Charley can't mass for a ground attack—ARVN's artillery would slaughter him. But isolated terrorist attacks can undermine any confidence the people have in GVN.

I went to a noontime party hosted by Colonel Nguu, the province chief, that day. I later described him as:

. . . an unforgettable character who reminds me of an old Chinese warlord. Has 17 children. "All from the same wife?" Sgt. Wilson asked. "No! Not from *one* wife!" Col. Nguu roared, as if the question were insulting. "From *many wives*." The Chief claims to have served in all 44 provinces of VN, with a concubine in each. Fat, laughs real loud, and drinks cognac like water . . . seems as corrupt as can be, although I don't really know that.

I read the name of 1LT Tom Lipscomb, my office mate at Ft. Bragg, in the *Army Times* under the column "Missing to Dead: Hostile." That means his body has just been recovered. Tom was listed as "the husband of Mrs. Cheryl D. Lipscomb, Columbus, Ga." That *has* to be him. They had 2 or 3 kids. He was a platoon leader in the 101st Abn.

12 July. Maj. Johnson called me down today for wearing fatigue pants and a civilian shirt—as if that will make a difference in winning this war. I said *Yes Sir*, and didn't mention

that my trousers are mud-caked from the rice fields. The highlight of my life will be the day I can tell a hard-ass major or a pompous, bird-brained light colonel to get screwed.

Seven of the twelve men who lived at CORDS were military, but usually wore civilian clothes. I was one of them.

Lieutenant Commander Madson was adviser to the Vietnamese Psychological Operations unit—but he never really understood PsyOps. He was a family man in his midfifties who fell in love with his Vietnamese secretary during that long year in Vi Thanh. After his tour, Colonel Madson divorced his wife and returned to Vietnam to marry the secretary.

Madson's assistant, Sgt. Willie Wilson, despised the Vietnamese, and was miserable.

Lloyd Craig had been, I felt, a good cop . . . back when he was a police officer in Milwaukee. In 1969, he was public safety adviser to the local police unit, but did *not* advise on traffic control. Lloyd drank a lot when he arrived. A year later, he was often drunk by midmorning and could hardly function as an adviser.

Sgt. Bob Howell had served in the military police and was adviser to the National Police Field Force. Bob was a real soldier, and the NPFF operated more like soldiers than policemen. The other police adviser was Enrique Gonzales, a Puerto Rican sergeant who, like Wilson, hated everything about Vietnam.

Paul Farrel worked for the Defense Intelligence Agency, or DIA. He didn't talk much about his work, but spent a lot of time with the spooks at OSA.

The CORDS compound was also home for two military men who dressed in civvies and *denied* they were army. Ted Hoffman was husky, blond, and about twenty-five. He had played college football and swore he was a DIA civilian. We all knew he was an army intelligence lieutenant with a lousy cover. And I never understood why Bouncin' Buddy Clark, a black army sergeant, claimed to be a civilian. He wasn't in intelligence, he served as administrative officer for CORDS's fifty or sixty Vietnamese employees.

Norm Olsen and Frank Gillespie were the CORDS advisers I knew best and admired most. I used them a lot in building Robert Cantwell, the civilian in my novel.

But Cantwell frustrated me. I'd somehow made him Ivy

League and condescending, and hinted that he could be CIA. Neither Frank nor Norm fitted that description . . . not exactly.

Why did I make one of my main characters a civilian?

Dozens of Vietnam books were appearing by 1987: memoirs of platoon leaders, army nurses, division commanders. But CIA spooks were the only civilians featured.

The new wave of Vietnam writers often *mention* the civilians who served there—but with contempt. They've created a stereotype of pasty-faced bureaucrats in white short-sleeved shirts and ties who worked in air-conditioned offices in Saigon or Da Nang. At 5:00 P.M. each day, they returned to heavily guarded government apartments for martinis and PX steaks.

I knew many of that type. But the new books ignore another group of civilians, a cadre of dedicated and brave men, and a few women, who spent years trying to help the Vietnamese win the war themselves.

Frank and Norm and a few hundred other civilians stayed in those god-awful provinces year after year, and gave the war what little continuity it had.

Most professional military men assigned as advisers—whether colonels, sergeants, or lieutenants—served mandatory one-year tours, then rotated Stateside. Career soldiers often returned to Nam a year or two later, but not as advisers. *Not if they could help it.*

And for good reason. Troop command was essential for an officer to climb that military ladder to bird colonel or general. The more men you led, the more combat, the better. Few regular army officers wanted to serve *one* tour as an adviser, but *two* MAC-V tours could be the kiss of death for a military career.

Willie Nelson sings "My heros have always been cowboys," and I've always admired cowboys fighting for lost causes. Frank and Norm weren't cowboys, but they committed the best years of their lives to a cause they must have known, deep inside, was lost.

Civilians like Norm and Frank are, to me, unsung heroes of a war that America, and the world, considered too distasteful to produce heroes. They ran the U.S. side of the pacification program, the countryside battle for *hearts and minds*.

The two men were very different, but had a lot in common. Both were children of Camelot, among the first to rush to President John F. Kennedy's stirring call for a new army of idealistic young men and women dedicated to development: the Peace Corps. But within a few years, they had answered *another* idealistic JFK call: *to support any friend, oppose any foe* ...

Yet Norm and Frank were cynical about the U.S. effort in Vietnam. That may seem contradictory, but it isn't. They knew that only honest and committed South Vietnamese officers and government workers, not America's military power, could defeat those little men and women who blended into the countryside under leaders who were fanatically dedicated to a cause.

We called them Viet Cong, from the Vietnamese term for Vietnamese Communists, or Charley, from "Victor Charley," radio language for VC.

The VC called themselves *Mat Trang*, or "The Front"—the National Liberation Front.

Charley described the pacification program as "the velvet glove that hides the iron fist of U.S. aggression."

Thomas Carlyle, the nineteenth-century advocate of Protestantism, coined that line, but I doubt that the Communists knew that. Nor would they know another Carlyle quote: "Be not the slave of words."

I turned back to chapter 2, mainly to study my fictional character. The setting was, in reality, Norm Olsen's office. I had made Robert Cantwell a lot more like Norm than Frank, but I did real justice to neither:

The entrance of a lanky, slow-moving civilian in his midthirties interrupted Dan's conversation with the secretary who claimed to be French.

"Monique, can you translate and type this by noon?" Then the tall civilian offered Dan a huge hand. "You're the new lieutenant? I'm Robert Cantwell."

Cantwell wore horn-rimmed glasses and looked East Coast. Dan knew this man would always be Robert, never Bob.

"Let's go to my office to talk."

An overhead ceiling fan pushed dry heat through Cantwell's sparsely furnished cubicle with its peeling yellow plaster walls. An M-2 carbine stood against the wall. A field phone sat on a government-issue steel desk. Wooden shutters opened at the back of the room to a view of a yellow building with a huge red cross painted across its side.

"Sorry to disrupt your talk with Monique." Dan sensed sarcasm. *No, it's probably my imagination.*

"Coffee?" Cantwell was already pouring Sanka into two cups. He added boiling water from a pot on a hot plate, then pulled a file. The civilian folded himself behind the desk, and motioned Dan to a steel chair.

"Lieutenant, you're going to Mobile Advisory Team 96 in Nuoc Trong village of Kien Hung District."

Dan knew that MAT teams were the U.S. Army's lowest-level advisory units. No one wanted a MAT assignment. Still, finally *getting* assigned was a relief.

Cantwell rose and pointed to Nuoc Trong on a map punctured by green, black, and red pins.

"Nuoc Trong is marked by a green pin. What does that mean?" Dan asked.

"The security rating, determined through the hamlet evaluation survey or HES, a monthly security report from OSA, USAID, and the military. A *green* pin means that Nuoc Trong is a *C*-level village: contested, but generally under GVN control. Black is *D*, meaning the village is far from pacified, and probably belongs to the VC. Red means the National Liberation Front runs the village.

"A blue pin means *A*-level, or safe twenty-four hours a day, and yellow marks a *B* village, under GVN control . . . almost all the time."

"Where are the blue and yellow pins?"

"There aren't any, 56 percent of our villages are *C*-level," Cantwell replied flatly. "But a year ago, after Tet of '68, only 18 percent were *C* villages."

Dan noticed black and red pins to Nuoc Trong's west and south.

"You'll bring MAT 96 to full strength, two lieutenants and three NCOs," Cantwell said. "That's unusual in Chuong Thien."

"I know that MAT teams answer to CORDS," Dan said. "But *who* runs the CORDS show? My briefings were . . . vague on that point."

"Okay, Lieutenant. First, CORDS is the *pacification command*. It's a joint military-civilian agency of about sixty-five hundred men and a few women under a single command. That's Bill Colby, the former CIA station chief for the Far East. Colby served with the OSS in the French underground in the Second World War. Then CIA in Korea. Bill first came to Vietnam in 1959 as the Saigon station chief. CORDS was formed in 1967, and Bill took over in 1968."

Cantwell sipped his coffee. "The CORDS team includes military from all branches, but most in Chuong Thien are army. We also have a couple of navy SEALS, and an air force light colonel who's adviser to the Vietnamese PsyOps unit. CORDS includes State Department civilians like me, and USAID.

"We run the *Chieu Hoi*, or 'Open Arms' program to bring in VC defectors. The *Chieu Hoi* adviser is Ben Salcedo, a Filipino who worked with Ed Lansdale to help President Magsaysay put down the Communist Huk rebellion in the Philippines in the midfifties."

Dan knew that Lansdale had been the thinly disguised hero of two best-selling novels. In *The Ugly American*, he was a freewheeling U.S. Air Force colonel who helped a threatened Third World country, obviously the Philippines, defeat Communist insurgency. In *The Quiet American*, which Dan was now reading, Lansdale was an idealistic CIA agent who found Vietnam over his head. Both descriptions were, he suspected, fairly accurate.

"We started Phoenix Program, or *Phuong Hoang*, after Tet of '68, to neutralize the VC infrastructure. CORDS runs the program. The phoenix was, or is, a bird from Asian mythology. Every five hundred years, the phoenix flies into the desert to burn itself to death. Another phoenix emerges from the ashes, to reestablish civilization." Cantwell paused. "Some say the phoenix represents death. I think it symbolizes resurrection."

Cantwell said *we* started Phoenix, Dan thought. Not *they*. And he refers to the CIA chief as *Bill*. Dan had heard about Phoenix, but wasn't sure the program even existed.

"Political—not military—officers give the VC units orders on whom to assassinate, villages to shell, outposts to attack. Phoenix targets those political leaders rather than the captains and majors who follow their orders.

"And despite what you may have heard, Lieutenant, Phoenix concentrates on getting those leaders to defect, or capturing them—not on cutting throats. Dead VCI are worthless for intelligence. But if dirty work is necessary, it's done by the PRUs, the Provincial Reconnaisance Units, made up of VC defectors who have nothing to lose, and who will be dead men if the Communists take over. The PRU adviser is a navy SEAL."

Cantwell added, like an afterthought, "Of course, *OSA* also works with the *Chieu Hoi* and Phoenix programs."

"What *about* OSA, the Agency? I've heard that the CIA ultimately funds and controls CORDS. Does it?"

"Lieutenant, you can hear a lot of things," Cantwell said carefully. "Let's talk about matters that concern you—like MAT operations."

Dan resented Cantwell's condescending tone. *But don't underestimate this guy*, he thought. *Cantwell obviously knows things they didn't cover in briefings at Pentagon East.*

"You'll be executive officer of MAT 96. You should take over when Lieutenant Burns, the present team leader, rotates Stateside in three months." Dan noticed that Cantwell said *should*, not *will*.

"You'll see a different war than if you were a lieutenant with a regular U.S. unit like the 4th Infantry Division or the 101st Airborne—but one just as real . . . in some ways, *much more* real. The war in Chuong Thien is fought pretty much like when the first of us arrived in '63 and '64. There were only a few hundred advisers in this sad country back then; now we're blessed with half a million GIs that hate the Vietnamese, have no idea why we're here, are scared shitless, for good reason—and blast away anything in the bush that moves."

"Have advisers been killed here?" Dan *had to* ask that question.

"A dozen over the past year, Lieutenant. We lost two last month. Those casualties don't sound high, but only 160 Americans are stationed in Chuong Thien, probably the lowest number for any province in Vietnam. Only thirty or forty advisers work outside of Vi Thanh.

"But only two of those twelve dead advisers were actually killed in combat, facing the enemy World War II–style. The others were ambushed in sampans, or hit mines or booby traps. One was at the wrong place when a Chicom B-40 rocket hit."

Why does Cantwell intimidate me? Dan thought. Because he's Ivy League, and I'm South Texas? Or is it because I'm here for 365 days, while this man seems to have dedicated his life to the war?

"There are 250,000 Vietnamese in Chuong Thien Province. Almost all are farmers, and most live under Viet Cong control, especially at night. So you'll be kept entertained, Lieutenant, here at the *Front Lines of the Battle for Hearts and Minds*. How's your Vietnamese?"

"I took the six-week course at Fort Bragg. But I didn't learn much."

"I wouldn't expect so," Cantwell said. "The advisers we get *today* can hardly order a meal in Vietnamese. There's only a handful of Americans who don't need interpreters. They all took the bedroom course."

Dan looked at Cantwell.

"Vietnamese wives—or girlfriends."

As Cantwell talked, a distant *whomp-whomp* roar grew louder and an airborne speck larger through the window behind him. A Huey settled on skids by the hospital. Two GIs set three stretchers in the helipad's dust, then scrambled back in as the chopper lifted. Vietnamese orderlies in white uniform rushed the stretchers inside.

"You'll get used to that, Lieutenant."

Dan looked at Cantwell.

"The wounded, dozens come in to the provincial hospital every day. More, when we're *really* having fun. Civilians, ARVN soldiers, wounded VC, kids, old women . . . mostly with shrapnel wounds."

"Viet Cong shrapnel?"

"Sometimes, but the local VC don't have that much ordnance. Most of the wounds are from heavy artillery. Uncle Sugar supplies ARVN with unlimited 105 and 155 shells. You'll see, when you get to MAT 96. We'll be firing intermittent H & I shells around you," the civilian's voice turned more caustic, *"to keep you safe at night."*

Cantwell stood, which told Dan the briefing was over.

It's strange that my mental picture was usually of Norm Olsen when I wrote about Robert Cantwell. At first, I thought Norm was East Coast. He was actually from Seattle, I learned later.

Norm was tall, quiet, and unassuming. He was an idealistic product of the sixties; answering Kennedy's inaugural call took him to Colombia as one of America's first Peace Corps volunteers. Norm then went to Vietnam with USAID in about 1964, where he served in Kien Phong Province, in the Delta.

Norm was deputy senior adviser for Chuong Thien Province, like my fictional Cantwell, and serving his third Vietnam tour when I arrived. Norm intimidated me—although he didn't mean to—when he briefed me at Chuong Thien provincial headquarters.

Later, I got to know the *real* Norm Olsen . . . I think. He was a sensitive and complicated man who sometimes covered shyness with what seemed, at first, to be sarcasm. He was also more formal than most men in such situations. Norm called me "Lieutenant" instead of "Tom," during my first couple of months. Even after that, I became *Lieutenant* again, when Norm was irritated.

A strange thing about Norm. Over the next year, he often *returned* from the field . . . but I seldom saw him leave. He did it that quietly. Norm would reappear in Vi Thanh, carrying a battered M-2 carbine and gas-mask bag stuffed with extra clips of ammo and dirty clothes. He'd have spent a night with a MAT team in Long Tri, the next couple of nights in Kien Long District with the People's Self-Defense Force, trying to build morale among demoralized village militia. Only a few men did that.

As my tour ended, I asked Norm how he felt about serving all those years for a cause that, I knew, was futile.

"It's like I've sat through three reels of a four-reel movie," Norm said. "I know how the story will end . . . but I still want to watch that last reel."

Norm's wife Betsy lived in a "safe haven" compound in Manila. She was an American adventurer who had also served *her* Vietnam tour, with the International Voluntary Services. IVS operated like the Peace Corps—but the Peace Corps didn't send volunteers into war zones.

Wives couldn't live in Vietnam, but could visit. Couples sometimes met in Saigon. That wasn't the best setting for a romantic rendezvous, but incredibly, Betsy made her way to Chuong Thien several times.

Betsy gave me quite a shock on her first visit after I arrived. The VC were walking 82mm mortar rounds across Vi Thanh around midnight, so I rushed to a sandbagged bunker. Frank and Norm and Lloyd were there, then I saw straight black hair streaming from a steel army helmet. I almost freaked out. I was face-to-face with a *Caucasian woman*! An honest-to-God *round-eye*, but you couldn't see those eyes through her glasses in the yellow lantern light.

Chuong Thien was a man's world and Betsy didn't belong there, not by my thinking. But I liked it when she came.

You might find a Norm on the Harvard campus, but Chuong Thien Province seemed where Frank Gillespie belonged.

Frank was in his early thirties, was physically fit, prematurely bald, and wore steel-rimmed glasses. I've never known a braver man, military or civilian. But Frank's was a calculated bravery. My admiration for him bordered on hero worship, and led to calculated risks of my own—because I couldn't let him down. I was proud when Frank asked me along on three-day trips across Chuong Thien, traveling by sampan along the rivers and canals, sleeping in village huts or with far-flung MAT teams.

A native of Cleveland, Frank graduated from Ohio University, then served in the Peace Corps in northeastern Thailand in 1962–63. There, Radio Free Thailand, the clandestine Communist station, and Radio Hanoi denounced him and other volunteers as American spies.

"My helping U.S. military intelligence as an interpreter didn't soften that image," Frank later wrote. "But it got me to isolated spots that I wouldn't have seen otherwise."

At first, I suspected, like many others, that Frank was a spook with a USAID cover. He wasn't, but the story still follows him.[1]

In the spring of 1964, Joe Granger, later to be the first U.S. civilian to be captured, tortured, and executed by the VC, talked Frank into leaving the Peace Corps to take a USAID contract in Binh Long Province, along the Cambodian border north of Saigon. Only eight hundred Americans, military and civilian, were then in Vietnam.

He reported to Col. Sam Wilson, a Special Forces officer who ran the Office of Field Operations, and would later command the U.S. Army Special Warfare School at Fort Bragg. Wilson retired as director of the Defense Intelligence Agency.

As he was leaving Vietnam a year later, Frank ran into Col-

---

[1] Even today, many *old Vietnam hands* think that most of Chuong Thien's CORDS team in those days, including me, were CIA.

onel Wilson in a Saigon bar. He had just learned that friends from his Binh Long advisory team had been killed in savage hand-to-hand combat.

The colonel tried to convince Frank to return to Vietnam. "Go to Thailand and marry that girl," he said, "then go back to the States. I'll get you back in Vietnam in a few months."

Frank married Urai in Bangkok a few days later. Her father had been an immigrant merchant from China who married in Thailand, then later brought his original family to Bangkok. Urai's Chinese stepbrothers were gold traders who worried that she was marrying below her social level. But they gave Frank a heavy golden wedding ring, fashioned as a dragon with ruby-inset eyes, nostrils, and tongue.

Gillespie was teaching in Ohio when Sam Wilson's men tracked him down. A few months later, Frank reported to an advisory team in Tay Ninh Province, on the Cambodian border, again on USAID contract. Urai moved back to Bangkok and taught sociology in a teachers' college.

Frank would serve in Indochina's war zones for almost seven years, then in Thailand and Indonesia for another decade.

In 1966, Frank took a regular USAID assignment in Laos. This time he brought Urai and Lisa and Russell, their two children.

Frank might not admit it, but he loved the adventure and freedom of operating in a nonconventional and clandestine war where the United States, officially, was not involved—but was.

In the spring of 1968, turncoat soldiers of the Royal Lao Army set Frank up. The guards who watched the Gillespie's Lao-style home vanished in the early morning. That's when three squads of Communist Pathet Lao came to blow Frank away. The PL pitched hand grenades at the windows, but they bounced off the screens. The house was on stilts, so the PL went under and sprayed AK-47 fire up through the floor. Expended bullets wounded Frank lightly. He was cut, crawling over the broken glass, as he tried to find an exit for his family to escape.

The Gillespies finally crawled into an iron bathtub. The Pathet Lao assumed the family was dead, and left.

Frank moved his family back to Thailand, then returned to Vietnam to serve in Chuong Thien Province from 1968 to late 1970. He was chief adviser to the New Life Development Program, at the forefront of the pacification program, when I arrived. Frank later replaced Norm Olsen as deputy senior adviser for Chuong Thien. In 1971, John Paul Vann made him adviser to the IV Corps inspector general's office, comprised of senior ARVN officers.

Frank looked after his men if they were in trouble. When they got into trouble because of their own screwups, Frank worried about that after they were safe.

Like one evening in 1969 when Rod Fernandez, a Filipino Civic Action worker, didn't return from Hoa Luu, about ten kilometers to our south.

At 8:00 P.M., Frank put on a steel helmet and flak jacket, loaded an M-2 carbine and M-79 grenade launcher, and grabbed a PRC-25 radio. Other than his Levi's and sports shirt, he looked—and acted—like a good infantryman whose buddy was in trouble.

"*Where the hell* are you going?"

"To Hoa Luu," Frank answered at the door of his Scout. "Fernandez is one of my men."

Damn! I thought. Fernandez is one of *my* men too, in a way. Most of his work is in agriculture. But the road to Hoa Luu is Indian country after six. Besides, I know Rod. He's horny as a rabbit and probably shacked up with some village girl that he's promised to marry ... along with a life of U.S. dollars and PX shoes. Rod will promise a woman anything, when he's in heat.

Frank could easily die tonight ... because of Rod's libido.

"Wait!" I grabbed my helmet and shotgun, and climbed into the Scout. This was dangerous and, worse, dumb. I didn't like it. If Fernandez is in trouble, he brought it on himself.

Frank didn't radio the TOC that we were leaving because he knew the colonel would order him to return.

Vi Thanh was pitch-black as we drove through.

"Frank, stop! Rod drinks at a beer joint somewhere around here."

Frank turned onto a mud trail through the palm trees and pulled up to a thatch hut with no sign. A kerosene light was glowing, so I took my shotgun and went in. Frank stood guard outside, with his M-2.

The table was covered with *Biere Larue* bottles, and Rod's arms were draped around two Vietnamese dollies. He had fallen in love—again. Frank and I paid for the beer, left some piasters for the professional ladies, and loaded Rod into the Scout.

I mentioned that night, years later when Frank visited IRRI. He didn't remember it. Frank did things like that, all the time.

The Revolutionary Development cadre were the front-line soldiers of New Life Development—and Frank's love in Chuong Thien. I found a 15 July 1969 diary description of the paramilitary civilians:

I went by jeep today with CPT Williams to Long My & from there rode a sampan north up the river to Long Tri, a newly opened village. By "new," I mean ARVN has just chased the main-force VC out. The Phoenix Program is, hopefully, neutralizing its political infrastructure. It's probably a "D" village.

Floating on that river, heavily armed, in an open sampan to a village that the VC have controlled for years—that's a bit scary. And our PRC-25 radio didn't work. I wouldn't have gone, but Williams acted like I'd stay behind because the trip is so dangerous.

A 10-man RD team is in Long Tri, mostly young men and women who live in these contested villages to make conditions that will shut Charley out. The RD cadre do civic action: build schools and medical clinics, mobilize villagers to dig wells, dredge irrigation canals, build roads. And find and eliminate the VC infrastructure. The RD role is like that of the VC "action militia"—to gain the people's confidence, propagandize, recruit. They are brave young people with a high casualty rate, the most motivated and idealistic I've met.

The RDs and I looked across the rice paddies from Long Tri at the next village in the tree line, one that Charley controls day and night. To approach that village with less than a company of infantry would be suicide. The RD team has been in Long Tri only 3 days & the VC have hit them every night, and sniped during the day. But someday, another RD team will go into that village, to push the VC out and extend the secure area. It's called the "oil slick" strategy, and it's a long, painful process.

We could probably whip Charley . . . if the sun never went down.

Many RD cadre were teenagers whom regular Vietnamese officers sometimes called *linh sua*—"milk soldiers." Once Capt. Bud Shields, a fellow Texas Aggie, and I were driving along the few klicks of open road in Kien Hung District. We offered a ride to a female RD in black pajamas. She'd slung an ancient M-1 Garand rifle across her back, and a bandolier of .30-caliber ammunition crossed her bosom. But most incongruous was the baby that the brave young woman cradled. We all soon laughed as Bud cracked jokes in pidgin Vietnamese while trying to keep the jeep on hardened tracks that, we hoped, couldn't conceal VC mines. The woman pushed the bandolier aside, unbuttoned her blouse, and offered a nipple to the crying baby. *Linh sua*, I thought. Milk soldier.

Agriculture, including the spread of IRRI rice varieties, was part of New Life Development, so I answered directly to Frank for all but army duties. That included Land Reform and the Agricultural Development Bank, which gave loans to farmers.

My main counterpart, Mr. Ming, was chief of the Agricultural Services. He was raised in Saigon, but had a B.S. degree in agriculture. Ming was frail, effete, and his handshake was limp. He hated Chuong Thien, and I could easily see why. It was one of the Delta's three exile posts for the most inept or corrupt officials. The others were Moc Hoa on the Cambodian border, and Ca Mau to our south.

Ming was also a coward who would leave Vi Thanh only if pushed. I pushed him a lot.

Ming's deputy was Vinh, a muscular ex-farmer with a high school education. The Vietnamese called him "Dr. Vinh," and considered it funny. I don't know why. Vinh was proud of his ten years of service as an ARVN sergeant, and was probably a good soldier. "The VC are like rats . . . and Dr. Vinh is the cat," he'd brag after a few glasses of *baxide*.

Thursday. At least I *think* it's Thursday but I'm not sure because the days are all the same. The war is strange; I think adjusting to a WWII-type situation would be easier. I sleep on clean sheets in the CORDS Compound and take hot showers, unless I'm in a village. I have ham and eggs for breakfast, then call the TOC to see where the main-force VC units may be today. I slip my .38 into the front of my trousers, pull my shirt-tail out, and grab my M-16. I sandbag the floorboard of my Scout, in case we hit a land mine, pick up an interpreter and some Vietnamese *ag cadre*, and go off to farms where IR8 or tilapia fish are being raised. We eat lunch with a farmer, then rest in a hammock for half an hour. But artillery always fires in the distance.

I've spent the last 3 days with José Ona, a Filipino rice specialist who studied at the International Rice Research Institute in Los Baños, Philippines. We have an experimental-demonstration plot about 8 miles up the Xa No Canal where we test IRRI rices, and run fertilizer and herbicide trials.

We furnish the seeds and inputs, and Ba Lien, a VN farmer, provides land and labor, but must follow our instructions. Ba Lien keeps the rice harvest—at least double what he grew before.

We use tight research methods. This is university-type work that will help tremendously in improving rice farming in the Delta.

Staying busy keeps me from being so lonely. I'm thankful to be doing something I believe in, and that may help me professionally after the Army.

My agricultural background also involved me in the controversial Agent Orange missions through Operation RANCH HAND, the U.S. Air Force defoliation program. RANCH HAND pilots had a motto: *Only we can prevent forests.*

I reviewed plans for spraying each area, made recommendations, and monitored results when missions went wrong. I disliked defoliation and usually advised *against* it. The army seldom listened. On 15 August, I wrote:

I'm waiting, with Lloyd Craig and 2 Land Reform cadre, to go by sampan up the Xa No Canal about 8 or 9 km to Thanh Binh hamlet.

Later—I was wrong, we didn't go to Thanh Binh (fortunately, maybe—Charley hit it twice this week), but went to Di An A, about 5 km SW.

The farmers there seemed enthusiastic about Land Reform. The cadre processed 10 applications for former French plantation land by noon. I told the farmers that I'm a farmer, too, back in my country, so I know how much owning your land means. I never mention, except to Ba Lien, that I'm in the Army.

The farmers said that they appreciated my going there, and even gave a round of applause. It's strange. Di An A has been a VC stronghold for years.

The farmers complained that our defoliation missions had destroyed their fruit trees and gardens. I asked if they had applied for compensation payment. The reply surprised me: they don't want money, but would I ask the military to be more careful and not destroy any more of their trees and crops? On Monday I'll go in to take Polaroid pictures of the damage. But the area is very insecure. The U.S. Air Force—and Army—pulled another bad screw-up in Long My District last week that will cost us a lot of ground and prestige. They defoliated an area officially declared as "pacified." The pilots read the map wrong, according to one report. But a VN told me that a request to defoliate that area was made 2 years ago, when it was a VC stronghold. The mission killed everything: a crop of IR8, bananas, fruit trees, gardens. To make it more sickening, a gunship hosed down the area ahead of the defoliation plane. The chopper killed 2 old women and some water buffalo, and wounded about 10 civilians.

I wish we would stop defoliation, or limit it strictly. Once again, we'll go in and dole out money to pay for what we inexcusably destroyed. Very goddamn big-hearted of us.

I remember a red-lacquered coffin in a hootch up the river north of Long Tri village, and Frank—or was it Norm?—paying off a family for killing a mother or grandfather or whoever the hell was killed *that time*.

I later wrote, as fiction:

"Welcome to *beautiful Ap Lan hamlet*," Robert Cantwell said as the sampan docked at a bamboo pier.

Dan stared at the naked trees with bare branches standing in a carpet of dead leaves. *"Christ"* was all he could say. It was like black-and-white photos he'd seen of eerie World War I battlefields.

"What will happen to those RANCH HAND sonofabitches?"

"Nothing, Lieutenant. They read the map coordinates wrong, that's all. They'll probably never know—or care— that they hit the wrong target.

"And the gunships? Those eighteen-year-old kids fly just above the treetops, they're sitting ducks for VC machine-gun fire. I don't blame them for being trigger-happy. I blame no one, I just wish to God these things would quit happening."

Robert left the sampan first and greeted a dozen boys and tired old men of the Ap Lan Self-Defense Force. They wore faded fatigue jackets with black pajama pants, and carried weapons discarded by armies of several wars: bulky M-1 Garands, M-2 carbines, a 1903 Springfield .30-06, some Winchester 12-gauge pump shotguns with sawed-off barrels.

The men followed their local guides cautiously along a trail through desolation that was once an orchard, then came to a rice field.

"This is—or was—the first crop of IR8 planted in Long Tri village, Lieutenant." The plants' wilted leaves lay flat and yellow in the water. "But don't worry. Our government will pay for the trees and the rice. The money will filter through the province chief and the district chief, of course, so it'll never reach these farmers. But Uncle Sugar means well."

A farmer leaned on a crutch. His right leg was gone from below the knee, but that could have been from the French war, Dan thought. The farmer spoke. Robert answered in Vietnamese, then translated for Dan.

"He asked if the trees are really dead. I said, 'No, the trees are just asleep. They'll come alive again, next year.' "

Another question.

"These people have a wonderful sense of humor, Lieutenant. He asked, 'Will the people also wake up next year?' "

A dog barked, and chickens and ducks scattered as the men approached a thatch hootch. "Now comes the *fun part*."

Inside, a dignified and elderly lady in white, the Buddhist color for mourning, served cups of green tea. As Dan's eyes adjusted to the dimness, a shiny red coffin materialized along a wall.

"I'll need some help translating *this*, Khang," Robert said. "First, offer my apologies, on behalf of the U.S. Government, for defoliating the wrong area, and for gunning down her husband and water buffalo. It was a mistake. A *bad* mistake. Throw in some flowery Vietnamese phrases, okay?" Khang nodded.

"Does she understand that I'm authorized to pay compensation for her losses?"

Khang talked with the woman. "She un'nerstand, Mr. Cantwell."

"How much does she think the dead water buffalo was worth?"

Khang spoke with the woman, then said:

"She say numba one buf'lo, sir. Worth at least twenty thou' p."

"That sounds high, but I'm not going to argue about today's buffalo market. We'll pay, with American taxpayers' money."

"Didn't taxpayers' money *kill* the goddamn buffalo?" Dan commented.

"Very astute, Lieutenant Bridges. You're a real philosopher. Now we'll discuss reparations for her dead husband. Khang, can you somehow ask how much *he* was worth? Use as much diplomacy as possible."

Khang spoke softly to the woman.

"*Muoi lam ngan.*"

"Holy Christ!"

"What did she say?" Dan asked.

"*Fifteen* thousand piasters."

"*God fucking damn.* That's from the theater of the absurd."

"Vietnam *is* the theater of the absurd, *Lieutenant.*"

Much has been written about the legacies—from skin rashes to cancer and deformed children—that Agent Orange left Vietnam veterans. Its use peaked in 1970, when 3.25 million gallons were sprayed across Vietnam.

Agent Orange was part of the Chuong Thien environment;

we were exposed continuously. To deny the VC cover, we burned away foliage around MAC-V and CORDS with the herbicide, and sprayed potential ambush sites along the canals.

I documented defoliated areas on the ground, but never worried about health hazards. I knew that the main Agent Orange herbicides, 2,4-D and 2,4,5-T, were used on farms across America. What I *did not* know was that the defoliant contained about two parts per million of *dioxin*, a highly toxic manufacturing byproduct. A few parts per *billion* of dioxin causes cancer in rats. *My* main concern was that Agent Orange drove peasant farmers to the VC.

23 Aug. Col. Nguu and the former Province Sr. Adviser had both earlier recommended defoliation of the Snake River, a few klicks SW of Vi Thanh. I went up in a chopper to look it over this morning. I can't approve the mission. The area has beautiful pineapple groves, coconut trees, rice. I don't know what will happen now. Col. Le Vasseur, the present PSA, canceled the mission, but Col. Nguu wants it sprayed, so now he's lost face. I feel strongly that spraying would be an unwise move psychologically, especially since all the VN know about the Long My screw-up. I say it makes no real difference whether we actually kill crops in pacified areas, or not. In this war, the truth matters little; its what the people *believe* that counts. If I were a VC propagandist, I'd love to see the US spray planes coming.

During the 3 days I was gone from Chuong Thien, two more buses hit VC mines, and an outpost was overrun.

09 Sept.—Tues. We haven't been mortared since Saturday night. But there has been a lot of activity, in spite of the "cease fire."

This morning I went to Long Tri village to see the crop damage from the defoliation screw-up a couple of weeks ago. Others were Ming, *Trung Uy* Chuong (VN S-5), Cpt. Bolich, Norm Olsen, and Maj. Lewis, the Long My District Sr. Adviser. We damn near walked into a VC-RD firefight. But Maj. Lewis said the shooting was just PF militia practicing. It's his district, he should know, but I thought something was wrong all along. When we got back, we found it *was* a VC firefight.

The defoliation damage was awful—80–100% of the crops destroyed. The sugar cane wasn't hurt much. They were probably spraying 2,4-D, which kills broadleaf plants only. But it's quite a shock to see, in lush VN, trees that look like West Texas mesquites in mid-winter.

On Sunday, Oahn, Bac, and Tri talked me out of going to Kien Long. I learned today that Charley rocketed the compound from only 50 meters away Sun night. One VC was KIA.

We nearly lost an ag cadre on Friday in Hoa An Village. The VC threw a hand grenade into his house, and shot it up. Killed his wife and one baby, but he got away. The Ag Service took up a collection this morning and I put in 500 piasters to help bury them. He must have been doing a good job, or the VC wouldn't have singled him out for assassination.

Vietnam veterans began claiming that Agent Orange had caused serious health problems in 1970, and the U.S. military rapidly cut its use. Only 0.6 million gallons were sprayed in 1971.

Veterans' suits against the Agent Orange manufacturers have been inconclusive. The corporations deny liability for health problems, but reached a 1984 out-of-court settlement of $180 million for vets who met a certain defoliant exposure level and have since died or become disabled, with no good reason. The cutoff time for application is 31 December 1994.

Sores beneath the skin of my groin (sebaceous cysts) began to plague me soon after returning from Vietnam. I've undergone surgery four times, but more keep returning. I'm not disabled, but it's damned uncomfortable. As this book goes to press, I face either another round of surgery, or a month of noncosmetic plastic surgery in my groin. Did my heavy exposure to Agent Orange cause the problem? I don't know.

After I submitted this manuscript in 1991, Owen Lock, my editor, sent it to outside reviewers for comments.

"How could Hargrove have learned about rice so quickly?"

asked Kenn Miller, author of another Vietnam book, *Tiger the Lurp Dog*. Owen asked me to respond.

To be honest, learning about rice wasn't hard.

First, the skills of growing crops are about the same, whether dryland cotton in West Texas, or irrigated rice in South Vietnam. All plants must have care, especially in their early, fragile days, and protection from insects and diseases. I learned that as a farm boy.

Also, I had studied the basics of crop science in agronomy classes at Texas A&M. Healthy plants need nitrogen, the most essential nutrient, plus phosphorus, potassium, and minor elements, depending on local soils. IRRI scientists had designed IR8 to convert those nutrients to grain more efficiently than traditional rice varieties do.

Then José Ona came to Chuong Thien soon after I arrived. With no one to oversee his local experiments, Joe gladly took me under his wing. Thus, I had a personal mentor who knew more about growing rice in the tropics than anyone I've ever met.

On 18 July, I wrote:

> Went out with Ming and "Dr. Vinh" this morning, and saw that irrigation water had overflowed the banks of our herbicide trials. I felt pretty low, but called Joe Ona in Can Tho on the land line, and found that it wouldn't ruin the experiment. Also, a farmer brought us some IR8 leaves with a disease—brown spots along the edges. Looks like some sort of blight to me, but I'll ask Ona.

> José Ona, he's an inspiring man. A product of IRRI who's been in VN for 3 years, pushing IR8 like hell, establishing experiments, demonstrations, farmer meetings across the Mekong Delta. He's an idealist, but an effective idealist. If peace ever comes to VN, it'll be more because of men like Ona than all the generals we've sent over here.

The only framed diploma that hangs in my office at IRRI today documents another advantage I had in learning about rice. It's not my Ph.D. from Iowa State, nor my B.S. from Texas A&M. The diploma is in Vietnamese, except for the words 1LT THOMAS R. HARGROVE. It's my graduation certificate from the IRRI Rice Production Training Course.

When I joined IRRI in 1973, veteran scientists who'd worked across Asia for a decade sometimes asked, smugly: "Have *you* ever been in a rice field?" They assumed that a science editor would know rice only on paper, not in the mud.

I had a perfect answer: "Yeah, I'm an IRRI RPTC graduate," pointing to the diploma. "But *I* took the course *the hard way*."

Today, few in the rice world are naive enough to bait me with *that* question.

Since its early days, IRRI has run RPTCs to train extension workers in how to use, and teach, the new rice technology.

During the war, Filipinos ran RPTCs to transfer that technology to Vietnamese rice specialists through a USAID contract with IRRI. In February 1970, they offered a course, in English, for USAID agricultural workers. Army officers who worked in pacification could fill vacant slots. I applied and was accepted.

The course was taught mostly in the fields of the National Rice Production Training Center on Hiep Hoa Island, near Saigon. Joe Ona was one of two instructors. Crops of rice had been planted on a "staggered" schedule so, in one intense week, we gained hands-on experience with every stage of rice production: planting seedbeds, transplanting, weeding, pest control, harvesting, threshing, and drying.

I learned a lot. But Joe Ona had already taught me most of the course's content, and I had worked with both rice and livestock, in country, for eight months before taking that course.

A few days after my return, I wrote in my diary:

27 Febr 70

Woke up last night to machinegun fire. It had been a long time. VC platoon probed the *Chieu Hoi* Center again. One man WIA. Lots of shooting, flares, then went back to bed.

Have sent resumes to every agency I know that works in intl agr development, but no job offers. Am beginning to think I won't be able to work overseas, after the Army.

Went to Kien Long yesterday with Khoui to look at some village swine projects. Many pigs dying from what seems to be hog cholera. Had lunch with the Vinh Phong village admin. chief, and got real sick later.

Set up 4 more New Hampshire chicken projects, with 50 chicks each: 2 in Vi Thanh, 1 in Long My, and 1 in Vi Thuy.

Just got back from a week-long IR8 training course on Hiep Hoa Island, near Saigon. José Ona and another Filipino, Bong Bolo, taught the course—and did an outstanding job. Bolo was formerly in charge of extension training at IRRI. Also in the rice course was Tex Bogg, a DSA from An Xuyen Prov, to the south of Kien Long. Tex is a civilian, fluent in VN, who's been in Nam for 5 years and has a VN wife from Can Tho. Two Army DSAs from An Xuyen also attended: CPT Martinez, a Cuban refugee, and CPT Swenson.

Our training was interrupted one morning when the U.S. Air Force dropped a "daisy cutter"—a one-thousand-pound bomb—on the riverbank opposite Hiep Hoa Island. It shook the ground, and threw a mushroom-shaped, smoke-and-dust cloud thousands of feet into the sky. I had never seen a daisy cutter explode, not even in Chuong Thien, but Joe Ona made us keep on identifying insect pests of rice, like nothing had happened.

One night in Saigon, after our field exercises, the two good captains and I were drinking beer in the Eden Roc Hotel, where Tex and Frank Schwenke were staying. A bar girl joined us, and Martinez bought her a couple of Saigon teas. After a while she asked: "Hey, honey, where you stay?"

"Here in the Eden Roc," Martinez answers.

"Good! Maybe so I come your room tonight? Show you time you never forget! OK?"

"Fine, I'm in room 602," CPT Martinez replies (602 was Tex Bogg's room). "You come at 11:30, and I give you beaucoup piasters."

"Numba one! What your name?"

"Tex. You knock real soft and say 'Tex, Tex,' and we'll have a numba one time." We paid for our drinks, and laughed as we walked back to the Ambassador BOQ where US military types stayed.

I've mostly described men I liked and respected when I arrived in Chuong Thien. But I must also describe one of those rare individuals, a total stereotype, that we all had to endure.

"Go over to the MAC-V orderly room and find Captain Roger That," Norm Olsen said that day I reported to Vi Thanh. "He'll process your papers."

"Captain Roger That? Who's he?"

"You'll see. Ask for the S-1."

The orderly room was an olive-drab wooden hut with large screened windows. The personnel officer, a captain in his midthirties, talked into a field phone.

"Well, get on the Lima-Lima and find out. We're fighting a *war* down here!" The captain patted the .45 automatic in his shoulder holster fondly. He looked up through plastic-rimmed, army-issue glasses and motioned me to enter, but did not motion me to sit. A black-lacquer name plate sat on the desk, inlaid with mother-of-pearl letters that read CPT G. A. PULLEIG. A cheap brass plate beside it featured an engraved map of South Vietnam, with the inscription WHEN I DIE I'LL GO TO HEAVEN, 'CAUSE I'VE SPENT MY TIME IN HELL. CAN THO, REPUBLIC OF VIETNAM, 1969.

Captain Pulleig had the whitest skin and shortest crew cut I had seen in Vietnam. A caricature of a buzzard chomping on a cigar was tacked to the wall above his typewriter. The bird wore a green beret and cradled a smoking M-16. His message, in bold black letters, was: **"Hearts and mind, my ass! I want to *kill* somebody!"**

"Roger that. Out!" Captain Pulleig barked, hanging up the field phone.

"Goddamn Victor Novembers."

"Who?"

"Victor Novembers, Lieutenant. Vietnamese. Our *allies* in this war, supposedly. Cowards who will never fight." He pointed a finger at me. "We could kick Charley's ass out of the Ca Mau Peninsula in a month with one good division of

American fighting men, led by professional, regular army officers."

I glanced at the captain's insignia. Adjutant General's Corps. Personnel.

"So you're the new lieutenant, just in from the World. Fresh meat for the Green Machine. You an RA?"

"No, sir, a two-year reserve officer."

Captain Pulleig sneered.

"Where'd you get your commission?"

"Texas A&M."

"Oh no! Another *rotcie*," Captain Pulleig rolled his eyes, and I stiffened. I didn't consider a Texas Aggie a "rotcie."

"Why does the army send these wet-behind-the-ears college boys *to me*?"

"I take it you went to OCS, sir?"

"That's a rog ... I *earned* my commission, after six years as an EM in Sam's Army." He held out a hand. I put my right arm forward, thinking the captain meant to shake hands.

"For God's sake, Lieutenant, give me your orders, *your records*!"

I withdrew my hand and gave the captain the manila envelope. The humidity had sealed its gummed flap shut. Captain Pulleig drew a Buck's hunting knife with a carved bone handle and twelve-inch blade from a scabbard and slit the envelope.

"I see that you ETS on the same day you DEROS."

I knew that ETS meant estimated termination of service, but asked "What does 'deros' mean, sir?"

"Date of expected rotation from overseas. Christ, don't you know *anything* about the army?"

"Not enough, I guess."

"Roger that. You don't know *nearly* enough." I now realized why Olsen had called the personnel officer "Captain Roger That." This guy isn't just a military prick, I thought. He's a real meathead.

"After Nam you'll go back to the soft civilian life, right, Lieutenant?"

"Yes sir."

"I *hate* civilians. If I had my way, we wouldn't have civilians like you in *this man's army*."

"If I had *my* way, I wouldn't be here either, sir." That wasn't exactly true, but I had to say it.

The captain jolted, then scowled.

"Lieutenant Hargrove, I suggest that you disappear for an hour while I cut your orders. I'm sorry that Advisory Team 73 doesn't have a fraternity club, but maybe you can go think about panty raids."

"Yes sir." At the door, I turned. "Captain Pulleig, may I ask how long you've been here?"

"Six months. Why?"

"You must have gone through hell." Then I hoped the comment didn't sound as sarcastic as I'd meant it.

"That's a rog," the captain replied, inserting a form into his typewriter.

Transition 4

Chuong Thien Province, 1988

We dock along the canal, and I follow Tran Van Rang. Ba Lien's palm-thatch home sits beneath coconut palms, surrounded by bougainvillea in a grove of banana, papaya, and mangosteen. The house hasn't changed, but it's so much smaller than I remember.

Children see me and start shouting. I walk inside.

He's in his seventies now, and his Ho Chi Minh beard is gray, but I recognize him easily. "*Chao, Ong* Ba Lien," I say, as we shake hands and embrace. Someone pours green tea, and we sit around the table as neighbors start to drift in.

I talk about my family, IRRI . . . anything to hold back the emotion as Ba Lien throws me back in time. The old farmer catalyzes memories that go beyond rice.

"Do you remember José Ona, the Filipino agronomist who brought the first IR8 seeds?" I ask. Dr. Vo Tong Xuan translates. "And how in 1970, Joe smuggled two kilograms of IR20 from the Philippines?"

Those seeds—the first in all of Vietnam—were precious, because IR20 was IRRI's first improvement over IR8. Yields were about the same, but IR20 had better grain quality and resisted several pests without insecticides. Ona and I gave the IR20 seeds to Ba Lien, in trust, because we knew he'd give them the care they deserved. By 1972, IR20 had replaced IR8 across the Mekong Delta.

Yes, Ba Lien remembers ... IR8, IR20, and Ona.

Tu Rang then leads me to Ba Lien's wife, who lies on a hard teak bed at the back of the room. She recognizes me, but she's sick. Do I have medicine? I wish I did.

We return to the table and sip tea.

"She's my aunt," Tu Rang says. "Ba Lien's wife reported your visits and helped us gather information on you."

Tu Rang's words are numbing, but don't surprise me. I knew, back in 1969, that farmers eight kilometers up the Xa No Canal from Vi Thanh either supported, or had to answer to, the VC at night. I bear no animosity, I'm still alive. I just wish I had medicine.

A shrill voice breaks my thoughts. A young woman rushes through the crowd and grasps my shoulder. Xuan asks her to slow down, then translates.

"The tall American!" she shouts. "I remember you so well. Do you remember me? I'm Ba Lien's granddaughter, the little girl you carried around the farm on your shoulders." She now balances her own baby on a hip.

All I can say is "Yes, but I can't do that now." I can't talk anymore, so I walk outside to the concrete patio where Ba Lien dries rice. The woman, Huyen Xuan Dep, follows.

"The round table was here on the patio before," I say. "Ba Lien gave a party for me here, just before I left Chuong Thien."

"You remember well."

We go back into the house. "What happened to the bomb shelter?" I ask. "It was in that corner."

"We don't need a bomb shelter anymore." I'd made a bad joke, and everyone knew it, but it was okay.

I pull a copy of *Field Problems of Tropical Rice* from my bag. I coordinated publication of the IRRI booklet, with 158 color photos to help farmers identify rice pests. It's now been published in twenty-two languages. I'm proud that Xuan and I raised German, Australian, Mennonite, Ford Foundation, and FAO money to print and distribute 160,000 copies of the Vietnamese edition—enough to give one copy to every agricultural production brigade in Vietnam. It was the largest press run IRRI ever made. We used thirty-six tons of paper and filled six ship containers with the booklet. To me, that's paying back a little.

Ms. Dep clutches, then flips through the booklet. She thrusts an open page at me. "This is our problem now!" It's thrip damage, so I introduce her to Nguyen Van Huynh, a University of Can Tho entomologist and, like Xuan, an IRRI alumnus. We all go to the field.

The rice looks bad, and Huynh confirms that thrips are the problem. The IRRI variety, IR13240, resists most pests, but not thrips. Huynh tells her how to save the crop, if she can get the chemicals. Pesticides are like gasoline: hard to find, and expensive.

We return to Ba Lien's home for more tea before leaving. I give the farmer a coffee cup embossed with the IRRI seal. That's not much, is it? His friendship may have saved my life.

Tu Rang speaks again, and I know it'll be something I don't want to hear.

"Ba Lien's two sons-in-law were both Viet Cong colonels. One was a Revolutionary Hero." The ex-VC loves telling me these things. I might be the same way . . . but *my* side lost the war.

"Ba Lien never told me *that*."

"How *could* he?"

That triggers another memory. Ba Lien was selected the "Outstanding Farmer of Chuong Thien Province" in the spring of 1970. President Nguyen Van Thieu would present the award in Can Tho, with all expenses paid by the South Vietnamese Government. Ba Lien turned it down. He was too busy, he said, preparing to plant the monsoon rice crop. Now I know he had other reasons for declining the honor.

About thirty Vietnamese have gathered at the canal to see us off. "We know it was hard for you to come here," Ms. Dep says, and she means it. Tears streak her face, and she kisses me the way Vietnamese do, by pressing her nose against my cheek and sniffing.

"We are deeply moved that you remember us after all the years."

I should have taken *her* own child for a ride around the farm on my shoulders, I think, and I wish I'd brought medicine . . . but it's too late now.

A dozen Vietnamese are crying as we climb back into the sampan for the trip to Vi Thanh. Me, too, I guess.

CHAPTER VII
Five Foot Two,
Eyes of Blue

19 October 1987, Detroit to Washington, D.C.

After clearing customs in Detroit, I found an airport restaurant and ordered an American hamburger. That's the first thing I do whenever I land on U.S. soil. All airline meals taste like army or, worse, hospital food to me. I know it's psychological, something I developed by flying so many thousand miles a year. But the best T-bone in Texas would taste like cardboard if served on a plane.

An easy two-hour hop would complete the trip. As the plane droned from Detroit to Washington, D.C., I read diary, then novel, searching for new facts to reconstruct as fiction.

"You look beat," the man beside me said. He was about my age. "Where did you board?"

"Manila." That led to a brief conversation about rice, IRRI, and living in the Philippines.

"I spent a year in Southeast Asia, a long time ago . . ." I had already sensed it.

"Vietnam?" I'm not psychic, only the odd phone call from someone when I'm thinking about him. But when Vietnam is heavy on my mind, I invariably meet someone whose mind is on the same track. That sense became uncanny . . . frightening actually, once in my life. But 1977 was a scary time.

"Yeah, you too?"

"The Mekong Delta in '69 and '70, then Saigon in '72."

"I was at Phu Bai, up in I Corps, in '68 and '69."

I had wondered for almost two decades, so I had to ask "What did 'Phu Bai is all right' mean?" The phrase was painted on buildings and scratched into latrine walls across Vietnam, like "Kilroy was here" in World War II. But I never met anyone who had the faintest idea *why*.

"Hanoi Hannah started that. I was there at the time."

Chuong Thien was too far south to pick up Radio Hanoi, so I never heard the famous Hannah's nightly propaganda appeals in English to U.S. soldiers to resist the dirty and unjust war of aggression.

Phu Bai was mainly a resupply depot, he explained. It was the apex of a rough triangle with Camp Owen, headquarters of the 1st Air Cavalry, and Camp Eagle, home of the 101st Airborne, the Screaming Eagles.

"Hannah would sometimes close her broadcast with 'Owen and Eagle will get rockets tonight, but Phu Bai is all right.' When she said that, Owen and Eagle would be hit. But we were *all right* at Phu Bai."

So Hanoi Hannah started the most popular GI graffiti in Nam, I thought. I'd like to work that into the novel, but how? I turned back to the book.

Chapter 3

The pilot caught Dan's eye as the Huey approached a cluster of huts along a canal. He jabbed a finger at Dan's chest, then to the village, and gave a thumbs-up sign.

That must be Nuoc Trong, Dan thought. He strained to see the village better as the chopper descended in a tightening circle. It doesn't look like much. A double line of huts—a few of concrete but most of palm thatch—stood along the canal, separated by a dusty street. A dozen brightly painted sampans were moored to a bamboo pier.

A beige stucco building with a tin roof, flanked by two

towers, dominated the northern side of the village. A giant
eye, with black lines radiating from its pupil, was painted
across the front of the building. What *is* that? Dan thought.
It seems to watch our approach.

A triangle of mud walls with blockhouses at each point
flew the saffron-and-red flag of the Republic of Vietnam and
guarded the southern approach to the village. Barbed concertina wire encircled the mud berms of the outpost, and a dry
moat bordered the wire. The moat was circled by still another twisting concertina barrier. A clear firing zone was
burned from the brush at the perimeter, obviously with the
herbicide Agent Orange.

A road ran north along the canal until both were bisected
by a muddy river, half a mile past the village.

Three broken columns rose from the river, like the rib
cage of a decomposed sea monster. The road was overgrown
on the river's opposite shore.

A swath of bare earth scarred the river bank. There,
women in black pajamas and straw hats mixed cement and
sand with shovels, while Vietnamese soldiers hauled earth in
wheelbarrows to build embankments.

The chopper descended toward a salmon-colored building
with an aluminum antenna by the outpost. Two men—
Americans, obviously, by their size—stood outside, watching the chopper circle. As the Huey drew nearer, a
bare-chested black man trotted out to guide it onto a helipad
cleared from the brush.

Dan unlocked his seat belt, grabbed his gear, and jumped
from the chopper. He clutched the brim of his jungle hat and
turned to protect his contact lenses from the dust stirred by
the rotor blades.

The black man handed a canvas mail bag to the door gunner, and took a bag in exchange. The other two men unloaded supplies. They first stacked three cases of Carling's
Black Label beer and a case each of Coke and Fresca at the
edge of the helipad. Next came four boxes of frozen hamburger and one-liter cans, olive like everything else Dan had
seen in Vietnam, with black labels: Spiced Beef, Chicken,
Ham (chunked).

Dan's mind drifted to Fort Benning, to his only friend
who'd served on a mobile advisory team . . .

What made those National Guard lieutenants make fun of Bernstein, riding back to the BOQ that afternoon? That OCS lieutenant from the Indiana Guard started it, the smartass who resented anyone who'd gone to college. I was Richard Bernstein's best friend in the company, why didn't I tell them to cut that shit out, for God's sake? Everyone was tired from a long day of artillery instruction. Most would head to happy hour and twenty-five-cent drinks at the officers club. But a few, like Richard, would drive for forty-five minutes back to wives who waited for their men in miserable, over-priced apartments in Columbus.

Why did they resent Richard? Because he was from a well-to-do Jewish family in New Jersey? No, he was over-weight, and wore those thick, steel-rimmed glasses, and talked about books and music and history—especially military history—instead of fucking and fighting. What a transition . . . from Princeton to infantry officers' school.

Dan received Joan's card a few days before he left for Vietnam: "Dan, I have lost my Richard . . ." Less than three months with a MAT team near Soc Trang, ambushed in a sampan on a Mekong Delta canal . . . shot through the head while trying to load a wounded sergeant on a Medevac chopper. Richard got posthumous Silver and Bronze Stars— but he never saw his son, born two weeks before he died. That smartass from the Indiana National Guard will never get a Silver Star. But the other side of Dan's mind responded, "No, but he's still alive."

Why did I know, from the day we met, that Richard would die?

I set the chapter aside. Did I still feel guilty, when I wrote that back in 1971, about not sticking up for a friend in Infantry School in 1968? Bernstein was clearly Michael Arnovitz, but who could know that?

Gail Arnovitz would. If my book is published, she might see my name and read it; or her son would—what was his name, David? I've never seen him . . . neither did his father, but he must be about seventeen by now. What I wrote might not seem flattering . . . but I meant it to be. I was in Chuong Thien when Susan sent me Gail's card. It was a stark winter scene, some birds sitting on a leafless branch against a gray sky. The message started "Susan, I have lost my Michael."

Did I write about Arnovitz's death in my diary? I found an entry:

6 October 1969.

I just learned that 1LT Mike Arnovitz was KIA in an ambush on 30 Aug. I was shocked. We went through IOBC [Infantry Officers Basic Course] together at Ft. Benning and then he was in the 2d PsyOps Gp at Ft. Bragg when I was with the JFK Center. Michael was an intelligent man, whose hobby was painting toy soldiers from armies around the world—authentic soldiers. His wife Gail was close to Susan. He was on a MAT team somewhere in the Delta . . . probably ambushed riding a sampan.

I'll ask Susan if I should edit out the fiction I wrote about Arnovitz. She knew Gail far better than I did. Gail and the new baby even stayed a week with Susan and Linda Lanning in San Francisco. My God, now I remember! That was the week of vacation Gail had set aside to meet Michael on R & R in Hawaii.

That must have been tough on the women, with Lee and me both in Vietnam. Linda was pregnant, and Gail and the baby were living reminders of what could happen—easily. What times those were . . . I continued reading the novel:

The men turned and squatted to avoid the fresh dust as the chopper lifted, tilted forward, and began to climb. Dan felt more alone than since he boarded the Braniff charter at Travis, how long ago? He checked the metal calendar tab clamped to his watch band. Today is 19 May. Ten days.

"Welcome to Nuoc Trong, fifteen miles up the asshole of Chuong Thien Province."

Dan felt like he'd heard that line before.

"I'm Alan Burns, and I'm really glad to have you on MAT 96." The black man was very black. He was in his early twenties, of medium height, and muscular, with curly hair.

"This is Sgt. Joe Culver and our radio man, Spec. Four Bob Saunders. Where's Enrique?"

"Aw, he's makin' some more of that goddamn Meskin food. You'd better have a stomach for beans and Spanish rice, Lieutenant, and ever'thing cooked in chili peppers and garlic and onions," Sergeant Culver said. " 'Cause you won't get nothin' else with Enrique cookin'."

"I was raised on the Mexican border, Sergeant. That's my kind of food."

The three men stood on the helipad, exchanging home states, family, job in civilian life, last army post.

Alan Burns had a B.A. in English literature. He was married, and teaching in a Chicago high school when the draft notice arrived. Vietnam was Burns's first assignment after OCS at Fort Benning.

SFC Joseph Culver was a bearish man in his midforties from Augusta, Georgia. His eyes and hair were brown, but his bushy moustache was flecked with gray. His beer belly could not weaken his barrel chest.

Sp.4 Robert Saunders was nineteen, and skinny. He wore fatigue pants, an olive T-shirt, shower shoes, and sunglasses. Saunders volunteered only that, before the draft, he'd worked for the phone company in San Francisco. He seemed to resent Dan's questions, and Dan sensed that the peace medallion dangling from Saunders's dogtag chain irritated Sergeant Culver.

A short, round man scurried from the team hut, wiping his hands on an army-issue towel.

"That little tamale-colored feller, that's Enrique," Sergeant Culver said. Inwardly, Dan winced, wondering if the black Lieutenant Burns would consider the sergeant's comment racist. *Was it, or does the built-in guilt of my Texas heritage make me oversensitive?*

"Very glad to meet you, Lieutenant," S.Sgt. Enrique Rodriguez said. "But I don't say I'm glad for you to be here, because I don't wish that nobody should be in this goddamn place ... Me, I leave here in about four months more, and I get my discharge and retire back home."

"Where is home, Sergeant Rodriguez?"

"Hobbs, New Mexico! The most wonderful town in the United States of America—and that means *the World*. Where are you from, Lieutenant?"

"McAllen, down in the Rio Grande Valley."

"Well, that's so nice. But you gonna be in this awful Chuong Thien Province for one year more, and me—I'm gonna be back in New Mexico so soon. I got nineteen years in the army, and they send me to this damn Vietnam on my last year! If I don't have so much retirement, I would tell the army *fuck you*. But what can I do?" He shrugged, and Dan thought . . . this is a very sad and lonely man.

"Enrique is a fine medic, but he also cooks for us. He deserves disciplinary action—maybe an Article 15—for his chow," Lieutenant Burns said. "It would kill most self-respecting Mexicans. When we're not eating rice with the Viets, Enrique feeds us Spanish rice with lots of beans, and tortillas, and enchiladas, and tacos that he makes from God-only-knows what . . . God and Enrique.

"But I'm beginning to like Enrique's food, so I asked the colonel to extend him for another twelve months. After a year of cooking for MAT 96, Enrique can open the best Vietnamese-style Mexican restaurant in Hobbs, New Mexico."

Of course, it was really *my* cooking that irritated the half-dozen men who ate at the "Delta Lily Lounge & Dining Club." That's what we named our refrigerator, gas stove, and wooden table. I liked to cook, and my favorite spice, red chili peppers, was plentiful.

One day I returned from three days in the field and went into the kitchen to start dinner. There was Enrique, cooking away. He never asked, he just . . . took over. As an officer, I felt the sergeant should have at least discussed his coup with me. But the other men seemed pleased, so I let it go.

"Sheeit, you have to tie me down to keep me here after 118 days more, Lieutenant Burns!" Enrique said. "I tell you one secret. The fucking army tell me to stay in Nuoc Trong for fifteen minutes extra, and I swim up that goddamn Xa No Canal outta here, VC or no!"

"Let's move you in, Dan," Burns said. "The MAT 96 team hut isn't the Hilton, but it's home in Nuoc Trong. It has four concrete walls and a leaky tin roof, but that beats hell out of a tent, like how we lived down in Kien Long."

The hut was divided into three windowless rooms, side by side but not connected.

"This is the radio room, kitchen, bar, library. Saunders monitors radio traffic here all day. We rotate after six. Whoever has radio duty sleeps here on the cot."

One wall featured a pin-punctured map, plastic overlays, and grease pencils like Cantwell's office in Vi Thanh. But this room had a PRC-25 radio instead of a field phone, and no desk or typewriter.

The two NCOs loaded the frozen meat into a portable, kerosene-fueled refrigerator. A two-burner oil stove sat among a stack of plastic plates, pans, a skillet, and a kerosene lantern. Adjacent was a metal folding table loaded with bottles of chili powder, oregano, bay leaves, and comino. Hanging from the wall were bunches of dried garlic and onion, and woven strings of red and black peppers that had obviously been mailed from New Mexico.

"That's the bar. Help yourself." A metal ice chest sat along the opposite wall, with a beer opener hanging by a piece of cord above it. "Just keep tab of what you drink. It's the honor system. Every couple of weeks we divvy up to buy more beer and pop. When we run out of American beer, Bob and I survive on *Ba Mui Ba*, Biere 33. Enrique won't touch the Vietnamese beer. He swears it's laced with formaldehyde. Saunders seldom drinks."

Each man's name was listed on a wall chart above the ice chest, with hash marks under two headings: "Soda" and "Beer." The "Beer" column was subdivided into two more columns: "Real beer" and "VN beer."

They walked into a larger room next door whose peeling walls were plastered with *Playboy* centerfolds. A walkway cut through cases of ammunition and plastic ten-gallon water containers.

On a card table in one corner were a transistor radio, a deck of cards, and a dozen dog-eared magazines that featured nudes, racing cars, and men's action stories, plus two issues of *Rolling Stone*.

Three cots, draped with mosquito nets, lined the three walls. A poster of a glassy-eyed GI sharing a marijuana joint with a VC guerrilla was taped above one cot.

A hand-printed sign beneath the poster read:

> On the war in Vietnam
> I sing this song
> I ain't got no quarrel
> With the Viet Cong.
> —Muhammed Ali, 1966

* * *

That's Saunder's bunk, Dan thought.

A color photo of a plump, middle-aged woman and six children stood on a cardboard box by another bunk. The youngest sat in his mother's lap, and the eldest daughter stood proudly by her side in cap and gown at high school graduation. A print of the Virgin Mary of Guadalupe and a plastic crucifix were taped to the wall by the photo. At eye level with the pillow, a heavy-breasted blonde, torn from a Scandinavian porn magazine, spread her legs toward the bunk.

"The third room is the 'officers club,' where you and I stay," Burns quipped. "I've set up your cot and mosquito net. That footlocker is yours."

Getting settled didn't take long. Alan lay on his cot and talked as Dan emptied his duffel bag. He stored four sets of fatigues, green socks, shorts, T-shirts, lightweight nylon blanket, and shaving kit in the footlocker. He added a second pair of canvas-sided jungle boots with steel-plate insole for protection against VC punji stakes, the sharpened bamboo-stick booby traps, poisoned with human excreta, that claimed 2 percent of the U.S. casualties in Vietnam.

Dan also placed copies of *Vietnamese Made Easy* and *Customs and Culture of Vietnam*, half a dozen paperback novels, and a notebook that he was using as a diary in the footlocker.

It's strange that when I drafted this text, I had Lieutenant Dan Bridges bring a diary to Chuong Thien—maybe because I regretted not keeping my own diary.

Dan hung his steel helmet and rifle from nails.

"I see you took the M-16 at weapons issue in Saigon," Alan said. "You should have taken a .45. We'd have scrounged an Armalite for you."

"I didn't know that," Dan replied. "But I picked up a revolver in Can Tho." He handed Alan a snub-nosed Colt Cobra from under his fatigue jacket.

"Neat." Alan spun the cylinder. "This one has an aluminum barrel, so it's from the newer batch. Where'd you get it?"

"From a sergeant at the Alamo Lounge in the Special Forces camp by the air field."

"The CIA has shipped thousands of these .38 specials to Vietnam, and the Green Beanies have sold half of them." Alan handed the pistol back.

"You'd better rig your web gear."

"Do you expect trouble?"

"No, but it pays to be ready. Always."

Dan started at his web belt and shoulder harness, and all the gear to hook onto it. He glanced at Alan's web gear hanging from the opposite wall, fixed it in his mind, and began to strap and hook poncho, clip holders, pouches, compass, first-aid kit, and—damn! he thought. Does the bayonet go on the left hip? He took another guilty look at Alan's web gear, then hooked his *canteen* to the left side of the belt, and the black bayonet to the right.

Of course the bayonet goes by your right hand. A real soldier like Sergeant Culver would know that *instinctively*. But if I stayed in the army for life, fixing my web gear would never come naturally. Thinking about "real soldiers" reminded Dan of Captain Pulleig. He grinned, then confronted the shoulder harness.

"You've been in country for nine months now?"

"Believe it, baby! I'm a genuine two-digit midget, less than one hundred days left in country. I'll ETS in Oakland, the day I reach the World. Then Uncle Sam and I go our separate ways . . . forever."

"When can I see the village?" Dan asked.

"We'll meet the chief and tour Nuoc Trong after lunch," Alan said. "But don't expect much."

Lunch was vienna sausages warmed in chili beans, and Spanish rice. Dan washed it down with a can of Coke. He wanted a second Coke, but the men seemed to hoard American drinks.

"Tell me about the chief," Dan said.

"His name is Nguyen Van Cam, and he can smell Charley a mile away," Alan said. "Cam hates the VC—*hates* them. I'll bet he's *personally* wasted more VC than an average ARVN rifle company. The chief has made our People's Self-Defense Force, the local militia, one of the most aggressive in Chuong Thien."

"Is he honest?"

"As honest as any Vietnamese can be in this situation. He's strong, a born leader. A good soldier, too. Cam fought with the Viet Minh in the early fifties."

"Then why does he hate the VC? The Viet Minh were Communist too."

"Fighting with the Viet Minh did *not* make a man Communist," Alan said. "Who *else* could a Vietnamese, who wants the French out of his country, join?

"Electing a former Viet Minh as village chief may be a sign that democracy can actually work here. In ARVN, there are lots of ex–Viet Minh captains and majors, but few colonels and no generals. Saigon discriminates against officers who fought with the Viet Minh—and that has lost Vietnam its most dedicated nationalists."

Alan pushed his plate back and stretched. "No more politics. Let me take a catnap before we visit the chief. This heat makes me drowsy, it seems like I'm always tired." The black lieutenant's shoulders were slumped as he left the kitchen.

"What about the dishes?" Dan asked.

"I'm a *soljer*, not a dishwasher," Sergeant Culver said. "China Doll, that's our hootch maid, comes in every morning to wash dishes and clean up. We all chip in and pay her. It don't cost much, and it's our only luxury.

"Lawrence Welk don't hardly ever come to Chuong Thien," he added.

"And you don't worry none if China Doll makes the dishes clean," Enrique said. "I know how filthy these goddamn people are, so I sterilize with hot water after she washes."

"The problem is, Lieutenant, these zipper-heads ain't even *civilized*," Sergeant Culver said.

"That's right," Enrique added. "You cannot even get a good piece of pussy in this goddamn country."

"Yeah, half the women have VD."

"But the others have TB," Enrique pointed out.

"What you gotta remember is to fuck the gals that cough," Culver said. "And get blow jobs from them that drip."

"You're *really* from Texas?" Specialist Bob Saunders said. "Man, I find that hard to believe. I took basic training at Fort Hood after the draft. Texas was the pits. It's so hot and dry and . . . *ugly.*" Dan didn't say anything.

"The lifers at Fort Hood made us miserable," the radio operator continued. "After three weeks we finally got passes, and I put on civvies and left the post. But *retired* lifers run Killeen—old redneck sergeants, with their bars and used-car lots."

This guy is a real jerk-off, Dan thought. But I'm stuck with the twirp when I take over, so I *won't* get pissed at his first, whining words.

"Then the army shipped me to Fort Blister, Texas. Now that's *really* a miserable place. I'm from northern California, so I'm used to green plants. But El Paso is nothing but sand, jackrabbits, rattlesnakes, and ignorant people who can't speak English."

"Texas is a fine state, Lieutenant. In fact, I'm thinkin' about retiring in Killeen in four years." Sergeant Culver glared at the radio operator. "I might open me a bar down there—or a used-car lot."

"*Lo siento mucho*, Sanders," Enrique added. "I'm sorry 'bout the sergeants who treated you, oh so bad, and then the peoples in El Paso who don't speak the English so good." Enrique is exaggerating his accent, Dan thought, making his bad English worse.

"You are from a farm?" Enrique turned to Dan. "Me too, I love farm work. What do you grow?"

"Mostly cotton, cattle, some tomatoes, vegetables. Where is *your* farm? Near Hobbs?"

Enrique turned his head. "I was never *really* a farmer, Lieutenant. I was a migrant worker. My family, we had a small home in San Antonio, but we lived most of the year in a truck. We went wherever crops needed to be planted, or hoed, or picked: Oklahoma, New Mexico, into California, Texas, the Valley. Maybe sometime your father was my boss.

"But I loved working with the plants, even though the life was not so good. I hope to buy a little farm in New Mexico, when I leave this goddamn army, and be a *real* farmer. Never a big one like your father, but . . ."

Alan reappeared. "Let's get Khang and visit the chief."

"Who's Khang?"

"Please fasten your seat belts," the captain announced. "We'll land at National Airport in five minutes."

The wheels were down, and the No Smoking light came on. As we touched the runway in Washington, D.C. I wondered why I set my novel on a mobile advisory team in a fictional village, instead of the provincial team in Vi Thanh? I don't know.

I felt compelled to write about advisers, an undocumented side of the war. But Vietnam had generated little literature, of any type, by 1971. Vietnam was *distasteful* to the American public back then.

I was an adviser, both agricultural and military. But MAT teams were the *front-line* advisers—like I consider platoon leaders in the regular U.S. Army. The MATs lived as tough and dangerous a life as the Special Forces—doing about the same job, building up units of local troops—but without the glory.

Robin Moore started the Special Forces mystique with his book *The Green Berets*. Then Sgt. Barry Sadler wrote and sang "The Ballad of the Green Berets," which stimulated the John Wayne movie. But no one wrote a Ballad of the MATs.

I drew MAT 96 from half a dozen MATs across Chuong Thien, but mostly MAT 54, the *hard luck team*. Khang, my interpreter, and I sometimes arrived by chopper, the "swing ship" that delivered mail and supplies to MAT teams every other day. When there was no swing ship, we hitchhiked on local farmers' sampans along those interlocking rivers and canals to reach isolated MAT teams.

I was always amazed, and embarrassed, by MAT hospitality. The three- to five-man MATs gladly shared rations and scarce beer and soft drinks with us, knowing that we'd return to province headquarters in a few days. Vi Thanh's beer supply was erratic, but we had such luxuries when the MAT teams didn't. When I could get beer and Coke, I'd bring a case of each to MAT teams that we visited.

The MATs—brave men and a few cowards, the idealistic and the cynics, devout Christians and drunks, and a few dopeheads. MATs may have been a cross-sample of all Americans who served in Vietnam.

But I don't think so. The army seemed fairly selective in its assignment of advisers—officers, at least. Most lieutenants, the group I knew best in Chuong Thien, were college graduates, and several had master's or law degrees.

All MATs had one thing in common: lonely men who welcomed someone—*anyone*—new to talk with.

I secretly wished I were on a MAT team, but I was too smart to volunteer. Hargrove would return to Texas sitting in a regular seat on the "Freedom Bird," not in the back, draped with a U.S. flag. Of course, I never made that trip from Vietnam back to the States; I stayed in Asia for a while, but that's another story.

What bothered me most was that I'm probably as qualified to write about MATs as anyone . . . except someone who actually led a team. I needed a former MAT leader to check what I'd written. But I didn't have addresses of any MAT leaders who made it, and my diary didn't help. Michael Arnovitz would have loved helping me, but . . .

What about Kinard? I had noticed his name in the diary and marked the page. It was an entry made on 28 October 1969:

> I got a note from David Kinard, who was in Co. D-1 with me in the Corps at Texas A&M. He's a 1LT, a MAT leader somewhere in Vinh Binh Province. He saw my name somewhere and wrote "Are you the same Tom Hargrove I think you are? You *must* be, you're the only man I know who could get an assignment as an ag adviser while a lieutenant in VN."

Vinh Binh was an ethnically Cambodian region of the Delta that was always rated down there with An Xuyen and Chuong Thien on the HES scale. Kinard had a B.S. in animal science and wanted to know if I could help *him* get the hell off that godawful MAT team. I tried, but it didn't work.

I think Kinard made it. Maybe he'd review my writing, if I can find him.

The plane's doors were open. I stuffed my manuscripts into my carry-on bag and filed into National Airport with hundreds of passengers.

CHAPTER VIII
A Message at the Vietnam Memorial

Washington, D.C., 25 October 1987

I took a cab from National Airport to the Lombardy Hotel, and called Susan. She was surprised that I was in Washington, D.C., and yes, she'd fly up to meet me.

I worked most of that week, but we took Sunday, 25 October, off for sightseeing with three old friends. We were all in international agricultural research, but working on different crops from separate global bases.

Ed Sulzberger was now information officer for the Consultative Group on International Agricultural Research, based in Washington. Before that, he was editor at the International Institute of Tropical Agriculture in Nigeria, then with the Asian Vegetable Research and Development Center, Taiwan. His wife Linda had visited Susan several times in the Philippines. Tiff Harris was communication head at CIMMYT, the International Center for Maize and Wheat Improvement, in Mexico.

We had lunch at the Old Ebbitt Grill, then went to see the Declaration of Independence and Bill of Rights, then to the Smithsonian Institution. Late that afternoon, we drank Cokes on the lawn of Smithsonian Mall, and caught a taxi to the Vietnam War Memorial.

I had visited the Memorial twice. The experience was incredibly moving. I had wanted to take Susan there but was uneasy about suggesting it. But before I left the hotel the previous morning, Susan told me *she* wanted to visit the Memorial.

"I'm glad . . . but surprised," I said. "Why?" I knew that Susan had her own problems in dealing with that era, and preferred to erase it, like Vietnam never happened.

"Tom, I've lived with Vietnam as long as you. What choice have I had? So maybe it's my Memorial, too," Susan said. "Besides, I want to leave a small U.S. flag by Michael Arnovitz's name, another by your cousin's, and one flag for your Texas Aggie friend that you've talked about so much . . . Joe Bush?"

Arnovitz. That shook me. We hadn't discussed Michael for years, yet he had been on my mind since leaving Manila . . .

> Five foot two
> Eyes of blue . . .

We expected to find plenty of stands selling miniature American flags at the Memorial's entrance, but there were none.

We found the three names among the 58,300 etched on that black marble wall: Jimmy Hargrove, my cousin and the first man from Rotan, Texas, to be killed in the war; Joe Bush, a Texas A&M friend and classmate, the first American soldier to die in Laos; and Michael Arnovitz.

We then walked silently to the three battle-weary GIs, frozen in bronze, staring at the Wall. Those hauntingly real statues have seen their own names, I thought . . . but I didn't say it.

Everyone was now ready to go back to the hotel, but Susan was determined to leave American flags by those three names. She left us by the Reflecting Pond and went to the Lincoln Memorial . . . its bookstore might sell flags. I appreciated Susan's motive, but it was turning dark and chilly, and even I was getting irritated.

Susan found miniature flags at a souvenir stand, but had to wait in line for twenty minutes to buy them. She finally returned with three flags. We walked back to the Memorial.

We arrived at block W18 and searched, again, for Arnovitz's name. Two men and a woman stood, also scanning that block. As we searched those names, we all heard: "W18, line 10—but his name was Michael."

"Richard M., line 10," one of the men answered. "That's him."

I was stunned. "Are you looking for *Michael Arnovitz*?"

"Yes, we are . . ." A distinguished man in his fifties turned to me.

"So are we, but . . . who are you?"

"My name is Newberg, and I'm from White Oak, Pennsylvania. I was Michael's ophthalmologist since he was a kid . . . he had such bad eyes. Remember, he wore those thick glasses? Michael's father was my personal friend. He died about a month ago, so I've been thinking about him, and Michael. I came to Washington for a professional meeting, and . . . I wanted to see Michael's name. But who are *you*?"

"I'm Tom Hargrove. I was Michael's friend in Infantry Officers' School at Fort Benning in 1968. I was in Vietnam when he died. We live in the Philippines now, but I'm in Washington for a week and . . . this is my wife, Susan . . ."

"Gail and I were army wives together at Fort Benning, then at Fort Bragg," Susan said. "After Michael was killed, Gail and David, the new baby, stayed with me in San Francisco . . . during the five days she was to meet Michael for R & R in Hawaii."

Susan gripped the miniature U.S. flag with both hands. "I bought this to place by Michael's name."

"You know, his father told me that Michael believed strongly in what he was doing," Dr. Newberg said. "Michael felt that the U.S. role in Vietnam was right."

"So did I, at first," I said. "But not when I left . . ."

"So you live in San Francisco?" Dr. Newberg was confused, and I could understand why.

"No, we live in the Philippines." I tried to explain about the International Rice Research Institute, the Green Revolution, but I don't think he followed me.

"Have you visited the Memorial before?" I asked.

"No, this is my first time."

"Mine, too," Susan said.

"Do you realize that the chances of our meeting here, at Michael's name, are incredible?" I said. "Far, far lower than the 1 in 58,000 names on the Wall. The Memorial has been open twenty-four hours a day for about five years. And we both appeared, from the Philippines and Pennsylvania, looking for Michael Arnovitz's name—during the same two or three minutes . . ."

"Yes, I know." The doctor shook his head.

The situation was now electric, and tears were streaking Susan's face. I was okay . . . I'd lost my head before, when Vietnam came back strong, but that was years ago. It wouldn't happen again. I choked back my own tears.

We didn't talk much more . . . what could we say? Susan touched Michael's name, left the flag, and we shook hands and walked away.

Then I turned and walked back to the doctor. "I *must* have your name."

He wrote, on the back of one of my business cards: J. A. Newberg, MD, and his Pennsylvania address.

Ed and Linda and Tiff had watched the scene, and were almost as stunned as Susan and I.

Susan was crying as I relocated the etched names of Jimmy Hargrove and Joe Bush. She left her flags, touched their names.

"Do you believe this?" I asked as we walked away from the Memorial.

"No . . . it's incredible," Susan said. "And it wouldn't have happened if I hadn't made everyone wait until I finally found those flags."

"I have something still stranger to show you when we get to the hotel," I said. "I was planning to discuss it after we returned from the Memorial."

Back in the room, I mixed us drinks.

"Susan, I've thought about Michael Arnovitz a lot lately," I said. "I wrote something about him a long time ago, and reviewed it on the plane to the States. I'm not sure I like what I wrote, so I wanted your reaction. I meant to show this to you earlier, but the time was never right. Then you said you wanted to go to the Memorial and put a flag by Michael's name. So I decided to wait until after that." I found chapter 3 of my novel.

"I wanted you to read this—it's one of those slices of life that I remember when I think of Michael. I changed his name to Richard Bernstein, but it's obviously about Arnovitz. It's a flashback, when my main character arrives at his MAT team." I handed Susan pages 4 and 5 of chapter 3, which described the mocking adaption of Ray Henderson's "Five Foot Two, Eyes of Blue" sung about Michael by National Guard lieutenants at Fort Benning so many years ago.

Susan read silently. Then she handed me the manuscript, and shook her head.

"You know, I have a haunting feeling . . . that Michael might like what I wrote," I said. "Somehow, I sense I got a message at the Memorial, communication from . . . someone or something . . .

"I know Michael wasn't killed in a sampan," I continued, "but I'm writing fiction, and five men died in sampan ambushes during my year in Chuong Thien."

Susan was silent, so I said, "After what happened today, I'd like to use Michael's real name, and write how and where he died in the novel. But first I'd have to clear it with Gail and the kid."

Susan finally spoke. "Tom, you *have* to write to Gail."

"Yes, I know."

Back in the Philippines, I stared into my computer screen:

10 December 1987
Dear Gail,
This letter may be painful for you, but it must be written . . .

Transition 5

Chuong Thien Province, 1988

As our sampan pushés through the muddy waters and memories of the Xa No Canal, I skim my wartime diary. I find words about how I hoped to return in ten years and find no more war and visit old friends doing well in a peaceful and prosperous Chuong Thien Province. Why did I write that, I knew it wouldn't happen . . .

It's been nearly twenty years, not ten. There's no more war, but peace didn't bring prosperity, and my host, Tran Van Rang, is *definitely not* an "old friend." What happened to Khang, Tri, Father Hoa, Monique, Duc, Captain Hong? I've heard nothing since the fall of South Vietnam. I guess they're all dead.

"Do you remember this place?" Tu Rang points to a gate facing the canal, emblazoned with a red star. "That's the old ammo dump. It's now a cemetery for fighters of the National Liberation Front."

The Vi Thanh air strip, the only one in Chuong Thien that could land fixed-wing planes, is now a military-run factory for making bricks.

We approach the wooden bridge at the edge of Vi Thanh.

Ahead, the canal is carpeted with water hyacinth. The scene is idyllic—but I still hate and fear those floating plants. Two decades ago, no sampan dared touch a hyacinth, because the Viet Cong used them to camouflage floating mines. We posted two Vietnamese soldiers with 12-gauge shotguns permanently on the bridge to blast any hyacinth that floated close to its beams.

The firing was constant, day and night, but I guess it blended well with our outgoing artillery. A lot of it supported Vietnamese operations, but most artillery was H & I, or harassment and interdiction, fired randomly into areas where the VC *might* be. Our H & I killed a few VC—and many more civilians. The flow of wounded and dying through our dismal hospital in Vi Thanh was steady.

But random slaughter wasn't restricted to South Vietnamese and American firepower. The VC's mortars and rockets also killed far more farmers and shopkeepers than soldiers.

This bridge must be new, I think as our sampan cuts through the hyacinth. A friend wrote that the VC finally blew the old bridge—with a hyacinth-camouflaged mine—two weeks after I left.

We moor at a dock, and I'm back in Vi Thanh.

Why have I returned? I left this sad village in June of 1970, but I've remembered her every day and night since. Most memories are bad. I owe this backwater province nothing, but she took a lot from me. I can't explain it, I just *had* to come back.

Dr. Vo Tong Xuan's jeep is waiting for us, and we drive through the village. Vi Thanh looks about like it did during the war ... I think. I see little change, but honestly, time has sharpened some memories of her, while blurring most.

I recognize a South Vietnamese government office, but now it's a war museum. The front is painted with revolutionary murals of heroic Viet Cong soldiers shooting down F-4 Phantoms with AK-47s, and angry peasants waving red flags.

We park at an artificial pond in the heart of Vi Thanh. I'd forgotten the pond ... but I see it's bigger now, and a cafe has been built over the water. That's where we meet Le Van Minh, the district agricultural chief. We sip iced coffee and talk about rice for a while. But Minh is about my age, so I finally ask "Where were *you* in 1969 and 1970?"

"I lived mostly in Vi Thanh," Minh says. "I carried a Saigon-issued ID card, but I was a VC captain at night."

Minh takes us to the People's Cooperative restaurant along the canal. We're served in the VIP room. Like the rest of the restaurant, the cement floor is slippery, its walls are bamboo, and its roof is thatch. Vietnamese food was always good in the old days, and so is today's lunch. But I want the meal to end, so I can explore Vi Thanh. It finally does.

I walk into the market. Pajama-clad women still hunker under conical hats before baskets of fish and vegetables. I want to take photos of rice being sold, but I see only a few scattered kilos. The farmers are hoarding their rice, and it's easy to see why. The legal exchange rate is 360 Vietnamese dong to the U.S. dollar—but the black market rate is almost 3,000 dong, and it's slipping fast. Rice is the farmer's buffer against paper money.

Outside the market, I face a cluster of buildings that look familiar, but they aren't ... I'm confused.

"May I help you?" The voice startles me. I turn to face a tall man.

"You speak *English*?"

"A little."

"I lived here, a long time ago ..."

"Yes, I know."

"You *remember* me?"

"No, but you look like an American, and you seem to be . . . *searching* for something."

"What *is* this place . . . or what *was* it?"

"The provincial headquarters, when this was Chuong Thien Province."

"But I remember it as yellow stucco, with a red tile roof, like a pagoda."

"Looters tore that building down in 1975, the night that Chuong Thien fell. This one is new."

"Where was MAC-V?" The Vietnamese points toward my old army post. "I will guide you," he says, but I'm already racing ahead.

Chapter IX
Write It in a Book

Texas, August, 1988

> What thou seest, write in a book,
> and send it to the seven churches
> which are in Asia.
>
> —*Revelation*, 1:11

I should call Bruce McAllister before leaving Texas, I thought as our 1988 home leave was ending. I hadn't met the novelist, but felt I knew him since we began corresponding after my long letter about rice and Vietnam. McAllister's second letter intrigued me more, and I answered:

> So you were a dove during the war. That's neat. Certain types of Vietnam vets, and doves from the '60s, experienced a lot in common back then, maybe more afterward. The war is over, and we're both veterans of an era.

About reviewing your final draft of *Dream Baby*. Thanks,
I'm flattered, but not until I've finished my own novel. I
might, subconsciously, steal some of your ideas. But I'll
check anything you write about rice and, if in doubt, consult
the world's top authorities, IRRI scientists. That's part of my
job.

Besides, authors of Vietnam books are special. I want to
help tell our generation's story. That time was so fiery, so
complex, it must come from different perspectives—the
doves, the hawks, those caught in the middle.

Maybe your book will help our kids understand us . . . or
help us understand ourselves, especially what happened *after*
the experience.

You wrote that you might go to Thailand to get the feel
of the jungle. Why not the Philippines? Our place could be
your headquarters. It's as much like Vietnam as anywhere
. . . except the *real* Nam.

The jungle begins at our back fence, and I can easily arrange for you to slog through rice paddies in stifling heat.

To experience the fear and uncertainty of the Vietnamese
countryside, you can visit Quezon Province to our south.
There are no VC, but plenty of NPA—New People's Army.
Farmers by day and guerrillas carrying AK-47s or captured
M-16s at night. The common NPA soldier probably thinks
he is fighting injustice and imperialism, but his leaders are
Maoists. What do you—or I—know about Maoists? None
are left in China. The only other Maoists I know of are Pol
Pot's boys in Cambodia, and the Shining Path in Peru.

Yes, the NPA could substitute nicely for VC.

If you want the excitement and decadence of wartime Saigon with its blaring rock and roll, GIs and pimps and bar
girls and dope pushers and brawls and MPs and underlying
sense of danger, visit today's Angeles City outside Clark Air
Base, about 4 hours to our north. The NPA have assassinated three U.S. servicemen in Angeles over the past few
months. One was killed having a quarter-pounder and chocolate shake at McDonald's.

I wasn't writing for McAllister . . . not really . . . but for me.
Those long letters had become like my diary, but I was now
storing thoughts on hard disk, not black ledger.

Bruce had reviewed some personal accounts of experiences

after the war, and I'd mentioned Owen Lock's request for a copy of the diary I forgot I wrote. Bruce's response reached me in Texas. It's message was clear:

Don't send the diary to Lock! Your diary is not the book. Let me say it again: Your *real* book is the story of the relationship of your diary and novel—to you, to each other, and to reality.

We want to hear a true story of self, guilt, anguish, glory, lies, reality . . . the diary that you never wrote, but did . . . and the novel that you wrote, but failed in the telling . . . the publisher who wanted your diary, but not your novel, and how you couldn't go back and change the diary. But then, in your new book, you *do* go back and change it—you make the diary better, more exciting. Maybe you tell us you have . . . maybe you don't at first, but later admit the trick.

Isn't that what Vietnam was about? Lies and tricks and reality?

In other words, Tom, your *real* book is about yourself: the story of a narrator who wants to make sense of his war experiences, and is trying to create "literature" from a novel that didn't capture it and a diary he doesn't remember writing. So you create another book from the failure of the first two.

We read stories from the old novel, then the diary version, and get the truth—if there's a difference.

Above all, don't send the diary to Lock. He'll read it, say "no" nicely, and forget it. You must put together you *own* book.

I dialed McAllister. He was working hard to finish *Dream Baby*.

"Thanks for the invitation to visit the Philippines, Tom, but an Asian trip just isn't practical right now.

"But how's *your* book going? Did you get my last letter?"

"About writing my own story? You're the second person to give that advice." I told him about Susan saying I should write nonfiction. But I still dreamed of writing a great Vietnam novel, even though I now suspected that the *real* Vietnam story transcends the war. Besides, could I separate the Chuong Thien in my memory from the Chuong Thien of my novel? Two decades had blended them so intricately . . .

We talked a while longer. I now wanted to review *Dream*

Baby; it was obviously different from my book. Bruce offered to comment on . . . whatever I sent.

Bruce's last advice was predictable: *"Don't send your diary to Lock!"*

Later I thought . . . *my* story would have to start with that red-dirt, West Texas cotton farm that led to Texas A&M . . . then A&M blended into Vietnam, and Vietnam dictated that rice would become my life . . .

CHAPTER X
Other Toys

Fisher County, Texas, 1944–1962

> I think it has something to do with the Civil War.
> In the South, all available boys were expected to
> go to war. Football is war, so to speak. So all
> available boys are to go out for football, which
> means you have to have girl cheerleaders.
> —Betsy Throckmorton in
> *Fast Copy*
> by Dan Jenkins

Michael Herr wrote, in *Dispatches*, that we had Vietnam instead of happy childhoods. He meant that the experience was so powerful, it became a new base for our lives. Herr's words are true—but I had a happy childhood that Vietnam never erased.

I was raised on a red-dirt, dryland cotton farm in West Texas. To me, that says it all, but it might not to others.

Thomas Jefferson would have been proud of my parents.

Tom and Bargy Hargrove epitomized the rural ethic he believed in so deeply. We were hard-working, honest farmers who raised a lot of what we consumed. We were close to the earth, but no one philosophized about it. We were an ordinary Texas farm family in the 1950s.

Like most older families in Fisher County, mine came from the Deep South, leaving behind what little the terrible Civil War had left them, to start a new life on the frontiers of Texas.

My great-grandfather, Wade Lafitte Hargrove, left Pulaski, Tennessee, in 1866 after fighting for the Confederacy. He moved first to Arkansas, then to Comanche County, in central Texas. The Hargroves were never military men, but he named his son Rafael Sims, apparently for Raphael Semmes, the Southern naval hero.

Rafael Sims bought a racehorse and moved to Oklahoma in 1900. The racehorse wasn't for track or derby, it was to ride in the 1901 Land Rush, to stake and claim virgin prairie farmland. But the Rushes of 1889 and later had been so chaotic and violent, authorities canceled the 1901 Rush the night before it began. Instead, lotteries were drawn for the limited land. The Hargroves weren't lucky, so after farming another year or so in Oklahoma, they moved back to Texas.

Rafael Sims Hargrove moved further west in 1907, to plant cotton on former rangeland around the new town of Rotan, about seventy miles west of Abilene. Rotan, at the end of the railway line, was sure to prosper. It didn't, but my Grandfather Hargrove did.

Rafael Sims died when Daddy was fifteen. But he left behind a close Hargrove clan: five brothers and a sister, all cotton farmers, and good ones. Cotton is in the Hargrove blood. Today, I'm one of the few Hargroves who do not grow cotton in West Texas. Most are prosperous.

My mother's family was also Southern. The Geddie side left their native Morayshire, in northern Scotland, in 1702. Daniel Geddie married Isabella Barcelona McPhail on the ship to Cape Fear, North Carolina. The Geddie and McPhail families intermarried, cousin and cousin, for generations.

Some of the Geddie family drifted to Georgia, Alabama, Mississippi. A few Geddies left the Deep South to settle new land on the Texas frontier in the early 1800s. Most of the men fought for the South in the Civil War. Defeat of the Confederacy forced most remaining Geddies to abandon their land and join relatives in Texas.

Mother was the daughter of Julius Fields and Fannie Davison, granddaughter of a Geddie. Granddaddy had run away from home at age fourteen, in the late 1890s, and drifted further west to be a cowboy. Marriage made Granddaddy give up that life he loved. There was no money in cowboying, and Fannie didn't like the loneliness of a rangeland shack. But farming wasn't much better.

Granddaddy was a real liberal, for West Texas in his time. During the Great Depression, the Fields had two sons and a daughter about college age. They could help educate only one. They chose my mother.

Granddaddy's reasoning: "A man can always find work. He can cowboy or chop cotton. But if a woman doesn't have an education, and marries wrong or is widowed, there's nothing left for her but to live off family charity."

Granddaddy also said, back in the 1950s, "If I was born a nigger, I'd of been a *mean* nigger." Years later, I understood what he *really* meant.

Mother graduated at age fifteen as salutatorian of her ten-person high school class in Hobbs, Texas. But the school principal ruled that the honor should go to the man with the second-highest grades—because, being a man, he should obviously get the scholarship that would help pay his way through McMurry College in Abilene. Mother protested, got the scholarship, and finished two years of college. That qualified her to teach school for sixty dollars a month.

At age seventeen, Mother started teaching grades one through seven in a two-room schoolhouse in Rough Creek, Texas—an area that was named appropriately. It was a harsh land of red-clay canyons and cedar breaks around Longhorn Valley, where outlaws had hidden stolen herds in the 1870s. Most of Rough Creek's inhabitants were God-fearing ranchers and farmers, or hard-drinking cowboys. On Sunday and Wednesday evenings, the Devout and Unsaved alike attended Rough Creek's main social event: hellfire-and-brimstone services at an open-air tabernacle.

Some Devout objected to the cowboys' sport of goat-roping on Sunday afternoon, but revivals drew a good crowd. So did the impromptu Kangaroo Courts. Mother inevitably stood trial for breaking some cowboy's heart. She always lost.

My parents married in 1936. Mother taught for a year before moving to the land Daddy farmed west of Rotan. Her paychecks helped pay for the first Hargrove tractor. The change from mule to tractor power meant Daddy could rent more cotton land. He was soon buying land, and is a successful farmer today.

The Hargroves raised three children. I was born in 1944. My sister Becky is four years older, and my brother Raford came four years after me.

Becky could get away with anything by yelling loud enough. I never liked Becky until she met Kenny McKinney. Marriage and kids, somehow, tamed her. She's a nice person today.

Raford had an uncanny talent for avoiding work. When Daddy sent us to hoe cotton across the creek on those hot Texas afternoons, Raford camouflaged himself and lay under hackberry trees, drinking ice water. A few years later, we were joined by Mexican braceros. We called those hired farm laborers "wetbacks" because most had crossed the Rio Grande—illegally—to work on Texas farms and ranches.

Raford loved having wetbacks! Now, he could drive the pickup into Rotan and shoot pool until quitting time at sundown, and Daddy couldn't monitor how much work he'd done.

That's how I remember our childhood. Becky and Raford may remember it differently.

The Hargrove farmhouse sat at the end of a dirt turnrow that ran along our cotton fields, half a mile from a gravel road. It was another six miles before you hit paved road for the last five miles into Rotan, population two thousand. Rain meant we were stuck on the farm until the road dried.

But rain wasn't a problem when I was a kid. The Great Five-Year Drought or simply, "The Drought," began in 1951. We were rainfed farmers whose crop of short-staple cotton depended on an unreliable average of twenty inches of rain a year. For five years, we never got two inches of rain at one time, and crops were sparse. Twice, there was *no* crop. That's when, some farmers claim, they learned that jackrabbits make good chili. Times were hard, but the Hargroves never ate jackrabbits.

In fact, I thought we were prosperous. We probably were, compared with most of our far-flung neighbors. We raised our own beef, pork, chickens, eggs, and garden. Even at the worst of the drought, there was always plenty of food in the Hargrove home.

The most exciting days, for me, were "Hog-killing Day" in the fall and the annual "Rabbit Drive" each spring.

When the weather turned brisk in October or November, three or four neighboring farmers would come to our farm to help kill and butcher a couple of hogs. On the next cold day, Daddy would help with another farmer's hog killing.

The men would shoot the hogs, then hoist them by the heels on a pulley to gut them before dipping the carcasses into a fifty-gallon drum of scalding water. We'd then scrape the hair from the hide with flattened-out hoe blades.

The women used the hog skin to make cracklings, or cooked it with lye and water in black cast-iron washpots to make gray lye soap. They cured hams and slabs of bacon with salt. We ground sausage and cut pork chops on the farm, then took the fresh meat to freeze in rented vaults at the Rotan locker plant.

Hog-killing Day was the only time we ate pork ribs. The women fried all the spareribs at noon for the men who killed the hogs. Today, pork ribs are still a special meal.

In the spring, before cotton-planting time, farmers and ranchers from miles around would gather for the annual rabbit drive. One group set up a half-mile-long "stand." Two other lines formed a V covering hundreds of acres. All rabbits unlucky enough to be in that trap were driven into the stand. Only shotguns with bird shot were allowed on a rabbit drive. At noon, the women laid out a country spread at the Hobbs Baptist Church: fried chicken, potato salad, green beans, corn bread, and huge glasses of iced tea.

Farmers claimed the rabbit drives were to protect young cotton from ravenous jackrabbits, but they were really the community's main social event.

In 1951, I started first grade at Hobbs, the local crossroads with a schoolhouse, Baptist church, and country store with a gas pump. My class had twenty kids, but that was in the fall so it included children of Mexican migrant workers who came to pull our cotton.

The drought whipped hundreds of farmers in Fisher County over the next couple of years. Dozens took jobs in Abilene or Lubbock or Fort Worth. My fourth-grade class dwindled to ten students. But every Hargrove stayed on the land, and all did well when the rains finally came.

Hobbs School had no blacks, of course. All schools within several hundred miles were segregated. So were restaurants and rest rooms. Blacks helped harvest our cotton, but no farmer would stand for black kids in our school.

The Hargroves went into Rotan for shopping on Saturday afternoon. That was exciting, because Rotan had two picture shows. One showed only Spanish films, but the Lance Theater had the latest Roy Rogers or Gene Autry or Superman films. Blacks were admitted . . . but only to the balcony.

But we had bussing back then. Rotan had a black elementary school, but all blacks in junior high and high school in Fisher County were bussed twenty miles to the nearest Negro school, over in Jones County.

The Hargrove farm didn't have electricity, but we always had electric lights and a refrigerator. The power was generated by a wind charger, a windmill-like device that generated and stored enough electricity in twelve-volt batteries to run those essentials. The system's fuel, wind, was abundant and free.

The Rural Electrification Program brought power lines to the farm in about 1954. That led to a four-party telephone, and our first television set in 1955.

I remember Lyndon B. Johnson for many things. But I first heard his name as a child—when he pushed through the program to bring electricity to farms.

We always had running water, drawn by windmill. But it was "gyp water," with gypsum and salt content so high, it could be used only for bathrooms and to water the grass. We paid Roy Kingsfield to truck household water from Rotan, and store it in a cistern. Water was expensive, so I never bathed in more than three inches of water until I left West Texas.

There was no stigma, at the Hobbs school, for wearing shirts made from flower-printed chicken-feed sacks. I enjoyed picking out the sacks of chicken feed at the Barnes Purina Feed Store in Rotan, for Mother to sew into my next shirts.

I had no friends until I started school, and few after that— because there were no other kids around. I sometimes entertained myself, when we weren't working in the fields, by riding Betsy, my mare. But mostly I walked, alone, through the mesquite pastures and canyons infested with rattlesnakes—my gun and me.

Guns. Like most farm and ranch boys, I always had them. First, I played my solitary game of cowboy and imaginary Indians along the creek and canyons with cap pistols. I later graduated to a BB gun, then became a real killer with my .177 pellet rifle.

Slick, our black farm worker, moved to Lubbock when I was ten years old. He left behind a Bible, a Harrington & Richardson 20-gauge single-shot, and a hundred-dollar debt to Daddy against future wages. I got the "hundred-dollar shotgun."

Joe Dismore, a neighboring farmer, later lent me my first real rifle—a Mauser .22 caliber. Joe had "liberated" the Nazi training rifle in World War II. That Christmas, I got my own .22. I was disappointed that it was a Stevens pump-action, but it was mine. I sent the jackrabbits and chicken hawks around the Hargrove farm into hiding.

The next Christmas, I got a 12-gauge Winchester Model 59. That beautiful automatic shotgun gave me equal status with my uncle, Rex Fields, when dove season opened in September and he brought his big-city friends out from Snyder, which had a population of twenty thousand.

We sat behind shocks of cut sorghum in the early afternoon, and shot as the beautiful doves swept by at sixty miles an hour. Later, we stationed ourselves under mesquite trees around muddy stock tanks as doves—pigeons, actually—flew in for water. The limit was fifteen doves a day, but no game warden had ever been around the Hargrove Place.

We returned home to clean our kill at sunset. Mother would roll the dove breasts in flour and fry them. They taste a lot like chicken dark meat, and were delicious.

I fantasized about being a soldier, of course, and hoped a war would roll across our cotton farm. I knew exactly where I'd hide in the canyons, picking off Germans, or Japs, or Yankees, or whoever the unfortunate invaders might be. War on the Hargrove farm wasn't likely, but if I were lucky there'd be a real one, like Korea, by the time I could join the army or Marines.

I guess it's good that, when war came, I'd outgrown that phase of life. Barely.

My sixth-grade class had dropped to only six students. It was hard to get good teachers at Hobbs, and my parents felt that we three kids weren't getting an adequate education. In the fall of 1956, we transferred to school in Rotan. I suddenly found myself in a seventh-grade class of thirty kids. But I soon adjusted to the big-city school life.

Susan Sheldon came to Rotan during the eighth grade to stay with Empress Day, her grandmother. "Miss Empress" was a pioneer teacher who demanded—and deserved—great respect. She began her career, riding sidesaddle to teach cowboys' children, in one-room schoolhouses on the ranches around Rotan. Miss Empress eventually taught three generations of Hargroves.

Anywhere outside of Texas was fascinating to me, so Susan Sheldon was the most interesting person I had met. That's why, years later, I married her. Susan had lived in exotic places like Kodiak Island and the windswept, treeless tundras of Adak in the Aleutian Chain. She had spent the past six years in the Philippines, and had been to Tokyo, Germany, Hong Kong.

Susan's father, Buck Sheldon, was a marine engineer who had worked on the atomic bomb in the Manhattan Project in World War II, then supervised construction of the docks for the U.S. Naval Base at Subic Bay in the Philippines. His next job was to build the docks for the port of Kuwait, so Susan and her mother left for the Middle East after one semester in West Texas.

My strongest childhood memory was *the day it rained*. We stood in the rain . . . almost four inches fell that spring day in 1957. We waded down to the creek behind the house and watched the water flow from the broken stock-tank dam. The five-year drought was over.

Daddy made a bumper crop that year, and the price of cotton was high. He made more dollars, when dollars bought four times what they buy today, than in any of his fifty years of farming. Daddy was tight with money, but we rode the train to Lansing, Michigan, to pick up our new Oldsmobile at the plant.

We drove to New York and Washington, D.C., then started the part of the trip that excited me most: the Deep South. We visited Civil War battlefields and museums in Vicksburg and Atlanta, and Confederate monuments across Dixie.

Becky drove Raford and me to school in Rotan each day in

the 1956 Chevrolet pickup until she graduated in 1958. I turned fourteen that year, and got my driver's license. I also got my first car at age fourteen. A few months later, I learned some facts of life from a Rotan girl, two years older but decades wiser, in the backseat of that two-door '54 Ford. I guess I disappointed her. I also wrecked that same first car at age fourteen.

Daddy bought me a replacement '53 Ford a few months later—but not because he was indulgent. If I didn't have a car, my parents' lives would be spent driving Raford and me to school, taking us to teenage functions in Rotan, or picking me up after football practice.

Football. That's my only bad memory of growing up in West Texas. I hated football passionately. To me, it made no sense to go out on a hard clay field for two hours every day after school for three months so two hundred and twenty-pound L. D. Daniels, whose IQ was about like our cocker spaniel's, could practice running over me.

But I had no choice. Uncle Ben Hargrove had played tackle on the first Rotan Yellowhammer team, back in 1920. Strong Hargrove farm boys had fought for the orange-and-white ever since. My father would be disappointed—heartbroken is a better term—if his sons didn't play football.

Besides, what really *desirable* girl would date a boy who didn't play football? How would she feel if she couldn't even wear your letter jacket with the big **R** . . .

To make it worse, I was a bench-warmer who never made first-string until my senior year. Even then, I played center, and the *backfield* got the cheerleaders and twirlers.

Did I tell my parents that I hated football? No, I wouldn't even hint at it. I was a West Texan, and a Hargrove.

I carried that terrible secret into my senior year. It was bearable then, because I knew that if I could last three more months—twelve games—I'd never have to wear a football suit again. Then something awful happened.

We Fightin' Hammers had always finished around last in our district. That suited me fine. But in the fall of '61, Rotan won seven of eight games and, oh, no! We were the Class-A district champions. That meant another two weeks of workout before the bidistrict playoff.

We kicked the hell out of Seagraves to win bidistrict, and that set me into secret depression. Regional championship came next. What if we win—then we go to quarterfinals, and maybe all the way to Texas state championship? I'll be playing football till almost *Christmas*!

We rode in a yellow school bus to Midland to play Wink, a far West Texas town, on a windy Thanksgiving Day. That afternoon, something happened that made me appreciate civil rights and integration more than any of Rev. Martin Luther King's eloquent speeches. Wink had a hotshot fullback named Simmons who was—would you believe?—black! No Rotan team had ever faced a Negro on the gridiron.

"Gonna get me a little black on my headgear, come Saturday," one Yellowhammer boasted in the Rotan locker room after practice.

"Step on the nigger's feet—that'll stop him," another player replied.

"I got a better strategy. When Simmons gets the ball, have someone toss a watermelon near the Yellowhammer goalpost. He'll head straight for that melon and ... Bingo! Another touchdown for Ol' Rotan High!"

What happened was predictable. Whenever the ball was snapped, eleven rednecks charged straight for Simmons. The black fullback would simply lateral the pigskin to a companion, who'd trot down the field and ... another touchdown for Wink.

Our defeat was humiliating, and teammates sobbed softly in the locker room after the game. It was tough, but I acted like losing our chance for the Texas Class-A state football championship was the end of my life, too.

After football, religion was the most important part of life in Fisher County. Rotan had half a dozen Baptist churches and a strong Church of Christ. Most citizens frowned on dancing, and many considered it satanic. Otherwise-devout farmers and ranchers were occasionally "churched"—struck from the roles of the more fundamental churches—for dancing. Rotan never had a school dance, and probably never will.

Mother and Daddy were respectably religious, but far from fanatic. We were solid members of the First Methodist Church, and attended ... most Sundays.

There was never much drinking around the Hargrove house, maybe some eggnog at Christmas. My folks weren't judgmental, they just didn't care for the stuff.

It goes without saying that Fisher County was, and still is, dry. I mean *bone* dry—that means not even beer could be sold in grocery stores. Two groups kept it that way: the churches, and the bootleggers.

The greatest Saturday night excitement was to drive around "the drag," our one-stoplight main street, until the Rotan chief of police parked in front of Wallace's Cafe. When Betty Porter served Chief Hughes his coffee and slice of apple pie, we knew it was probably safe to head for The Flat, Rotan's black section.

One of us, usually me, would get out near Club-Foot Sam's shack while the car circled the block, watching for the chief. I'd knock at the back door and yell softly "Sam! Six beers!" I'd pass over six one-dollar bills, and Club-Foot Sam would hobble out with six cold quarts of bootleg Jax.

We'd drive north of Rotan with the radio tuned to Wolfman Jack from XERF, the fifty-thousand-watt station in Ciudad Acuña, Mexico, across the river from Del Rio. But once we had parked under the river bridge, we'd dial KOMA from Oklahoma, waiting for the DJ to broadcast the thirty-second *kissing tone*. That helped a lot of guys who didn't know how to make the first move. No girl could refuse you at the kissing tone.

If we were lucky, the evening moved into some real heavy petting. I kept an old army blanket in the trunk of my '53 Ford, just in case Sue Ann Reynolds or Betty Mueller might get in the mood to go lie in the riverbed sand by the foot-deep Double Mountain Fork of the Brazos.

When I was fifteen, a Baptist preacher launched a fresh antidancing crusade. One ringing sermon was:

> I'll tell you why them kids want to dance. It's the Devil's work. Yeah, Ol' Satan himself . . . he knows that listenin' to that rock 'n' roll music and dancin' belly to belly will work up passion . . . then them kids will get in a car and drive down out to the canyons to relieve that passion! Yessir, the Devil is listenin', and he smiles when he hears that music. But he laughs, fellow Christians, when he sees them kids start dancin'. Because Ol' Satan knows that *he* will soon possess those once-innocent souls . . .

Mother and Daddy didn't dance, but that was because they never learned or, maybe, they were too bashful. Mother said—

openly—that the sermon was ridiculous. She knew that parking under the river bridge was likely to work up more passion than dancing . . . even if belly to belly. My parents encouraged me to have dances, for friends whose parents would allow it, at the farmhouse.

My junior class went to the Texas State Fair at Dallas one weekend in the fall of '60 when we didn't have a football game. There, I walked through the education pavilion, because it was the most direct route to the "Amazing Gorilla Woman." I noticed a booth with a sign A&M COLLEGE OF TEXAS.

On the front cover of a free eight-page brochure, a Texas Aggie senior kissed a beautiful Texas girl under a giant Texas A&M ring. The Aggie wore a starched khaki uniform, a Sam Browne belt, and knee-high, spit-polished senior boots with military spurs.

Those boots. That girl. There was no longer any question about where I'd go to college. It could only be Texas A&M.

Transition 6

Chuong Thien Province, 1988

I'm in a tropical ghost town, the skeleton of a U.S. Army post deep in the Mekong Delta. I pause at a plank hut. Its olive paint is peeling and time has rusted the screens away, but . . . something is hauntingly familiar.

My God, this is our old orderly room. I walked through this door and reported for duty in July of 1969, carrying an M-16 and a duffel bag and wondering if I'd live through the next year.

I feel the ghosts of American soldiers—GIs and officers who survived, as well as those who died, in Chuong Thien

Province. The MAC-V camp is my personal Vietnam War Memorial. No other U.S. veteran has seen it since the war ended.

A half-dozen plank buildings still stand. All are rotting, but not even thirteen years of tropical neglect and monsoon rains can wash away that cold and sterile look of an army camp.

The chain-link fence is gone. So are the sandbagged bunkers and barbed concertina wire. That makes the camp look . . . naked? Only an empty concrete pillbox, its firing slits choked with jungle vines, still guards MAC-V from attack across the Xa No Canal.

A dozen laughing children surround me as I walk through the unguarded compound. They chant something friendly, but it's not "Okay, *Ong My*, okay!" like before. These kids have never *seen* an American.

I leave the old orderly room. I don't recognize the next two sheds. Then I come to—was this the mess hall, or the club? I don't know, it's been too long.

The missing screens make the barracks look hollow, lonely. That makes me feel almost . . . homesick. How can I think that?

MAC-V is so much smaller than I remember. Most enlisted men never left this camp during their one-year tours. That must have been worse than navy duty. A ship had more room.

"Why haven't squatters moved in?" I ask.

The Vietnamese stranger, my unofficial guide, explains that the military—to me, that's the Viet Cong—took over all U.S. military posts in 1975. But one hundred thousand Vietnamese troops are now in Cambodia.

"We're desperately short of housing, but the old American camps sit empty." He shrugs.

"Where was CORDS?"

"You've already walked past it." Tran Van Rang, the ex–VC political officer, has caught up. I turn back, but see only an empty lot and two broken posts—the gate. We parked our jeeps inside those columns. Then I spot the concrete light post. From there I find, and stand on, the concrete slab that was my quarters.

I locate the kitchen and porch where we set up the Delta Lily. Col. Thomas Le Vasseur, the province senior adviser, didn't like our improvised bar. Colonel, I wish you could see the Delta Lily now. The Viet Cong have shut it down, for good.

I walk back to the light post, my position when we had trouble. I remember the night we learned that Ho Chi Minh had died. The VC dropped thirty-eight 82mm mortar rounds on us, then a platoon entered Vi Thanh. The South Vietnamese troops defending the village never left their bunkers. Am I bitter about that? I guess not . . . those soldiers wanted to live through the night, too.

I had my M-16, a shotgun, and a sack of ammo and grenades. I lay behind this post and watched buildings burn through the barbed wire as we waited for the VC to attack.

There were red-and-yellow streaks, then a blast. The Chicom B-40 rocket exploded in front of this light post, but I wasn't touched.

At dawn, Frank Gillespie went into Vi Thanh, and returned with bad news—the VC had Duc, the head of our security force. The ex-ARVN soldier was with his "second wife"—Americans would call her a mistress—when the mortar rounds started falling. Duc was running home, to his real wife, when the VC grabbed him. I had been a guest in that home, to celebrate his son's first birthday, a few days earlier.

Duc knew our defenses and weapons, and that meant the VC now knew everything they needed. During the next days our guards moved claymore mines, bunkers, firing positions.

The VC took half a dozen prisoners deep into the U Minh, the "Forest of Darkness," that night. Five were released after a week of indoctrination. But not Duc—he worked for the Americans.

Our insurance covered Vietnamese employees that the VC killed or wounded but, ironically, not those who were captured. I wanted Duc's family to eat, so I carried him on the payroll—illegally—for the next three months. His wife appeared every two weeks, said, "I'm Mr. Duc," and I paid her Duc's salary. It was our private joke.

CHAPTER XI
Cross the Bassac at Can Tho

Los Baños, Valentine's Day, 1990. Chuong Thien Province, 1969–70

A letter from Vietnam arrived on 14 February, Valentine's Day, 1990. Its address was simple: "Thomas R. Hargrove, International Rice Research Institute, Philippines."

Then I saw the return address: *Khang*, Nguyen An. Can that be *my* Khang? No, he's dead. He'd have written after 1975 if he'd survived, he had my address.

But the letter was postmarked Sa Dec . . . Khang's home town north of Can Tho.

I closed my office door, poured a cup of strong coffee, and opened the letter.

A news clipping fell out. There was my photo, taken in Chuong Thien Province in 1988. I looked stunned, and for good reason. Tran Van Rang, the Viet Cong political officer for Vi Thanh, was explaining why he didn't kill me in 1969. I saw the words CO VAN HARGROVE in the headline, and remembered that *co van* means "adviser."

I unfolded the handwritten letter:

To Dear Mr. Tom,

I am Nguyen An Khang, your interpreter in Chuong Thien Province. I was surprise when I read on the Police Department weekly newspaper publish in Ho Chi Minh City dated 10 Jan 1990 printed your picture taken in Vi Thanh and your idea concerning relation between VN and USA government.

It's very lucky and happy because I looked for your address a long time to contact you since I returned to my home in Sadec in March 1975. That's where you and me once stop at my house on the way from Saigon go to Can Tho, then Chuong Thien.

It *is* Khang, who else could know that we visited his mother in Sa Dec in 1969? She was a poor but gracious Confucian-type widow who wore a high-necked, traditional *ao dai*. She made a wonderful lunch for her son and the American *co van*: *cha gio* or spring rolls with crab and pork, roasted chicken, and rice. I appreciated the lunch, and felt guilty because I knew she couldn't afford it—but it took too long. We *could not* be on the road to Can Tho after dark.

Finally, we were barreling down the next forty miles of flat Delta road toward the ferry that crossed the Bassac, a mile-wide branch of the Mekong River. Can Tho lay on its other side.

An M-16 lay by my right hand in the front seat, Khang cradled an M-2 .30-caliber carbine, and the floorboard was sandbagged. I hate driving fast, but I drove madly in Vietnam. A speeding jeep was a tougher target for snipers, and the driver was more likely to survive if he hit a road mine. Besides, we *had* to cross the Bassac before the sun set.

Lyrics of a Billy Walker cowboy song about a Texas outlaw on the run swirled through my head:

> Cross the Brazos at Waco
> Ride hard and I'll make it by dawn
> Cross the Brazos at Waco
> I'm safe when I reach San Antone . . .
>
> *Cross the Bassac by sundown*
> *We're safe when we reach old Can Tho . . .*

I turned back to the letter:

In late March 1975, the Secretary of General Consulator in Can Tho advised me to try to go from VN out to the sea, there were many US Navy ships ready to pick up all of us.

But I couldn't evacuated to USA because my wife having pregnancy about 6 months. So I have to return to Sadec.

I burned all my documents and pictures of us because when VC liberated I am afraid the Communist govern't will revenged and savage who worked closely with Americans . . . I changed my name, became AN, NGUYEN HUU. But my neighbor told the security service I was CIA's employee so they came to my house, arrested me on 19 June 1975.

Nineteen June . . . a special date. I never remember 3 March, my birthday, or Susan's, which is sometime in November. I have trouble with 25 December. I knew this was Valentine's Day because the IRRI Secretaries' Association had sent IRRI scientists a reminder, with an order form for flowers they were selling. But on 19 June, in 1969, I shipped out to Vietnam . . . 19 June is probably a special day for Khang, too.

I was sent to Re-Education Camp in Sadec for 6 months. After that I have to stayed at home while my wife selling stuffs in market. We saved money enough to escape oversea by boat before Christmas 1980. But the secret police known and arrested me again for Re-Education Camp until December 1982.

Two and a half years in reeducation camps—the Communists must consider Khang a hard core. How can he write this, the police *must* read his mail . . . maybe he doesn't care any more. . . .

I always remember our memories when we worked together in Chuong Thien as "Dangerous and happy." Do you remember Mr. Ba Lien, old farmer in Vi Duc . . . times we spent in Long My, Kien Hung etc.? Specially when we stop to visit the sorghum demonstration located the side of road from Hoa Luu to Vi Thanh—and we are very lucky when we arrived to Vi Thanh and heard the TOC report what was happened after we just left overthere.

Dangerous and happy . . . those days were always dangerous and sometimes happy, but often, tragic. What happened on the road from Hoa Luu? Maybe the next jeep was ambushed, or a VC squad moved in. Things like that happened every day in Chuong Thien.

Won't Khang be surprised to learn that "Ba Lien, old farmer in Vi Duc" is still alive, and I visited him eighteen months ago? And that Ba Lien's granddaughter, the little girl I carried around the farm on my shoulders, now has her own children.

Khang would also remember Joe Ona, and the demonstrations of IRRI varieties that we ran on Ba Lien's farm. After Vietnam, the Filipino agronomist spread the new rice technology in Iran, then Belize. He's now working in Timor, a former Portuguese colony and one of the southernmost islands of Indonesia.

Khang's letter also catalyzed memories of an exotic farewell dinner that Ba Lien gave for me in June of 1970, two days before I left Chuong Thien. In typical Vietnamese fashion, it was the best he could offer.

Late that afternoon, Khang and I sipped orange soda with Vi Duc farmers on the concrete patio where Ba Lien dried rice. I hadn't touched the bottle of *baxide* that sat on the round teak table because I knew that, later, farmers would propose far too many toasts in my honor.

Ba Lien's wife served the main dish, a bowl of meat in a thick brown gravy. I caught snatches of Vietnamese conversation, including the words *con meo*.

"Khang, what will we eat *this time*?"

"Never mind, Tom. You like."

"This isn't *con meo* ... cat ... or is it?"

"Numba one food." Khang laughed, dipped chopsticks into the dish, and dropped morsels into my rice bowl.

I shrugged. My first exposure to what might be called *exotic* Vietnamese food, a year earlier, wasn't so bad. Our host was *Dai Uy* Hong, chief of the Revolutionary Development cadre. I only learned what I'd eaten the next morning.

"Trung Uy!" The captain always addressed me by the Vietnamese term for first lieutenant.

"How you like my pig last night?"

"Good pig, *Dai Uy*! I ate *beaucoup*."

"Not pig, *Trung Uy*. Meat was *con cho*."

"Dog? Why didn't you tell me?"

"I know 'Mericans. If I say 'dog,' you will not eat. So I tell you 'pig,' and you like too much."

I soon learned to enjoy dog.[1] In fact, I guess I ate every creature that flew, swam, or slithered through Chuong Thien Province—except I somehow avoided the giant fruit bats. Roasted rats were delicious. They were grain-fattened, caught in the rice fields and as clean as rabbits. Snake tasted like chicken, and I could tolerate lizards, turtles, and eels cooked in slimy black skin. But I hated eating the embryos from eighteen-day-old duck eggs.

"Eat duck egg, then you will drive your jeep around Vi Thanh, looking for *companionship*." The local boys swore the eggs had aphrodisiac powers. What I remember is getting sick, back in the CORDS Compound.

I'm the guest of honor, I thought that 1970 afternoon, *and Ba Lien cooked this cat especially for me.* Maybe it'll be like dog; it can't be as bad as unhatched ducks. I plucked the piece that seemed most succulent with my chopsticks, and chewed.

How does cat taste? Close your eyes and *imagine* . . .

Cat meat tastes a lot like you might think . . . but worse. It's rancid, like rotting meat, and it *expands*. The more I chewed on that chunk of cat, the bigger it got. I almost choked, swallowing.

Thank God for rice whiskey. I chased the cat with a straight cup of *baxide*.

Khang saw what was happening. I had let my interpreter become too Americanized. He thought this was funny, and dropped another piece of cat into my bowl. I remembered feeding fish bones to Ba Lien's yellow tomcat. I liked the cat *then*, but not now.

Only Khang spoke English, so I said, as pleasantly as possible, "Khang, your ass is grass if you give me one more piece of goddamn cat! I'll *fire* you."

Khang translated for the farmers, "The American adviser

---

[1] When my parents visited the Philippines in 1978, my father and I toured the mountains of northern Luzon. One evening in Bontoc, an Igorot tribal town, I took Daddy for a beer in a restaurant whose sign illustrated its specialty: a head-and-shoulders painting of a German shepherd that looked like Rin Tin Tin.

I ordered a plate of roasted dog . . . not because I wanted it, but so Daddy could tell Fisher County farmers of another exotic experience in the Philippines.

Daddy declined, but I ate some dog. It was rancid and tough. Had I changed? Or had Philippine canine cusine not reached the level of excellence found in Vietnam?

loves cat," he said, "and wants more." A farmer courteously dropped a tiny paw, its fur removed, thank God, into my bowl. I covered it with rice, but had to accept another piece. It was worse. I gulped more *baxide*.

"Maybe I won't fire you," I said in a tone I hoped the farmers wouldn't catch. "But I'm going to beat the hell out of you when we leave," Khang and I both knew, of course, that I'd never do it.

The sun now hung low and orange against a cloudless sky. Darkness would come suddenly. I said a few words of thanks and farewell, embraced Ba Lien, and rushed to my Scout.

Once Ba Lien's home had left my rear-view mirror, I slammed the brakes and flung my door open. I was vomiting, and Khang was laughing, as I fell from the Scout and rolled into the roadside canal.

I've often thought about eating that cat. My West Texas upbringing definitely made me a carnivore—a meat-eater. But I had never, until that cat, eaten the flesh of *another* carnivore. Buddhist and Hindu vegetarians sometimes think that Westerners smell bad, because *we* eat meat and *they* don't. That cat was the first time I had eaten another carnivore.

The night after I ate the cat, American advisers threw another farewell at the MAC-V Compound. Khang gave me a VC flag, courtesy of his brother Truong, and the Phoenix Program. Things were okay now, because I was leaving Chuong Thien Province.

At noon on Valentine's Day 1990, I searched my novel and found my first *fictional* reference to Khang, in chapter 3. Sergeants Joe Culver and Enrique Rodriquez had talked with Dan Bridges while Lieutenant Burns, team leader of MAT 96, slept.

Alan Burns came back into the radio room. "Let's get Khang and visit the chief."

"Who's Khang?"

"Our interpreter. He's an ARVN soldier, a kid who learned about five hundred words of high school English before he got drafted. Khang isn't Henry Kissinger, but he tries."

Alan walked through the open door of a hootch by the militia outpost and approached a net hammock slung between two wooden posts. He touched the shoulder of a Viet-

namese youth who slept in crumpled fatigues. The boy
swept hair from his eyes, then slowly swung bare feet to the
clay floor.

"Khang, meet our new adviser, Lt. Dan Bridges."

"I hope we be numba one friends for chure, *Trung Uy*."
He shook hands, then rubbed his eyes.

"We want to visit the chief, then show Lieutenant Bridges
the cultural attractions of Nuoc Trong," Alan said.

"What means 'culture traction'?"

"Never mind, Khang. Let's go."

A skinny pig slept in the shade of the canopy before
Nuoc Trong's only cafe. Several shops had yellow signs
with bright red letters in the roman script that Portuguese
missionaries had brought to Vietnam a hundred years earlier.
Signs of the more prosperous-looking shops were also let-
tered vertically in Chinese calligraphy.

Dan glanced into a shop. It offered essential goods, but
few luxuries: canned sardines, cigarettes, needles and thread,
Vietnamese beer and soft drinks, hard candy, dried fish,
soap, dried roots, and one bottle of French cognac.

A stocky man in his midfifties met the three men at the
door of the police station, a two-room concrete building with
a tin roof. Muscles rippled beneath Nguyen Van Cam's
black, collarless shirt, showing that he was more a farmer
than a politician.

The chief smiled as they shook hands, but his hard black
eyes bothered Dan. *This man has seen, or done, something
bad.*

"Mr. Cam offer you *chi*, *Trung Uy* Dan," Khang translated. A boy set three chairs around a table, then brought a
teapot and clear pyrex glasses. *Ong* Cam poured enough
steaming tea to sterilize each cup, swirled it, and flicked the
liquid onto the floor.

"The chief ask do you have sons?"

"No, I'm not married."

"Mr. Cam hope when you return to your country, Texas,
you find good wife, raise many sons."

"No daughters?"

"Girls numba ten. Mr. Cam have four sons, no daughters.
Numba one man."

"How old are his sons?"

"Mr. Cam have sons that are twenty and seventeen and

sixteen year old, but they die last year. One son still 'live, age fifteen."

"I'm sorry, where is his fifteen-year-old?"

The chief and Khang talked in Vietnamese.

"You arrive very bad time, Mr. Cam say. Chuong Thien is hot now, but monsoons come soon."

Why did the chief ignore my question? Dan thought.

Alan and the chief discussed an ammunition shipment for the Nuoc Trong militia, and cement, tin roofing, and rebar, or reinforced steel bars, for the new outpost.

"Mr. Cam hope *Trung Uy* Dan must come soon to his home for a numba one party," Khang translated as they left. "*Beaucoup* to drink, plenty good foods."

"*Cam an*, thank you."

"We'll go through the Nuoc Trong market now," Alan said. "It's a good introduction to a typical Ca Mau Peninsula village."

Barefoot women in baggy black pants and white blouses carried naked babies on their hips. Vendors squatted, flat-footed, under cone hats of straw in front of baskets of onions, red and green peppers, tomatoes, fist-sized eggplants, cucumbers, and ginger root. A boy peed in the dust between the rows of baskets.

Dan picked his way around red puddles. A woman spat a stream of blood into the street.

Dan was startled. "What's *that*?" Then he watched the woman calmly put a round, carrot-colored disc into her mouth.

"Betel nut."

The woman's red-stained mouth reminded Dan of an old, sad clown.

By the canal, the smell of the fish market overpowered all others. A woman displayed a pan of fresh gray fish, each a foot long, with snowy bellies and jutting dorsal fins.

"Are those sharks?"

Alan nodded.

"But Chuong Thien is landlocked. We must be fifty miles from the ocean."

"Forty miles—pick your direction. Charley controls the rivers and canals west to the Gulf of Siam, and east to the South China Sea. But we can buy fresh ocean fish every morning."

The next vendor lifted the lid from a tub, and wormlike coils tried to slither up its sides.

"Relax, those aren't snakes," Alan said, "they're eels."

"They're . . . hideous."

"You'll eat eels—and a lot worse—over the next year. Not bad, if you've never seen them alive. I could handle eels if the Vietnamese would only remove that slimy black skin.

"I'm not saying there's anything wrong with black skin," he added.

The woman's betel-stained smile seemed hellishly red as she pushed the squirming black mass down with her hand.

"Look, lobsters." Dan pointed to a tray.

"No, crawfish. They're from the Xa No Canal. Look at their claws." The six- to nine-inch crustaceans had ridiculously long, bright-blue pincers the thickness of a pencil.

"Those crawfish were cheap in Kien Long—because no one would eat them," Alan said. "There was a lot of killing, and the Vietnamese claimed that crawfish ate corpses thrown in the canals. That didn't bother us. A five-gallon can cost two dollars, so we ate crawfish every day: fried, boiled . . . soul food. Of course, that was before Felipe joined the team."

"So now you eat *Mexican* crawfish?"

"*Now*, I won't *touch* a damn crawfish," Alan said. "One morning a dead man floated by our tent, face down in the canal. The body was bloated like a balloon. He could've been VC, an ARVN, a PF, or some poor damned farmer caught in the middle. He had been stripped, and dead Vietnamese all look the same.

"We fished the corpse from the canal, and I rolled him over with my boot. What a sickening fucking sight—*no face*, just skull and white slivers of rotting meat. The rest was gnawed away."

Dan thought about taking catfish off a trotline after turtles had gotten to them. *The dead man must have looked like that.*

"I don't know if crawfish or turtles ate his face . . . maybe both . . . but I haven't eaten either since."

Dan grimaced.

"Sorry, I shouldn't start your first day in Nuoc Trong with a story like that. Color me a flaky black lieutenant who's getting short. Those crawfish are better than shrimp. Buy them, if they get cheap again. *But you'd better hope they don't.*"

"That doesn't bother me," Dan lied.

Those crawfish—they *were* cheap—and Alan Burns explained why. Vietnamese thought they fattened on bodies, Communist and capitalist and neutral, dumped into the brackish rivers and canals of Chuong Thien. We ate them a lot at the Delta Lily, that spring of 1970. Sergeant Willie Wilson wouldn't touch the crawfish after a MAT lieutenant told about finding the body in a canal. But the rest of us were less finicky.

You see, I became the Lily's unofficial procurement officer because I enjoyed taking Khang to barter for food in the Vi Thanh market, which I described in my fictional Nuoc Trong.

We probably ate better than any advisory team in Vietnam during my last three months in Chuong Thien, although the men started bitching about the monotony of New York strip steaks, night after night.

It started when I met Sergeant Shaw, who worked at the officers club at Can Tho Air Base.

"Can you get Viet Cong rifles down there?" Shaw asked when he learned I was stationed in Chuong Thien, and came to Can Tho every two weeks to pick up the Vietnamese payroll.

"Sure, Vietnamese soldiers are always giving us weapons—or trying to sell them."

"Let's step into the kitchen, Lieutenant. I know it's rough in Chuong Thien, so I'm gonna make a small contribution to your men's morale."

The sergeant opened a standing freezer and pulled out a frosty box labeled NEW YORK STRIP STEAKS, 10 OZ. (24).

"These steaks look spoiled, right, Lieutenant?"

He marked the box CONDEMNED with a black felt pen.

"If I served this meat at the O-club, some important officer might get food poisoning. That would hurt the war effort, and be mighty unpatriotic . . . so could I turn this meat over to *you*, to throw away?"

What could I say? "*Thanks*, Sergeant Shaw!"

"But Lieutenant . . . I sure would appreciate one of them

Chicom rifles. The kind with the bayonet that folds up into the stock?"

Now I understood . . . airmen in Can Tho might pay big bucks for VC rifles to bring home as war trophies.

"You mean SKSs? I have two, back in Vi Thanh."

"Need any coffee, Lieutenant?" He handed me an olive-colored one-gallon can. "How about some pork chops? Artichoke hearts in oil?"

Back in Vi Thanh, I set out strip steaks and frozen asparagus for dinner, and stored the other steaks in a freezer that held bottles of blood plasma. Sergeant Shaw got his first VC rifle two weeks later.

But not his last. Norm Olsen donated the next rifle for the good sergeant. Vietnamese soldiers in Chuong Thien had an inexhaustible supply of rifles they'd trade for a $2.40 case of American beer or Coke. Not bad, when converted into cases of steak. Sergeant Shaw soon introduced me to his friends. The sergeant who ran the Can Tho Air Base mess hall and the Green Beret's Alamo Lounge wanted VC weapons too, and we had developed a taste for New York strips.

We served two cases of Maine lobster tail at my farewell party, the night after I had dined on cat with Ba Lien. I hope Sergeant Shaw got a good price for his new Chinese AK-47 assault rifle, still packed in cosmoline.

I set the novel aside and searched my diary. The first of dozens of references to Khang was on 24 September 1969, soon after I hired him:

Khang and I are at Kien Thien district town. We arrived by swing ship and will go by sampan south on the canal to meet Binh, head of a 3-man Land Reform team in Ninh Quoi village.

Later. We are at NQ, on the border of An Xuyen, better known as Ca Mau, VN's southernmost province. MAT 104 has moved into Ninh Quoi. For safety, we should stay with those 4 Americans tonight. They'll have security, and radio communication with the outside world. But we'll sleep where the VN Land Reform cadre sleep . . . I'd rather not, but we have to take the same risks the VN do.

The next day, I wrote:

I am angry at Binh. The village chief gave a party in our honor, with plenty of *Ba-Mui-Ba* ["33" brand beer]. Binh drank too much, and bragged loudly, in VN and English, about the American who wasn't afraid to stay in the village with his LR team. *The VC controlled Ninh Quoi until 6 mo. ago, for God's sake!* The crowd *had* to include VC agents. In villages like NQ, an adviser shouldn't even *decide* where he'll stay until after dark—much less, announce it.

No doubt, Charley knew we would sleep in the NQ village chief's home. Maybe he could have gotten to us, maybe not. I didn't want to learn the hard way, so Khang and I stayed with the American soldiers of MAT 104, beside the Popular Force outpost.

Binh's mouth will get him—and maybe us—killed some day.

But having my own interpreter is wonderful. Khang is hard-working, eager to learn—and can handle a carbine. He is the 16-yr-old brother of my friend Mr. Truong.

Khang's brother Truong . . . his role in the Chuong Thien war was another reason I had felt sure my interpreter was dead. Truong was a chubby man in his midthirties with curly hair. He had a dangerous job.

Truong was head of the Special Police, which ran the Phoenix Program.

The VC feared and hated Phoenix because it was effective. From 1968 to 1971, about 17,000 VC sought amnesty, 28,000 were captured, and 20,000 were killed, according to William Colby, then CORDS director and later head of the CIA.

Despite Phoenix's image, killing was never its main purpose. In 1988, I located the former Capt. Harvey Weiner, who had been Phoenix adviser for Chuong Thien. Harvey objected strongly to my use of the word "assassinate" in a description I'd written of *Phung Hoang*:

Phoenix was designed for neutralization by capture, because the Viet Cong Infrastructure held crucial information. But actually, most VCI were killed in battle, because many wore two hats: soldier and VCI. Most of the hard-core VCI in

Chuong Thien were killed when they surfaced during the 1968 *Tet* [Lunar New Year] Offensive, before my arrival. The new recruits were not committed Viet Cong, and were quite susceptible to switching sides. I focused on the *Chieu Hoi*, or "Open Arms" program. Most of the VCI that were "neutralized" actually became *hoi chanhs* [VC defectors]. Some were accidentally killed in air strikes.

But not a single VCI was assassinated, that I knew of, in Chuong Thien Province in 1969–70.

I also mentioned Khang on 27 September 1969:

Before we left for Long My, Lloyd Craig, the police adviser, said "Tom, if that sniper between Duc Long and Long Binh fires at you, *don't shoot him*! He's been sniping for months, and hasn't hit anyone yet. But if someone kills him, the VC may replace him with another sniper who can shoot."

Lots of people have been shot at, but none hit, on that road lately. Last week a sniper shot 3 times at Frank Gillespie, Khang, and 1LT Rascke, and never even hit the jeep.

Last night SFC Bill Haley and CPT Sands and I had a party. We cooked a pot of chili beans on the Delta Lily stove, and Sands brought a can of jalapeño peppers from his family in Arizona. It was good, but made me feel homesick.

Haley is a rice-and-hog farmer from Arkansas who recently got a Silver Star. He keeps re-upping, and has been in Chuong Thien for more than 2 years. I ask his advice a lot on ag projects.

Haley came upon a beautiful field of IR8 on a VN operation last week above Mickey's Ears (where the Snake River that separates Duc Long and Kien Hung districts meanders into two big curves that gave the area its name). The crop was planted uniformly. It was well-headed, with no weeds.

That's my first reliable report of farmers growing "Honda Rice" in totally VC territory. But many who grow IR8 in supposedly "secure" areas (in reality, there are none in Chuong Thien) obviously support the VC.

Speaking of IR8, last week the Ag Service harvested our trials of new IRRI experimental rices on Ba Lien's farm. They were to weigh the grain from samples we cut from each plot. Seeds of the best might be multiplied and recommended as varieties for farmers across the Mekong Delta. I thought our job was done. Then Joe Ona arrived to check our results. That's when I learned that the ag cadre had *stored* the samples—and rats had eaten them. *I was sick*, and Joe was sicker. The experiment was wasted. I've learned my lesson: don't assume *anything*, no matter how simple, in Vietnam.

By late Valentine's day, 1990, a Vietnamese scholar at IRRI had translated the news clipping that Khang sent. The headline was:

THE DOCTOR AND FORMER U.S. ARMY ADVISER HARGROVE: THE U.S. SHOULD RAPIDLY ESTABLISH DIPLOMATIC RELATIONS WITH VIETNAM

The first paragraph was about how Tran Van Rang claimed he knew and followed me in 1969, but did not have me killed . . . and why. It was straight from the three articles I'd written about my 1988 return. The second paragraph read:

In June, 1989 the former Lieutenant Hargrove, having visited the old battlefields around Vi Thanh, Chuong Thien Province, and others in Moc Hoa and today's Hau Giang Province, returned to the USA and expressed his opinion in three articles.

I noted that the Communist paper had changed my 1988 return to 1989, then had me going back to the *States*, not the Philippines. But the next sentence really irritated me:

Dr. Hargrove's opinion is that it is best not only to forget, but also to clean up the aftermath, of the war. Otherwise, the U.S. younger generation might make the same mistakes.

What *I really* wrote was that we veterans, *American and Vietnamese*, should *reconcile*, *but never forget*, the war, because if we forget, *our* children or grandchildren may make the same mistakes.

Dr. Hargrove's articles connect a bloody past with a bright future. . . . he said it was dangerous and difficult to publish them—because he wrote what he witnessed, and that is usually unacceptable to the U.S. Government.

Dangerous? Hardly. But yes, the articles were *difficult* to publish. The finest magazines in America rejected them . . . *Harper's*, *Atlantic Monthly*, the *New York Times Sunday Magazine*. Still, they convinced Owen Lock to offer me a Random House contract to write a book. But that forces me to throw away the text I wrote for my novel.

"Something bothers me about our meeting with the chief," Dan said as he and Burns left the market. "He ignored my question about his fifteen-year-old son. Did I say something wrong?"

"Nothing was wrong with the *question*. Vietnamese love to talk about their children, especially sons. But you hit a sensitive spot. I've heard that the chief's boy is a regular soldier with the 34th VC Local Battalion."

"Even though his father is a village chief?"

Alan shrugged. "Welcome to the Nam, Dan. And to civil war. Lots of families have sons fighting on both sides.

"But it's different with Cam. Charley overran Nuoc Trong during the '68 Tet Offensive. The VC were after Cam—he had just been elected village chief—but he was in Vi Thanh. So the VC troops rounded up the villagers to watch, and beheaded Cam's father, his wife, and his three oldest sons, here in the market. The youngest son left with the VC unit.

"The chief doesn't talk about it—but if that boy's still alive, and with the local VC . . . he knows."

The street turned at the northern end of the village, as if deflected by the giant eye staring from the temple.

"That eye is . . . *eerie*."

"*The All-Seeing Eye of God*. This temple is Cao Dai."

"Are they Buddhist?"

"Yes . . . and no, they believe in some of everything. Caodaism grew from the nationalist movements of forty years ago. It's a blend of religions and philosophies that the Vietnamese have adopted, or were forced to adopt, over the past four or five centuries. They make saints of whomever they feel has served mankind best. The Cao Dai believe that one God looks over the Buddhist and the Hindu, and the Christian and the Jew. They've blended those religions with Chinese Taoism, Confucianism, even some Islam.

"See the triangle?"

Dan noted a thin gold triangle painted around the eye.

"Each corner represents a Cao Dai saint. One is for Trang Trinh, who founded the Cao Dai in the 1920s. The story is, Trinh was such a fanatic, the French arrested him as a nut case. But Trinh converted his French psychiatrist to Caodaism in the insane asylum.

"The second corner is for Sun Yat-sen, because he established the first Chinese Republic, free of European colonialism.

"The third corner is for Victor Hugo."

"You mean the author of *The Hunchback of Notre Dame*?"

"Yeah, the Cao Dai founders knew their French literature. They felt that only a great spiritual leader, who truly understood the suffering of the poor, could have written *Les Miserables*.

"The Cao Dai priests claim to talk with their saints in seances. They say Hugo is their most prolific spiritual communicator—he gives guidance in poetry. The Cao Dai have a small library of literature, in French, that they claim is from Victor Hugo, at their holy city in Tay Ninh, on the Cambodian border."

"Can we go inside?"

They walked through a garden with shrubbery precisely trimmed in geometric patterns. One was a triangle.

"Khang, tell the *bonze* that the new *trung uy* would like to visit the temple."

The *bonze*, or head monk, had a scraggly white beard and wore a black skullcap, white trousers, and a purple robe that fell past his knees.

"*Chao Ong,*" Alan said, bowing at the waist and gripping the *bonze*'s right hand while covering the other side with his left hand.

The *bonze* offered a hand to Dan. It felt like parchment.

A sweet and heavy smell of incense permeated the temple. A painting of the symbolic Eye stared between two flickering red candles. Joss sticks smoldered in an urn before the altar. Red-lacquered plaques were painted with gold Chinese calligraphy.

A green dragon with a forked red tongue twisted among plaster figurines before the Eye. "Who are the statues?"

"This one is Mr. Jesus Chris'," Khang translated as the *bonze* pointed to the images. The Oriental figure looked nothing like Jesus to Dan.

"There is Mr. Sun Yat-sen. This one Mr. Confucius. That one Mr. Trang Trinh, father of Cao Dai. Mr. Lao-tse over there. And Mr. *Bonze* say that one is Mr. Mohamy."

"*Who?*" The black-bearded figure looked different, more fierce than the others.

"Mr. Mohamy. You know. Far 'way from here, where people ride big funny cambels—Mr. *Mohamy!*"

"He means *Mohammed*, Dan, in the land where men ride camels. The Cao Dai recruit the best saints from everywhere."

"This is hard to believe."

"Don't underestimate the Cao Dai. There are about five million in the Delta, and they had lots of political force, including their own army, until President Diem broke their power ten years ago," Alan said. "Today, some Cao Dai support Saigon, others are VC, but most stay out of politics."

They thanked the *bonze*, and left the temple.

"Let's go back," Alan said. "Enrique acts like my mother if we aren't home by sundown."

The market was now empty. Alan greeted two Vietnamese militiamen in the street, and waved to a table of farmers sipping tea and beer in the cafe.

"You seem to know the Vietnamese well," Dan said.

"This country . . . this village . . . it can get under your skin. If only Vietnam weren't so torn by the goddam war. It's such a strange mixture of cultures: their own, plus Chinese, Cambodian, Indian—all tinged, on the surface, by the French. Now American culture is creeping in. The Cao Dai may be talking to President Kennedy ten years from now."

I hope not, Dan thought. John Kennedy got us into the

Vietnam War . . . he's no hero of mine. But I won't say that to the black lieutenant.

"But the Cao Dai will somehow make Kennedy Asian," Alan continued. "Asia's cultures run deep and strong. Stronger than yours. Or mine."

Alan looked older in the setting sun.

"Let me tell you what may happen after I leave Mother Green and Nuoc Trong. I don't discuss this in the team hut, but I've enrolled for a semester of French at the University of Chicago. Then I'm applying for admission as a doctoral student at the Sorbonne in Paris. If things work out right, I'll return to Vietnam within two years."

"You're kidding."

"No, I'll go to Tay Ninh, to study the writing of Victor Hugo, his *ghost writing*. I'll compare what Hugo wrote in the 1800s with what the Cao Dai have documented through seances. If the French language and structure fit Hugo's mid-1800s style, I'll have my doctorate research, *plus a book*! If it doesn't, I still have a Ph.D. dissertation."

"That sounds solid."

"I'm glad you're on the team, Dan. The others are good men but to them, Asia is a bunch of *gooks*. God, I hate that term!

"You'll command the team when I leave. Can I give some advice, for when you take over?" Dan nodded.

"Treat the Vietnamese as *people*, good and bad, right and wrong. Don't call them *gooks*, or think of them like that. But also forget the idealistic bullshit that all people are the same. The Vietnamese *think* differently, Dan. You have to shift mental gears with them. The mind-set you use with Joe and Enrique and Bob won't work with the chief."

Alan watched his boots kick dust as they walked.

"Never make a Vietnamese lose face—unless you *intend* to, as a weapon. And be careful about making friends, as well as enemies, in Chuong Thien Province.

"This may sound hokey, but always remember that the Viets watch you constantly—because you're an officer of the Army of the United States of America. We both know that lieutenants are one step above whale shit at the bottom of the ocean—but the Vietnamese don't. You're nothing to the army . . . just another MAT team leader who can be killed, and replaced easily. But you can be a *god* in Nuoc Trong."

"Lieutenant!"

Sgt. Joe Culver walked toward them, carrying a 12-gauge Winchester pump shotgun with a sawed-off barrel. The bandolier across his chest was for M-16 clips, but Culver had filled it with shotgun shells, .00 buckshot.

"It's getting dark, so I came to make sure you're okay."

"What's for chow?"

"Prob'ly Meskin food. Spanish rice and beans and somethin' cooked in tomatoes and garlic and chili peppers."

"Like last night?"

"Do you think ol' Enrique's cookin' us Oysters Rockefeller, Lieutenant? If he did, he'd fuck the oysters up with chili powder."

"Let's have a beer before we face our Mexican chef's culinary delights."

"What does mean 'culin lights'?" Khang asked.

Sergeant Culver ordered a round of "33" at the village cafe. They poured the warm beer over ice and watched a brilliant red ball of fire set in the west.

A hundred yards away, a troubled man sipped *baxide* and watched the same fiery sunset. The chief wondered if he would see his last living son again.

I set the novel aside and reread Khang's letter:

I have migration form for Orderly Departure Program to leave VN since 1985 but I can't apply because the Embassy of USA in Bangkok requested proof I worked closely with Americans before 1975. But I burned my i.d. and all such papers.

A copy of Khang's ODP application was enclosed. His first reference was Thomas Hargrove (Texas citizen). Next came Richard Burke, Lt. Richard Peace (U.S. Army Engineer), then Terry J. Barker (This is the last American).

A mimeographed letter from the U.S. Embassy was attached: "Before your case can be considered further, we must have these documents." There was a check mark by: "Photocopies of papers that show you worked for the U.S. Government or a U.S. organization."

Now my family have 2 sons, 17 yrs and 13 yrs, and one daugter 15 yrs. So if you still thinking about our friendly memorial, and love my childrens, would you please help me by contact the U.S. Embassy, prove I worked with you since 1969–1970 and continued until March 1975? My family hope very much your letter.

Sincerely

Khang

I didn't write to Khang that night, I had to do something more important. But the *next* night, I wrote:

Khang, it is strange and wonderful that, after 20 years, you saw my photo in a Vietnamese newspaper and located me.

. I've thought about you a lot since 1975, especially in the past 6 months. Your life must be hard—but I'm so glad to finally know that you're alive.

My first reaction was to write to you. Then I thought: no, it is *more* important to immediately notify the Orderly Departure Program in Bangkok that An Nguyen Huu is undoubtedly Nguyen An Khang, and to confirm that you indeed worked for CORDS in Chuong Thien Province.

Next, I wrote to a friend with the Mennonite Central Committee, who helps process Vietnamese applications for ODP.

Then I wrote letters to Frank Gillespie, Norm Olsen, Chauvin Wilkinson, Harvey Weiner, and Dick Burke, asking them to also contact Bangkok.

Those letters were in today's mail, so now I can take the time to write to you personally.

Your letter stirred deep emotions. "Dangerous and happy" . . . we *did* often have fun, didn't we? Like the time we took Woody Dickerman, the American war correspondent, to a Vietnamese wedding near Long My? The farmers there played their usual trick of "ganging up" to drink the Americans under the table. Each one would propose, and drink, a toast of *baxide*. But Woody was a hardened war correspondent, and drank all the *farmers* under the table, one by one.

Remember when you and I were the first to drive the

newly opened road from Vi Thanh to Kien Hung? We were scared, but it was exciting. But the VC blew up the ferry 2 weeks later, and closed the road again. We arrived right after the explosion. I photographed what remained of an ambulance truck on that ferry, marked with a huge white cross . . . splattered with blood.

How about when I sent you up in the back seat of "Bird Dog" to throw Land Reform propaganda leaflets over the Old Frenchman's Plantation? Leaflets jammed the rudder and almost crashed the spotter plane deep in VC territory . . .

We were young, back then. Others died, but we couldn't. We could have, of course, easily.

What happened to Oahn? To Bac? To *Dai Uy* Hong?

What about Mr. Duc, chief of the "Land to the Tiller" program? He was a truly good man.

Mr. Ming, the Ag Services Chief? "Dr. Vinh," his deputy? Did you ever hear from Monique, after 1972?

What about your brother? I'm sorry but I can't remember his name.

Of course I remembered Truong's name—but I knew better than to mention Khang's brother in a letter that today's Vietnamese police would probably read. Truong may have changed *his* name and gone underground, like Khang tried to do.

You may wonder how I'm in contact with Olsen, Gillespie, and the others. Khang, I'm writing a book. The setting is Chuong Thien Province in 1969–70, and you are part of it. I tracked those men down, because I wanted them to check some of my facts . . .

Dangerous and happy . . . how can Khang *remember our memories* of Chuong Thien as *happy* days? I turned back to the novel.

Aromas of frying ginger, fish, and garlic wafted across the unpaved road as the men walked to the team hut. A dozen children followed at the heels of the three strange *My*, or Americans, who had come to live in Nuoc Trong. They pulled at the curious hair on the giant soldiers' arms, and begged to be lifted far into the sky.

"Okay, Sa-lem. Okay, numba one! *Ong My, Ong My!* Okay Salem, numba one!" The chants for "Mr. American" made Dan feel good.

"Okay *number ten!*" Alan swung a boy, in T-shirt but no pants, over his head. The child, grinning and chanting before, began to howl. Alan set him down, and he tottered to the arms of a laughing young mother at the door of a hootch.

"Kids—I reckon they're the same ever'where," Sergeant Culver said. "They sure make me miss home."

"Do you have children?"

"Yeah, my oldest boy, Darrel, is twenty and doin' okay. He ain't educated, but he's got his own diesel truck. Him and Alice've got the cutest two-year-old you ever saw. They named him Joey, after me." The sergeant stopped and scratched.

"But my other kid's nineteen, and Mike's been nothing but heartache for me and the ol' lady. We tried to raise him decent, Lieutenant, but he got into drugs, smokin' marijuana, all that shit, when he was sixteen. I guess it's my fault. I was over here lootin' and shootin' with the Big Red One, and left Mama to raise the kids as best she could. Mike barely got out a high school, but we got him into the University of Georgia. That's tough, on a sergeant's pay."

That may help explain Culver's animosity toward Bob Saunders, Dan thought.

"Mike's got hair to his shoulders, and he's doin' drugs and protestin' in peacenik demonstrations—while I'm over here in this pile of shit, payin' his tuition. Raisin' kids is fun when they're little, Lieutenant, but it ain't easy when they grow up wrong."

They paused at Khang's hut. "You need me more today, *Trung Uy* Alan?"

"No, Khang. Have a good night, but remember, we have to work tomorrow, so don't let the *con meo hung* bite you."

"Nevah happen!" Khang laughed and disappeared into his hootch.

"What's a *con meo* . . . whatever you warned Khang about?" Dan asked.

"*Hung* mean pink, and *con meo* means cat," Alan said. "I think you can figure it out."

"Oh."

* * *

At the team hut, Sergeant Culver pulled three cans from the ice chest.

"Who wants beer? I'm buyin'." He punched a worn opener into a can, spun it around, and punched two more holes, side-by-side. "We call that a 'dry county hole' back in Georgia."

"Why doesn't the army send beer in pop-top cans?" Dan asked.

"They'd bust ever' can," Culver answered, "the way them forklifts load and unload those crates at the Saigon docks."

"I think maybe it's so that Vietnamese who get beer black market can still open. These goddamn gooks are so fucking dumb, they could never learn to use the pop top."

"Thank you, Enrique, for that int'lectual philosophy. You may be right," Culver said.

"I've been to three Pollack weddin's, seventeen rabbit drives, ten hog-killin' days, and a one-legged goat fuck—but I ain't *never* seen such people. These gooks could fuck up an anvil with a rubber hammer."

Dan was dry, and the beer tasted crisp.

"What's for supper, Enrique?" Sergeant Culver asked.

"I bought canned tortillas at the PX in Can Tho. I'm gonna cook some hamburger with onion, garlic, some peppers, and comino and make nice tacos. Not so good as Mama makes in New Mexico, but I hope so much you like. I also cooked a little Spanish rice and some frijoles."

Specialist Bob Saunders wandered in, drinking a can of Sprite.

"God, do we have to eat *that crap again?*"

Enrique glared at Saunders across the gas burner. "You don' like my food after I work so hard? No one makes you to eat. Cook for yourself!

"All'a the time you bitch, bitch, bitch 'bout Enrique's cooking. Tell me jus' one thing—*do you like anything in the whole fucking world?*"

Enrique enjoys jokes about his cooking from Alan and Culver, Dan thought. But that hippie radio operator sends the wrong vibes.

Sergeant Culver opened more beer, and offered a can to Saunders.

"No thanks, Sarge. Alcohol dulls your senses, and destroys

brain cells." Culver shrugged and passed fresh beer to Dan and Enrique.

"Lieutenant Bridges, did you meet Captain Roger That when you came through Vi Thanh?" Saunders asked.

"You mean Captain Pulleig?" Dan rolled his eyes.

"What a prick!"

"He's an off'cer," Sergeant Culver snarled. "And you're a scraggly-ass Spec Four."

"No offense. I wouldn't *dare* make fun of the great military leaders of Chuong Thien Province. Let's change the subject. What about Monique?"

"The secretary at CORDS headquarters?"

"He's met her, all right!"

"We talked for a few minutes, while I was waiting to see Robert Cantwell. Her English is good, but she said she was French."

"*Half* French," Culver said. "Her old man was a French sergeant, kinda like me, and we were buddies. But he stayed in this backwater swamp after Ho Chi Minh kicked the Frogs' ass out in '54. Left his ol' lady and family in France and settled here permanent—beats hell outta me why anybody'd be fool enough to do that. He was a good mechanic, fixed motors and sold parts in Vi Thanh. But the old soljer died three months ago. Monique and her mama made me go to his funeral, but I didn't like it. The service was mostly Catholic, and that was bad enough, but they mixed in a buncha strange Buddhist shit—seemed almost *heathen* to me."

"Monique is sad," Alan said. "*She* says she's French, but the Vietnamese don't consider her French—*or* one of them. Racial prejudice isn't restricted to Mississippi."

"Prejudice in America ain't only in the South, sir," Sergeant Culver said. "*I've been to Detroit.*"

"Monique *is* pretty," Dan said, to change the subject.

"Monique is *beautiful*," Alan said. "Lots of Eurasian girls are. But it's best to tell yourself they're ugly . . . you avoid a lot of trouble that way."

"With due respect to my commander," Sergeant Culver said, "I'd be after Monique if I was you, Lieutenant Bridges."

"Why not *you*?"

"I'm too old, and too married. Besides, Monique don't care

much for old sergeants like me and Enriq'. But an officer and gentlemen might interest her."

"Why do you say that?"

"Aw ... you get nothin' but bullshit 'round a buncha horny GIs. But I never did hear, reliable, of Monique takin' up with any soljer," Culver said. "Or even an off'cer."

"I wouldn't mind to screw her a little bit," Enrique said, stirring meat and spices in a garlicky skillet. "Most Vietnamese don't have nothing to hold onto. Me, I like my women to have big tits and some ass, like when I was in Korea back in '52. Also, these women, they don't have hardly no hair on—"

A flat *whump* interrupted Enrique. Three bursts of automatic rifle fire rang from the outpost.

"Incomin'!" Culver yelled, bolting for the sandbagged bunker outside the door. Enrique reached the bunker, then scurried back into the hut, turned off the burner under his skillet, and dived back inside.

Whump! Whump! Whump! The explosions grew louder. Dan was lying flat on the bunker floor, smothered by the other men. The staccato firing continued.

"Are they attacking? My rifle's in the hut!"

"Three short bursts means we're being mortared."

Whump!

"No shit?"

A few minutes later, Sergeant Culver said "It's over," and pulled himself from the pile of humans. "Charley usually walks a few rounds across Nuoc Trong, then saves his shells for the next party ... unless he's *really* pissed."

The men returned to the team hut. Saunders took the radio handset:

"Crystal Drifter, Crystal Drifter, this is Drifter Foxtrot. Over."

"Crystal Drifter, here. Over," the TOC at Vi Thanh answered.

"Report Victor Charley mortar fire. Five eight-deuce mike-mike's, over."

"I read you five 82 millimeters. Are you still under fire? Over."

"Negative. Over."

"I've logged it. Keep us posted. Over."

"Roger. Out."

"We'd better find the chief and see if anyone in the village got hurt," Alan said. "Enrique, bring your first-aid kit—and your weapon." Alan broke open an M-79 grenade launcher and loaded a fat round of barbed flechettes.

"Joe, take the Prick-25. Saunders, stay here on the radio!"

Culver slipped the PRC-25 radio onto his back, hooked two smoke grenades to the harness, slung the bandolier, and cradled his shotgun. Enrique strapped on a .45, then grabbled a metal satchel marked with a red cross.

Khang appeared as they walked into the village. Someone shouted. The chief motioned from an alley between two huts.

"Mr. Cam say one mortar round hit the home of Mr. Luu, his brother," Khang said. "But he don't know if anybody hurt."

"Let's find out."

Only wooden frames of the hut stood. Broken furniture, pottery, and clothing were strewn across an earthen floor compacted smooth by years of bare feet and sandals.

A girl lay on a hard bed of polished black teak in the hootch next door. Her face contorted under a flickering oil lamp as an old woman clutched her hand and watched. The chief knelt and spoke softly, then drew back the sheet.

A jagged, red wound tore across pubescent breasts. She could have been beautiful, Dan thought . . . I'd have expected more blood.

The girl's breathing was a gurgle. A cherry-pink froth bubbled from gray lips . . .

Like a kid blowing bubble gum, Dan thought. Why do I think so absurdly?

"This little girl has a bad lung wound," Enrique said, opening his kit. "She's gotta have a Medevac chopper to Vi Thanh—fast."

Black blood was now seeping from the girl's mouth, and Dan didn't want to see more, so he followed Culver outside and leaned his rifle against the hut. The sergeant pushed the talk button, which triggered an electronic rush.

"Crystal Drifter, this is Drifter Foxtrot Mobile. Over."

The response was metallic: "Come in Foxtrot Mobile. Over."

"We need a Medevac, do you copy?"

"Go, Foxtrot."

"Urgent life-or-death—but nonoperational. Child, female civilian. Chest wound, diagnosed by a Uniform Sierra. *Me.*

Lima Zulu is Whiskey-Romeo five-niner-zero-niner-seven-five. Area is secure, we'll mark with smoke. Do you read?"

"Loud and clear Foxtrot. I read Landing Zone is WR590975. Over."

"This is Drifter Foxtrot Mobile. That's all." Then Culver added "But if that chopper ain't here *real* soon, this gal's a goner. Out."

The sergeant hooked the handset back on his shoulder harness.

"Does she have a chance?"

"No, but we gotta try."

Dan walked into the road and stared across the canal and rice fields at a dark tree line, barely visible.

"Don't try to figure it out. Not now."

Dan turned. It was Alan.

"The VC mortared Nuoc Trong from that tree line, Dan—and the girl that we're watching die, without having really lived, was as much a target as us Americans or the militia."

"Did you know her?"

"Yeah, I'd met her in that hut, with the chief. It was a miserable hootch, but it was all the family had." He shrugged.

"I've lost all feeling for this shit, but you're new, so you'd better learn how to handle it. You'll hate things that you see and do here, Dan. But you'll never forget them: corruption, cruelty, cowardice . . . and one hell of a lot of suffering.

"That's the toughest part, Dan, suffering. You'll learn to walk past fellow humans who are in terrible pain, yet do nothing. It won't bother you, because you can't help all the hurt people you'll see here. If it gets to you . . . *you'll* be as hurt as them."

Alan gazed at the tree line.

"You'll see bravery . . . and sacrifices that'll break your heart. The bravery will go unrewarded and the sacrifices . . . for nothing.

"You'll make terrible mistakes, Dan, *like I have*. Some will kill innocent people. You'll dream about those fuck-ups, like I do. They'll wake you in the darkest hours of early morning."

Alan's face had turned gaunt and chiseled, like an ebony carving from Africa. His eyes were far away, and his healthy appearance now seemed camouflage for a disease in his soul.

"It's no use, you'll have to learn. Just remember—MAT 96

lives with carnage and loneliness. Don't try to change that, you'll only hurt yourself."

"Maybe I understand," Dan said.

"Understanding, in Vietnam, is a curse, not a blessing."

Alan turned back to the hut where the girl lay. He dropped his grenade launcher in the dust by the blown-away door. Dan picked up the weapon and followed.

"Roger, Crystal Drifter," Sergeant Culver spoke into the mike. "Cancel the Medevac. Patient has terminated. Out."

An ancient wailing, as primeval as war itself, drifted from the hootch. One candle now lit the head of the cloth-draped body. Another flickered at the soles of bare feet that stuck from beneath a frayed red blanket.

The old woman was painting the girl's toenails cherry pink. Dan winced at the color.

"Let's go," Alan said. "It's time for chow." Enrique's tacos and beans were good, but the black officer didn't eat. "I'm hitting the sack," Alan said.

"Watching another Vietnamese die doesn't bother me . . . it just makes me tired."

Transition 7

Chuong Thien Province, 1988

The ex-VC political officer leads me past the decaying barracks of the army ghost town, to a white, two-floored building across the road. We're now in headquarters of the Vi Thanh People's Committee.

This building is familiar. It was the provincial office of the Chuong Thien Land to the Tiller program when I was agricultural and land reform adviser.

I meet Committee Chairman Vo Thanh Tong. We sip tea at a table whose glass top displays leaflets of Viet Minh raising the revolutionary flag over Dien Bien Phu in 1954 and, twenty-one years later, Soviet-made tanks entering the city I still call Saigon.

The land reform cadre gave me a dinner in this same room in June of 1970, a few nights before I left Vi Thanh. We drank farewell toasts of *baxide* from blood plasma bottles that the distiller had collected from the stack behind the Vi Thanh hospital.

Le Van Minh, the agricultural chief, briefs me on local rice production in 1988. Three agricultural graduates, Dr. Vo Tong Xuan's students from the University of Can Tho, work in what is now Vi Thanh District. Rice production is higher than ever. Sixty percent of the district's 17,500 hectares is double-cropped with IRRI varieties, mostly IR13240 and IR64. But they need more help, especially training.

We move to the second floor. The standard triad—Ho Chi Minh, Marx, and Lenin—stares down at me while I stare out the window at those concrete slabs and rotting U.S. barracks.

Steaming plates of Vietnamese food arrive. A banquet is beginning. Tu Rang surprises me by pouring toasts from a bottle of French cognac. Then I see that the *Maxime* is a blend of cognac flavoring and local alcohol.

"I was born and raised in Vi Thanh. I joined the Revolutionary Forces during the 1968 Tet Offensive," Ut Tong, the chairman, says. "I've *seen* Americans, but I never *met* one, until today. But I've learned about the hardships you took to return here, and of your feeling for the Vietnamese people.

"Last week in Moscow, something happened that may change the world," Ut Tong continues. "President Reagan and Premier Gorbachev shook hands and pledged to work for friendship and peace between the people of their two nations.

"Will you shake hands and drink a toast with Tran Van Rang, who was once your enemy, but is now your host?"

"I'll gladly drink with Tu Rang," I respond, and raise my glass. "But please, don't compare us with those two men. There's a big difference. Reagan and Gorbachev were never enemies in Chuong Thien Province."

Tu Rang and I touch and drain our glasses, then shake hands firmly. The ersatz cognac isn't bad.

More dishes arrive. This banquet is costing the People's

Committee a lot, I think, but Vietnamese have always spent more than they could afford on hospitality. More toasts. Some are to cooperation with IRRI and the University of Can Tho, but most are to the American who returned.

Then I remember the prestamped postcard I'd brought to mail to Harvey Weiner. He's now an attorney in Boston, but the VC once set a price on Harvey's head.

As an intelligence captain, he was coordinator of Operation *Phung Hoang*, the Phoenix program. To me, Harvey would have seemed more natural in a tuxedo than in jungle fatigues. But I remember Harvey's interest in IR8, and I'd written, in my diary, about an afternoon when he helped vaccinate 250 Rhode Island Red chicks against Newcastle disease at the Vi Thanh orphanage.

Harvey left a month before I did, cynical and despondent. We never wrote, but the alumni office of the London School of Economics had sent me his address.

"Does Vi Thanh still have a post office?" Yes, Tu Rang says.

"Will you mail this?" I scribble:

4 June 1988
Vi Thanh
Chuong Thien Province, SVN

Dear Harvey,

I liked Chuong Thien so much, I stayed. Why don't you ever visit, or write . . .

Tom Hargrove

Tu Rang was a prime Phoenix target, and probably set the price on Harvey. He likes the joke, and promises that the card will be clearly postmarked "Vi Thanh." I'm pleased with how I'll reestablish contact with an old friend.

The feast finally ends, and Ut Tong and Tu Rang walk Xuan and me to the jeep.

"American and Vietnam share a heritage," Ut Tong says. "The war left deep scars on both countries. But now we must forget the past."

"No . . . we must *reconcile*, but we can never forget the

war," I reply. "Because if we *forget*, Ut Tong, our children or grandchildren may make the same mistakes."

We three old enemies embrace, then I climb into the jeep.

I did it, I returned to my old mistress, I think as we churn northward through the mud. The war took a lot from her, and she seems to have mellowed. The Chuong Thien I knew before would have killed anyone foolish enough to drive her roads in the night.

I'm leaving her, for the third time. But I know she'll lure me back. Maybe Chuong Thien Province and I have finally made our peace.

CHAPTER XII
Whatever Happened to the Class of '66?

Texas, 1976

> There is a Reaper whose name is death,
> And, with his sickle keen,
> He reaps the bearded grain at a breath,
> And the flowers that grow between.
> —Henry Wadsworth Longfellow,
>   "A Psalm of Life"

I didn't want to know what happened to the Texas A&M Class of 1966 until ten years after graduation. I'd outgrown being a Texas Aggie, with its military tradition that few knew of, and fewer understood, even before graduation. I rejected it forever, in Chuong Thien Province.

I'd heard about a few classmates, of course. Bad news travels, even to dropouts of the loyal network of Aggie alumni. We seemed to have paid a high price for that heavy gold A&M ring embossed with an eagle, the Lone Star of Texas, and crossed rifle, saber, and cannon—a ring I no longer wore.

It's hard to explain why I cut myself off from A&M. Aggies are known for loyalty to the alma mater. Four years together in the Corps of Cadets built a camaraderie that few colleges can offer.

But I put that era behind when I came home in 1970—forever, I thought. A&M was no longer part of my life. I paid no dues to the Former Students' Association. I threw away, unread, copies of the *Texas Aggie*. I didn't answer letters from old friends.

But had I *really* broken those A&M ties? Maybe not. It's hard to deny values that were burned deeply into your psyche when young. Graduates of Jesuit schools say you can't. So do former Marines and flower children committed to causes of the sixties . . . and Texas Aggies.

By mid-1976, I *needed* to know what happened to Charley Griffin and Stonewall Jackson, Stanley Griffith, and Jerry Harbert. I hope Andy Denny, that crazy bastard, made it . . .

But on home leave in Texas, I kept putting off that first call. Then, after three weeks of vacation, I realized that I'd be on a plane back to Asia in a few days.

Jack Gaden should be easy to locate, I thought . . . if he's still in Round Rock, Texas. Gado will know where Bob Rutledge is, and Bob was my first sergeant, then company commander, so maybe he's kept up with the old Spiders. Spider-D was the nom de guerre, even before we had a war, for A&M's Company D-1.

I dialed the number that 555-1212 had given. The voice at the other end of the line sounded familiar, so I said, "Gado! This is Tom Hargrove."

A moment of silence . . . maybe I've reached the wrong person.

"*Hargrove?* You're still *alive*?"

"Why wouldn't I be?"

"It's hard to say, the stories I've heard . . . where *are* you?"

"On the farm in Rotan."

"You're in *Texas*? I can't believe that! Is your father alive?"

"Daddy? He's as healthy as a horse. And why shouldn't I be in Texas?"

"The story is, you disappeared into Southeast Asia after the army," Gado explained. "The last I heard, you were running a rice plantation in Sumatra, and you'd sworn never to return to America except to bury your father."

I could understand how, after stories are told a few times, the International Rice Research Institute in the Philippines could evolve into an Indonesian rice plantation. But leaving Asia only to bury my father—that made no sense. I shifted the conversation.

"Gado, remember those nurses in Dallas?" That started us swapping Aggie stories. Corps Trips ... hazing, and upper-classmen we hated ... how Gado tended bar in the evenings at the South Gate Lounge for a few short weeks during his senior year. Jack Gaden was the world's worst bartender. He considered it unethical to charge Aggie buddies for beer.

Gado told me about other Aggies and gave me phone numbers. I mentioned my work at IRRI.

"Rice—didn't you do something with rice during the war?"

"That's how I got into this business. I might still be growing dryland cotton out here in Fisher County if there'd been no Vietnam." That wasn't true, of course. I knew, at age eighteen, that I'd escape West Texas.

The conversation shifted to what *had* to come next. Gado had served in Korea and was discharged a captain; he'd missed the Vietnam scene.

"But our class got hit hard, Tom. We lost a lot of friends. You heard about Gene Oates?"

"I read it in an *Army Times* list in '69—a platoon leader with the 25th Infantry. Remember how we used to eat summer sausage and rat cheese with Gene down at Ed's on Sunday afternoons?" "Uncle Ed's" was a Bohemian beer joint near the campus, an A&M tradition for fifty years.

"I heard that Roy May bought the farm, too."

"I don't know *how* that story got started. Roy got hit, with the 1st Infantry, but he made it. So did Larry Kennemer." May and Kennemer were commanding officers in the Texas Aggie Band.

"Kennemer's photo made the cover of *Newsweek* in early '67," Gado said.

"I saw it." I was in graduate school at Iowa State University, studying late at the library. During a break, I browsed through the "Current Periodicals" section, and picked up the latest *Newsweek*. There was Larry. His chest was bandaged, and he looked tired, awfully tired. Larry was being Medevacked out after the 173d Airborne took on North Vietnamese Army regulars at Dak To, one of America's first big fights with the NVA.

"I ran into Kennemer in late 1968 at Fort Bragg," I said. "Would you believe, he'd re-upped and joined the Green Berets."

"Yeah, Kennemer spent forty months in Nam . . . there and over the fence into Laos . . . you must know that Crocker got shot up bad, but he survived." Larry Crocker was a friend in my Spider-D Class of '66, but I didn't even know he went to Vietnam.

"Crocker was an adviser somewhere in the Mekong Delta," Gaden said.

"So was I. How about Andy Denny?"

"Andy flunked out of A&M the semester he should have graduated. He later went back and finished his degree, but that was after the army. Andy wound up a sergeant on a Duster somewhere in II Corps." A Duster, I knew, was a twin 40mm Bofors killing machine that was designed for air defense, then modified for perimeter fighting on the ground. But I never saw a Duster; sophisticated weapons like that weren't issued to South Vietnamese troops deep in the Delta.

"Denny ran into Jack Blake just before *he* got it."

"Blake? Wasn't he a vet?"

"Yeah, probably the only veterinarian killed in Vietnam. Jack ran scout dogs. His jeep hit a mine." No, I didn't know about Blake.

"Surely you heard about Joe? You were close buddies at A&M."

"Yes, I was in Nam when Joe made world headlines." In the spring of 1970 I read, in *Stars and Stripes*, President Nixon's claim that no U.S. serviceman had died in the secret but escalating war in Laos. Be careful, Dick, I thought. Stonewall Jackson—but he was then Capt. Mike Jackson—had written a couple of months before. His letter was partly to let me know that he'd come home from Nam okay . . . but mainly to tell me that Capt. Joseph Bush had received Silver and Bronze Stars . . . posthumously. Joe was killed when a North Vietnamese regiment overran a Lao Army camp near Muong Sui. I guess he wasn't supposed to be there . . . not officially, anyway.

A few days after Nixon's statement, *Time* ran the last photo Joe sent to Mickey in Texas. He was squatting in front of a sandbagged bunker in Laos—holding a can of Asahi beer.

"Did you know that Mickey later found poetry that Joe had written—before shipping out to Laos—that seemed to predict his death?"

"No . . . how did Mickey take Joe's death, and all the publicity?"

"She's one hell of a woman, Tom. She sent Joe's grave marker back to the U.S. Army." Gado's voice turned caustic. "Mickey told 'em to send another stone, please."

"Really? Why?"

"The army had engraved the standard epitaph on Joe's marker—that he died for his country in the Republic of Vietnam. Mickey made the army send a replacement stone that read *Laos*. I guess it was another U.S. cover-up."

"Maybe not, Gado. Tombstones for Vietnam were assembly-line business in those days. Besides, the manufacturer probably never *heard* of Laos.

"Gado . . . how many men did we lose over there?" I meant how many *A&M men*, of course, and how many from our class.

"One hundred and eleven Aggies died or were missing in action in Indochina.

"Fifteen of the Aggie casualties were from the Class of '66. We took more casualties, Tom, than any A&M class since World War II. Thirteen were army and two, air force."

"I didn't know . . . that sounds like a lot."

That night I got out my 1966 Texas A&M yearbook and calculated. A&M commissioned ninety-three army lieutenants in 1966, plus two in the Marine Corps and thirty-seven in the air force.

Almost one man in seven who took an A&M army or Marine commission that year died. But only half of our class went to Vietnam. Even in those days, the United States needed officers in Germany, Korea, Fort Hood.

That meant almost one in three of us who went to Vietnam as army officers, died there. Those are World War I casualties . . . maybe higher.

Two days later, I flew back to Asia. I'd left Texas without calling any more of the Class of '66.

In 1989, I got statistics from the U.S. Military Academy. West Point commissioned 579 fresh second lieutenants in 1966. Thirty of its Class of '66 died in Indochina, one of every nineteen men.

West Point's total losses, for all classes, were 258 graduates—a little more than double those of the far-smaller corps that A&M sent to the war.

More ironic, James Webb, a Vietnam veteran and former secretary of the navy, called the registrars of Harvard, MIT, and Princeton in the 1980s, according to an article by James Fallows published in the *Atlantic* in April, 1993. Webb asked each university for two figures: how many males graduated from their undergraduate colleges from 1962 to 1972, and how many of those men died in uniform?

Of 29,702 graduates of the three elitist universities, only twenty died in Vietnam.

Why did A&M, and my Class of '66, take such heavy casualties? Partly because we were Southerners, mostly macho Texans. And so many of us volunteered for infantry, Airborne. You'd have to know what Texas A&M was like, in those days, to understand. . . .

CHAPTER XIII
We Happy Few Brothers *or* We are the Aggies

Texas A&M, 1962–1966

> We few, we happy few, we band of brothers;
> For he today that sheds his blood with me
> Shall be my brother; be he ne'er so vile,
> This day shall gentle his condition.
> > —William Shakespeare,
> > *Henry V*

> Ye are better than all the ballads
> That ever were sung or said;
> For ye are living poems,
> And all the rest are dead.
> > —Henry Wadsworth Longfellow,
> > "Children"

Today's Texas A&M University is America's seventh-largest educational institution. A third of A&M's forty-three thousand students are female.

It's amazing how few remember that A&M was one of the world's largest all-male, military schools through the 1960s, or that Texas A&M, not West Point or Annapolis, was America's main source of officers in World War II. It's hard to explain how females could be excluded from a land-grant university, operating on state and federal funds—but A&M was only for men until 1970.

Texas A&M was still the Agricultural and Mechanical College of Texas in September 1962, when I hugged Mother, then shook hands with my father in front of those long, barrack-style dormitories of stark red brick. We "fish," or freshmen, were lining up for our first formation as Daddy put on his Stetson and pointed his 1961 Oldsmobile back to the rolling mesquite plains of West Texas.

We wore Levi's, T-shirts, and pointed cowboy boots or tennis shoes that Sunday afternoon, but next morning we'd draw uniforms and rifles.

"Each of you fish! Look at the man to your left," David Lyons barked. But we learned quickly to address our cadet first sergeant, like all upperclassmen, as Mr. Lyons, *sir*. The creases in Lyon's uniform could cut butter, and the three rockers below his stripes told us he was God. "Lock eyes with the man to your right . . . next, the man to your front, and behind you.

"Now . . . remember their faces—because those men won't graduate from Texas A&M with you. Most of your fish buddies will take Highway 6 before this semester ends."

Highway 6 runs both ways—our constant reminder that the Aggies were happy to put any fish who didn't like A&M on the two-lane road back home.

A&M was steeped in tradition, mostly military and macho. The A&M Corps of Cadets was far more army than the *real* army. Assignment to companies in one of the three army brigades, or to squadrons in the two air force wings, was compulsory for the first two years.

We wore khaki uniforms in the fall and spring, and fatigues and jump boots when it rained. In the winter, we switched to World War II-style "pink-and-greens": salmon-colored woolen trousers and, for dress, olive blouses.

Seniors strutted in knee-high boots of shiny brown leather, like Gen. George Patton in old photos. Every fish dreamed of the day he'd wear those boots. Many think the boots meant cavalry, but they were the mark of an officer, of any branch, in the pre–World War II army. And A&M prided itself in being *Old Army*.

Juniors were called "sergebutts" for the permanently creased rayon uniforms they were privileged to wear. The main job of the "pissheads," or sophomores, was to whip the new class of fish into shape. They'd been fish a year before, and accepted the responsibility with a vengeance.

Hazing was officially forbidden, but it was part of daily fish life for a year. A complaint bought you a one-way ticket onto Highway 6. The pissheads had ways of doing that.

The entire Corps stood formation and inspection, then marched to chow, three times a day. Those days began at 6:00 A.M. with the bugle call *Reveille*, blown by a real cadet bugler, not a recording. That's when the "whistle jock," a rotating duty for fish, threw himself at attention against the wall in each Corps dorm, blew shrilly, and shouted the first of three calls before formation:

> Spider-D. First call to chow!
> Fall out in forty-five minutes.
> Uniform is: piss pots and jump boots.
> Menu is: bullneck: bacon and cackle.

Announcing the menu didn't mean much, because only seniors could skip chow. But that first call gave us fish time to polish brass and whip a fresh spit shine on our army shoes or jump boots before formation.

The mess hall was the most miserable place on earth for fish. We ate at attention, eyes locked forward except when serving the sergebutts and seniors.

The mess hall had a special vocabulary, and its use was compulsory. Bullneck was any meat, and cackle was eggs. Knife, fork, and spoon were saber, pitchfork, and shovel. Salad was rabbit; ketchup, blood; salt was sand; and pepper, dirt. Worcestershire sauce was Winchester; tamales were mummies; bread was deal; butter, grease; water, sky; milk, cow; and ice cream, cold cow. I'll skip the terms for mustard, stewed tomatoes, and mayonnaise.

The pissheads spat a stream of "cush" questions to make our chow more fun: "Who plays left tackle on A&M's second string?" "What is inscribed on the plaque of the Memorial Students' Center?" A wrong answer meant you lost cush, or dessert. Several wrong answers, and you left the table without eating. If one fish left, his fish buddies also had to "request permission to leave the table, sir." Hopefully, another fish buddy would smuggle food back to your "hole," or room, after the hated pissheads had left.

"I don't know" was not an acceptable answer to any upperclassman during that first long year. The only response—other than the correct one—had to be stated in five seconds:

Sir, not being informed to the highest degree of accuracy, I hesitate to articulate for fear that I might deviate from the true course of rectitude. In short, sir, I am a very dumb fish and do not know, sir.

For fish and pissheads, it was call to quarters at 7:30 each evening. Hit the books, at your desk, "four on the floor" (meaning chair legs), and no talking until a thirty-minute shower break at 10:30.

That break was another ordeal. Fish had to "hit the wall," and make that wall ring, when meeting an upperclassman. You snapped into a tight brace, with heels, back, and head pressed hard against the concrete. Meeting a pisshead in the hall often led to fresh rounds of hazing in his room, maybe on the "pink stool": back against the wall with legs in a square sitting position, eight pounds of M-1 rifle on extended fingertips. Hazing sessions usually ended with a stack of upperclassmens' jump boots or shoes to spit shine before morning formation.

An unbuttoned pocket meant that all buttons were cut from your khaki shirt and trousers. Twice, sadistic pissheads sliced the buttons from *all* of my uniforms. I spent the next long weekends sewing buttons back on.

The bugler blew taps at 11:00 P.M., then it was lights out, unless a cadet sergeant gave you a study pass to stay at the books a little longer . . . or to shine boots and sew buttons.

We lived an army life, but didn't come to A&M to be soldiers. We studied animal science, petroleum engineering, veterinary medicine.

I was so naive that I registered "cotton production" as my major. What else would a West Texas farm boy study? A tired professor marked through my words and scribbled "agronomy"—the study of crops and soils. A year later, I changed to a double major in agricultural science and journalism.

A few Aggies were army brats, but most were sons of farmers or engineers, many from families that had sent sons to A&M for three generations.

Yet serving as an officer was part of the A&M tradition, although most Aggies served only two- or three-year tours. A&M's first president, the Confederate general Lawrence Sullivan Ross, was revered as a "soldier, statesman, knightly gentleman," and that's been the A&M creed since 1876. The senior class of 1917 quit college to enlist as a unit. But they didn't go to France together because all were commissioned army officers and sent to different units.

In World War II, A&M was America's largest source of officers, Medal of Honor winners, and, of course, officer casualties.

In the midsixties, A&M was second only to West Point and other service academies in commissioning officers. Most Aggies took army or air force commissions, but the more gung ho opted for the Marine Corps.

When an Aggie died, A&M extinguished lights across campus at midnight. The Aggies filed out and walked, silently in darkness, to the center of campus. Buglers from atop the administration building played A&M's own mournful version of an old army dirge: "Silver Taps." The Ross Volunteers, A&M's crack drill team, fired a twenty-one-gun salute with 1903 Springfields, then all returned, without speaking, to the dorms.

Graduates of Texas A&M, wherever, meet yearly for Aggie Muster on April 21—the day that, in 1836, Gen. Sam Houston kicked hell out of the Mexican Army at San Jacinto. That battle gave the Republic of Texas its independence, and we remained a nation for ten years. Texas joined the United States in 1846. We seceded in 1861, but that's another story.

The most famous Aggie Muster was held during the early days of World War II: on 21 April 1942 on Corregidor, the island fortress built to guard Manila Bay. "The Rock" was the last Allied stronghold in Asia. Japanese artillery and bombers were pounding Corregidor with two-thousand rounds per day as twenty-five surviving Texas Aggies attended the Muster, convened by Gen. George F. Moore, Class of '08 and commander of Philippine coastal artillery. The Aggies answered a traditional Roll Call for the Absent deep in Malinta Tunnel, next to the lateral tunnel of Gen. Douglas MacArthur, who had slipped through Japanese defenses a month before to organize Allied forces in Australia. The Roll Call was substantial; it followed the fall of Bataan, on Luzon's mainland, and the Bataan Death March. Ten Aggies had already died on Corregidor. Within fifteen days, all the Aggies who mustered were dead or prisoners of war. Twenty Texas A&M men died defending Corregidor; nineteen were officers, mostly young lieutenants and captains.

The Cuban missile crisis was in the fall of my fish year. The cadet commander of Battlin' B-1 wrote to Lyndon B. Johnson, then vice-president, volunteering his company to go whip up on Castro. LBJ answered with a personal letter. He appreciated the Aggies' offer, but felt obliged to give the U.S. Marines a chance if we had to invade Cuba.

Only in Texas could there be an A&M ...

I had requested assignment to A&M's army Company D-1, or Spider-D, because of its hell-raising reputation. We called ourselves "the last of the Old Army."

Besides, Spider-D was Jim Lanning's company, and "Big Hoss" was the kind of Aggie I wanted to be.

Hoss and I were farm-and-ranch boys from Fisher County. That's a strong bond, even though our farms were forty miles apart. Big Hoss was a junior when I was a fish. We couldn't be friends on campus, but often went together to Huntsville, the nearest campus with girls, after Saturday morning drill. But a fish had to sign in at the company by 1:00 A.M. Sunday morning. Hoss and I sometimes got weekend passes to drive about two hundred miles north to Denton, where Texas Women's University had a lot of girls in about the same situation as us Aggies.

The Lanning-Hargrove relationship went beyond Big Hoss and me. I was a sergebutt when Hoss's younger brother Lee Lanning reported to Spider D. Lee was a junior when Raford Hargrove reported to the company. For ten years, Company D-1's roster carried a Lanning or Hargrove brother. From 1962 to 1968, Spider-D had both Lanning and Hargrove brothers, two years apart. We always helped one another.

Hoss's roommate was the toughest man I've ever known. Lee Sanders was a middleweight boxer in California before his father, an air force sergeant, sent him to A&M to become an "officer and a gentleman." Lee never started fights—but loved to hang around redneck bars where a cowboy or truck driver might pick a fight with *him*. I couldn't have imagined that Lee would get all the fighting he'd ever want within a few years—with his company of 101st Airborne infantry on Hamburger Hill.

I was a stereotype Texas Aggie, born to raise hell and make babies ... and there's a war brewing over there in Southeast Asia. A lot of Aggies wanted a piece of the action. By late 1965, when I was a junior, the Big Red One and the 173d Airborne and the 1st Air Cav and the 3d and 6th Jars up by the DMZ were kicking ass and taking names.

Hoss and Lee Sanders were already army lieutenants and in infantry, Airborne, Ranger schools, into the Pipeline to Vietnam. But what if men like them finish the job before *I* get a chance to kick some ass?

A hundred coffins a week were being shipped back to the States, and I knew how many held army and Marine lieutenants. But Aggies had an arrogant saying: "Only the good die young."

The flower movement and war protests had begun, but the Age of Aquarius bypassed Texas A&M. My greatest internal conflict about the war was: should I go for a Marine commission, or stay army and go infantry, then Airborne Ranger? To prove how macho I was, I taped *pinups*—color shots of dead Viet Cong torn from *Life*—on my wall.

That also impressed girls, of course. Texas women were always patriotic, even in the turbulent sixties.

Yes, A&M was all male, but our lives were not without women. Lots of coeds wanted to be dates on A&M football weekends, or on Corps trips where, the morning of the game, four thousand Aggie cadets marched in precision behind the world's largest military, marching band, the Fightin' Texas Aggie Band, down the streets of Dallas, Fort Worth, Houston or Austin.

The Aggies and dates, everyone in A&M's section of the stadium, stood during the game because the Corps was the Twelfth Man, each ready to don a helmet and go onto the field if A&M needed him. We sat at halftime, but were proud to stand again when the Aggie band marched onto the field like a legion of the Roman army.

The Twelfth Man tradition dates back to an A&M–Clemson University game in 1912. A&M's injuries were so high that only eleven men remained on the field, with no reserves. Cadet King Gill had not made the Aggie team, but the coach called him from the stands at halftime. He suited up and stood by the sidelines, ready to go into the skirmish. Gill was never sent in, and Clemson won the game—but A&M had another tradition: the Twelfth Man. Old Army.

The Corps parties that followed out-of-town games were the ultimate of Texas A&M hell-raising. My first was in the Fort Worth Coliseum, after we played Texas Christian University in

1962. I don't remember, or care, who won the game—but I remember the TCU theology student that I taught to drink bourbon and Coke. We left the Corps party and found Bill Braden's 1953 Chevrolet in the parking lot. Her panties were rolled at her feet when the front door opened, and lights came on. We were in the backseat of a '53 Chevy, but it wasn't Bill Braden's. The theologist's passion had cooled by the time we found Bill's car.

During the 1963 basketball season, A&M played its traditional rival, the despised "Teasippers" of the University of Texas. The game was on a week night in Austin, but word spread that as many Aggies as possible, especially freshmen, *would* be there. Passes were issued to all.

When the final whistle blew—regardless of who won—the Aggies were to rush across the court, to clean out the Teasip side of the stadium. The UT stadium offered open seating, but we sat by unit.

It was a wonderful battle, a melee of swinging fists, cursing, kicking, as 1st Brigade swept the left side, the 2d and 3d Brigades took the middle, and the air force and band fought on the right. The Marines, of course, just fought. We fled in cars before the UT campus police could take over.

A few days later the *Daily Texan*, UT's student paper, ran an editorial OUT, DAMNED AGGIES!

"Texas A&M College should be abolished," the editorial started, and gave some pretty convincing reasons why:

Granted, a state-supported school should not be a training ground for "gentlemen." But if a college is incapable of training its students to be anything more than animals, it should not exist . . .

The Army tradition is too much ingrained at Texas A&M to allow the school to be a real institution of higher education. Compulsory military training must be done away with and the curriculum must be broadened, de-emphasizing the ability to kill.

If men cannot learn how to behave like gentlemen at a state school, at least they should learn to behave like Twentieth Century human beings . . . The state is throwing money down the drain by providing a school which "trains" men like the Romans trained gladiators . . .

We loved it! Company G-2 renamed itself "Gladiator-G." The East Gate drugstore offered "Gladiator Sundaes," and the Aggie Band started playing "The Gladiators March" at parades. Old Army.

A&M's biggest spring event was Military Weekend. It kicked off on Friday night with the Combat Ball. Uniform: fatigues and jump boots. The theme during my fish year was War in Cuba. In 1965, it was War in Vietnam, and we decorated Sbisa Mess Hall with mortars, sandbags, camouflage nets, punji stakes, and M-60 machine guns. We boogied to the Beatles, then danced slow and close to sad country songs. The fake setting was a lot of fun, but we would soon see the real thing.

Sandi Chandler was my 1965 date. She wore a Chinese slit skirt, but didn't win the big event: the crowning of Combat Cutie, and presentation, for the photo, of a symbolic M-1 rifle. She should have won, her heart was in it. Old Army.

Saturday night was the formal Military Ball. It started with the Spider-D banquet in a brown-bag restaurant, where you brought a bottle in a paper sack, in dry College Station. The light bounced off the brass on our dress uniforms, and our dates wore formals. The banquet was interspersed with toasts and A&M songs. First was our company marching song. Its lyrics were rousing, but not very deep:

> Spider-D is like dynamite
> We always give 'em a hell of a fight
> And we don't give a damn 'cause
> We're from Spider-D

But any Aggie function was, and still is, closed by the more serious "Spirit of Aggieland":

> Some may boast of prowess bold
> Of the schools they think so grand
> But there's a spirit can ne'er be told
> It's the spirit of Aggieland
> We are the Aggies
> The Aggies are we . . .

The Military Ball wasn't much fun—not like the Combat Ball. But we snowed our dates with the dress uniforms and shiny brass and polished leather and bravado of young men who'd soon be at war. That paid off at the next round of parties, under Whiskey Bridge on the sands of the Brazos River, or in the Saber Motel, just off the A&M campus.

I was well-known because I was vice-president of our junior, then senior, class and editor of the Texas A&M *Agriculturist*. As a fellow class officer, I became close to Joe Bush, the head yell leader, who led the Corps in precision yells during football and basketball games.

Joe was a man's man: witty, wiry, ready to fight for what was right. I never remember anyone's eyes, but Joe's were steel blue.

Joe's hometown, Temple, was an hour's drive from A&M. His girlfriend Mickey lined me up with dates on weekends, and we hit the local German and Bohunk dance halls.

We requested branches for our army commissions during our junior year. Joe's father, an Aggie, had served as an officer in the horse cavalry. Naturally, Joe requested armor, which had replaced the cavalry, to carry on the "jock" tradition. There was no question about *my* branch.

So I was shocked and embarrassed when my commission orders arrived in the fall of 1965.

The *medical services corps?* But I *clearly* specified *infantry* as first choice, then armor and last, artillery.

I checked at the Trigon, A&M's three-sided equivalent of the Pentagon, where military science cadre told me that my uncorrected vision was below the cutoff for combat arms.

So I'll work in a *fucking hospital*? I thought. Maybe supervise the collection of *bedpans*—while my friends lead infantry platoons?

No way! Four other Aggies were also angry about the army's insensitivity. We requested waivers for combat-branch commissions, and the army sent us to Fort Hood for tests: running, shooting, sticking bayonets into things.

The weekend party we threw when the army changed our commissions to infantry should go down in Texas A&M history.

Looking back, it all seems so . . . naive? And the price we paid . . .

CHAPTER XIV
Each Army Hath a Hand

Texas and Iowa, 1966–68

> The sun's o'ercast with blood; fair day, adieu!
> Which is the side that I must go withal?
> I am with both: each army hath a hand;
> And in their rage, I having hold of both,
> They swirl asunder and dismember me.
> —William Shakespeare,
> *King John*

> And but for these vile guns,
> He would himself have been a soldier.
> —William Shakespeare,
> *King Henry IV*

Texas A&M was boring by my midsenior year in 1966. The military tradition that had drawn me now seemed Mickey Mouse and intellectually stifling. I was sick of standing formation and wearing khaki.

Sandi Chandler's letter didn't help. She'd played "Old Army Girlfriend" for almost two years. Sandi had loved Aggie traditions, and partied with the best of us.

But we'd been drifting apart. Sandi's letter was honest, and one I knew would come. She wrote that it had been good, but let's face it . . . it's over.

Still, it hurt. But Sandi made it easier by closing with: "P.S.—Kill a Cong for me, okay?" Old Army.

As a senior, I could leave A&M for weekends after Saturday morning drill. I dated coeds who took me to parties at regular universities. I listened to rational—and to radical—"civilian" students who were convinced that America's deepening involvement in the Vietnam conflict was immoral.

Slowly I realized ... A&M is out of step with my generation, I'm missing "Life in the Sixties." *And that war, over in Southeast Asia, may not be as much fun as the Combat Ball.*

Graduation loomed, and I prepared for the military, but with little enthusiasm. I'd spent the past four years in the army.

My academic adviser called me in that spring. "Tom, you're going to graduate school," Dr. R. C. Potts, A&M's associate dean of agriculture, said. He was one of the finest men I've known.

Before I could protest, Potts had called Dr. Hal Taylor, my boss for a $1.25-per-hour student job writing about cows and cotton and corn for the Texas Agricultural Extension Service. Hal wrote to his old friend Dr. Bob Kern at Iowa State University.

Hal and Bob were different, but had a lot in common. Both had Ph.D.'s in agricultural communication at a time when that was rare, and they'd gotten them after World War II through the GI Bill, which helped support veterans for college education. Hal had been an army Ranger who was captured at the Battle of the Bulge, held POW in Germany, then escaped and made his way back to the U.S. lines. He later met the German resistance agent who got him out. Bob was proud that he'd fought across Europe as an infantryman, never firing his rifle.

Taylor and Kern shared something else. Both had received the ACE Professional Award, the highest honor awarded to one communicator each year by Agricultural Communicators in Education, a U.S.-based, six-hundred-member professional society.

Kern offered me a twenty-two-hour per week graduate assistantship as an agricultural writer. The pay, $212 per month, wasn't much, even in those days. But grad school poverty forced me to learn a craft. I was soon rewarming, at night, press releases that Iowa State had paid me to write during the day, and free-lancing them to farm magazines. Checks were usually $25 or $50, but once I got $200.

In 1988, I accepted the ACE Professional Award—the first agricultural journalist to receive that honor while working outside the USA. I thought back to two decades before, and wondered. *Why* did Hal and Bob and Dr. Potts do such a big favor for me? Because graduate school would help my professional growth? Or did they conspire, maybe without *realizing* it, to keep me out of Vietnam? The answer, probably, is a little of both.

When word spread that I was going to Iowa State, Leroy Shafer, also a Fisher County Aggie, told our buddies: "I never thought Hargrove would ever go to one of those *Ivy League* schools."

The Iowa State campus was like Berkeley, after Texas A&M. Hell, Iowa State had women and war protestors, students who smoked dope, and even a few long-haired *hippies*! But most grad students were conservative males who studied electrical engineering or plant breeding while avoiding the draft.

My technical communication class in the fall of 1966 had twelve graduate students. But the 1967 class shot up to thirty students, mostly male.

I was avoiding the army, too, in a way. Graduation from A&M found me commissioned an infantry second lieutenant, but with a two-year deferment to finish my M.S.

Letters from my Aggie buddy Big Hoss Lanning, written from the field in Vietnam, added to my guilt trip. Upon his 1964 graduation from A&M, Hoss had requested an infantry commission. But the army was less kind to Hoss than to me, two years later. He was commissioned in the corps of engineers. That hurt, and I had sympathized.

The army sent Hoss to Germany, where he requested, again and again, orders to Vietnam and assignment to infantry. He finally got the orders, but not the change of branch.

After serving six months in Nam as a combat engineer, Jim Lanning was finally reassigned to the infantry—and his tour was extended to eighteen months. Hoss took command of a rifle platoon, then later a company, with the 25th Infantry, frontline troops in a war with no front lines.

I read about Vietnam in the Des Moines *Register*, watched it too vividly on TV. Texas A&M was far in the past, and that war was *really* beginning to scare me.

We grad students studied for a few hours each night, then headed to downtown Ames at 10:00 P.M. to drink draft beer and talk politics at the Sportsman's Lounge. My new friends weren't scornful of the men fighting in Vietnam, but all preferred the pursuit of higher knowledge over the war. Graduate school offered an almost indefinite escape from the draft—the M.S. program, then a doctorate. When you finished, you'd probably have a wife and kid.

Vietnam . . . No sir, I won't go to *that* party unless they ask me. That was my line, but I felt guilty about my dull, safe life in Ames while the blacks, Hispanics, and poor whites had no choice. Also, my Texas A&M buddies were leading platoons that were being shot to hell, or dodging SAMs over Hanoi. A decade would pass before I learned what a price my class was actually paying.

In November 1966, I found a letter from Jane Raymond in my mailbox at the Iowa State grad dorm. We had shared a fairly passionate summer when I worked on the Abilene *Reporter-News*, and she was executive secretary for the Abilene chamber of commerce. I tore open the letter:

> Kim and Alice and I went to see *A Man Called Horse* last night. It was a real good movie.

Then I stopped:

> By the way, a Hargrove from Rotan was killed in Vietnam the other day. Was he kin to you? I'm enclosing the clipping.

> Maybe I'll start a night course at Hardin-Simmons next semester. I'd like to finish my degree . . .

For me, the war began when I read that clipping. I wasn't that close to James W. Hargrove, it was mostly a farm kid's hero worship for an older first cousin who'd escaped the red dirt to become a genuine navy fighter pilot . . . a jet jockey who traveled to places I swore I'd see myself someday— Naples, Yokohama, Manila.

Jimmy had graduated from Texas Tech, then enlisted in the navy. He'd been a navy lieutenant, then was RIF'd, the military term for reduction in forces, in the mid-1960s. Jimmy joined the army air corps to keep flying—but as a warrant officer, that twilight zone between enlisted man and *real* officer, and flying choppers, not jets. His UH-1 was shot down in the Mekong Delta on a rescue mission to extract survivors of a company of ethnic-Chinese Nungs and their Green Beret advisers who were pinned down by a VC battalion.

Jane Raymond's nonchalant reference to Jimmy's death angered me. My God, doesn't she have any *feelings*? Texas men are dying and ...

We dated twice when I went back to Texas that Christmas, but the magic was gone.

In the spring of 1967, economists William and Paul Paddock published an alarming bestseller, *Famine 1975*, warning that the 1970s would be a "Time of Famines." Both Paddock brothers were Iowa State alumni, and one (I don't remember which) returned to give a lecture at his alma mater. I attended.

The Paddocks' predictions for Asia were bleak. By 1975, the industrial nations would be forced to adopt a "triage" policy, they wrote, like armies on a battlefield. Food aid and technical assistance would go to the few developing countries with hope. Other nations would have to be written off. India and Egypt were beyond saving.

Dr. Don Wells, my academic adviser, knew that I wanted to work in international agricultural development. In the spring of 1967, Wells introduced me to Dr. Francis Byrnes, who had completed his B.S. in agricultural communication at Iowa State. Byrnes had dropped by to visit his alma mater, while back in the States on home leave from the Philippines.

Byrnes had an exciting job. In 1963, the Rockefeller Foundation had recruited him to establish a communications department at the fledgling International Rice Research Institute. He talked about international work, and gave me a copy of the *IRRI Reporter*. It featured an article about a revolutionary new rice variety developed by IRRI: IR8. That was my first real exposure to the crop that would dominate much of my life.

I would join IRRI six years later and, in 1979, take the position that Frank Byrnes held back then. But a lot would happen in the meantime. Much of it would revolve around IR8.

During the 1967 Easter break, I wore my uniform so I could travel at military standby fare, 50 percent discount, to the West Coast to see Susan Sheldon. She was my old girlfriend from the eighth grade in Texas who had lived *everywhere*. Susan had finally returned from Kuwait to America, where she had never lived, at age eighteen. She'd dropped out of Macalester College in Minnesota, and wound up at the fringe of the flower and protest scenes in San Francisco.

We were married in the summer of 1968, when I received my master's degree—and orders to Fort Benning.

Transition 8

The Plain of Reeds, 1988

Moc Hoa . . . I once gave a woman my pistol to kill herself on these acid soils of the Plain of Reeds. Her name was Mrs. Phan Thi Suong, and she was a fine agronomist.

Memories of that night—nineteen years ago—come on strong, because it happened in Moc Hoa, here on the Cambodian border.

It's 9 June 1988, and we've left sad Chuong Thien Province. Dr. Vo Tong Xuan is showing me how pioneer farmers are transforming a war-torn wilderness into a rice bowl. New seeds from IRRI and technology developed at the University of Can Tho make it possible.

Only the Viet Cong grew rice on the Plain of Reeds during the war, and they didn't grow much. The Plain could support little more than the reeds that gave its name. Its 1.4 million acres of sour marshes have a pH, or acidity rating, of three to four. That ranges from like the worst acid rain to the acidity of a human stomach.

But gunships were a worse problem than acidity when I was last here. These empty swamps threatened Saigon with attack from the southwest, so the Plain was made a free-fire zone, patrolled by Huey Cobra choppers and Puff—customized C-47 cargo planes that gunned down anything that moved.

But you didn't call that magic dragon "Puff" when you needed her. The radio code was Spooky.

Puff carried awesome firepower: three multibarreled Vulcan

Gatling machine guns that each fired six thousand 7.62mm rounds per minute, 2.75-inch rocket pods, 40mm grenade launchers, parachute flares, and laser to mark targets for fighter planes and bombers.

The marshes of the Plain of Reeds were deadly then, so I had imagined them as ugly. Instead, I find the former VC stronghold beautiful and eerie, like a Vietnamese Everglades of reeds and a few acid-loving Melaleuca trees. The acid turns the water emerald green and clear, not muddy like in the rest of the Delta.

Only a handful of westerners have seen the heart of these swamps since the Viet Minh made the *Plaine des Ajoncs* a bastion for their fight for independence from France in the late 1940s. During *our* Vietnam War, a few Green Berets and U.S. advisers to the South Vietnamese Army came in, mostly on clandestine operations. Did those soldiers find the swamps beautiful? Probably not.

We drive past thatch houses on stands of dried mud six feet high, but water will soon reach their doorsteps.

"In 1969, there was a small agricultural experiment station here on the Plain, near Moc Hoa," I say. "Is it still here?"

"No, it was destroyed during the war. But we're about to pass its site." Xuan points to the right.

I see only rice fields, but I remember Mrs. Suong—that's not her *real* name, of course—working here. Many Vietnamese women are willowy, graceful, and vain. She was short and plump, and seemed to carry tragedy. Mrs. Suong was also intelligent and knew her soil science, so CORDS hired her to run the Moc Hoa Agricultural Research Station.

In August of 1969, CORDS was filming a television program about Mrs. Suong's research to find farming uses for these acid soils. Because I was an agricultural journalist in civilian life, CORDS detailed me from Chuong Thien for a few days to help with the film. I was glad to learn that Joe Ona would give technical assistance. We were starting a friendship that would last at least two decades.

But Joe and I arrived in Moc Hoa at a bad time.

We quit work at 4:00 P.M. that day to be back in town well before sundown. Ona and I made small talk with Mrs. Suong as we drove through empty streets. We knew why they were deserted, but we'd been ordered to keep it quiet. The military would soon announce a special curfew. After 7:00 P.M., anyone on the streets would be shot.

"What's *wrong* with you?" Mrs. Suong finally said. "Don't you know what's going on?"

"No," I lied.

"A North Vietnamese courier was killed here last night carrying orders for an NVA regiment to attack from Cambodia and overrun Moc Hoa—tonight."

"Where did you get that information?"

"*Everyone* knows."

"Okay, it's supposed to be secret, but I learned the same thing—officially—this morning. MAC-V intelligence says fifteen hundred NVA troops will hit."

"What happens to us Vietnamese who work for the Americans if the NVA take Moc Hoa?" It was a statement, not a question. "What about *me*? My husband is a major with the South Vietnamese Army."

"The North Vietnamese could never take Moc Hoa." I felt guilty saying that, because I'd been briefed. If the CORDS compound couldn't hold, the signal would be a smoke grenade, then a flare. We'd then move, one by one, across the road to the OSA compound—the heavily fortified Embassy House.

We reached Mrs. Suong's home. She eyed my M-16. "Do you have another weapon, maybe a pistol, that I could borrow—only for tonight?"

She couldn't know about the Colt Cobra tucked into the front of my trousers. I loved my pistol. Its aluminum frame and two-inch barrel made it easy to conceal. But I had a rifle, and I'd be with soldiers and, if things got *really* bad, the CIA tonight. Mrs. Suong would be alone.

I showed her the blue-black revolver. "Do you know how to use this?"

"*Teach me, I can learn!*"

"Calm down, it's simple." I released the cylinder and ejected the cartridges. "Pull back the hammer, like this, then squeeze the trigger. Don't jerk, squeeze it. Try it."

She clutched the .38 special with both hands, pointed it down the empty road, and jerked the trigger. Click. She snapped the pistol three times, then handed it back. "Load it, please."

"But you don't know how to *aim* the pistol yet. Line the front sight up with the *V* on the receiver."

"Never mind. I surely won't have to use the gun . . . but if I do, it will be at *very* close range." She slipped the pistol into her purse, and turned to enter her home. "I will pray for you tonight."

I stood for a few seconds. Damn, I thought. *I* should pray for *her*. And I never really *gave* her that pistol—she just . . . took it. Then I remembered a handful of extra cartridges in my knapsack.

"Mrs. Suong!" She turned. "Here's more bullets. Now *please* let me teach you how to reload that pistol."

"I already know, thank you." She dropped the cartridges into a pocket and scurried inside.

How *could* she know how to reload a .38? I thought.

Back at the CORDS compound, I wrote about Mrs. Suong in my diary:

A very brave woman—she will live alone in Moc Hoa tonight . . . It's 6 p.m. now. I've emptied clothes, etc. from my barracks bag and stuffed it with ammo and hand grenades. We have no Claymores set up. This place is poorly prepared . . . a Shadow aircraft is circling, loaded with sensitive electronic spotting devices . . . Thank God "Puff" is circling.

A constant roar of outgoing artillery pounded all routes to Moc Hoa that night. We watched Puff spray solid streams of red tracers through the darkness, and Arc Light—B-52s—cratered the land with 750-pound bombs along the Cambodian border, four kilometers west.

As the ground rocked, a cold reality hit my stomach. My God, Mrs. Suong didn't want my .38 to kill North Vietnamese . . . *she took it to kill herself!* That's why she wouldn't learn how to reload the pistol. I guess that's her right, if the NVA take Moc Hoa—but what if they don't even hit? She's scared, and this madhouse of B-52s and Spooky and artillery could panic anyone.

The next morning was bright and sunny as I drove to the research station.

I was relieved to find Mrs. Suong supervising laborers who were transplanting IRRI rices into experimental plots. The gunships and bombs had killed hundreds of NVA and turned the main force back. But the threat wasn't over. Taking a provincial capital, even for a few days, would be an NVA propaganda victory. Moc Hoa probably won't get advance warning of the next attack. Well, I won't be here.

"I came to say good-bye," I said. "I'm catching the ten o'clock Air America flight to Can Tho, then south to Vi Thanh."

"This is yours." Mrs. Suong drew a handkerchief-wrapped packet from her bag. "Thank you."

I unwrapped the revolver to slip into my trousers. Then I thought about Mrs. Suong and her few options, and handed it back to her. "You may need this more than me. Keep the pistol, and leave it with Gleason Rohlfs at CORDS headquarters the next time you're in Can Tho. He'll get it back to me." I wheeled the jeep toward Moc Hoa.

It's nineteen years later and we're in Tuyen Thanh village, a few kilometers past Mrs. Suong's research station. This land was marsh two years ago, but rice fields now stretch for kilometers. Most of the early monsoon crop is planted to IR13240, the most popular variety in the Delta.

A woman farmer is pulling weeds in a field. What's her story? I ask Xuan to translate.

Tran Thi Tam is a widow with six children. The government lets her farm these 1.6 hectares because her husband died fighting for the Viet Cong. She expects to harvest six tons, plus another four tons from her second crop.

Ten tons of rice, where only reeds grew before. Farmers have opened more than three-hundred-thousand hectares of new land across the Plain, and more land goes into production every day.

I wish Mrs. Suong could see this, I think. Her research, two decades ago, helps make it possible.

Years after I left Vietnam, I learned of the tragedy that haunted Mrs. Suong when we met. She once had a lover, a student leader and classmate at the University of Saigon who was drafted into the South Vietnamese Army. The young man was brilliant, and quickly rose to first lieutenant, then aide to the commanding general of Quang Tri Province.

But her lover was also a "mole"—a Viet Cong infiltrator. His cover evaporated when South Vietnamese troops captured top-secret VC documents that he'd written. His family was influential, and appealed to Saigon's upper echelons for mercy. They proposed that, in trade for his life, he turn double agent and feed VC intelligence to the general. It didn't work. A few days later, Mrs. Suong learned that her lieutenant had been "killed in a Viet Cong ambush."

Mrs. Suong returned my Colt Cobra, and we exchanged Christmas cards for several years. But we lost contact in 1975, and I often wondered if she survived the war.

One day in 1979, I received a letter postmarked Omaha, Nebraska. Mrs. Suong didn't mention the night she took my pistol, but worse things had happened to her since . . . like the four different ships of Thai pirates that boarded her flimsy craft packed with Vietnamese "boat people" for pillage and rape before it reached Malaysia.

Mrs. Suong somehow made it to America. God knows, I hope she's found the peace she deserves.

Chapter XV
A Bridge Over Troubled Waters

Chuong Thien Province, 1969

> When you're up to your ass in alligators, you forget that you came to drain the swamp.
>
> —Vietnam saying, late 1960s

In March, 1990 I reviewed my diary and saw an entry about that muddy Snake River, which took so many lives, and its destroyed bridge:

17 Jan 70
Khang and I did something *incredible* yesterday. We flew to Kien Hung by swing ship, then returned to Vi Thanh *by jeep* on the old French Road. We must have been the first men,

other than VC, to make that trip by road since the Viet Minh blew the Snake River Bridge in 1945.

Vietnamese troops had just opened the Kien Hung side of the road. CPT Bud Shields, my Aggie buddy, drove us to the Snake River. The three of us would cross with Bud's jeep on the new ferry, but the ferry wasn't there, so Khang and I crossed the Snake by sampan. Bud drove back to Kien Hung alone. CPT Olson and his Vietnamese counterpart had set up a CP [Command Post] for an operation on the Hoa Luu side of the Snake. VN 105-mm howitzers were dug in, and firing. We rode to Vi Thanh in Olson's jeep.

The Snake River crossing was the setting for a chapter in my novel:

Chapter 4

Enrique's Spanish omelet tasted bitter, not spicy, the next morning. No one mentioned the lung-shot girl they'd watched die the night before, but her last, bubble-gum breaths had haunted Lt. Daniel Bridges for hours that first night on MAT 96 in Nuoc Trong.

At 8:30 A.M., Dan left with Alan and Sergeant Culver to visit the new outpost being built on the Snake River.

The chief and Khang were waiting at the village cafe. They shook hands, then Cam poured tea.

A skinny pig was scavenging for scraps thrown under the tables by last night's customers. The animal was so sway-backed, Dan wondered how it could stand.

"Do you want Chinese soup?" Khang translated for the chief.

"For sure," Alan replied, "but first, *cafe sua*."

An old woman in white pajamas shuffled away, then returned with pyrex glasses of coffee.

"If you think we're killing time, Dan . . . you're right." Alan stirred the sweet condensed milk at the bottom of his glass. "Rule one of staying alive in Chuong Thien is *never* ride the morning's first sampan on a canal, or jeep on a road."

"Why not?"

"If Charley mines the road in the night . . . let the local

traffic detonate the mines." Alan sipped his coffee. "If Mr. Charles sets an ambush—he can spring it on *local* troops.

"That's how I inherited MAT 96 . . . I was XO down in Kien Long. The team leader, a lieutenant named William Jackson, hit a mine on the road at about 8:00 A.M. He should have known better. Blasted the jeep into the canal and blew Bill's leg away . . . He was bleeding to death—and would be dead if he hadn't sandbagged the floorboard. But we got Bill on a Dustoff chopper to Can Tho, and he made it."

"You're gonna like Chuong Thien," Sergeant Culver said. "It's a real kick in the ass."

Alan turned to Khang. "Has the chief requisitioned sheet metal for the barracks roofs at the outpost?"

"Mr. Cam say he ask for tin from the Khien Hung district chief beaucoup times, but no have."

"Bullshit! Robert Cantwell sent Major Nghia enough tin roofing for the outpost *and* dispensary."

"Mr. Cam don' know 'bout that. But Mr. District Chief got no tin for roof."

"I bet *Tu Tau* Nghia's home has a new sheet-metal roof," Alan muttered to Dan. "That sonofabitch has three wives, God knows how many concubines, and drinks cognac like water. We may not win the war by building these outposts, but we'll *lose it* by helping corrupt bastards like Major Nghia."

The scavenging pig sniffed at a sleeping dog under a table. He woke in a snarling crouch, lips curled over broken yellow teeth, then sprang!

The mongrel clung to the pig's snout for a second. The pig knocked over a stool fleeing the cafe, outraged and squealing.

"Tell Mr. Cam I'll try again," Alan said. "And I'll sit on the next roofing from the minute the chopper unloads it at district headquarters till I see it nailed to the roofs of those fucking barracks!"

Bowls of steaming soup arrived. Alan poised chopsticks between his thumb and first two fingers, then picked and dropped slivers of fresh red peppers into a broth of simmering pork, shrimps, and rice noodles. Dan's use of chopsticks was clumsy.

The aroma of the noodle soup blended with other village smells—a pungent mingling of decaying plants, the lingering smell of burning coconut husks, a dank smell of stagnant water and drying fish, a sweetness of smoldering joss sticks, blended with the odor of decaying human and animal wastes. The village had an organic smell of death and decay . . . from which new life springs.

The smell is timeless, Dan thought. It seems to carry a message: that life was like this—before what? Everything that we understand, or our ancestors remember? Yes, and life will be this way after the jungles of time have taken our dreams, our wars, our empires . . . like time has taken the empires that have swept this village.

The smell took Dan back to Fort Sill, when Capt. Carl Ayler opened his footlocker.

"That *smell*!" the captain said. "I didn't think it could follow me home, but *the trunk carries it*."

"I don't smell anything."

"I hardly noticed the smell when I was in that damned Vietnamese village, and I knew I'd forget it when I left. But it's filling this room. *Of course* you smell it!"

Dan caught only a faint, musky odor.

Did the trunk really hold the smell, or was it in the captain's head?

Alan rose and dropped a blue bank note on the table.

Two sampans waited at the boat landing. "The black eyes painted on the bows are to watch for water spirits," Alan explained as Dan followed, almost tipping the canoelike boat.

"Sit flat on your butt and cross your legs, like the Vietnamese." Dan's knees stuck awkwardly from both sides of the craft.

"Sampans were made for gooks," Sergeant Culver said. "Not for long-legged Texans."

The sampan's nose cut northward, then picked up speed. They passed houses anchored on land, but with backs on stilts over the canal. The Nuoc Trong market looked larger from the water; then the village slid behind them, and they were on open canal.

"This country is like a table top," Dan said. "You can see for half a mile, even from a sampan."

"Lock and load, Dan," Alan said. "PF troops have burned the mangrove along the canal with Agent Orange, then cut the dead foliage. But the stubble's growing back, so there's cover ahead. A sampan is *not* a good defensive position in an ambush."

Dan thought of Michael Bernstein. "Were you ever ambushed in a sampan?"

"I'm *alive*, aren't I? There are damned few men who can describe a sampan ambush, firsthand. But we're probably okay, the chief sent a PF squad to walk both sides of the canal ahead of us this morning."

A mass of dark green water hyacinth blocked the canal ahead of the sampans. A soldier fired three rapid shotgun blasts, like he was cutting a path through the floating plants.

"That's to make sure Charley hasn't hidden a surprise for us in that water hyacinth."

"Like what?"

"The VC camouflage floating mines in hyacinth clumps and send them down the canal. A sampan going to the Nuoc Trong market hit a mine last week. Blew the family away—four people—but Charley hoped to get one of *us*.

"We try to steer past the hyacinth, but that's hard in the late dry season when the water's low."

Ten minutes later, the sampans passed about forty men and women working on the new outpost, then moored where the Xa No Canal met the Snake River.

Dan saw the three broken columns he'd watched from the chopper coming into Nuoc Trong. Remnants of a destroyed bridge.

He stepped to shore and walked on a gravel road overgrown with grass and shrubs.

"Stay on the clear, hard sections," Alan said. "The PF troops have secured the perimeter—but no one knows if Charley set booby traps last night. Let the local troops go first. Follow a Vietnamese soldier, and step *exactly* in his footprints."

"Who built this road?" Dan asked.

"The French—but the jungle and the VC have taken it back," Alan said. "Our new outpost will provide security, so GVN can put a ferry here."

"Where does the road go?"

"Nowhere now, but when the outpost is finished, this segment of road will connect Vi Thanh and Kien Hung. Before World War II, you could drive south from here to Ca Mau, or northeast into Cambodia. A Frenchman could drive from Nuoc Trong to Hanoi . . . for a while."

Alan threw up his hands.

"Can you *imagine* driving from Chuong Thien to Hanoi? *That is unfucking real!*

"The French didn't have choppers during *their* Indochina War, so they had to move troops overland by truck. Roads in the Delta required a lot of bridges, so . . ." Alan waved at the skeleton of the French bridge.

"The ferry will reopen the road. A new bridge may come . . . someday."

"But is opening the road *practical*?" Dan asked. "You said that most traffic is by water—and the VC control the canals and rivers. Can we keep a road secure? Even if we *can* . . . won't the VC bypass us on the water?"

"I'm a ragged-ass lieutenant who's getting short," Alan said. "I do what I'm told, and don't look for answers to sensible questions."

Now was the time. "Alan, that girl last night."

"Yeah?"

"We watched her die, but this morning was . . . like it never happened."

"This is today, Dan. One gook girl's death is no big deal in Chuong Thien Province." Alan said *gook*, Dan thought. Why?

"You'll see so much of that shit, it won't . . ." Alan paused. "*Forget it*, okay?"

Dan stared at the destroyed French bridge, looming from the dark river waters. *Learn from me,* the broken white columns seemed to warn. *Go back where you belong, this land is cruel. It will destroy you, too.*

I turned back to the diary.

I'm interested in the Snake River area because 3,250 hectares [8,125 acres] of former French plantation land lie on the Kien Hung side. It's 95% VC-controlled, but troops are building new outposts on both sides of the river.

The Old French Plantation is an excellent place to send a Land Reform team. I'm trying to direct LR to contested areas, where land redistribution will give the greatest political payoff. Farmers who live under the VC were applying for land last week at Ngoc Hoa and Hoa Hung villages, then leaving by sampan. They'll return for the titles later.

Bud Shields had a close call last Tuesday. He stayed overnight in Dinh Anh village, and drove back to Kien Hung district town the next morning. Then he returned to Dinh Anh—and found soldiers digging a 6-kg mine from the road a few klicks from the village. The plunger was depressed, but the fuse had failed. Bud was the only person on the road that day.

Rod Fernandez got drunk last Saturday and hired a sampan to go to Ngoc Hoa at 5 in the afternoon! He lay under a piece of canvas at the bottom of the sampan—went to see what he claims is his "girlfriend" (wife??).

1LT Clyde Aderhold was killed over here . . .

Aderhold. I was standing in drizzle at the Can Tho Air Field, about to board the 1420 Air America flight to Vi Thanh. I wore a .45 and felt uneasy because I carried a fat black satchel with the Vietnamese payroll—about $2,500 in piasters. A civilian was leading us onto the runway.
  "*Hargrove!* Whatcha doing here, buddy?"
  The lieutenant looked familiar. I glanced at his nametag.
  "Herb Sennett! I haven't seen you since Fort Benning. Where are—"
  "I'm sorry, but we're boarding now," the Air America civilian interrupted. Flights that carry six passengers don't need much boarding time.
  "Gotta go, Herb. I'm in Chuong Thien, Advisory Team 73, where are you stationed?"
  "Tom, quick! Did you hear about Aderhold?"
  "Clyde? What . . ."
  "You two were close at infantry school, right?" Sennett grabbed my arm. "Clyde got it. He was a platoon leader with the 197th Infantry Brigade."
  "Please hurry—the others have boarded."
  All I could say was "Thanks, Herb," as I dashed across the airfield with the bag of money. I got in just as the Porter's doors were closing.

As the Porter climbed steeply, I thought about eighteen months earlier, sprawling under an oak tree during a ten-minute break at Fort Benning. I'd asked the chubby lieutenant beside me where he was from.

"Athens, Georgia."

"That's a beautiful town," I said. "Thank God General Sherman missed those fine colonial homes when he marched to the sea in 1864. The most magnificent mansion is the home of the president of the University of Georgia."

"I know," the lieutenant drawled. "I lived in that house for sixteen years." Clyde was the university president's son.

Michael Arnovitz, now Clyde Aderhold, I thought. That's 66 percent of the best friends I made at infantry school . . .

I read my next diary entries:

22 January 1970. Am flying on Air America to Can Tho for a meeting of ag/land reform advisers in the Delta. I didn't drive this time, partly because the VC ambushed Captain Nghia, Chuong Thien's *Chieu Hoi* chief, and his driver on that road last week. Both survived.

Just learned that 1LT Clint Ward, Texas A&M '67, was shot down over Laos. Missing and presumed dead. Clint was on Corps Staff, and Leroy Shafer's roommate their last 2 years at A&M. A real nice guy—and straight, for an Aggie. With Joe Bush, Clint makes two A&M friends killed in Laos— quite a few for a war that we aren't fighting.

27 January. I'm at Camp Alpha, Tan Son Nhut AFB, waiting for my flight to Hawaii to meet Susan for R&R. It's delayed 3 hours so far.

Left Vi Thanh on 24 Jan. Doug Lovejoy met me at TSN. Incredibly, Jeanne has been in Saigon as a tourist for 3 weeks. They had a cocktail party Sat. night and I met so many people that Susan and I knew back at Ft. Bragg. All are with PsyOps in Saigon.

The war seemed a long way off. I hadn't been in Saigon since coming thru, 7½ months ago. People wore sports jackets and ties to Doug's party. American girls even came in cocktail dresses.

I described Saigon as a "dying city" when I arrived in VN, but it now seems a bustling, overcrowded metropolis. Maybe Saigon represents a dying *society*, but not a dying city. I stayed at the Central Palace Hotel, downtown. It's for USAID, but I wore civvies and faked it.

SGT Conrad, the medic with MAT 104, was wounded by a grenade blast when the VC attacked the Kien Tien District Advisory Team HQ last week. If all the grenades Charley threw into the team hut had gone off, Norm Olsen said, the entire team would be dead. Norm threw quite a surprise at me, the morning I left. He asked if I'd like to take a district—be District Senior Adviser for either Kien Hung or Kien Thien when Bud Shields or CPT Rowen leaves. It was like he'd hit me between the eyes with a hammer! I felt complimented. Rowen wasn't worth a damn, but Shields is an outstanding DSA. The other captains available—Pulleig ("Roger That!") and Johnson—couldn't handle the job. If I take it, I may be the only lieutenant in Nam serving as a DSA. It would be a great job, and I'm tempted—responsible for everything in the district: military opns, outposts, pacification and development, etc. I'd probably get Kien Thien. It has no roads, and is our second-least secure district after Kien Long. I told Norm that I'll give an answer after R & R. But I doubt that I'll take it. My other work, particularly Land Reform, may be more meaningful.

Especially if my aerial drop of LR applications works! Doug Lovejoy and others in the 2d PsyOps Group like the idea.

I'd had PsyOps print blank land titles, in the type and format of any legal land transfer title in Vietnam. On the back, we printed certificates that authorized farmers to use those land titles, once they had been processed, as collateral for loans for rice seeds and fertilizer. We dropped thousands of the leaflets over former French and Chinese plantations.

My scheme worked! Hundreds of farmers came out of VC areas to claim free land, and credit for inputs.

The leaflets were only a psychological weapon, of course. The farmers could have claimed land titles, and credit, without those air-dropped applications. But the leaflets were a *catalyst*, they gave an *incentive*. Like the safe-conduct passes that the *Chieu Hoi* program dropped. A VC could defect without one, but thousands of war-weary *hoi chanhs* came in, clutching those leaflets.

Khang was almost killed while dropping my land reform leaflets over the Old Frenchman's Plantation from the Vietnamese Bird Dog, a Cessna that ordinarily directed air strikes. Leaflets stuck in Bird Dog's tail rudder, and sent it into a nosedive. The pilot managed to shake the leaflets loose before the plane crashed.

My next diary entry was made en route back to Chuong Thien after R & R:

5 February 1970. It's 0635h and I'm in the Air America Terminal at Tan Son Nhut.

Our R & R flight was 12 hours late leaving Saigon for Hawaii. If we'd arrived 17 hours late, we'd have gotten another day in Hawaii. Instead, we were cheated of half a day of R & R. Typical Army.

But R & R was just great. I feel so much better now. I was getting edgy and jumpy before I left. Susan met me at the Aloha R & R Center at Ft. De Russey, on Waikiki Beach. We stayed at the guest house of the Bill Maximers; he's the head lawyer for Dillingham Corporation and an old friend of the Sheldons.

Why did I write that R & R was idyllic and restful? It wasn't, and my diary entry wasn't sincere. Susan had grown more independent after eight months without me, and I'd grown more . . . *something*. We didn't know each other well, when we met in Hawaii.

We had a terrible fight in that guest house by beautiful Diamond Head. *"Go back to Vietnam! You love it a lot more than me!"* Susan screamed. We made up, but I realized that she'd never understand. I wouldn't either, of course, and we learned not to discuss Vietnam.

Later. Am now in Can Tho—there was heavy fighting in Chuong Thien while I was gone. Three VC battalions hit a VN Marine base camp in Kien Long—23 friendly KIAs.

VC overran the camp, but the VN Marines retook it. Got 83 VC bodies—no telling how many were dragged away.

That reminds me of watching "Puff, the Magic Dragon"—a heavily armed C-47—work in the night as the VC tried to overrun an outpost in Kien Thien a month ago. Puff circled, dropped flares, sprayed the perimeter with miniguns.

Puff's fire is like a sheet of flame. She killed a lot of men that night, but the VC didn't take the outpost.

8 February. Am back in Vi Thanh from R & R. In Can Tho, I found that Air America hadn't manifested me. On 6 Feb, I talked an Army Otter pilot, who was flying to Rach Gia, into dropping me off at Vi Thanh.

While I was gone, Col. Nguu, the Chuong Thien province chief, was with a convoy along the newly opened road from Vi Thanh to the Snake River. They crossed the Snake by ferry, then drove to the VN Marines' new camp on the Kien Hung side. The first jeep hit a VC mine. Killed 4 VN soldiers, and one policeman who will probably die.

11 February. I was wrong. The mine killed 5, wounded 1 seriously. Mr. Tho, the Kien Hung deputy district chief, died. Everyone, VN and U.S., always said he was a crook. Frank Gillespie says "No, Tho was never corrupt. I asked him myself; he *told me* he's not." The S-2 also got killed.

5 March 70. This afternoon we carried a wounded PF soldier from Vi Duc to Vi Thanh. He had drunk a liter of *baxide* & fallen off his Honda. What a war!

Talked to Ben Salcedo, the *Chieu Hoi* adviser about the 27 Febr VC "probe" of the CH Center. Ben doesn't think *any* VC attacked. Two APTs [Armed Propaganda Teams, made up of *hoi chanh*, or VC defectors] had ambush sites around the Center. Things had been pretty quiet, so Ben was going to send the APTs into the boonies, where a man can get hurt. So, being sensible men, they attacked their own *Chieu Hoi* Center, then counterattacked, and turned back the human waves of Hated Cong.

The incident would be funny if a child had not been wounded by the firing. Not seriously, tho.

2315h. Hectic night in the province. VC activity seems to be increasing. Called lots of Medevacs, many of them Life/ Death. VC captured 3 PSDF [People's Self-Defense Force] at 1600h near Hoa An, and released them, minus weapons, a couple of hours later. 31st Regt was rocketed. The local priest reports that some VC were trying to enter Vi Thanh by the Catholic Church.

29 March. The disclosure of the death of CPT Joe Bush (A&M '66) in Laos in Febr '69 is causing a lot of commotion in the States.

A PF [Popular Force] outpost was overrun, from *inside*, last week. At 0800h the platoon leader took a patrol outside the outpost. Other PFs were repairing the barbed-wire perimeter. Only 2 PFs were inside, and they were undercover VC. They opened fire and killed the others, then killed the wife & 2 or 3 children of the platoon ldr (the PFs' families live in the outposts with them), then loaded up a sampan & got away clean. 20 M-16s, some pistols, and ammo and, maybe worst of all, 6 tactical radios were stolen. PsyOps is making "Wanted" reward posters of the 2 ex-PFs.

I turned to the next chapter of my novel, set three weeks after Lt. Daniel Bridges arrived in Nuoc Trong:

Chapter 6

Bluish clouds darkened the afternoon sky on 28 May 1969, and a few fat raindrops splattered the dust like bullets. The first of the monsoon rains then fell in heavy sheets that hammered the tin roof of the MAT 96 team hut. Two hours later, the rain ceased, and the sun drove steam from pools of muddy water. Nuoc Trong almost glowed at sunset, its air cleared of dust.

Dinner was over. Sergeant Joe Culver leaned his chair back and belched.

"Damn good chow, Enrique," he said. "These peckerheads may give you a lotta shit about your cookin', but you're gonna make a Meskin outa me yet!"

Enrique beamed. "I'm so glad you like it."

Those two sergeants are different, but close, Dan thought. I wonder what Joe Culver thinks of Alan Burns. He must respect him—Culver's old army, and would respect any officer who's deserving, and Alan is a good leader. But could that redneck sergeant *ever really like a black officer*?

I feel sorry for Saunders. I'm probably his best friend on the team, and I can hardly stand that damn whining wimp. He brings it on himself. How *can* you like someone who obviously despises you as an officer, but kisses ass to get what he wants? Saunders isn't *really* so bad, but I wish Alan would make him quit wearing that peace medallion. He wears it, of course, to piss the sergeants off. Saunders smokes dope, that's clear from his talk, the terms he uses. I hope to God he never turns on while he's on radio duty. Joe and Enrique would break his scrawny neck.

Enrique interrupted Dan's thoughts. "You did not eat hardly nothing, Lieutenant Burns!" He pointed at Alan's plate. "How you gonna to stay healthy if you don't eat?"

"It was good, Enrique, but I'm not hungry. I feel tired. I'm turning in early."

"I think maybe something is wrong with you," Enrique said. "Look at me, damn it." Then he added, "Sir."

"Enrique, do you *have* to play mother and doctor and baby-sitter and—"

"Yeah, all the time you make the funny joke, I laugh so much." Enrique stretched his chubby body across the table and pulled down one of Alan's eyelids, then the other. "Lieutenant Burns, your eyes don' look so good."

Dan looked closely. "Jesus, Alan, you're . . . as pale as a black man can be. And Enrique's right. Your eyes look . . . sick." He saw a yellow tinge in the corners of Alan's eyes.

"When you pee, what color is it?" Enrique asked.

"Damn it, nothing's wrong with me! You're like an old woman!" He mimicked Enrique: " '*When you pee, what color is it?*' "

"Jus' tell me."

"Okay, my urine is darker than usual. But *your cooking* could cause that!"

"Bullshit! I think you must call one Dustoff chopper right now, Saunders, to take Lieutenant Burns to the 76th Field Hospital at Can Tho!"

"Nothing's wrong with me!"

"Nothing but the hepatitis."

"Hepatitis." Alan whispered. "No."

"It don't surprise me none. You never listen to Enrique when I tell you don' eat what the goddamn Vietnamese cook, I would not feed that shit to a fucking *dog*!" Enrique turned to the other men.

"And *you* are gonna get the same hepatitis if you don' be more smart."

Enrique turned to Alan. "Maybe you'll go home early."

"But I don't want to go home *hospitalized*, for God's sake."

"I'm so sorry 'bout that. But the fault is of you, not me."

"Go ahead and call a Dustoff," Alan said. "I'll go to Can Tho—to prove that Enrique's wrong. But don't make it 'emergency' ".

"A couple of days of R & R in Can Tho will do you good, sir," Sergeant Culver said. "But stay clear of the girls in the Ben Xe Moi district, you're too close to your P-C-O-D."

"P-C-O-D?" Dan asked.

"Pussy cut off date."

Bob Saunders picked up the radio handset.

We should have seen that something was very wrong with Alan, Dan thought. The lethargy, the depression . . . and now, the yellow in his eyes.

Dan knew that Alan would never return to Nuoc Trong.

On 28 April, I wrote:

TOC again. It's harder and harder to make myself write. Things are dully routine. VC activity has slacked off a lot, except for the routine. 4 hamlet chiefs assassinated, a grisly hand grenade murder in Vi Thanh which, for once, wasn't blamed on Charley.

2 May. A man confessed to the murder. But he bought his grenade from a VC, so he'll be tried as a VC.

* * *

Two days ago, U.S. and VN troops invaded Cambodia . . .
we'll remember that day for a long time. Either as the beginning of the end of the VN War, or as the start of a *real* mess
. . . I wonder if I'll be able to visit Cambodia after my discharge on 19 June.

Yesterday, Duc, Khang, a Land Reform cadre, & I drove to
Vinh Tuy, down by the "Bowling Pin." That part of the old
French road has been open 5–6 days now. We're going to
distribute another old French plantation around there. Duc is
so damned aggressive. Last week we ran a PF operation into
the Snake River area just to get farmers out to apply for
land.

I wanted to be the first American to drive the new road, but
1LT Maxey of MAT 56 beat me to it. Am now waiting at
the Hoa Luu ferry to cross the Snake River and go back
down to Vinh Tuy. So, another road opens that has been
closed since WWII.

I remember being proud of the Hoa Luu ferry, and those
roads we were opening in Chuong Thien Province. Then I read
my next diary entry:

11 May. Charley blew up the ferry at Hoa Luu. I've crossed
on it at least 3 times a week, lately. Killed 2 VN soldiers,
blew an ambulance to bits, and sent the ferry & a 2½ ton
truck into the Snake River.

Transition 9

The Plain of Reeds, 1988

The Plain of Reeds is a tropical version of what West Texas must have been like for my ancestors. The Plain, like Texas, offers pioneer settlers both land and a new life after a terrible civil war.

The Plain is the main "resettlement area" for the Mekong Delta. Land is free, for those strong enough to tame the marshes. Some of its thousands of settlers come by choice, but as on many of the world's frontiers, more come by fate. The Vietnamese government sets quotas for overcrowded areas to send families here.

Everywhere I see new roads, homes, schools, even hospitals being built. These swamps are beginning to generate rice, and that means employment, income.

"We're now farming 40 percent of the Plain of Reeds, and opening new land fast." Dr. Vo Tong Xuan is proud of what his scientists have done.

But how? I know that the Plain's soil acidity peaks during the six-month dry season. The early monsoon rains bring fresh water, but farmers could never use it because that water absorbs enough acid from the soil to kill any rice planted.

Later in the monsoon, the rains sweeten the water, but then it's one to three meters deep. Farmers could only plant a single crop of primitive but hardy "floating" rices that have adapted over centuries to elongate with rising water and to tolerate acidity. But floating varieties yield no more than a ton per hectare, barely enough to feed a family of six.

We pull up at the meeting hall of the Moc Hoa People's

221

Committee. "I want you to meet a *real* VC," Xuan says as I shake hands with Nam Tam, committee chairman. In five days of travel across the Delta, Xuan has introduced half a dozen hosts as "real VC." It's always true. Former Viet Cong who fought as local guerrillas now hold most public jobs.

Xuan and Mr. Tam talk as we're served tea and pineapple beneath the standard portraits of Ho Chi Minh, Marx, and Lenin. My Vietnamese was never good, but I know what Xuan is saying.

Tam starts his briefing. "You are the first IRRI scientist to visit Moc Hoa since the war ended. But you are even more welcome because you're an American and, like most of *us*, a veteran of the war. I've fought Americans, but I never met one."

Tam explains how the Plain is becoming a rice bowl through technology from the University of Can Tho and fast-maturing rice varieties bred at IRRI. Memories of the war, and thoughts on how to heal its scars, intersperse his talk. That seems natural to me.

New canal systems are being dug, by machine and hand, to divert fresh water from the Mekong River to the Plain. First, the farmers burn the straw from the previous rice harvest. Then, early in the monsoon season, they "flush" the acid from the fields with fresh water from the canals and early rains, then drain them. Next, they broadcast IRRI seeds directly onto the mud. They then irrigate with fresh canal water.

The floating varieties took about five months to mature. But farmers harvest the IRRI rices in about three and a half months, before the deep water drowns the crop.

The farmers rest the land as the water deepens through the main monsoon season. When the water level lowers, they transplant another crop of a taller variety, usually IR42 or IR64. Again, fast growth allows a second harvest before the dry season turns the soil acid again.

The Viet Cong developed the "direct seeding" technology to escape U.S. gunships, Xuan says. Farmers learned to burn the straw, rush in to throw pregerminated seeds onto the field . . . then stay away until harvest. Their crops were mediocre, at best. Often, there was no crop at all.

The briefing ends, and we go for lunch at a restaurant built over an artificial pond. Between courses, Tam talks about his guerrilla days.

"For thirty-four years, I knew only war on the Plain of Reeds," he says. "I was a Viet Minh soldier for nine years, then fought in the American War for twenty-one years. At Liberation, I was a captain ... then I had to fight for four more years against Pol Pot's invaders from Cambodia."

During the American War, Tam says, he and other VC lived on sampans, three per boat, for six months of the year. They fought South Vietnamese troops in the same type of sampans "but the government troops had heavy artillery support." The best defense from U.S. gunships, Tam says, was to lie still in the open marshes. To hide near the few melaleuca trees was suicide—they were obvious targets.

"My comrades died around me. I should have been killed more times than I remember," Tam says. "That's why every day of peace is precious to me."

"What about food?" I ask. "You must have gone hungry."

"Not really. We lived off the land, and the Plain was a good provider. We caught fish, turtles, snakes, swamp rats." Most scarce was the food vital to all Vietnamese—rice. "But our supporters sometimes smuggled rice in."

Tam pours from a bottle of reddish liquor. "Chairman Ho Chi Minh taught us not to confuse people with their governments," he says, toasting with his glass. "Even when we killed one another, we never hated U.S. soldiers, or the American people."

The day before, Xuan and I had visited a Viet Cong cemetery and war memorial. Over tea, I asked the curator of thousands of graves how he felt about Americans.

He answered with a one-line poem: "Even in the swamps of the Plain of Reeds, the beautiful lotus flower blooms." He meant that good people are found everywhere. The curator had never heard of the Vietnam War Memorial in Washington, D.C. I offered to send him a leaflet that describes the Memorial. He promised to display it.

Tam continues: "Would you carry a special message to U.S. veterans? I think that most feel as you and I do. Tell them that the war left a common bond between America and Vietnam. Ask if they will call on their politicians to normalize relations." He toasts.

The liquor is smooth. I ask about the coiled cobras printed on the bottle's label.

"This is a specialty of Moc Hoa, rice whiskey blended with cobra venom."

The drink symbolizes my Vietnam. It disguises something deadly. Maybe that's what makes it intoxicating.

CHAPTER XVI
Madness with a Method
or Follow Me

Infantry Officers School, Fort Benning, Georgia, June–August 1968

> Though this be madness, yet there is method in't.
> —William Shakespeare, *Hamlet*

Fort Benning was at its busiest since World War II when I reported to the Infantry Officers Basic Course on 20 June 1968. I had just finished my M.S. degree at Iowa State University.

IOBC was for us who were already commissioned lieutenants and automatically classified, from a less-complicated era, "officers and gentlemen." Officers, we were. But the army placed less value on the second character during the height of the Vietnam War.

For new lieutenants, Infantry School was nine hard weeks of tactics, weapons, artillery, booby-trap courses, and a lot of leadership training. Not as much spit and polish as the Corps at Texas A&M. We were never unnecessarily hazed; that was for cadets in OCS, Officers Candidate School.

But the army pushed us to the limit, while never asking the impossible. I remember being tired and sleepy at Benning, and walking all the time.

I could say that was in the days of the Old Army, but I won't. There was *never* an Old Army—that's how old-timers always describe the army of a few years before. I learned that at Texas A&M.

Susan and I rented a dismal apartment in Columbus, Georgia. Having a wife at Infantry School was tough. My day began numbly at 4:30 A.M. when I broke starch on a crisp fatigue uniform that cost a dollar to launder—more than ⅟₅₀₀ of my salary. I'd pop open a can of Coke and stumble to the Corvair to race to Benning in time for the 5:30 formation. We were usually dismissed around 6:00 P.M., unless we were on overnight maneuvers. Those were long days.

The romance of the army was gone, for me. But hearing the OCS cadets sing as they marched in precision stirred something deep, instinctive. We had sung most of the same songs at A&M, marching to chow each evening. That, somehow, seemed . . . natural? Soldiers had marched and sung pretty much the same since Caesar's legions. Confederate and Yankee soldiers sang many of those songs, and their grandsons modified them in the Spanish-American War. Another generation marched to new versions in World War I, and GIs carried the songs on into World War II and Korea. Soldiers will sing that way centuries from now.

> Liza Jane, dressed in brown
> *Li'l Liza Jane*
> Has her fun in Columbus town
> *Li'l Liza Jane*
> Hey, Li'l Liza
> Li'l Liza Jane . . .

Some were "jodie calls":

> I got a gal in Phoenix City
> She's got a wart on her left tittie
> *Sound off*
> One, two
> *Once again*,
> Three, four,
> One, two, three, four,
> *Sound off!*

But some songs were new, and reflected what was happening in 1968. One was to the tune of the hit song "Poison Ivy":

> Viiiet Naaam, Vietnaaam
> Late at night when you're sleepin'
> Charlie Cong comes a'creepin'
> Around . . . around
> A punji stake'll get you . . .
> A punji stake'll get you . . .

Yeah, there was a war going on, and Fort Benning was geared for Vietnam, throwing an IOBC class like mine into the Pipeline every two weeks. OCS and Noncommissioned Officers Candidate School were throwing in hundreds more officers and NCOs every month.

My class had two hundred and sixty officers from three backgrounds: about one hundred and fifty were infantry and intelligence officers, newly commissioned through ROTC or West Point; the others were mostly National Guard and Army Reserve lieutenants who'd become officers through *their* version of OCS. Two lieutenants were former NCOs who had received direct, or battlefield, commissions. They were tough.

You might expect the two former sergeants to be contemptuous of us green lieutenants, but they weren't. The ex-NCOs shared their experiences. They *knew* what awaited and wanted to help us, and the men we would lead, come home alive.

Lieutenant Gilreth was from a coal-mining family in West Virginia, and had already served three years as a Green Beret sergeant "snoopin' and poopin'," as he put it, in Nam and Laos. I don't remember the other ex-NCO's name, but he'd been "top"—the first sergeant—in a 173d Airborne company in Vietnam. He wanted the war to end so he could resign his commission and resume his career as an NCO, where he was comfortable.

Those who haven't been through Infantry Officers School may think it's a quick course in killing. There was a lot of that, of course, but the main focus was on leadership: how to motivate men to do their jobs in the most difficult of situations—combat. The Infantry School slogan was, after all, *Follow Me!*

Twenty-one years after Fort Benning, the International Rice Research Institute sent me to a three-week management-training course at an isolated castle in Heemskerk, Netherlands.

Of the fifteen participants, I was the only one who had been exposed to many of the concepts taught in that expensive instruction.

Like the top-management concept of learning by role-playing. We did that a lot at Benning. A regular army major taught one class in "Leadership by Example." First, he played a tape, narrating a hypothetical situation: You're a green second lieutenant who's just taken command of your first platoon. The unit hasn't had an officer for the past year, so the platoon sergeant has been acting platoon leader. He's respectful enough . . . outwardly. But the NCO obviously resents you, for taking over *his* platoon. He won't exactly sabotage you, but likes to watch you fall on your face.

"I'll play the sergeant now," the major said. "You, Hargrove, you're the new lieutenant. How would you handle this situation?"

I appealed to the sergeant's sense of pride. I respected his experience and abilities, so I'd give him full support, but I expected *his* support in return . . . something like that. I guess I wasn't too good. The major-turned-sergeant called me *sir* and said he'd *always* backed me, but still acted smartass. The next lieutenant, Herb Sennett, used the "put yourself in my place" routine, and did no better.

Lieutenant Gilreth, the ex-sergeant from the coal mines, was next.

"Major, you're *really* gonna play sergeant?" Gilreth asked. That's right, the major assured him.

"Sir, that means I can talk to you like you're a *real* sergeant? Not like a major?"

"Yes, *sir*, Lieutenant."

"Then . . . *Lock your fuckin' heels!*" Gilreth roared, and we jumped. The major looked confused, but popped to attention.

"You better get your shit together, *Sergeant!*" Ice dripped from Gilreth's voice as he spat that last word as *only* an ex-sergeant could say it. "And fast! If you don't, then your ass is grass, and I'm gonna play lawn mower!"

"But sir . . ."

"And about this 'silent contempt' shit. It *will* cease. Do you understand me? You *do*, Sergeant, so you are dis-fucking-missed!"

The major saluted and about-faced. Then he turned.

"Okay, *I'm a major again*," he said. "I take it you spent time as an NCO?"

"Eight years, sir," Gilreth answered proudly. "Special Forces."

"Well, the leadership method you demonstrated might work for *you*, but would you recommend it for an inexperienced officer like, say, Lieutenant Hargrove?"

"*Absolutely*, sir," the ex-sergeant answered. "I've been in the army long enough to know there's only one way to handle a sergeant who doesn't respect his officers."

The major dismissed his class on Leadership by Example early that day.

I disliked one group: the National Guard and Army Reserve lieutenants. They were volunteers, but for a force that would stay in the States. Few had been to college, and most were so damned gung ho about playing army. It was like Infantry School was the biggest experience of their lives, so they played Sergeant Rock at Benning to tell war stories on weekend drills back in Cleveland or Detroit. The ROTC graduates had college degrees, and were a little older but far more mature. We were in for two years and for us, Vietnam seemed inevitable.

One sultry Georgia afternoon, we were waiting for transport back to the main post after M-60 machine-gun instruction. The trucks were an hour late, and the instructor, a regular army sergeant, passed the time sipping from a concealed pint of vodka and talking to a group of National Guard lieutenants . . . northerners. The topic was blacks.

"I'll tell you the truth, Lieutenant. Niggers don't carry their weight," the sergeant said. "Not in Nam, not here. Look at this civil rights shit, while our country's in trouble."

"I agree," Lieutenant Thompson from the Ohio Guard said. "Only one thing can save our country, Sergeant. A military coup."

These are imbeciles, I thought. Thank God that jackass will lead a platoon of Ohio guardsmen—not infantrymen in Vietnam.

Bayonet drill. We're spaced ten feet apart on a parade ground the size of a football field. A drill sergeant with a portable loudspeaker will work us into a frenzy for Mother-Green-the-Death-Machine.

"What's the spirit of the bayonet?" the sergeant screams through the bullhorn.

"To kill! To kill!" we scream back.

"Who we gonna kill?"

"The Cong, the Cong!"

Then we remove bayonet scabbards and move forward aggressively, on-line, to the drill sergeant's chant:

"Upper butt stroke, *thrust*! Shoulder stroke, *slash*!"

"What's the spirit of the bayonet?"

We scream, again and again, how we'll kill the Viet Cong.

I thrust and stroke and sweep my bayonet to the sergeant's commands. But I can't reach the mind-bending madness that the sergeant wants—because other naked bayonets are thrusting and shoulder-slashing to my left, my right, and ahead of and behind me. I glimpse a couple of Guard officers who are really on a trip. If I get just a little out of step, the spirit of the bayonet will slash into *Hargrove*'s back. If I'm killed in this war, I want it to be by a Viet Cong—not an eighteen-year-old from the Indiana National Guard.

Hargrove, at twenty-four you're too old for this shit, I thought. And I was. I'd have loved Infantry School at age eighteen . . . but I went to Texas A&M instead.

Most of the Infantry School cadre were fresh from Nam, and took their jobs seriously. Instruction was generally good, but some seemed a bit unrealistic.

"Never drink the water in Vietnam. Don't even take a drink with ice cubes," an army public health doctor warned us sternly. "Don't eat anything that's not from a U.S. army mess or a C-rat can." That bothered me.

"I'm sure that's good advice for regular American units, but what about *advisers*?" I asked. "How can an officer assigned to the South Vietnamese Army refuse to eat Vietnamese food?"

His answer wasn't very good.

At the end of Week 1, Susan was required—*Command Performance* was the term—to attend a seminar for new infantry wives given by Lt. Col. Martin Anderson, his wife Sue Ann, and the colonel's liaison to the infantry wives, a captain recovering from a bad shoulder wound.

Colonel Anderson lectured our wives on patriotism and the long-haired peaceniks who were undermining America and its fighting men. After a couple of years in San Francisco, Susan didn't consider long hair, or war protests, so bad.

"A lot of you, and your husbands, have been to universities," the colonel said. "Well, be advised that I never went to college, but I'm proud to say I graduated from the finest school in the world—The United States Army Infantry Officers School."

The colonel sent the wives on a tour of Fort Benning, beginning with the hospital.

"It's good to have babies in the army—and it's cheap. Sue Ann and I've had six.

"We want you to appreciate what your husbands are learning here at Benning—and their jobs when they get to Vietnam," the colonel said as the wives passed bleachers facing a simulated Vietnamese village. "So you'll get to see your men in action, from those bleachers, later in the course.

"You'll watch your husbands and other officers run a sweep-and-clear mission—it was called *search-and-destroy* until the new DA directive six months ago—on those thatch hootches. The operation will be as much like Vietnam as we can make it."

The shot-up captain grimaced. Susan didn't think he liked his job.

"But don't worry, your men and our fake gooks will fire blank ammo, and the explosives won't carry shrapnel."

Susan found Infantry School hard to believe. I didn't.

I made three good friends at Fort Benning, civilians like me who were serving two-year tours. Michael Arnovitz and Clyde Aderhold would die within a year. I wonder if Johnny Krebs made it?

The Oklahoma City attorney was commissioned as an intelligence officer. Krebs took the infantry compass course twice—and failed both times. Once, he got lost and a sergeant had to search the woods for him.

We got a rare treat at noon on July 4: the rest of the day off. Everyone but Krebs. Johnny had to take the compass course a third time, and he'd damned well better pass it. The word was, failing the course three times meant that you lost your commission and went to Nam as a "grunt," an enlisted rifleman. I thought that losing a commission was unlikely, if you were smart. The army needed lieutenants too badly in 1968.

Susan and I invited fellow officers over for an Independence Day barbecue that afternoon. Johnny promised to drop by when he finished the compass course.

We waited until sundown, then started grilling ribs and chicken without Krebs. At 8:00 P.M. I answered the door.

Krebs looked awful. His fatigues were torn, caked with mud, and his face and hands were scratched.

"You look like hell," I said, handing him a Schlitz.

Krebs looked at his boots. "I failed the compass course."

"Oh ... sorry."

"I got lost, and they sent the sergeant back into the woods to find me again."

"Have another beer."

After three despondent beers, Krebs said "I may as well tell you the worst part. You'll hear it anyway."

"Nothing could be worse than getting lost, for the third time, on the compass course. You'll lose your commission and go to Nam as a grunt. You'll probably get killed."

"Yeah, something could be worse. I lost my compass."

CHAPTER XVII
The First Casualty *or* Fighting Soldiers from the Sky

Fort Bragg, North Carolina 1968–69

> The first casualty in war is truth.
> —Senator Hiram Johnson

> Veritas et Libertas
> *(Truth and Liberty)*
> —Slogan of *USAJFKCENSPWAR*

I didn't go to an infantry unit after Fort Benning. Instead, an army computer caught my M.S. in agricultural communication, and assigned me to the 4th Psychological Operations Group at Fort Bragg, North Carolina.

The field was traditionally known as "psychological warfare," but the army had renamed it a few years before. *PsyOps* is probably a better term, psychologically, but to me, *PsyWar* was more accurate.

At 4th PsyOps, I found orders to report to a Major Stilwell, the S-1 or personnel officer, over on Smoke Bomb Hill. "The Hill" was the U.S. Army John F. Kennedy Center for Special Warfare (Airborne), known by its catchy military acronym USAJFKCENSPWAR.[1]

It was appropriate that the Special Forces nerve center bear President Kennedy's name. His passion for James Bond novels reflected a fascination for the covert. Kennedy gave the Special Forces its power, and authorized its elite troops to wear the Green Beret.[2]

The JFK Center was the foremost training and research center for counterinsurgency and clandestine warfare in the Free, and Not-So-Free, World. Almost every non-Communist nation sent officers to The Hill. The largest groups were from Vietnam, Thailand, and Laos.

Half a dozen Special Forces officers interviewed me. Late that afternoon, Major Stilwell offered—yes, *offered*, not assigned me to—a position as propaganda instructor, JFK Special Warfare School.

By then I knew that Major Stilwell was the grandson of Gen. Vinegar Joe Stilwell, chief of staff to Generalissimo Chiang Kai-shek and World War II commander of U.S. troops in China, Burma, and India. Vinegar Joe's son, Gen. Joseph W. Stilwell Jr., commanded the JFK Center in 1964–65. Cider Joe

---

[1] Today the Hill has a more diplomatic name: the JFK Center for Military Assistance.

[2] A beret also symbolized the far left in the midsixties. European and North American revolutionaries often wore black berets. They were emulating Che Guevara, the Argentine Communist who, with Fidel Castro, orchestrated the revolution that toppled the Fulgencio Batista regime in 1959, establishing Cuba as the Western Hemisphere's only Communist state. Che disappeared from the public eye in 1965, then reemerged, as a guerrilla leader in Bolivia, in 1966. Soldiers of Bolivia's 8th Army Division, allegedly with U.S. Special Forces advisers, killed Che in a battle with Communist guerrillas in 1967. Bolivian leftists later claimed that Che was captured alive, then executed in the field.

Figure 1 (Transition 1). Former Viet Cong political officer Tran Van Rang and I in the lower Mekong Delta, 1988. Rang is explaining that he could have had me killed eighteen years ago, but didn't . . . and why. *Vo Tong Xuan.*

Figure 2 (Chapter II). President Lyndon B. Johnson inspecting IR8, soon to be called the *miracle rice* of Asian agriculture, at the International Rice Research Institute, 26 October 1966. Philippine president Ferdinand E. Marcos (to LBJ's right), IRRI Director Dr. Robert L. Chandler (center), leaders of the IRRI program to breed and select improved semidwarf rices, Dr. Peter Jennings (standing, far left) and Henry M. ("Hank") Beachell. *Courtesy of the International Rice Research Institute.*

Figure 3 (Transition 4). At the Ba Lien home in 1988. Ba Lien stands to my right. His granddaughter, Huyen Xuan Dep, examines the Vietnamese edition of the IRRI booklet *Field Problems of Tropical Rice*. Ba Lien's wife, second from his right, was seriously ill, but left her bed to be in this photo. *Vo Tong Xuan*.

Figure 4 (Transition 18). Two decades before, I had carried Huyen Xuan Dep, Ba Lien's grandaughter, around the farm on my shoulders. In 1988, I regretted not carrying Ms. Dep's own daughter, but I made up for that in 1990. Ba Lien walks in front of me. *To Phuc Tuong*.

Figure 5 (Chapter XI). Interpreter Nguyen An Khang (right) and I on a river in Chuong Thien Province in 1969. To the left is Nguyen Thanh Tung, a land-reform technician.

Figure 6 (Transition 6). This slab of cement was once my quarters. In the background is the MAC-V water tower and concrete bunkers. I don't remember the abandoned building. *Vo Tong Xuan.*

Figure 7 (Transition 16). Our old olderly room was being used to raise pythons for their skin and meat when I visited Vi Thanh in 1990. *To Phuc Tuong.*

Figure 8 (Chapter XIII). (Above) The "fish" of Company D-1, or Spider-D, in 1962. I'm wearing a fatigue jacket and campaign hat, holding the beer sign. (Below left) Me, sporting new corporal's stripes as a *pisshead* (sophomore), in 1964 [*Jerry Harbert*]. (Below right) With date Sandi Chandler at the 1965 Combat Ball.

Figure 9 (Chapter XIII). The last photo that Captain Joe Bush sent to his wife Mickey, from a Lao army camp near Muong Sui in 1969. *Courtesy of Mickey Bush Hunt.*

Figure 10 (Chapter XIV). This photo of Larry Kennemer on the cover of the 1 January 1968 issue of *Newsweek* increased my guilt trip: I was safe in grad school while so many of my Aggie buddies were leading platoons in Nam.

Figure 11 (Transition 15). War and peace. Nurse Luu My Thanh wore camouflaged fatigues and jungle boots, like her Green Beret counterparts, at a Special Forces camp near Can Tho in the mid-1960s (Right). [*Courtesy of Luu My Thanh.*] (Below) The registered nurse, who now sells cigarettes on Can Tho streets, displays her mutilated photo album of happy times—the war years—in 1990. *Tom Hargrove.*

Figure 12 (Transition 16).
(Above) With Susan Hargrove
in the "Vi Thanh Hilton." (Right)
Susan during one of her few
moments of peace, floating on
a sampan. The lotus blossums
to her left were picked from
swamps along the Mekong
Delta canal. *Courtesy of Lynn
Johnson.*

Figure 13 (Chapter XXXIII). Capt. Harvey Weiner (right) and I inoculating baby chicks against Newcastle disease at the Vi Thanh orphanage in 1969 or 1970. *Courtesy of Harvey Weiner.*

Figure 14 (Chapter XXXIII). Monique—beautiful and tragic, born of a mixed marriage in Vietnam but, in her mind, French. This is the *real* Monique, on whom I based the Monique of my fiction, at CORDS headquarters, Vi Thanh, 1969. *Harvey Weiner.*

Stilwell died in a C-47 crash over Pacific waters in 1966. That was strange—C-47s *never* went down.

Meanwhile, the computer alerted the USAJFKCENSPWAR PIO. He also offered a position, as a public information officer. Communication would be my business after the army, I thought, so I turned the PIO job down. PsyOps seemed more interesting than writing press releases.[3]

Those were the glory days of the Special Forces, and Green Beret lore and legend dominated Smoke Bomb Hill. John Wayne had left a gift that never let us forget where we were: a twenty-foot Green Beret soldier, tough as steel, but cast in bronze. We marched to a famous song at our few formations:

> Fighting soldiers from the sky
> Fearless men who jump and die
> Men who mean just what they say
> The brave men of the Green Beret . . .

> Silver wings upon their chest
> These are men, America's best
> One hundred men, we'll test today
> But only three will win the Green Beret . . .

> Back at home, a young wife waits
> Her Green Beret has met his fate
> He has died for those oppressed
> Leaving her one last request

> Put silver wings on my son's chest
> Make him one of America's best . . .

---

[3] In Vietnam, I would turn down PIO jobs in Saigon and Can Tho, because I wanted to get closer to the action. I maneuvered a lot in the army, just to stay out of public information work. I know that some Ph.D.s became unwilling enlisted infantrymen—but I never saw it. The army seemed fairly good about placing soldiers, or at least officers, in slots where special skills were needed. I quoted Susan in this chapter, so I asked her to review it, November 1990. That was a mistake. Reading the above footnote made her furious. "If I'd known you turned down press-officer jobs in Saigon and Can Tho," she yelled, "and then you'd been killed in that miserable Vi Thanh—I wouldn't have shed a single damned tear. Anyone with that little sense *deserved* to get shot!" By then, Susan had been to Chuong Thien Province. But that's in a later chapter.

That song, written and sung by Special Forces Sergeant Barry Sadler, had been America's No. 1 single in 1966. It sold 12 million copies in the United States, and was recorded in a dozen languages. Whenever I remember Fort Bragg, I think of "The Ballad of the Green Berets."[4]

Susan had been a weekend hippie while working in San Francisco a year before. She almost flipped out at the Special Warfare chapel. A *church* with stained-glass windows showing godlike Green Berets vaccinating children and teaching Asian soldiers to calibrate the M-60 machine gun in a jungle camp surrounded by sharpened bamboo stakes? She couldn't believe it. This place was freakier than Infanty School.

The common denominator for PsyOps instructors was a master's or doctorate degree in psychology, advertising, communication, sociology. A few instructors lacked those social-science credentials, but had years of experience in psywar or counterinsurgency.

Special Forces officers were in charge, but our group included Marines, WACs, navy, air force. Enlisted men and officers had about the same status as instructors.

We had a draftee specialist fourth class with dual doctorates in psychology and physiology. We had Green Berets who'd run armed propaganda teams in Vietnam, and an advertising man from Madison Avenue who looked out of place in fatigues and jump boots.

We even had a Jesuit priest, a paratrooper sky pilot, fresh from a Vietnam tour as chaplain with the 173d Airborne. But Major Crasswell was *not* our chaplain, we didn't have one. *Our* priest specialized in bending minds.

He was a gentle man who seemed to have no moral problems with using his skills to teach propaganda, but was torn among Order, emotions, and libido. After his third cognac, the priest invariably confessed: "My life is lonely . . . so terribly lonely. I've met widows of men I knew in Vietnam . . . intelligent and charming women who are lonely, like me, yet . . ."

---

[4] Another popular song of that era, "I'm Proud to Be an Okie from Muskogee," was also a redneck response to sixties protest music. In Vietnam, I met a black lieutenant who really came from Muskogee, Oklahoma. "You don't smoke marijuana in Muscogee," I said. His response: "That's what you *white dudes* think."

Major Crasswell probably left the cloth soon after I left Fort Bragg.

The group included three or four highly paid civilians with impressive educational backgrounds. I'm not sure who paid their salaries.

PsyOps wasn't secret, but working at the Special Warfare School required a Top Secret clearance.

"Why do you make me list three references?" I asked the army intelligence sergeant when I submitted forms for *my* Top Secret clearance. "I'll name friends, of course. People who'll say I'm the salt of the earth."

"We know that, Lieutenant," the sergeant said. "But when our FBI man goes to *your* three references, he'll ask *them* to give three more names, and so on. The spooks will finally ask about you in them redneck bars where you hung out."

Fisher County had no redneck bars—or *any* bars—but I got the sergeant's point.

Sure enough, an FBI agent was in to Rotan two weeks later, checking me out. That worried Mother, but gave my home-town's two thousand farmers, ranchers, merchants, and good ol' boys something to talk about.

I'd worked hard for, and was proud of, my primary MOS, or "Military Occupational Specialty": 1542, Infantry Officer. To me, infantry was the heart of the army.

But I also liked my new MOS: 9305, Psychological Warfare Officer. My tactical slot at the JFK Center was Radio Propaganda Officer (Airborne). Within a month, I taught all radio and television propaganda courses. I was also secondary instructor for print-media propaganda, which focused mainly on psywar leaflets.

That part of my job wasn't too different from teaching sophomore journalism or junior advertising at a university. PsyOps is, after all, persuasive communication.

In fact, the word *propaganda* carried no negative connotation until British psywar of World War I associated the craft with lies and deceit. The word stems from the Congregation for Propagating the Faith, established in 1622 by Pope Gregory XV for Roman Catholic missionary work.

But the JFK Center crest symbolized a sinister and fascinating side of PsyOps: a shield, with a torch that stood for light, liberty, and truth. At the shield's top was a horse's head, the knight on a chessboard—"the only piece capable of moving indirectly and of striking from, and within, enemy territory."

Those symbols were fairly conventional, considering the JFK Center mission. But they stood against a background of white, gray, and black: for the three types of propaganda. Those noncolors represent the *source* of propaganda, not its degree of truth.

"White" propaganda openly acknowledges its source. Radio Hanoi may have broadcast lies, but it was a white station, because the transmissions were clearly from North Vietnam.

The origin of "gray" on the propaganda color chart is . . . gray. It avoids identification as friendly or enemy. Gray propaganda leaves its source to the imagination of the target.

Black, in the shadowy world of intelligence and insurgency, means secret or covert, something that requires the cover of darkness. On the JFK shield, it symbolized the clandestine craft of black propaganda: counterfeiting your enemy's communication to attack your own country—in the enemy's name.

Black propaganda is one of the most secret and elusive weapons of war, hot or cold. Little has been written about the covert profession, where a skilled artist wants no public recognition.

Black propaganda refers to counterfeit radio broadcasts, fake leaflets or letters, any political communication that masquerades as produced and spread by a source other than the true one. The black propagandist buries subtleties in his fake messages to discredit the alleged source. Black messages often appear to originate from their own target audience—those the propagandist seeks to influence or undermine. Black often claims to come from a revolutionary group within the propaganda target.

Nations advocate causes contrary to their own national policies through black channels. A black propagandist can use words and promote actions that his "white" counterpart wouldn't touch. After all, he is the "voice of the enemy." If exposed, the true source denies everything. "*You* said that—not *me*!"

The British were, and probably still are, the masters of black propaganda. In World War II, Germans accepted counterfeit Nazi radio broadcasts—British black—because, for example, the programs ridiculed Winston Churchill, the U.K.'s own prime minister, as "a flat-footed bastard of a drunken old Jew."

Germans couldn't believe the British could broadcast such messages, so they accepted the transmissions as authentic. Indeed, the Brits lifted 99 percent of their black broadcasts from "straight" Nazi propaganda.

But English propagandists buried insignificant items in those broadcasts ... like assurances from the *Wehrmacht* medical corps that venereal diseases could not spread through blood transfusions. Thus, wounded German soldiers on the Russian Front had no reason to worry about getting transfusions of blood taken from Polish and Russian prisoners—*even though 12 percent of the blood donors had syphilis*.

Nasty, but I loved it.

I also researched and taught a course on rumor as a psychological weapon. The planted rumor is the oldest—yet still the most common and destructive—form of black propaganda.

Psychologists and sociologists at Ivy League universities pioneered rumor research after World War II, funded by U.S. Army and Navy contracts. The military wanted to know how and why rumors spread, how much they had hurt the war effort, and ways to counter rumors in future conflicts.

But those research findings could help black propagandists *tailor* rumor campaigns as offensive weapons.

I first learned of the VC rumor campaign to sabotage IR8 at Fort Bragg, and used it as an example in my rumor class.

Vietnam, with its complicated conspiracies and deep-seated hatreds, was a natural battleground for black propaganda. Associated Press correspondent Malcolm Browne was intrigued with black propaganda "because it is so close to the Vietnamese way of life."[5] He defined black as "the art of putting words in the other guy's mouth and then blaming him for them."

Brown, who won the 1964 Pulitzer Prize for his war coverage, wrote that grenades tossed into crowds by unseen VC were often thrown by operatives of the Saigon government posing as VC agents (or vice versa), with follow-up plans to incite public anger against the alleged terrorists:

When something happens in [Saigon], residents often suspect black propaganda at work, or even double black propaganda ("The Viet Cong threw that grenade, knowing that we

---

[5] Browne, Malcolm. 1968. *The New Face of War* (rev. ed.). The Bobbs-Merrill Co.

would suspect the government of throwing it with the idea of blaming it on the Viet Cong"). South Vietnam is a nation in which twisted, devious thinking is the rule, and nothing is accepted at face value. Another sample: "The government deliberately lost that battle in order to alarm the Americans into giving us more aid." And conversely, "The Viet Cong deliberately lost that battle to give the Americans a false sense of security."

Americans are widely regarded as gullible people ready to swallow all black propaganda. Perhaps we have, on too many occasions.

I wasn't with PsyOps in Chuong Thien Province, but PsyOps operatives knew I'd taught at Fort Bragg, and often asked my help. I also sought PsyOps support, because I knew the power of communication and propaganda.

The South Vietnamese, with a little help from their friends, to paraphrase the Beatles, probably used black propaganda better than the Communists. The reason was simple: an authoritarian society won't allow propaganda attacks on its own political system. That's why British black propaganda worked, but German black didn't, in World War II. Soviet black has also generally been lousy.

But my theory on Vietnamese black may not be valid; I never worked on a black operation. But I was one of the few Americans who *recognized* black . . . sometimes.

Black propaganda and intelligence are intimately associated, and should work hand in hand. An example:

In 1968–69, Capt. Doug Lovejoy and I were friends and instructors on Smoke Bomb Hill. But in 1970, Doug was S-2, intelligence officer, for the 2d PsyOps Group in Saigon. Doug was well qualified for the job. He had a master's in Asian Studies from the University of Chicago.

Doug analyzed Viet Cong and North Vietnamese propaganda. His weekly reports on VC-NVA PsyWar trends, classified SECRET, reached every intelligence officer and PsyOps unit in Vietnam.

U.S. Marines had picked up some interesting Viet Cong leaflets near Da Nang, in northern I Corps. Like all unusual Communist propaganda, those leaflets landed on Doug's desk.

An ultraleft Viet Cong group had printed the leaflets on a

"jelly-roll press," a jungle mimeograph machine that didn't need electricity.[6]

The crude leaflets attacked, viciously and with standard Communist rhetoric, the U.S. and its "running-dog lackeys," the South Vietnamese Government and Army. Doug was sure, by analyzing its dialect and specific Vietnamese phraseology, that the leaflets were written by local boys of that region.

But the VC leaflets also denounced—angrily—North Vietnamese *revisionists* who were "betraying the Revolution, and impeding the Vietnamese People's just struggle for true independence."

Doug knew that North-South conflicts split the Communist ranks . . . an excellent "wedge" for U.S. and South Vietnamese propaganda to exploit. He published the text of the leaflets in his Secret PsyOps report.

A MAC-V SOG colonel came to Doug's shop the next week. A unit that called itself the *Cutthroats*, in Nam, was probably okay. But you'd better be careful when dealing with agencies that had wimpy names like *Studies and Observation Group* (SOG), or *Social Research*. They usually answered to Langley, Virginia.

SOG was the top secret liaison of covert military agencies with the CIA.

Special Forces officers led SOG, and Green Berets comprised most of the task force's personnel. But SOG also drew on soldier-spooks from the navy SEALs (because they infiltrated, and gathered intelligence from, enemy territory by *SEa-Air-Land*). Men from two other clandestine forces served with SOG: the Marine Corps Force Recon, and the air force 90th Special Operations Wing.

The SOG colonel held a copy of Doug's secret intelligence report. "I'd like to meet the officer who prepared this."

"*I* wrote it, sir!" Doug said, ready to deny that he deserved praise for a job well done.

"Captain, are you *sure* the map coordinates you published—where the Marines found those leaflets—are correct?"

"I think so, Colonel. But I'll double-check."

Doug returned, embarrassed, five minutes later.

"Sorry, sir, my clerk made a typo. The report put the coor-

[6] *We* also taught how to make and use jelly-roll presses at Fort Bragg.

dinates as Juliet Whiskey 324793. But the *actual* coordinates were JW 344793."

"That's what I thought. You're doing a *fine job* . . . *Captain*."

Doug shut his office door . . . and figured out the *real* source of those Viet Cong leaflets.

I didn't remind Doug that a U.S. PsyOps intelligence officer shouldn't fall for his own country's black propaganda. I doubt that I'd have caught the trick either. But it taught me new respect for the Studies and Observation Group.

The head of instruction in print media propaganda at the JFK Center, and my boss for those courses, was Capt. Jane Gunther, a WAC with a master's degree in journalism. She could have been pretty, but wasn't. Captain Gunther was army, and bitter that God had made her female. I've never met a woman who was—and I know the term is contradictory—more a military prick. Her swagger stick was authorized, but officers hadn't carried them for forty years.

Captain Gunther ordered me to snap to attention when she entered the two-desk office that we shared. I stood, but not very straight. The WAC once made me so angry, I slammed the wall when she left our cubicle. It didn't hurt Captain Gunther, but I broke the sheetrock, and fractured a knuckle.

Major Isenberg saw bad trouble brewing, and moved me into an office with Tom Lipscomb, a Special Forces lieutenant who had requested a Vietnam tour. He died there, six months later.

Meanwhile, Susan and her pets and I settled into a red-brick, two-bedroom duplex on the post. It was standard second-lieutenant housing, but the nicest we'd lived in as a couple.

The phone rang a few weeks later. It was Lee Lanning, from Fisher County and two years behind me in Spider-D at Texas A&M. Lee was also a new second lieutenant, just out of infantry and Airborne schools. He was now a platoon leader with the 82d Airborne while waiting for orders to Ranger School—and *praying* for a Vietnam tour.

Lee had married Linda Ann Moore, the daughter of cotton farmers near Roby, only ten miles from Rotan. Linda had been twirler for the Roby Lions, and star guard on its girls basketball team. We'd known each other since high school.

Linda was usually Lee's date at A&M football weekends and on Aggie Corps trips. The Aggies called her "Old Army

Moore." The three of us, and whatever dates Linda scrounged for me, had partied in College Station, Austin, Fort Worth, Houston.

In 1989, the Lannings wrote about our reunion at Fort Bragg. Lee first, then Linda:

> We heard that you had married Susan, who we'd never met, and were at Bragg. I called, and you said "come on over, we live just a few blocks away."

Linda will pick the story up from there:

> Tom must have figured he'd screwed up badly by inviting us. He was nervous, and said that Susan was doing laundry at the PX. She drove up a few minutes later, and Tom went out "to help carry laundry baskets." He was probably telling Susan that he'd let the infamous Lannings in the house. Susan was nice, but wary, over the next few hours. She'd heard too many stories about our A&M days.

I showed the Lanning letter to Susan.

"It's basically correct," she said. "But I wasn't doing laundry at the PX. The lines were too long. I'd been at that Laundromat outside the gate—the one with a bar and pool tables."

Fayetteville was tough, all right. Soldiers claimed there were bars in town where customers were frisked at the door. If you didn't have a gun or a knife, you could rent one from the bartender.

Lee was stereotype infantry back then, and had no use for whiffy PsyOps. But the obvious connection with Langley, Virginia, intrigued him.

Lee's favorite line, after a couple of beers, was: "Come on Tom. Show me your suicide pill . . . *please*?"

Linda and Susan soon became friends, and lived together on the West Coast while Lee and I were in Nam.

October 1969. Our commander, Gen. Edward M. Flanagan, had given an hour's notice for a 4:30 P.M. emergency meeting of all JFK Center officers and NCOs. Tension was high, and rumors spread at the coffee bar.

We're jumping into the mountains of Laos. We'll tie up with nationalists to set up a third government behind the Communist lines, was one analysis. I didn't believe the rumor, but thought: Could I really set up and run a clandestine radio station in the jungle? I've taught it but . . .

General Flanagan made a dramatic appearance in the JFK auditorium. He wore starched fatigues, spit-shined jump boots, and a jaunty Green Beret. This man was a *soldier* . . . and he looked mad as hell. Something serious has happened.

"Men, I have bad news," the general said, and we waited for it.

"The 82d Airborne has pledged more to United Fund than the JFK Center. I know you'll agree that this is unacceptable, and an insult to the Special Forces.

"No one is *forced* to contribute to United Fund; it's voluntary. But you are *encouraged* to pledge as you leave. Finance NCOs have set up desks at the door to take each man's name, rank, company, and amount of pledge.

"I will review the pledges of each officer and NCO. Am I understood? Thank you."

I filed out with the others, relieved that we weren't jumping into Laos—but pissed off about the twenty dollars that the finance sergeant told me was expected from second lieutenants. How the hell will *United Fund* help win the war?

A few days later, I learned that the JFK Center had outpledged the 82d Airborne. I could care less.[7]

No, I wasn't gung ho anymore, but Texas A&M left a leg-

---

[7] In 1989 I bought an interesting paperback, *The Los Baños Raid.* I had lived in Los Baños for sixteen years, so I wanted to read more about the daring airborne and amphibious raid behind Japanese lines in February 1945. Paratroopers of the U.S. 11th Airborne, supported by Filipino guerrillas, had freed 2,122 American, Canadian, and British civilians held in a makeshift internment camp on the campus of the University of the Philippines at Los Baños. Today, the IRRI research center sits on the UPLB campus, adjacent to where the internees were held.

When I started reading that evening, I realized that the book's author was General E. M. Flanagan, my boss in 1968–69.

I showed the book to Susan. She reminded me that in 1969, she read a piece that General Flanagan had published in the "Humor in Uniform" section of *Reader's Digest.* It was about a Laotian officer, newly arrived at the JFK Center. He wanted to light a cigarette, and assumed that a red lever marked PULL FOR FIRE was another wonderful American device, like a water fountain or a Coke machine. He pulled the lever—and triggered a fire alarm.

Susan mailed the story to me in Vietnam.

"You helped evacuate the JFK Center that day," she wrote. "Why didn't *you* write the story, and sell it for three hundred dollars?"

"That's why Flanagan is a general—and I'm a lieutenant," I wrote back.

acy. I hated being a "leg" in an airborne outfit. I had jumped four times with the Texas A&M skydivers. *I could do it*.

Besides, Susan and I *needed* the $110 per month hazardous-duty pay. Enlisted men drew $55 a month to jump from the same planes—but officers cost more.

I applied for Airborne School, and started running an hour each afternoon.

Lieutenant Colonel Dandridge called me in. "I have bad news, Tom," he said. Higher officers often used first names with subordinates. But it didn't work the *other* way. Not between lieutenants and colonels.

"The higher brass has turned down your Jump School application."

"But *my job*—Airborne Radio Propaganda Officer—*requires* that I jump!"

"Yes, but the JFK Center must *stick to its budget*," Colonel Dandridge said.

"We *pay* Fort Benning for each man its Airborne School trains. You're an infantry-type second lieutenant, with a PsyOps background. Both trades are in, shall we say *high demand*? in Nam. You'll ship out soon, so to put silver wings on Lieutenant Hargrove's chest would be a waste of JFK money."

Clandestine warfare has to stick to a budget? Like the Iowa Agricultural Extension Service? That blew my mind.

A monetary constraint on something as important as Jump School? That's absurd. I started looking for ways around the decision. Army regulations specified that, if I proved tough enough, I could qualify for Special Forces while at Bragg.

The JFK Center had a Special Warfare course that was designed mainly so officers like me, who landed on the JFK staff because of credentials, not training, could wear Green Berets. The academic portion was self-study, but quite a few weekends would be spent in the field.

You *had* to jump to wear a green beanie. I applied for the course, and kept running.

Twice during that time, the JFK Center held Operation GOBBLER WOODS, a one-week war game for Special Forces, counterinsurgency, and PsyOps trainees.

An entire North Carolina county was our host—*guinea pig* might be a better term—for GOBBLER WOODS. I can't imagine a county in antiwar California doing that, but there weren't many war protesters among those patriotic Southerners.

Some Green Beret trainees were designated guerrillas; we called them "Aggressors." Others stayed loyal to the government of a hypothetical country.

Farmers, teachers, housewives all helped make GOBBLER as authentic as possible. The North Carolinians loved our army games, and I liked those Tarheels. I didn't realize that my ancestors on Mother's side had started life in America as cotton farmers in that region.

Farm families often hid Aggressors in their barns, and smuggled them food at night. They sometimes dined on home-cooked southern fried chicken and mashed potatoes.

PsyOps instructors were billeted in a high-school basketball gymnasium. We ate from a portable army mess, or had cold C rations.

While the counterinsurgency trainees planned their next ambush or search-and-clear mission, my PsyOps students generated propaganda messages. We prepared leaflets for air drops and broadcasts for transmission over local stations that got caught up in the spirit of GOBBLER. Those stations sometimes broadcast both guerrilla and loyalist radio propaganda.

My trainees were loyal to a decent, but threatened, government, so most of our propaganda was white. The Aggressors were dirty; they used a lot of black. But we used that term carefully in rural North Carolina in 1968.

My loyal propagandists spoke to first through fifth grade classes at local schools ... telling the kids how reporting on the Aggressors was their patriotic duty. We offered rewards to children for informing on parents who helped or hid guerrillas. It wasn't authorized, but it worked. Kids like Cokes and milk-shakes and cheeseburgers.

GOBBLER WOODS was a lot like Vietnam, à la North Carolina. And like in Nam, we were never quite sure which side was winning. The more romantic Aggressors, probably. The North Carolinians, rebels at heart, gave them more support.

Susan's parents, the Sheldons, had returned from the Middle East for a year. I took leave, and we flew to San Francisco to spend Christmas of 1968 with them.

I called Don Siegler a Californian but still, my first cousin. I hadn't seen Don since he spent summers as a kid on the Hargrove farm in West Texas.

Don and I thought similarly, but had aligned with different camps, on the Vietnam issue. To Don, the war was senseless and a threat to America's political and economic future. I couldn't argue with that.

And Don accepted that I was in the army, almost certainly bound for Nam. We got along well.

I admired how Don used tricks taught at Fort Bragg—even though he'd had no Special Forces training—to beat the draft and stay out of Vietnam. Like how he constantly changed his address, then denied receiving notices to register with his local draft board.

Don now runs his own public relations firm. But I thought, back then, that he had the imagination and intelligence to be a great black propagandist.

I told Don about Fort Bragg: PsyOps, white and black propaganda, rumor, GOBBLER WOODS. I was probably a little too proud of my PsyOps trainees.

Black propaganda didn't anger Don, but GOBBLER made him furious.

"How *could* you practice psychological warfare on children . . . use them to train soldiers for Vietnam? . . . tell little kids *it's their duty to turn in their parents as traitors*? Duty to who? Fort Bragg?"

I'd never thought about it, but encouraging kids to rat on Mom and Dad *was* kind of dirty.

What the hell, it wasn't a very nice war.[8]

I now had hard second thoughts about going to that war. Through PsyOps, I'd read the books of Mao Tse-tung, Ho Chi Minh, Vo Nguyen Giap, Che Guevara. I'd also taken a graduate course in History of Eastern Asia at Iowa State University.

The Communists had stacked the Vietnam cards. Even if we kicked the hell out of Charley in the swamps and jungles, we'd lost the war on the home front.

I wouldn't try to *avoid* Vietnam. No, I didn't tell Susan, but I secretly hoped for orders. It's hard to explain why. But I wouldn't volunteer. If orders never came, I'd sit the war out at Fort Bragg.

That's when the PolWar team was assembled, to develop a course for training officers for political warfare: a program to

[8] How times change. My cousin reviewed this chapter in late 1990. He corrected or added a few details, and concluded with: "I would prefer not to be mentioned by name when describing violations of federal law, because I'm trying to persuade a major defense contractor to hire my firm."

build a cadre of *political officers* into the poorly led and demoralized South Vietnamese military.[9]

Communist political cadre made sure the Viet Cong and North Vietnamese troops *thought* the proper way at each level, down to the ten-man rifle squad. VC troops studied the writings of Uncle Ho and Giap before and between engagements. After combat, political officers led self-analysis sessions. Each soldier *confessed* his weaknesses to his comrades, and was *criticized* by them.

Most religious movements, especially the more fanatic ones, use the same techniques. In an atmosphere of intense nationalism, such political indoctrination built dedication to a cause . . . a resolve that *our* Vietnamese lacked.

PolWar wouldn't duplicate the VC system. It was organized along the lines of the Chinese Nationalist Army in Taiwan. The Nationalists had worked with Soviet Communists in the 1920s to develop the political officer system that Mao, then Ho Chi Minh, later adopted.

The Chinese Nationalists had an active team of PolWar advisers in Saigon, helping build the program with ARVN. Our course would support that effort.

Ideally, PolWar should have started at the rifle squad, but that would take years, and time was running out for South Vietnam. The first ARVN PolWar officers were at division level. In a few years, PolWar would reach battalion level and, eventually, company, platoon, and squad.

We began writing lesson plans and designing audio-tutorial training modules on persuasion techniques. I thought, then, that a Nam tour was unlikely. I might go in and out of Vietnam for a few weeks at a time on TDY, temporary duty. But those assignments should be fairly safe.

Then one morning I found an amazing inch-high sheaf of papers in my in-box. *How could this happen? There must be a mistake.* My record is excellent, so the JFK Center wouldn't fire me. These orders to Nam simply couldn't have been cut.

My orders were pretty vague . . . MAC-V, the Military Assistance Command-Vietnam. I wonder if that time, the army computer picked up my M.S. in *agricultural* communication.

---

[9] Most of my hosts, when I returned to Vietnam twenty years later, had been VC political officers during the war. They're called People's Committee cadre today, but their jobs haven't changed much.

Agriculture = Pacification = MAC-V/CORDS, which led to Chuong Thien Province.

If my educational keyword had been entomology or agronomy, instead of the generic *agriculture*—what would the computer have done? Maybe I'd have gone to a PsyOps unit in Nam, or to the infantry, or wound up a PIO . . .

And what happened to the PolWar program? I don't know. It just . . . faded away. I've read dozens of books on Vietnam. None mention PolWar. I've never met anyone who has heard of it.

It's like the political warfare program never existed.

Transition 10

Hanoi, May 1988

I can make out a few B-52 craters as we approach Noi Bai Airport, about forty kilometers out of Hanoi. But I can't say the craters *scar* that lush countryside, like so many writers have. Farmers have filled in most craters, and converted the others to fish ponds.

I expect to see military aircraft—MIG 21 fighters and captured C-130s and Caribous—as we taxi along the tarmac, but there are none.

All passengers must write out two detailed copies of the customs declaration by ballpoint pen because Hanoi's international airport has no carbon paper. Uniformed officials check my two cameras and laptop computer three or four times, but I convince them to spare those sensitive instruments from the Soviet-made X-ray machine.

I'm met by Mrs. Le Thi Binh, an editor with Agricultural Publishing House, the main ag publisher in Vietnam. We take a Ministry of Agriculture car on the thirty-minute drive into Hanoi. The rice crop looks excellent.

"Is this your first visit to our country?" Mrs. Binh asks.

"Yes." Then I correct myself. "I mean, this is my first visit to the *North*." I explain that I was in the South almost twenty years ago, and she asks why.

My answer is *"Toi trung uy, co van My."*

Mrs. Binh doesn't seem surprised that I know some Vietnamese phrases, nor that I was an adviser with the U.S. Army in Vietnam. But her nonsurprise, surprises *me*.

Do I have children? I tell her about Miles and Tom G, ages fifteen and fourteen. She also has two sons, eight and ten.

"How old are you?" I ask. That's not an impolite question in Vietnam.

"How old do you think?"

Mrs. Binh looks twenty-five or twenty-six, so that's my answer. But she has a ten-year-old, so she must be older. She doesn't tell me her age, but later I ask if she remembers the war.

"No."

Either her age, or her memory, is wrong.

I'm taken to the *Thong Nhat*, or Unification, Hotel. I must rest this afternoon, Mrs. Binh says. Meetings with Agricultural Publishing House start at 9:00 A.M. tomorrow. Do I want to see anything special while I'm in Hanoi? Yes, Ho Chi Minh's mausoleum. Mrs. Binh will take me there at 7:30 A.M.

The elevator doesn't work, so a porter leads me up wide, high stairs. My luggage is heavy with IRRI books that APH may want to translate. I'd been told not to tip in Hanoi, but that handing out cigarettes is okay. I offer a Winston to the porter. He asks for the pack, and I give it to him.

Room 327 is dark, partly because the wooden shutters are lashed shut. They shouldn't be, so I slash the cotton cord, and greenery frames the Hanoi street below. Even with the sunshine, the room is dismal. It's from the French era but hasn't been improved—or, apparently, cleaned—since the French left in 1954.

Decadence and deterioration best describe the room. Its floor is teak, the ceiling is twelve feet high, and the bathroom is the size of most hotel rooms.

A naked bulb dangling below a ceiling fan throws bleak, yellow light on two hard beds draped by gauzy mosquito nets.

The air conditioner is broken, and a minirefrigerator is, for some reason, installed in the bathroom. It doesn't work either.

The bathtub is enormous, and chipped, and sits on four legs on a permanently stained tile floor. The toilet seat was carved decades ago, from a single piece of teak. There's even a bidet—and some of this may work when the water comes on, maybe later today.

I'm dirty and sweaty but can't bathe, so I search for an electrical outlet to recharge the batteries of my laptop computer. Two broken sockets are covered with mold. I finally plug the computer into the one good outlet, and leave.

Having the afternoon to explore Hanoi, without official escorts, suits me fine. First, I ask the desk clerk directions to a bank. A bicycle ricksha pulls up as I walk along a wide, tree-lined boulevard.

"Change monies?" The driver wears shorts and an olive pith helmet.

"No. I'm going to the bank."

"*Troi oi!* Bank give you six hundred to one. I change for two thou'."

"No thanks." I'd been warned about black-market deals on the streets of Hanoi. The embroidery and souvenir shops are the only safe places to change money at the black rate.

The cyclo driver shrugs, and I walk on. But he reappears at the next intersection. "Two thou' five hun'red."

It's now 3:00 P.M. and hot, and the bank isn't where the hotel clerk said it was. I can't eat until I get some *dong*.

What the hell, I climb into the cyclo, and the driver passes the word to another driver. We pedal among droves of drab-gray bicyclists for fifteen minutes.

The Communists released carefully selected propaganda film to show that the U.S. "carpet-bombed" Hanoi. That's not true. The railway yards on Hanoi's outskirts were the main target. Hanoi itself was hardly touched. A few overgrown air-raid shelters nestled among red-tiled colonial buildings are the only remnants of the war that I see.

We pull up by *Hoa Binh*, or Peace, Lake in the heart of Hanoi, and I get out to take photos. When I return to the ricksha, the driver hands me a six-inch bundle wrapped in newspaper. I try to count the money, but the largest Vietnamese bank note is five thousand *dong*. I assume I've received two hundred fifty thousand dong, and pass him a green $100 bill.

The driver, whose name is Hai, takes me to a restaurant. I climb stairs to an airy, sky-blue room with a green-and-white tile floor. Its main decor is a poster of Iron Maiden, a British heavy-metal rock group.

My meal of spring rolls, roast chicken with mint leaves, French bread, and a bottle of Hanoi Beer costs 4,500 dong—less than $2 by the black-market rate, or $7.50 if you have ethics. Half the cost is for the beer.

My watch band had broken that morning. I love the Rolex that my father-in-law gave me before he died, and can't risk losing it. I ask the waiter to explain to Hai that I need to get the band fixed.

Hai pedals me to a watch-repair stand in a market. A crowd gathers as I wait.

"Lien Xo?" a man asks.

I think hard, then say: *"Toi khong Lien Xo, toi phu My."*

"Troi oi! My—'Merican, no Russian!" About twenty-five men form a half-circle, staring at me.

"Lien Xo numba ten!" the man shouts, then raises a thumb. " 'Mericans *soi mot,* numba one."

He then shapes his right hand into a V and simulates a plane diving and dropping bombs. "Boom, boom, boom! 'Merica numba one!"

I ask Hai to explain, but his English is about like my Vietnamese.

" 'Mericans numba one," he says. "Russians—*Lien Xo*—numba ten."

I understand why the North Vietnamese don't like Russians, but not why the crowd seems to have loved the U.S. bombings. I know I missed something, and I'll always wonder what.

CHAPTER XVIII
A Walking Contradiction

Texas A&M University, 15 January 1989. Chuong Thien Province, 1969

IRRI business brought me to my alma mater in January, 1989. It was so different from the A&M College of Texas that I'd known, and the changes were more than opening its classes to women. The student body of Texas A&M University was now five times its size in May 1966, when I took what I thought would be my last, and best, look at A&M—through the rear-view mirror of "Old Grode," my battered 1960 Chevy.

The university's annual operating budget for running the main College Station campus was an incredible $500 million. The statewide A&M University System had a budget of $800 million. A&M's 7,400 graduate students were almost the equivalent, in number, of the entire student body of twenty-three years ago. Among the scientists on A&M's graduate faculty was Dr. Norman Borlaug, 1970 Nobel Peace Prize Laureate for developing the Mexican dwarf wheats at the International Maize and Wheat Improvement Center, or CIMMYT. Those new wheat varieties, with the IRRI rices, triggered the Green Revolution.

The 1988 Corps of Cadets was twenty-one hundred strong— half the size of the Corps that I had served in. But Texas A&M remains America's largest source of military officers, outside the service academies.

I had just returned from a heavy Tex-Mex lunch with Dr. Robert M. Rutledge. Bob was managing about $150 million in assets, as president of the A&M University Development

251

Foundation, and has been described as "one of the biggest bankers in Texas."

But I knew Bob when he had a tougher job—fighting to keep A&M Administration from disbanding Spider D-1. Bob was first sergeant, then commanding officer, of the company with the highest esprit de corps at A&M in the midsixties. But we also had the lowest grade-point average, and led the Corps in fish dropouts and disciplinary problems.

"An Owen Lock asked you to return his call," Bob's secretary said, handing me a yellow tab of paper with a New York phone number.

Owen Lock—Lee Lanning's editor at Random House. The call must be about my novel. Rutledge offered a watts line, and I dialed.

"Tom, I read what you wrote about returning to Vietnam," Lock said. "I liked it—and the piece about finding your diary."

"Thanks. How about those sample chapters from my novel?"

"I glanced at them, but that's not why I'm calling. If you can send me twenty-five-thousand words—*good* words—I'll offer you a contract for a full-length book, to be published under the Ivy imprint."

I couldn't believe it! I was excited, but also a little confused. "You mean . . . *you might publish my novel?*"

"Not your novel," Lock said. "I want to read the *rest* of the story. I want *nonfiction*—what it was like to be an adviser in the Mekong Delta, and how it felt to go back in 1988. Almost nothing has been written about the pacification side of the war. It doesn't have to be a typical war book. You may have killed in Nam, maybe not. I don't care.

"You might even include a bit about rice, and what you're doing today."

"But . . ."

"Tom, you can write bits and pieces about Vietnam for years. I want to do you a favor and help you *consolidate*, put your experiences together."

I didn't expect this. "Thanks, I'm flattered. But it was so long ago . . ."

"It shouldn't be hard. Lee Lanning said he thought most of your fiction was about things that really happened."

Thanks a lot, Lee, I thought after hanging up. But I couldn't be *too* mad at Lanning; he'd asked Lock to review my writing.

I liked how Lock said he wanted to *help* me. But what Lock doesn't understand—not clearly—is that while the novel *is* based on fact, it didn't all happen to *me*.

I'd brought my draft novel to College Station, to work on when I had free time. That night in the Aggieland Inn, just off the A&M campus, I reviewed my novel to see how much I could salvage as nonfiction. I turned to chapter 6. The story is true, and it happened to dozens—maybe hundreds—of advisers. But I can't write about that execution . . . murder? . . . as nonfiction. I don't even remember the lieutenant's name. Khang and I were with a MAT team somewhere in Chuong Thien Province . . .

Chapter 6

Billows of low, hot smoke made ghosts of the troops as flame consumed the thatch hootches.

An explosion! Then a second explosion, and the burning roof disintegrated!

Dan dived for cover, and rolled into green, scum-covered water.

"What you doin' in that shit trench for anyway . . . sir? That was just a buncha ammo goin' off." Sgt. Joe Culver laughed as Dan pulled himself from the rancid ditch. "The gooks must of hid them fireworks in the roof of that hootch. We got us some honest-to-God VC this time!"

Dan was scared, but made himself grin.

"I didn't see *you* charging the hootch, Joe. Where's the chief?"

Popular Force militia appeared and disappeared through the monsoon drizzle and gray smoke. A teenage soldier was stripping the wrist watch from a pajama-clad corpse in the mud. Two soldiers poked rifles into the door of the single standing hootch, then eased inside.

The chief appeared in the acrid smell of cordite. He wore a black-pajama uniform with a Smith & Wesson .38 revolver, the type issued to village chiefs, strapped to his waist. Two soldiers followed, rifles leveled at a prisoner with hands tied behind his back.

"Looks like Cam's got him a real live Charley, Lieutenant. The chief's a bloodhound!"

"*Troi-oi, Ong* Cam! Viet Cong *fini. Soi mot*, number

one!" Dan said in a pidgin mixture of Vietnamese, French, and English.

"Khang!" Dan called. "Where did the chief take this prisoner?"

Khang and the chief spoke in rapid Vietnamese.

"Mr. Cam find him hide in bunker in hootch. He must be 'bout eighteen year old, no ID. VC for chure."

"We'll send him to Vi Thanh for interrogation. I'll call a chopper."

Khang translated. Pause. The chief cradled the prisoner's chin in both hands, and locked his eyes. He spoke a stream of hate-filled words, then turned away. The young man lowered his head, and said nothing.

The chief then whirled and drove a boot into the prisoner's stomach. He doubled and fell into the mud. The two soldiers pulled him to a kneeling position.

"Mr. Chief he say no need chopper. VC numba ten, kill his father, his wife, three of his son. VC make too much peoples sad. Now Mr. Cam take care of VC."

"Khang! Tell the chief he can't kill our prisoner."

Translation. The chief spoke vicious words. "Is no good to send VC to Vi Thanh. Mebbe so intell'gence turn him loose, and he kill more peoples. Mr. Chief say he make chure this VC make no more troubles."

The chief spoke sharply. A militia sergeant kicked the prisoner's back. The bound man pitched forward.

A sergeant pulled the shaking prisoner back to his knees. The boy's face was taut and covered with slime as the chief circled him, catlike. I've never seen this side of the chief, Dan thought. How do I handle it?

"He can't kill that man, Lieutenant!" Sergeant Culver said. "We ain't even sure he's a VC!"

"Khang! Tell the chief that I'll have to report him to Vi Thanh if he kills the prisoner!"

The chief shrugged and drew his revolver. He pressed the muzzle against the back of the kneeling man's head. Dan heard a cold click as the chief drew the hammer to full cock.

"Chief! For God's sake, don't—"

The explosion drowned Dan's words. The prisoner pitched forward into a puddle of water. Blood rushed from the gaping wounds the bullet tore as it passed from the back of the teenager's head through his face.

The chief holstered his revolver and snapped an order to the sergeant. He spat on the body, then walked back into the smoke.

What an obscene sight! Nothing has less dignity than a goddamn corpse, Dan thought as the sergeant dug into the dead man's pockets.

Dan took the handset of the radio that Sergeant Culver carried. He pressed the talk button, and heard the electronic rush.

"Swampy Eagle Six, this is Eagle Mobile. Over."

"Eagle Six here. Over." The voice came from Major Clyde Bommel, S-3 or operations officer of Advisory Team 73, circling in the C & C chopper.

Dan clenched the mike. Do I report a murder? Execution? KIA? I know my responsibility as a U.S. Army officer. But if I report this, Nuoc Trong will lose its best VC fighter, and the only man who can really *lead* its Popular Force unit. Without the chief, the VC will slaughter those men. If I don't report it, *I've* lost . . . what? Self-respect?

But *I've got to survive in Chuong Thien.* They lectured us on the rules of warfare at Benning . . . but not how to handle shit like *this.* What would Alan do?

"This is Eagle Six. Continue transmission. Over."

"Eagle Mobile here," Dan answered. "Report three enemy hootches and . . ." he thought. "About five hundred rounds of Victor Charley ordnance destroyed. No friendly casualties."

Dan hesitated, then pressed the talk button again. "Two enemy Kilo-India-Alphas. That's two Victor Charleys killed in action. Now moving to pickup point. Will mark with smoke. Out."

That night, Dan wrote to his almost-fiancée:

But really, Janice, what could I have done? I *tried* to stop the chief from killing the prisoner. Besides, the VC didn't execute most of *my* family. It's an eye for an eye over here.

Dan addressed the envelope and scribbled "free" where the stamp would go.

But he tore the letter to shreds the next morning and

mashed the pieces into the mud with his boot heel. He had a terrible hangover.

Back in 1989, in the College Station motel room, I turned to the next chapter of my novel. It also happened, in a way. It was about a letter that was never written, but *could* have been.

Chapter 7

27 May 1969. Specialist Bob Saunders met Dan at the door of the MAT 96 team hut with a stack of envelopes.

"Here's your first mail, Lieutenant. You're lucky, getting letters after only a month in country. When I got here, the army screwed up my records, and sent all my mail back to the States—scared the hell out of my folks, and it took two months for letters to catch up.

"The personnel sergeant at Vi Thanh did it on purpose," Saunders added. "He was a lifer, and didn't like me."

Dan ignored Saunders's complaining as he sorted through the envelopes. Each letter was originally addressed to 1LT Daniel Bridges, MAC-V Receiving Center, then the APO number for Saigon. But an anonymous mail clerk had marked out that address and forwarded the letters to MAC-V IV Corps HQ, Can Tho. Another clerk had, in turn, scratched through the second address and scribbled Adv Tm 73. That address was changed to MAT 96.

One letter was from Mother, the next was an overdue Phillips 66 bill, then Grandmother . . . then Dan found *that* letter, in familiar handwriting.

Dan wanted to be alone when he read Janice's letter, so he opened and skimmed his mother's letter first: . . . everyone misses me, but the feeling around McAllen is that I'm okay because "Danny always lands on all four feet." Coach Griffith asked for my address so he can let me know how the football team does this fall. But I really don't *care* how the McAllen Bulldogs perform on the gridiron. It's dry, but rain surely must come soon. Your cousin Clarence had another fight with Edith, and they may file for divorce. Big goddamn deal, that's nothing new. Grandmother's stomach ulcers bother her a lot. Daddy bought a new Hereford bull . . . that's more interesting.

Dan pulled a beer from the ice chest and walked to the

cubicle called the "officer's quarters." He flung himself on his cot, and tore open the blue envelope:

April 30, 1969
Austin

Dan,

You flew away two days ago and I have no idea where you'll be when you read this letter. But I pray that you're somewhere . . . well, as safe as possible.

First, about Mother and Daddy. They know, of course, but, honey, they won't *dare* ask where I stayed that last night in Dallas—not while I'm in this mood.

Now, I'm sorry that my first letter to My Man Serving His Country isn't a classic love letter. But it *is*—in a way you probably won't understand. I have to write what's happening in my head. Tell me I'm wrong, Dan (if I am, but I don't think so).

Dan, I *know* the army sent you to Vietnam—but I also know something that's a thousand times harder for a woman to accept. *You wanted to go.*

Like when you requested infantry. With your M.S. degree, you could have been commissioned in the finance corps, or medical services. But no, *Daniel Bridges had to be macho infantry*.

You proposed to me—sort of—during your Christmas leave last year. You wanted to marry and start a home, a family. But it wouldn't be fair to *me*, because you'd probably get orders to Vietnam, and I shouldn't be a "waiting wife" before I'd really been a wife.

You tried to get your orders changed. I suppose you made a halfhearted attempt. *You* may even believe you really tried. But a woman knows *some* things.

I guess I must accept all of that. I have little choice, *do* I, if I really want you?

Dan, I'll probably be available when you return—if *you* still want *me*. And vice versa.

But I'll always wonder—am I less exciting than Vietnam? (For *your* sake, baby, you'd better hope I'm less dangerous.)

It's tough competition, Dan, to be jealous of a war.

This letter may sound like I'm feeling sorry for myself. Maybe I am. But I'm terribly afraid that I'll lose you.

I could lose you in the *obvious* way, like Joan Bernstein lost her Richard. Have you ever thought, my dear Daniel, that *you* are flesh and bone like Richard . . . like Richard *was*, and *you could be killed* over there? Just like—how many are dying now? A hundred or a hundred and fifty American soldiers a week? And for what, Dan?

Most of those poor GIs, like you, probably thought they could never die.

But *every* woman who has a man at war shares that fear. What haunts me is a different type of fear . . . an instinctive fear . . . that I'll lose you in another way. It's a horrible way that comes in my dreams.

I can't explain, because I don't understand it myself. I'm really not afraid—not *too* afraid—of losing you to another woman. I have a (naive, perhaps?) faith that God, or someone or something, meant us to be together.

On a less romantic, but more practical side, I doubt that you'll meet another woman who has what I can offer. I may not be Raquel Welch, but I'm intelligent, and I can be more than your lover and, later, mother of another generation of horrible, roughshod Bridges boys.

I can talk with you seriously, share life as your partner, understand your problems and make them mine.

There aren't many women, Dan, who can hold you intellectually. You know what's waiting, in Texas.

So how can I explain my (irrational?) fears? Let me try. I wake at dawn dreaming about a "big woman," a real bitch who is stronger, and far more sensual (to you) than me.

That Big Woman doesn't exist, so I can't even compete with her. But she's there.

I tell myself that you're a man, but not a cheating man. But I know that you're ready for that awful Big Woman. And I sense that once a man crawls into her bed, she'll never let him go.

That Big Woman, Dan, is that goddamn Asian war. I think, I fear that you're already obsessed with her—and I despise that Bitch like I've never hated a *real woman*!

I've said too much, so I'll close and mail this before I change my mind. Take care of yourself, my Dan, in a war where you arranged your own invitation, a party that,

I think, you could have skipped. My next letter will be
nicer, I promise.

I love you, more than you know,
Janice

P.S. Do you understand? I had to write this letter because
I care for you so much. *Do you?* My words may seem
harsh, but they're truly how I feel. I send you love and
prayers from by the Trinity River.

Dan crumpled, then tried to smooth the letter. I *know* how
Janice feels about the war, so why did she bring it up
again—and in her first damned letter? He stored the letter in
a tray of his footlocker to read again . . . maybe.

Dan pulled a slim folder of photos from the footlocker.
The first shot was a close-up of Janice peering with green
eyes through the plastic photo holder. He flipped to another
photo, of Janice in a yellow halter and Bermuda shorts, lying on a giant white towel spread over the grass. I took that
shot thirteen months ago, Dan thought. His mind drifted
back to the lake, on that last sunny April afternoon before he
left for Fort Benning.

"Let's swim," Janice said. She stretched, then her hands
darted behind her back, and her halter fell away. A band of
white skin highlighted her breasts against a suntan.

"Janice! This is a *public lake!*"

"No one's around!" Janice stood, unsnapped her bermuda
shorts, and let them drop.

Janice pretends to be so straight, but she's all woman—
and knows it.

Dan's mind flashed back to the letter. How can Janice
think I could get caught up in this senseless shit? I've already seen enough to know I want to stay alive for a year,
then forget about Nuoc Trong and Chuong Thien Province.
Forever. And how do I answer this crap about the "Big
Woman"?

"Damn!" Dan bent the can double, and returned to the radio room. The smell of Enrique's spices frying on the oil
burner filled the room as he opened another beer. That reminded him of South Texas . . . and Janice.

She's a wonderful girl, Dan thought, *but she didn't have
to write that letter.*

Dan never responded to the hard parts of Janice's first letter, and he knew why. *Maybe Janice was right.*

That was one of the few chapters of my novel that Susan had read. I'd shown it to her because . . . I thought I *should*. My wife scribbled a few notes in the margin, and handed the chapter back.

"I felt that way," Susan said. "But *I* would have written a better letter."

Transition 11

Hanoi, 1988

A soft click of bicycles wakes me at 6:30 A.M. Hanoi is bustling, and my windows are wide open, but a city with few cars and trucks generates little sound. The air conditioner hasn't worked for years, and the ceiling fan quit spinning in the night. There isn't even that subliminal buzz of electricity, somewhere.

There's still no water, so I can't bathe. I shave with lukewarm drinking water from a wine bottle from the French days, then go downstairs.

No one in the restaurant understands my order. Then I say *cafe sua*, and the waitress brings a pyrex glass of coffee blended with sweetened canned cream.

At 7:30, Mrs. Le Thi Binh, from Agricultural Publishing House, arrives in a twenty-year-old Soviet Volga. We're driven to the huge Ba Dinh square, dominated by a six-floored edifice of granite.

The procedure is much like my two visits to the Mao Tsetung mausoleum in Beijing's Tiananmenn Square. A government guide moves the half-dozen foreigners to the front of an incredibly long line, mostly schoolgirls in blue-and-white uniforms.

An honor guard goose-steps to the mausoleum, where soldiers place a wreath of flowers before a granite slab. We follow in a silent column of two's. Guards search handbags for hidden cameras at the entrance, and even make me open my wallet. Then we file up cold marble stairs.

Vietnamese soldiers flank the sepulchre, holding Chinese SKS rifles in stiff salute.

The body is waxen, but anyone would recognize the frail face, wispy beard, and simple gray tunic. For three decades, this revolutionary defied French, Japanese, and U.S. armies to unify Vietnam.

Two flags, the bright red of fresh blood, drape the embalmed body of Ho Chi Minh. One is the Communist Party flag, with hammer and sickle. The other is the flag of the Socialist Republic of Vietnam, with its five-pointed yellow star.

To me, a third flag should be there. Legions of brave and brutal Viet Cong guerrillas rallied and were slaughtered for Uncle Ho in South Vietnam under a blue and red banner, with a bright yellow star. A lot of my friends died in that carnage, fighting against what that flag symbolized. Why do I feel almost . . . *insulted* . . . by the absence of the flag of *Mat Trang*, the National Liberation Front?

Every American of my generation remembers exactly where he first learned of President John F. Kennedy's assassination. I also remember 4 September 1969. It was after a lavish lunch that a cattle trader in Long My gave for Ming, the Chuong Thien agricultural chief, and me. The main course was Martell—French cognac—but we also had eel, fresh shrimps cooked with chilis and whole garlic cloves, and pickled duck eggs. I later learned that Ming was selling certificates that allowed our host to ship cattle to Saigon without health inspection.

The lunch lasted until the Martell ran out at 3:00 P.M. We then stopped at the plank hut that quartered the MAC-V team of army advisers for Long My District. Sergeant First Class Walker, a friend whom a mine blast would kill later that year, had just heard a chilling announcement over Armed Forces Vietnam Radio. Ho Chi Minh had died on 3 September—the day before.

This means trouble, I thought. The U.S. and South Vietnamese agreement to Hanoi's call for a temporary cease-fire didn't reassure me.

We set out on the fifteen-kilometer drive to Vi Thanh. I realized that the left rear tire on my Scout was low, a few klicks out of Long My. I was nervous as we stopped to change tires—and scared, when we saw that the spare was flat.

The Scout was pulling left as we drove through Indian country, the stretch of road a VC sniper used for target practice. The Vi Thanh we had left that morning was grim and dismal, but the village looked lovely when we finally clanked in on a wheel rim.

U.S. PsyOps units printed and dropped millions of leaflets that day. One side was a black-bordered portrait of Ho Chi Minh. The other simply announced his death, and the cease-fire.

But the VC honored only truces that worked to their advantage. Vi Thanh was mortared heavily that night, and a VC squad entered the burning village to kidnap Duc, the head of our security forces.

In 1988, the Communist party finally admitted that Ho Chi Minh had actually died a few days before its announcement, but on an inauspicious date. The Party held back the death notice until 3 September. Vietnamese think that way.

This fiery little man once fought with Americans against a common enemy, I thought, standing by Ho Chi Minh. OSS officers who parachuted into the rain forests of the Tonkin Delta in World War II found Ho's Viet Minh the only resistance fighters who were serious about killing Japanese.

The Viet Minh helped American flyers, shot down over Indochina, reach U.S. lines. An OSS medic even nursed a malaria-wracked Ho back to health in a Tonkinese guerrilla camp.

Ho drafted Vietnam's Declaration of Independence, copying its opening words from the Declaration he admired most. He read "All men are created equal" to thousands in Hanoi in 1945, as the Japanese were signing unconditional surrender aboard the battleship USS *Missouri*. To Ho, America was the only world power that could pressure France to give up its colonial rule of Indochina. He even called on President Harry Truman to make Vietnam an interim U.S. protectorate before full independence.

Did it have to end like it did?

We leave the mausoleum, and Mrs. Binh takes me to a nearby park. There, we visit the austere two-room cottage where Ho lived and worked throughout his presidency. A portable typewriter and a copy of *The Making of a Quagmire*, by David Halberstam, sit on a desk by his bed.

Nearby, bulldozers are pushing earth and cranes lift blocks of stone. There's not much construction in Hanoi, so I ask what's happening. The government is building a new mausoleum, a multimillion-dollar national shrine to honor, forever, the remains of the Father of Vietnam. I look back at the simple cottage, and wonder how Uncle Ho would feel about that.

That afternoon, we drive through the rustic North Vietnamese countryside. The rice crop looks remarkably good, for a country that projects a rice deficit of 1.5 million tons in 1988, and is appealing to the world for food aid, mostly rice.

I kill time by reading and editing Bruce McAllister's *Dream Baby*. The novelist had offered me three-hundred-dollars to review his manuscript, but I turned the money down. I might want a favor from an author with connections, someday. Besides, the novel's plot fascinated me.

· It was based on actual CIA experiments with psychics during the war. In the novel, the spooks put together a special team, led by a Green Beret captain and a lieutenant, with an army nurse and a South Vietnamese major who was fluent in Russian. All had *talents*, or *gifts*—psychic powers. The captain saw danger in blue, the lieutenant could leave and hover over his body during combat, the nurse saw the deaths of living men through her dreams.

The team was traveling through North Vietnam, disguised as Russian agricultural advisers, with a string of pack horses carrying two tons of C-4 *plastique* explosive in bags marked *IR8*. Their cover was bringing new rice seeds—bought in the Philippines—for distribution to farmers in the Red River Delta. But their mission was to blow the dikes that hold back the Red River. Twenty million gallons of muddy water would move at $\frac{1}{16}$ the speed of a .45 bullet to flood Hanoi—and end the war.

That's why McAllister had written to IRRI in 1987, wanting to know the role that *rice* played in the war.

Water buffalo stand in deep ponds, only their eyes and noses above water, at the entrance to the Dan Phuong Cooperative, twenty-two kilometers west of Hanoi. The People's Committee chairman greets us, and introduces a delegation of local farmers.

I'm briefed in an ancient Buddhist temple that doubles as the communal meeting hall and library. I present copies of *Field Problems of Tropical Rice*, in Vietnamese, to the chairman.

Farmers in this cooperative still grow IR8. That surprises me. Aren't newer IRRI seeds, with insect and disease resistance, available? Yes, but farmers here claim that none yield as much as the hardy variety that introduced me to rice. They expect to harvest a bumper crop this season: 6.5 tons per hectare.

The chairman adds that the village militia shot down a U.S. F-4 Phantom during the war. Dan Phuong's final claim to fame: actress Jane Fonda visited here during her 1968 propaganda tour of North Vietnam.

The briefing ends and the chairman asks if I, as an IRRI scientist, have any advice or comments. I'm tempted to say a few words about Jane Fonda, but instead I open a discussion on the good and bad traits of IR8.

At Hanoi's outskirts, we park by a checkpoint while Mrs. Binh returns the visa that authorized me to travel outside the city, to a soldier.

A girl crashes her bicycle into the back of the Volga—that's strange. She spends a lot of time inspecting her bicycle *behind our car*. I don't like it—my instinct says *Get the hell out of this car, it could blow!* But this is Hanoi in 1988, so I sit tight.

As we drive away I realize: Hargrove, you're a hell of a lot less cool than you think.

I *must* do one more thing on this last day in Hanoi.

"Can we stop at the Red River dikes, before returning to the hotel?"

Mrs. Binh agrees, but doesn't seem pleased. Nor had she liked the questions I'd asked about the Red Dikes, over the past three days.

We pass the rail yards and cross the Red River on the Paul Doumer Bridge. Both were key targets of B-52s and F-105 Thunderchiefs during the war, especially during Operation LINE-BACKER, which was dubbed the "Christmas Bombing of 1972."

The three-thousand kilometer of dikes took twenty-five years to build, a century ago. They're about fifty feet wide and thirty feet high. I carry the *Dream Baby* manuscript and walk a few hundred feet along the dikes, then return to the car. I hope that will be a good omen for McAllister's book. I'd like to take a good photo for Bruce, but decide against it. Mrs. Binh doesn't like my interest in those strategic Red Dikes.

CHAPTER XIX
Christmas Bells, the Clanging Chimes of Doom *or* A Star in the East

Christmas 1989, Los Baños, Philippines. Christmas 1969, Vi Thanh and the fictional Nuoc Trong village, Chuong Thien Province

The boys were sixteen and seventeen on Christmas morning, 1989. Susan and I were glad that they'd finally outgrown dragging us from bed before dawn to rush down and see what's under the tree, like on so many Christmases past. The Hargrove family slept until nine.

I had worked on the book all Christmas Eve, but left my computer when IRRI friends—the Lampes, Neues, Nunns, and LaRue Pollard—arrived.

We had a lot to be thankful for, good friends and health, plenty of food, that Christmas Eve. We dined American-style, and didn't finish even one of the two Butterball turkeys stuffed with southern corn-bread dressing. We also had dishes of giblet gravy, cranberry sauce, candied yams, and mashed potatoes instead of our usual rice.

Our Christmas feast didn't *embarrass* me, but it was a sober reminder that hundreds of millions didn't have even enough *rice* to eat that Holy Night—and that we few rice scientists had the opportunity *(or obligation?)* to change that.

A few days before, my IRRI Communication and Publications Department had shared a Filipino Christmas feast: *lechon*, a whole roasted pig; grilled fish; *pancit*, a dish of noodles, shrimp, and vegetables; and of course, rice.

I'd read about rampant anti-Americanism—but experienced little of it in my seventeen years in the Philippines. Politicians are the problem, like everywhere. True, we were always foreigners, but in a friendly land where we enjoyed wonderful camaraderie at work, and Filipino hospitality in our daily lives.

We expatriates sat back after dinner over coffee, champagne, pumpkin pie, and chocolate cake with fudge icing and whipped cream. Then Susan put leftovers away while Diding and Mila washed dishes. At midnight Uli Neue, a German soil scientist, and I finally drove the maids to their barrio in Los Baños, where they'd spend Christmas with family and friends.

Our two maids and gardener, plus a driver three days a week, might seem extravagant, even exploitative . . . if you've never lived in the Third World. But hiring servants is more than a luxury in the Philippines. It's expected—almost a moral obligation for anyone who earns a middle-level North American or European salary, or even a third of that. From 20 to 40 percent of the Philippine labor force is jobless, and millions work for a dollar a day. The population is growing at a steady yearly rate of 3 percent. Yet the Catholic Church fights— vehemently—any serious government programs to control the birth rate.

Our maids are also security. Our home had been robbed twice in the past three months. The first robbery took the family's new video-8 system. In the next break-in, Susan lost her jewelry, mostly pieces that her father had given her as a girl in the Middle East—plus our *replacement* video-8.

The Hargrove family sat around the tree and opened presents on Christmas morning. The kids got more than they needed, but nothing special. Then came the surprise.

At 10:30 A.M., Ernie and Jean Nunn walked up the hill to our home, rolling two shiny Yamaha 80cc motorbikes that we'd hidden in their guestroom. One was red; the other, blue.

Tom G and Miles instantly changed from teenagers to excited little kids . . . Christmases past.

As the kids revved the bikes and barreled off on their first rides, I read the *Manila Bulletin*.

The news wasn't good. Could eighty thousand men and women *really* have died in Romania? The world seems to think that the fall of Eastern European communism will lead to a unified Europe ... but it might lead to a late twentieth-century feudal period, where each religious, geographic, and ethnic group fights for its own piece of the action.

The Panama invasion concerned me more, especially coming within a few days of the sixth coup attempt in Manila since the nonviolent "Peoples' Power" revolution ousted Marcos and swept President Corazon Aquino into Malacañang Palace in 1986.

Elite of the Philippine officers' corps led the December coup of 1989, and their compadres put the mutiny down. Leaders of both sides were from a military oligarchy, fellow graduates of the Philippine Military Academy, patterned after West Point. PMA instilled into its graduates the best—and worst—of military traditions. I understood both. PMA cadets lived a lot like Texas Aggies.

Much of the five-day battle for Manila was fought in luxury hotels and office buildings of Makati, the financial district. The coup attempt would cut Philippine tourism by 50 percent in 1990.

Filipino soldiers must be the world's best marksmen, I thought. What other army could shoot millions of bullets during a failed mutiny—yet kill only seventy-nine of their friends, loyal and rebel?

On the afternoon of 1 December—Day 1 of the coup attempt—Philippine Air Force F-5s blew away the rebel troops' fleet of three aircraft: a single Sikorsky helicopter gunship and two World War II T-34s that PAF pilots call *Tora-Toras*—from the 1941 Japanese command to launch dive bombers against Pearl Harbor.

But U.S. Air Force F-4 Phantoms from Clark Field flew cover for the Philippine jets, turning the tide against the rebel troops.

The American Embassy assured the world that its F-4s flew only for psychological support, and the U.S. pilots never pulled a trigger. I believed, and hoped, that was true.

Three weeks later, officials of President Aquino's government had resumed their angry attacks on the U.S. for having

Clark Field and Subic Naval Base on sovereign Philippine soil.
I understood, and basically agreed with their position.

But one thing seemed ironic: *Cory sure as hell didn't find
U.S. air support an insult to national dignity on 1 December*.

Now we've sent twenty thousand American soldiers to bring
democracy to a corrupt banana republic in Central America?
I'd been down that road before . . .

Susan had given our maids Christmas Day off, so we four
Hargroves had the house to ourselves. Not having help at
lunch and dinner frustrates me, because *the maids really* own
our kitchen. I love to cook, in the States, but the Hargrove
kitchen in the Philippines is an unknown jungle. I often can't
even find pans and spices. But exploring the kitchen gives Susan a rare sense of independence.

I wrote from 11:00 A.M. until noon, then ate a quick lunch
of warmed-over turkey and dressing. I knew that returning to
my computer would irritate Susan . . . but I *had* to finish the
book.

Writing about Vietnam on Christmas 1989 made me think of
another Christmas past. I was tempted—but I'd sworn not to
jump ahead of my story again. I'd avoid the trap I wrote myself into in 1971–72, when I raced forward too fast.

My new strategy was to consolidate two stories—nonfiction
and fiction—into one. I wasn't sure I could do it, and I hadn't
yet reached Christmas of 1969 in the nonfiction that I was
writing for Owen Lock.

But today seemed the *right* time to review my Christmas of
twenty years ago. First, I skimmed diary entries of Christmas
week, 1969:

22 December 1969. Almost Christmas, but doesn't seem like
it. Susan is flying to West Texas to spend the holidays with
relatives. I guess my gift and the flowers that I wired
through the Can Tho PX will wait in SF till she gets back.
Hope the flowers don't wilt.

Last night at the Delta Lily, Norm Olsen talked about an in-
credible man who's made quite a reputation in the Delta:
Derrick King, a large, moustached Australian. John
Lippincott had also told stories about King, back at Ft.
Bragg. King advises and goes into VC areas with APTs,
Armed Propaganda Teams. He pins white, printed cards to

the shirts of dead VC: "This man would be alive today, if he had *Chieu Hoi'*d."

I'm in Vi Thanh tonight, because of this damn TOC duty. But I sent Khang to Long Binh with the agr. cadre to vaccinate water buffalo.

We immunized 103 buffalo in Vinh Truong, and another 115 in Hoa An, against rinderpest disease last week. Also, 100 hogs in VT for hog cholera the week before. We walk along the canals, asking each farmer if he wants his animals vaccinated. We vaccinated all the animals from Vinh Truong to Hoa An. Troops won't go into that area, except as armed units, but we've had no trouble.

Several farmers down south, in Kien Long District, have made a spontaneous complaint to me. They are afraid to work their fields because U.S. choppers gun down anything or anyone in that area: men, water buffalo, houses. The farmers said that about 400 buffalo had died of disease in the past 2–3 months—but choppers shot another 200 buffalo. Maybe they're lying, but I doubt it. These farmers didn't ask for money—just would I please ask the U.S. military to quit shooting them and their buffalo?

I asked the farmers if the VC harass them. The answer was no, but they don't like paying VC taxes. I didn't ask if the VC drafts their sons. They do, of course, but so does GVN.

One American was killed, and 3 wounded, this morning at the Vi Thanh air strip. A charge with C-4 plastic explosive went off when they put the fuse in.

The idea of a hamlet-to-hamlet vaccination program probably won't work here, not with the quality of our local ag cadre. I want to make livestock vaccination purely commercial, where one good man in each village charges to vaccinate his neighbors' animals, for a profit.

A gruesome sight at the Vi Thanh air strip yesterday, but one I'm getting used to: 14 wounded and 6 dead VN soldiers from the 21st ARVN Div came in from the U-Minh

Forest. They were piled in the Hueys like logwood. One ARVN soldier, shot in the chest but still alive, lay on a stack of corpses, resting his head on a dead soldier's feet. A free-lance French photographer was there, and rushed up to get some bizarre shots. That's his job. People at home *should* see photos like that, and the scene isn't atypical—but I felt angry when he ran to the choppers with his camera as men were unloading their wounded and dead friends.

Ran a test on the 170 kg of grain sorghum seed that I bought in Can Tho. Only 23% germination—they claimed that 60% of those seeds would sprout. Maybe the germination rate was high before, but sorghum seeds lose viability fast in the tropics.

Returned today from the Cahn Dinh Canal in Kien Long, SE of the district town. My Land Reform cadre are making remarkable progress there. One LR team has set up a mobile land redistribution center in a palm-thatch hut along the canal SW of KL district town. That's several km past the last SVN outpost, and in VC country, but we've issued dozens of GVN titles to former French plantation land.

Amazing . . . why do the VC let those farmers take land titles from Saigon? Either: 1) the VC in Kien Long aren't as strong as we think (that's not likely), 2) the farmers don't think the VC will learn they've applied for land (less likely), or 3) the Communists like our land redistribution, because the package includes loans, funded by the U.S. Government, to increase production on land they consider theirs. The additional rice will also help feed VC troops, of course. Chuong Thien now has the second-highest rate of land redistribution among the 16 provinces in the Mekong Delta. I'm proud of that, as adviser to the Land to the Tiller program. Especially considering that we hover at the bottom of the list, in all of VN, in security.

Thank God we're not with those poor bastards in An Xuyen, just to our south. Its capital, Ca Mau, is nicer and safer than Vi Thanh. But An Xuyen Province is always rated *last* in security.

It's now 3 a.m., 23 Dec. I'm still on TOC duty, and can't go to sleep. Only 2 VC sightings tonight, both here in Duc Long District. MAT 54 reported 150 VC to its north. Another 50 VC were spotted outside of Vi Thanh. We pulled artillery on both units.

Binh, that fine, diplomatic Land Reform engineer, left us a couple of weeks ago. I knew something would happen to the obnoxious bastard. The exact circumstances are vague, but it's about Binh and a GVN official's wife. Binh claimed that *she* seduced *him*, and that the accuser was sleeping with her too. I'm not going to miss Binh, nor is *anyone* in the province. But I must admit, he *did* know how to organize. He did more than any three other GVN officials. That's why I haven't clobbered the fool.

But we haven't heard the last of our man Binh yet, as Lloyd Craig and Harlan Grosz said.[1] He was vice-president of the University of Saigon student body during the anti-U.S. riots. One night when Binh was drunk, he told how he helped organize and lead the riots. His best friend was student body president—but is now the VC vice-minister for education. I think Binh told me that as a threat. He does nothing without a reason. Binh would fit into a radical, fanatic organization like the NLF, or VC, better than he fits in GVN. Binh will probably be an important man in this country, someday—unless someone shoots him first.

I like and respect CPT Harvey Weiner, Phoenix adviser. He's an interesting fellow from the East Coast, has a law degree from Columbia, then got another degree from the London School of Economics. Harvey is miserable in Nam, he's definitely not the killer type—misses London, the opera, etc. Naturally, the Army put this peace-loving soul, who hates the Army even more than I do, into the seamiest, most sordid job over here. It's almost funny.

Harvey jokes a lot about his work. Today, I went to the Phoenix office. Harvey probably saw me coming because, as

---

[1] A U.S. civilian adviser to the Land Reform program, working out of Saigon, and a good friend.

I walked in, he was counting out a stack of piasters to his VN interpreter. "That was an excellent assassination. I'll use you for my next killing. Only next time—try not to leave so many survivors, OK? Oh, hi, Tom!"

From the newspaper clippings that Susan and Mother send, the Song My Massacre must be the Stateside story of the year.[2] 1LT William Calley will probably have more influence in forcing U.S. troops out of VN than Ho Chi Minh. Conservatives are yelling "The media and war protesters are trying to undermine the U.S. military." But I agree with Frank Gillespie: "The U.S. military is doing a pretty good job of destroying itself."

I'm not sorry to see the publicity. Too many soldiers have been given too much power over here, with too little control. Maybe this [My Lai] incident will stop some of it—like those choppers gunning down buffalo in Kien Long.

But something bothers me. How can we prosecute Lt. Calley, when hundreds of 19-year-old Cobra pilots, and our B-52s, kill so many innocent civilians from the air, daily and routinely?

I've personally called, *or at least paralleled and legitimized*, so much artillery fire, and so many air strikes on targets that ARVN reports as VC. Those explosives have killed far more Vietnamese civilians than Lt. Calley's men wasted, that tragic day in Song My.

But a man must draw a line. Calley's men murdered old men, women, children in cold blood, and he was responsible. You can't rationalize that. Lt. Calley's actions will haunt America.

Most U.S. advisers who work with the Vietnamese daily are sickened by Calley's actions. But "regular" American soldiers may feel differently.

Christmas Day, 1990. Vaccinating water buffalo and calling artillery . . . agricultural development and murder from the air

---

[2] Later called the My Lai Massacre.

of farmers and the buffalo they depend on for survival. Do those words of two decades ago hint at emotional problems that would follow?

Maybe not. *Maybe it was all okay* back then; and the *heavy* trip began in 1977. If so, *why did I erase the diary from my memory?*

I then found the fiction I'd written about Christmas Eve. I created some of that chapter from imagination, but most from memories of MATs in Chuong Thien, and of that holiest of nights in an unholy 1969:

Chapter (?)

Cease-fire. Christmas Eve, 1969.

The men of MAT 96 started their Christmas party at 5:00 P.M. by opening an "imperial quart"—a one-liter bottle—of Old Crow and loading Christmas cassettes onto Sp.4 Bob Saunders's stereo deck. They should have unwound by 6:00 P.M., but hadn't.

"Let's have us a little snort for the Meskin ... imagine ol' Enriq' gettin' R & R in Bangkok for Christmas." Sergeant Joe Culver poured bourbon into four plastic cups, then added Coke to three.

"No more of that shit for me, it fucks up your consciousness," Saunders said, pushing his cup back to Culver.

Dan and Joe Culver ignored the radio operator. "I'll drink to Enrique," Dan said.

"I'll drink to *anything*, tonight," Culver said, chasing his straight bourbon from a beer can. "Goddamn lucky little fat-ass Enrique, fuckin' them Thai dollies like a rabbit while we spend Christmas Eve in Nuoc Trong."

Elvis crooned:

I'll have a blue Christmas without you ...[3]

"Back in the *Old Army* we used to say 'Go to Bangkok, then die ... 'cause you'll never live again,' " Culver reminisced.

[3] "Blue Christmas." Jay N. Johnson and Billy Hayes. Recorded by Elvis Presley.

"Think about it," Saunders said. "Almost two thousand years ago . . ."

"Yeah," Culver said. "It was one thousand nine hundred and sixty-nine years ago tonight."

"Actually, it was nine months earlier," Saunders said, "when God knocked up that nice Jewish girl—and the world's never forgotten it."

Dan laughed, then saw veins bulge on Culver's neck.

"That ain't funny, Saunders! Don't you *never* joke about Christmas like that. You tell that kinda cheap crap again, I'll kick your scrawny ass so hard you'll have to take off your fatigue jacket to shit!"

"Don't be so uptight, Joe," Dan said. "Bob didn't mean anything."

"Yeah, Sarge, lay off."

"*You* knock that crap off too, Bob," Dan said quietly. Trouble could come easily tonight.

"Aw, both of you are prob'ly right," Sergeant Culver said, splashing the bourbon he'd poured for Saunders into his own cup. "It's just that we oughta be home with our families on Christmas Eve, instead of gettin' fucked up in gook country."

"Where were you last Christmas Eve?" Dan asked.

"At my mother-in-law's farm in Georgia," Culver said. "The ol' lady and me sat and watched logs burn in the fireplace, sippin' her mama's eggnog. Later on, we snuck out and put Santa Claus's presents for little Joey, my grandkid, under the tree.

"I think Joey had already figgered out there ain't no Santa Claus. But it don't hurt to pretend."

Christmas Eve, 1968, Dan thought . . . right after my orders came. An electric and emotional time of . . . fear, love, pride, guilt, sex . . . part of the package was an instinctual, animal excitement of realizing that it could be my *last* Christmas, and wondering where I'd be a year later.

Well, here I am. At the end of the line, an infantry lieutenant commanding a MAT team—and who the hell back home knows what a *MAT team* is?—of two sergeants and a draftee hippie. We're in a village no one has heard of, in Chuong Thien, a province that few know exists. Trying to mold forty Vietnamese farmers into Commie killers, when

20 percent of the PF unit probably sympathizes with the VC, and the rest don't care who's in control, as long as they can plant their rice. Those troops are commanded by a fanatic and vengeful man whose purpose in life—what life the VC have left him—is to kill more VC. The chief does a good job, but as brutally as *them*.

This is my strangest and most screwed-up Christmas Eve. But last Christmas was special . . .

Dan's last stop before leaving Fort Sill, Oklahoma, for 1968 Christmas leave was to sign out at the orderly room. The thick sheaf of papers in his in-box surprised him—but not really. His first thought was, do I *have* to yell *Figmo*? That's so damn corny . . . yeah, the soldiers expect it.

Dan shrugged and shouted "Figmo!" self-consciously, and just loud enough for the troops in the orderly room to hear that standard announcement: *"Fuck! I got my orders."*

He then drove straight to the Rio Grande Valley on his first leave since reporting, eight months ago, to the Infantry Officers Basic Course at Fort Benning. The Fort Sill assignment, as an infantry training officer, came after IOBC. Now he was going home!

Dan stopped only once: for a noon hamburger at a truck stop north of Dallas. He called Janice, home for the holidays from the University of Texas, from a pay phone. But Dan didn't mention his orders.

"Dan . . ." Janice ran to the driveway before he killed the motor in front of her parents' Spanish-style home in McAllen.

They hugged, and laughed. Dan held Janice at arm's length as a fiery sun disappeared behind a flat Texas horizon.

"UT has been good for you . . . you've never looked greater." Dan meant it. "You've changed your hair."

"The Joan Baez look? A lot of us wear our hair straight. It's practical—and says that we oppose racism, the war . . ."

How do I handle this? Dan thought.

"Janice, I'd better tell you now. My orders came this morning. I ship out from Travis Air Force Base on 19 April."

"No . . . you said you wouldn't have to go."

"I was wrong. I'm assigned to MAC-V, that's the Military

Assistance Command, Vietnam. I'll be an adviser to Vietnamese troops. That's all I know."

Janice turned, placed both hands on her hips, and stared at the sun's last rays. She then whirled. "You *volunteered* . . . I know you did. *Didn't you?*"

Dan locked her eyes. "No, Janice. I did *not* volunteer, and I don't *want* to go. But that big army computer finally caught my number."

"Maybe you didn't exactly *volunteer*, Daniel Bridges, I don't know. But I *doubt* that you tried to avoid it . . . even though you said you would.

"*I* feel strongly about American intervention to support a corrupt government in a civil war ten thousand miles from our shore. I *thought* you felt that way too."

"*Where you been*, Lieutenant?" Joe Culver said. "I poured you two fingers of Black Bird five minutes ago, but you keep starin' at the wall."

"And *I've* been explaining how we've gotta end the war to Sergeant Culver," Saunders said. "We have to redirect our emotions, our talents. We have to fight for *peace.*"

"Fightin' for peace is like fuckin' for chastity," Culver said. "There's only one solution to the Vietnam problem. First, you put all the *good* Vietnamese on a ship, and sail it four hundred miles out to sea. Then you nuke the country, and wipe out every livin' thing, from north to south.

"Then, you nuke the ship."

Dan sipped the Old Crow and tried to joke with his men. But he soon drifted back to South Texas . . .

"Be macho—go off to war," Janice had said.

"*But don't give me that bullshit about how you don't want to go,*" she said hotly. How do I handle this, Dan thought. He felt awfully uncomfortable.

"Dan, *I'm so afraid that you'll die over there.*"

"No, I won't."

"Can we cut a deal?" Janice was making a declaration, not a proposal.

"Don't talk about the war, and I won't say one damned word about how I feel about it. We'll live like there's no tomorrow for the next two weeks. Then what happens, will happen."

Dan held Janice and said that he loved and would always

want her, and a year wasn't so long. He hated to leave her, but had no choice.

But Dan knew, no matter how strongly he denied it to Janice or to himself, that he *wanted* those depressing orders to fight for a lost cause. That also made Dan feel *proud*? He knew that made no sense, and that Janice could *never* understand. That made him feel . . . *distant* from her. Like he had a secret, one he'd like to share but couldn't.

On Christmas Eve, a week later, Dan and Janice went to a BYOB party at Brent and Carolyn Zeigler's. The ex-fullback for the 1964 McAllen Bulldogs had, predictably, married the head cheerleader after graduation. Brent then finished a degree in physical education on a football scholarship at San Angelo State College.

Barely four years out of McAllen High School, the Zeiglers were back as solid citizens. Brent was now assistant coach of his former football team. Dan found it ironic that Zeigler also taught high school history. He had no sense of history, but that mattered little in McAllen, Texas. Football was far more important in molding the character of young people.

The Zeiglers made their three-year-old daughter the party's center of attention. Dan had to hold the newest Zeigler baby, and pretend he was cute.

Dan avoided the crowd around Coach Zeigler, teary-eyed when reminiscing about those glory days when the McAllen Bulldogs swept to bidistrict championship. Dan hated football, maybe because Texas tradition *forced* him to play.

He found himself talking to Joseph Medrano, his class valedictorian. Joe was now in graduate college at Rice University.

"You'll be in *Vietnam* in three months?" Medrano said. "That's unbelievable. And terrible. I don't know *anyone* over there."

"What about Danny McCombs? He got drafted last year. He's in the Central Highlands with the 25th Infantry."

"Yeah, but that dumb fucker McCombs couldn't have graduated from McAllen High School if he hadn't made Texas all-state tackle."

"And Frank Rodriguez?"

"Rodriguez got busted," Medrano said. "Judge Elliot gave him a choice. Enlist, or five years in Huntsville. The local cops were ready to make McAllen mighty uncomfortable for Rodriguez, if he fought the charge. He *was* selling dope, of course—to kids in junior high."

"I didn't like Frank either," Dan said. "But he's a Marine now, up by the DMZ."

"Rogriguez had a mean side. You remember how he loved to fight?" Medrano continued. "*That's* why he chose the Marines."

"What you're *really* saying, Joseph, is that *I'm* the only *upper middle–class college graduate* you know who'll go to Vietnam," Dan said, a little hotly. "The only one from *our* crowd.

"The rest of you will breed two kids, like Brent Zeigler, or get medical deferments, or go to grad school until . . ." Dan saw Janice sipping a glass of white wine and watching them from across the room.

"Let's change the subject. What will you do with a Ph.D. in . . . sociology?"

I don't really *resent* Medrano and the others, Dan thought. But I'm a reminder. *I make them uncomfortable!*

No one asked Dan and Janice to stay when they thanked the ex-fullback and cheerleader, and left the party early. Dan pulled his '62 Ford under the yellow lights of McAllen's Dairy Queen. He ordered two thirty-cent Cokes, and poured an inch from each cup onto the driveway. Dan refilled the cups with BYOB Old Charter—from the brown paper bag he'd taken to the party.

Janice sipped her drink and shuddered. The speakers blared rock and roll into the still Texas night as they tried to talk.

"Let's leave this awful damn place," Janice finally said.

Dan drove fast to the McAllen city limits, then turned onto a gravel road as Janice rubbed the inside of his thigh, then bit his ear. He wheeled onto a bumpy turnrow, then got out to open a barbed-wire gate to a Bridges family alfalfa field.

As the Ford bounced the last hundred yards to *their* parking place, Janice guided Dan's right hand under her skirt, along her thigh . . . until he touched nylon.

"Feel. I'm so hot, my pants are wet." She pressed against his hand.

Dan braked the car hard. They moved to the back seat and tore clothes away, then lay naked, exploring again.

Janice kissed across his chest, then bit at his stomach and teased with her tongue ... "Lieutenant? You keep driftin' away from us." Sergeant Joe Culver's voice jolted Dan back to Nuoc Trong. "We're talkin' about last Christmas Eve. What were *you* doin', a year ago tonight?"

"Me? I was home in South Texas with my family. Nothing exciting. How about you, Bob?"

"Last Christmas was fucking outstanding!" Specialist Saunders said. "We never left my bird's flat in L.A. Man, we had everything. Smooth sounds, sweet red wine, and Acapulco Gold. Wine and weed, that's how to spend Christmas Eve."

"One of *my* favorite Christmas Eve pleasures," Sergeant Culver said, pouring from the Old Crow, "is playin' stomp-ass with hippies."

What if that redneck sergeant decides to settle scores with our wimpy radio man tonight? Dan thought. Culver's pissed—*really* pissed—about catching Saunders smoking grass on duty. So am I, and Saunders deserves the ass-kicking Culver would deliver. But *I can't let that happen* on my team. *Not on Christmas Eve.*

The PRC-25 blared: "Eagle Foxtrot, Eagle Foxtrot, this is Eagle Delta. Over."

Saunders scowled, like he shouldn't be disturbed by radio transmissions during the Christmas holidays, then took the handset.

"This is Eagle Foxtrot. Over."

"Foxy-Boxy, stand up and stand by. The following traffic comes to you from the Delta Rats of Eagle Delta. Over."

The transmission was roughly to the tune of "It Came Upon A Midnight Clear":

> If I could shoot my rifle clear
> Away up in the sky
> Then I'd quit living on rice and beer
> And live on angel pie
> Piss on the earth, good kills to men ...

Drunken voices blended in poor harmony with radio static. The men of Eagle Delta—the radio code for Lt. Ben Hibino's MAT 103 in Long Tri—were as lonely as those of MAT 96. They were breaking strict radio procedures to cheer other MATs on this merriless Christmas.

"Can we sing something back?" Saunders asked.

"Why not?" Dan said. "What can the colonel do, if he learns. Send us to Nam?"

"How about 'Deck the Halls with VC Balls'?" Sergeant Culver suggested.

"No, that's an old one."

"Eagle Base, Eagle Base! This is Eagle Echo. Over." This metallic radio voice was different, and sounded urgent.

Eagle Base was the TOC in Vi Thanh. Eagle Echo was MAT 54, the "hard-luck team" in Hoa An, fifteen klicks southeast of Nuoc Trong. Its last two commanders, both U.S. lieutenants, had been killed last month, within three weeks of one another. Also, a U.S. sergeant and two Vietnamese interpreters.

"This is Eagle Base. Over," Vi Thanh answered.

"Dustoff request! Information follows. Emergency life or death. Do you read me? Over."

"Shit!" Sergeant Culver said. "It's not a Medevac." The *Dustoff* code meant the medical evacuation was for an *American*.

Maybe the VC are using this religious cease-fire to launch another mass attack, Dan thought. Like the Tet Offensive of '68.

The radio voice transmitted standard data from a medical-evacuation form.

"Priority One—Urgent, Operational. Civilian, male Caucasian. Identification of wounded personnel confirmed by a Uniform Sierra."

"The report *must* be for real, a U.S. adviser confirmed it," Dan said. "But what American civilian would be with MAT 54 tonight?"

The transmission continued: "Nature of injury: sucking chest wound . . ."

"Robert Cantwell . . . he's the only civilian crazy enough to spend Christmas Eve with MAT 54."

"Short, fat man in red suit with long white beard. Shot down with three elf support troops and eight deer. I repeat, eight tiny reindeer, one with red nose. All Kilo-India-Alpha. Repeat, all Killed In Action. Ordnance captured: one bag of toy AK-47s and one highly damaged airmobile sleigh, thought to be Soviet made."

The tension broke, and even Saunders laughed. Sergeant Culver slapped his back, and poured bourbon into his cup.

Dan was asleep by the radio at 2:00 A.M., when Bob Saunders stumbled to his cot.

"There's a star in the east!" he shouted, shaking Dan's shoulder. "A star in the east!"

Dan was confused, but lurched out the door behind Saunders.

A parachute flare flickered through blackness to the east, reflecting off the giant eye of Nuoc Trong's Cao Dai temple. A .30-caliber machine gun at the Popular Force outpost fired three short bursts, ricocheting red tracer bullets across the canal as another flare lit the night. But there was no return fire. It was probably a false alarm.

"Go to bed, Saunders."

"Yeah. Peace on earth, Lieutenant, and merry fucking Christmas."

Christmas Day, 1989. I remember, vaguely, calling a Dustoff chopper for Santa with a sucking chest wound . . . something like that. But weren't there *real* casualties on Christmas Eve? The VC never respected a cease-fire, not in Chuong Thien Province.

I reloaded my diary on my computer hard disc and word-searched for *Christmas* again:

Christmas Day, 1969
Well, it's Christmas Day, and I have TOC duty again. We had a huge Christmas meal at the MAC-V mess hall: shrimp cocktails, turkey and dressing, ham. It was a real morale builder.

As usual, we have a holiday truce. But Charley hit an outpost in Kien Long last night. No friendly casualties, but 2 VC KIA and one AK-47 captured. The Swingship took ground fire at 1330h from bunkers at WR355535, the abandoned French plantation in northern Kien Long. I authorized return fire and the Swingship's .30 calibers got one VC KBA.

At 1400h, Shotgun reported 47 men in bluish-gray uniforms

at WR386647. That's also French plantation land, where *only* Charley goes, in southern Kien Long.

KBA . . . I wasn't sure of the term, so I hit *word search* and found those initials four more times in my diary. Yes, it meant *killed by air*. Shotgun was the code for a single-engine Cessna observation plane, flown by army air corps pilots. Shotgun usually carried a forward air controller, or FAC, to call artillery or air strikes, and gather intelligence.

Norm Olsen, I remember, got mad when he learned that I'd authorized a Huey to return fire during a cease-fire—even though we got a KBA.

I'd written "Charley," the standard slang for Viet Cong, for those forty-seven enemy soldiers in Kien Long. But their bluish-gray uniforms could only mean *NVA,* regulars of the North Vietnamese Army that had entered Chuong Thien Province a few months before.

I have little confidence in cease-fires since the VC ambushed an RD team in front of Norm and me near Long Tri during the truce after Ho Chi Minh's death.

We began our Christmas Eve party in the Delta Lily at 6:30 last night. Had turkey, canned ham. Maybe forty CORDS, MAC-V, OSA, and VN employees. SFC Billy Dewey, a black "ordained Baptist minister," refused to give the predinner prayer "because it's not right to pray where alcoholic beverages are served." That's funny. Billy was at the CORDS compound, dog-drunk, last week. The Delta Lily party broke up around nine, when the VN who are Catholics went to mass. That's when we all piled into the OSA jeep: Harvey Weiner, Paul Marion, Willie Wilson, Harry (I don't know his last name, but he's CIA), and Dennis Depries. We drove to TOC to harass 1st Lt. Gene Griffiths, the S-5 or civil affairs adviser, who had TOC duty. We raised hell, sang Christmas carols over the radio net.

Harvey Weiner sent a radio message, supposedly to Phoenix operatives:

Proceed to eliminate VCI suspect. Description: short male

Caucasian, heavily built, with white whiskers. Confiscate sleigh, OD Model M6161/70, and all VC toys.

Then back into Vi Thanh, where we watched floats in the Catholic procession. Then over to the OSA, which is really the CIA, compound. Dennis is a navy SEAL, Lieutenant (jg), and adviser to the PRUs—the Cutthroats who go in to get VCI.

The PRUs, I thought. Those men of the Provincial Reconnaissance Units were all *hoi chanh*, or VC defectors. They had nothing to lose. Every PRU faced certain death if their former comrades won the war. The CIA, with a little help from its Green Beret and navy SEAL friends, had trained the PRUs well in eliminating the Viet Cong infrastructure, or VCI.

Dennis was drunk, and started shooting 40-mm flares from an M-79 grenade launcher. The VN also blew smoke grenades, and lit Vi Thanh with flares last night.

And today it's Christmas. Opened my presents. Susan sent a green-felt Santa stocking *stuffed* with packets of vegetable seeds: watermelon, okra, cucumber, onion, etc. Such a thoughtful, practical gift. I'll give those seeds to local farmers. Susan's stocking also included a *C-Ration Cookbook* from Tabasco, and a stainless-steel Case pocketknife. I got a 3-foot synthetic Christmas tree from Mother and Daddy, a Buck Owens C&W cassette tape from Grandmother, cheeses from Raford and Lana, a 1,500-piece jigsaw puzzle from Becky and Kenny—oh *a bunch of things*. Probably more than I'd have gotten if I were at home.

I bought Susan a Sony transistor radio at the Can Tho PX. And Ba Lien gave me a holder to keep a teapot warm, carved from a coconut husk. That's for Mother. I bought a VN teapot to go in it, painted with three old men and a deer: the Chinese symbols for long life, good fortune, and happiness.

Christmas Day, 1989. I'd forgotten the stocking, but the seeds that Susan packed into it obviously meant a lot. So did *all* my presents, that Christmas.

I mentioned that green Santa stocking to Susan late Christmas Day, and she showed it to me. She'd hung it for me in Los Baños in 1989, as she had every year after 1969. I'm awfully insensitive . . . I never really noticed that stocking before.

But how did Susan get the stocking back? She didn't remember. I probably returned it through APO.

I pulled out my Vietnam letter file. I never asked Susan to save the letters and cassette tapes I sent from Nam, but she did. She'd stored them, in chronological order, in a steel box for .30-caliber machine-gun ammunition that I must have lifted at Fort Benning or Bragg. That seemed symbolic, but Susan used the ammo box for convenience. Keeping Vietnam letters in an ammo box isn't her brand of symbolism.

I found a 22 December 1969 letter to Susan:

Tell Mother and Daddy thanks for making the color prints, and I'll try to give them to *Sai* Ngoc, the Cambodian Buddhist monk in Kien Hung, before Christmas. I want to start a chicken project with one of those Cambodian monasteries, because they're full of VC sympathizers.

Could you ask Raford to send me a Texas Aggie sticker. I want to put it on the jeep of my friend CPT Bud Shields, an A&M graduate from West. Bud is District Senior Adviser for Kien Hung. His village can be reached only by chopper or sampan. VC surround Bud's team, and all bridges are blown. He can drive to only one little village. That's why his jeep deserves an Aggie sticker. I wish I could give it to Bud for Christmas.

A mimeographed Christmas letter from Dr. and Mrs. Don Wells was enclosed with my letter to Susan. Wells was my major adviser a year before, during M.S. studies at Iowa State University. His letter expressed the Yuletide mood for 1969:

Dear Friends,

'Tis the fourth day before Christmas 1969 in the Wells House. The last year of the "Sickening Sixties" is almost gone. In many ways, we shall not be unhappy to see it go.

It has been a year of international turmoil and violence, of fear and uncertainty, of confrontation and death . . . a year of frustration in our country, as we've sought to hold onto a way of life we thought was good, as we've fought to hold back the agonizing realization that we can no longer control the forces that affect our lives.

What comes next is not easy to foresee; uncertainty has become a hallmark of daily life. Scott is now at Ft. MacArthur in California, but will likely move on in a few months ...

We're asking again: what kind of life do we want, and what kind of world will allow our children, and their children, to determine the kind of life they want? We're re-examining some long-held values about technological progress and material wealth as measures of men. We're reappraising some cherished assumptions about life and death and the nature of man, about the causes of poverty and violence and prejudice and extremism, about killing in the name of national security and social welfare ...

Our goals—peace, freedom, justice, a brotherhood of man—are surely ones with which you agree. Perhaps what we are trying to say is: they are more important today than ever before, in man's brief history. How we translate these into personal and collective action will determine whether the Seventies will become years of hope or years of hopelessness ...

When I reread that letter in 1989, I was struck with two thoughts.

First: Don and Ann Wells wrote eloquent and thought-provoking words. A reflection of the soul-searching that the turbulent sixties activated.

Second: Should Wells have sent that message to me, in Chuong Thien Province? Probably. The letter didn't hurt my morale, but impressed me enough to forward it to Susan. I knew our war was unpopular, and for good reason. It had blurred right and wrong, and would claim hundreds of thousands more lives before it ended.

It would all be for nothing. I knew that, too, back in Chuong Thien Province.

Would I send a similar letter to a U.S. soldier in Panama in 1989? No, *it wouldn't be right*. But 1969 was different.

I turned back to my diary:

1800h. The ceasefire officially ends now, at 6 p.m. Christmas Day. A SVN outpost N of the Snake River took a few rounds of sniper fire this afternoon. I saw a PF soldier lying by our Korean-run hospital today in very bad shape— shrapnel wounds in both legs and groin. Maybe the wounds were from a mine or booby trap set long ago, maybe not. Regardless, that militiaman is another casualty of our "Christmas Truce."

11:45 p.m. Christmas Day is almost over, and Chuong Thien is fairly quiet. MAT 54 reported 60 VC near Hoa An, and a VC flag flying over Ho Than hamlet. Vi Thanh artillery is firing again.

Christmas 1989. What else, besides the green Santa stocking, some scribbled diary notes, and fading memories, are left from Christmas of 1969? I did a mental inventory . . . more than I'd have expected.

Grandmother died soon after my *next* Vietnam tour, as a civilian in 1972, but I still listen to the Buck Owens tape. I lost the pocketknife that Susan sent. I noticed the synthetic Christmas tree in Miles's room the other day. It stayed in the Delta Lily until April 1970. The tree irritated Sherwin Liff, a State Department civilian who often irritated *me.* Maybe that's why I left the tree up so long after the holiday season.

The jigsaw puzzle . . . we spread its fifteen hundred pieces on a card table in the Delta Lily. Each man would stop for a few minutes, from time to time, to fit in a piece or two.

China Doll, our cook and hootch maid, had never seen a jigsaw puzzle. She was fascinated watching, day by day, a scene materialize from that perfect land, America—snow-blanketed corn fields, fat Holstein cattle, and strong men bridling horses in front of a red barn.

We finished the puzzle a month later. I left the winter scene, which was like no farm I'd known in Texas, on the table for a day. Then I broke the puzzle apart and repacked it in the box.

China Doll fled to our tiny kitchen, crying. She couldn't understand how we Americans could work so hard, for so long, to make that beautiful picture, then destroy it.

Chapter XX
My Days Among the Dead are Past *or* A Name in the Dust

New York, 1990. Vi Thanh, Can Tho, Saigon, Bangkok, Nuoc Trong, 1969–70

> Yet leaving here a name, I trust
> That will not perish in the dust.
> —Robert Southey, "My Days
> Among the Dead are Past"

Real life is seldom like it's *supposed* to be, like on TV or in books.

But 26 January 1990 was an exception. The meeting of communication heads of the International Agricultural Research Centers, held in New York City, ended at noon. I'd fly to Washington, D.C. the next day, but had that afternoon off.

Maybe I'm naive, but it was exciting to go to 201 East 50th Street—Random House—to meet my editor. Owen Lock took me for a three-hour lunch in an expensive Manhattan restaurant with deep leather seats to discuss the book, and writing in general. Lock may have considered it part of the job, like when I entertain visitors who are awed by the International Rice Research Institute. But this was a very special lunch for me, like an author's lunch with his editor in Herman Wouk's *Youngblood Hawke.*

My three trips to Nashville weren't like this, I thought. I'd spent them walking from one publishing house to the next, trying to sell my songs on Music Row.

Interest in Vietnam was peaking, I felt. Dozens of new war

books were hitting the shelves—*too many* books. That worried me, because *my* book wasn't out there.

"How long do you think the Vietnam market will hold?" I asked Lock.

"As long as boys play football, men will read good war stories." I liked that answer.

But then came: "That *doesn't* mean you can take your time finishing the book, Tom. Quit rewriting each chapter ten or fifteen times. Can you wrap it up in six months?"

Impossible, but back in the Philippines I set a goal: to finish a rough draft by 19 June 1990.

Why that date? Because the U.S. Army discharged me on 19 June, twenty years before.

I had left Chuong Thien Province five days earlier. Her terrible fascination had become a little scary, but it was over. I was glad I'd never see that miserable, tragic, waterlogged land again.

Frank Gillespie, Norm Olsen, Chauvin Wilkinson, and Khang drove me to the Vi Thanh air strip. Wilkinson was a first lieutenant from Louisiana who, like me, had a master's degree in agriculture. He'd taken over my job, and Khang would be his interpreter. I was to catch Air America to Can Tho at 10:00 A.M., then connect to Saigon the next day.

We talked about the good times, ignoring the bad, until we heard a distant drone. It was louder and stronger than the Porter that made the daily Air America run.

A blunt-nosed plane appeared on the horizon, then dived almost straight down to the runway. The army air corps Otter was even uglier than a Porter, but carried incredible loads. This flight wasn't manifested, and left no cargo. But *someone* must have expected it, because a Vietnamese sergeant drove a jeep onto the runway to deliver a canvas bag.

I strolled over to talk to the pilots as the Otter's powerful nine-cylinder radial engine idled.

"You're *leaving here*?" the army warrant officer said. "If you've spent a year in this goddamn place, you deserve a direct flight out. Hop in. We're flying this ugly bird to Ben Tre, but we'll drop you off at Can Tho."

I shook hands with Norm and Chauvin. Then Frank said the right words, the right way, at the right time. Words that meant more than the medals I never deserved, expected, or received. He made me feel good, like maybe it was worth it.

Frank said "You're a good man, Tom."

"Khang, give me your notebook." I scribbled, c/o Mr. and Mrs. Tom Hargrove, Rt. 2, Rotan, Texas 79546.

"If you ever need help, a letter to that address will *always* reach me."

South Vietnam was doomed, and I expected its fall sooner than it came. But I couldn't tell Khang that. Not when *I* was leaving Chuong Thien, and *he* couldn't.

Yes, I felt that guilt trip, exploited so well by television serials of the late 1980s, about leaving friends behind. But Vietnam was TV *news* then, not entertainment. No way would I get drunk in Saigon, reenlist, and come back teary-eyed, two days later, to my buddies in Vi Thanh.

Yet somehow, I'd return to Chuong Thien three times—once during the war, and twice in peace—over the next two decades.

Knowing that would have blown my mind, on 14 June 1970. Another friendly chopper pilot gave me a lift on a UH-1, or Huey, from Can Tho to Saigon that afternoon. I caught a beetle-like Citroen taxi from Tan Son Nhut to the USAID hotel on Le Loi Street.

I had Frank Gillespie's authorization, which he was not authorized to write, to wear civilian clothes. No one checked my ID when I signed in as a USAID employee of CORDS/Agriculture in Chuong Thien. I slept in a private, air-conditioned room for the next four nights—instead of paying five dollars a night to wear a uniform, and share a room with three other junior-grade officers in the Rex BOQ.

I left the USAID hotel in civvies each morning, then had French-style coffee in a nearby restaurant and changed clothes in the men's room. I reported to MAC-V as an army lieutenant should—in fatigues—then returned back to the hotel as a USAID civilian.

Looking back, I wonder what might have happened if the MPs had caught me. (Also, what would my fate have been if the VC had captured me, a U.S. officer in civilian clothes, in the Chuong Thien countryside?)

Leaving Vietnam was a lot like arrival—four days of filling in forms at Pentagon East, but with more red tape. In-country discharges were rare, and the army wasn't set up to process them.

I'd arranged "circuitous routing." The little-known program

let a soldier return to the States via the Middle East and Europe, by taking the equivalent air miles on American military planes. The key flight was a weekly U.S. embassy run from Saigon to Bangkok, then to New Delhi the next day, and Karachi the third day. Travel from Pakistan to Europe was from your own pocket. But you got a free "space-available" military hop to America from any U.S. base in England, Germany, or Spain.

Susan had flown to Tehran two months earlier, and was staying with her parents. We'd get to know one another again through a "second honeymoon." Then we'd explore Iran for a few weeks and travel together through the Middle East to Europe.

But the embassy flight left Saigon at dawn on the day of my discharge. The next free ride was seven days later. No way would I spend that week in Saigon. I'd go to Cambodia. The Khmer regions of Chuong Thien had fascinated me, so I'd see the *real thing* . . . as much as I could, anyway.

I'd always wanted to visit the twelfth-century temple complex of Angkor Wat. But some uninvited guests—the North Vietnamese—had moved in a month before, and made those ruins an ammo dump. The NVA knew that the culturally sensitive Americans wouldn't blow away eight centuries of history.

The U.S. Army discharged me at 9:30 A.M. on 19 June. A spec four clerk knew that was why I'd spent so much time at S-1, personnel . . . and was waiting.

Two minutes after I became a civilian, the clerk stopped me at the door—to tell me how fucked-up officers were and how deeply he despised us.

I started back to find his commander, then thought: I'd taken such bullshit from enlisted men only twice during two years in the army. The other time was *exactly* a year ago, on the bus to Travis for my flight to Vietnam.

Neither EM had ever met me. Only my former rank—and the thrill of getting away with insulting what had been an officer a few minutes before—caused the incident.

This must be the highlight of the kid's miserable tour, I thought. Is it worth my time to spoil it for him? To me, spending a year in Saigon, being at war but not seeing it, would be worse than Chuong Thien.

Besides . . . I don't have time. I have two thousand dollars—

green dollars—in back pay, I thought. If I hurry, I can catch the Air Angkor flight to Phnom Penh.

But I paused to read, for the last time, that incredible inscription on the concrete memorial block at the entrance to Tan Son Nhut:

THE NOBLE SACRIFICE OF ALLIED SOLDIERS WILL NEVER BE FORGOTTEN.

I missed the Phnom Penh flight, and the next plane was two days later. So I bought a ticket to Bangkok.

Frank had given me Urai Gillespie's phone number, in case I wound up in Thailand. Urai recommended the Opera Hotel; she'd heard it was cheap, clean, and fairly decent. She was two-thirds right.

For four dollars a night, I got a Spartan-but-immaculate room with linoleum floor, private bath, and air conditioning. The sweet smell of Thai marijuana wafted in the Opera's hallways, and the porter made it clear that room service was limited only by one's fantasies.

The lobby walls were lined with framed, and autographed, eight-by-ten photos of Special Forces A-teams. The Opera was an unofficial Bangkok hotel for Green Berets on R & R from Nam.[1]

---

[1] I was awfully tired when I arrived in Bangkok in the fall of 1974. I'd spent fourteen days in southern India, Bangladesh, and Thailand, then a strange and harrowing week back in Vietnam.

I wanted to soak in a hot bath and sip ice-cold Singha beer. My IRRI expense account would cover all but the beer at any of Bangkok's first-class hotels. But for nostalgia, I took a cab to the Opera Hotel. It was packed, but I lied to the manager about how often I'd stayed there in the *old days*. He thought he remembered me, and found a room.

Most Green Berets had left Southeast Asia by the mid-1970s, but Thais are clever. The Opera had now attracted a new clientele: U.S. Peace Corps Volunteers from remote areas of Thailand. The PCVs liked the Opera's cheap rooms and laid-back atmosphere. Opera management had replaced the Green Beret photos in the lobby with eight-by-tens of Peace Corps groups. But that sweet marijuana smell still lingered.

I gave the room boy my Wellington boots to shine, took a hot bath while drinking a couple of Singhas, and crashed.

The next morning I was on Thai 624, flying back to Manila. An hour out of Bangkok, I admired the glossy shine on my boots. Then I remembered the se-

I took Russell and Lisa Gillespie to the Bangkok zoo the morning of 20 June 1970, and bought them peanuts to feed the elephants. But that night, I drank Mekong Whiskey with two Thais in shiny black suits on the overnight train to Chiang Mai, that ancient mountain center of Buddhism and opium. They liked the VC flag that Truong, Khang's brother with the Phoenix Program, had given me.

19 June 1990, Philippines. I didn't meet my self-set deadline, I thought, but I *must* move the book out of Vietnam—at least, until I write about Saigon in 1972.

My diary is packed with entries that I haven't written about. But I *have*, really.

The diary is a blend of carnage and agricultural development. Only the dates and locations changed with the passing months.

But the *real* story of the war deep in the Mekong Delta is locked in my *fiction*. It's far truer than my diary:

Chapter ?

12 June 1969. Dan shaved in front of a cracked mirror nailed to a support post for the MAT 96 shower, a fifty-five-gallon oil drum. He was uneasy.

Lt. Alan Burns had been confined with hepatitis in the 76th Field Hospital at Binh Thuy, on the outskirts of Can Tho, for the past three weeks.

The colonel had just radioed a command that Dan both dreaded and, in a strange way, wanted. Burns would be Medevacked to the States on 15 June for treatment and early discharge. First Lieutenant Daniel Bridges would take command of MAT 96. That scared Dan.

Alan could handle the Vietnamese, he thought, *but can I?* The chief would never have killed that prisoner in front of Alan. And can I hold this screwed-up team together like Alan did?

But Dan also felt pride. This is my first *real* command—even if it's only a ragged-ass MAT team with three unhappy men. But being adviser to the chief makes me almost a commander, behind the scenes, of the forty Nuoc Trong militia.

cret pocket sewn into my right boot, where I carried a green $100 bill for emergencies. I unzipped the pocket. My $100 bill was gone.

I couldn't pull it off without Joe Culver. Thank God that redneck's not one of those arrogant sergeants who'd try to take the team away from a green lieutenant.

The colonel had also ordered Dan to catch this morning's swing ship to Vi Thanh, to turn in Alan's field gear. He'd then take Air America to Can Tho, to return the black officer's personal items. Alan would give a final briefing at the 76th Field Hospital in Binh Thuy, on the outskirts of Can Tho.

Dan announced his new command to the men of MAT 96.

"Congratulations, Lieutenant." Sergeant Culver thrust a huge hand forward. "You have my full support."

"We'll miss Lieutenant Burns, but I'm so happy that *you* will be our new boss," Sergeant Enrique Rodriguez said, also shaking hands.

"I can take Lieutenant Burns's gear to Can Tho, if you're too busy," Specialist Bob Saunders said.

"I'll bet. How about helping me pack for Alan?"

Dan arrived in Vi Thanh with two duffel bags, and found the MAC-V supply sergeant. He signed over the equipment issued to 1st Lt. Alan Burns to S-4, logistics, Advisory Team 73.

I'd better have Monique confirm my flight to Can Tho, Dan thought, and lugged Alan's personal duffel bag toward the CORDS office.

But why ask Monique? The MAC-V orderly room clerk could check that flight.

She won't remember me, we've met only that day I arrived in Vi Thanh. I'll look silly as hell. But I'm not interested in Monique, I just want to talk to a real, live female. Janice is waiting in Texas, and we have something special . . . then a kneeling prisoner fell dead, and blood and mud mixed in a puddle under a corpse, and Dan spoke into a handset "Two enemy Kilo-India-Alphas."

Fuck it! I may be dead, too, before this year's over. That's strange . . . I've never really *thought* about dying before.

Monique was studying a Vietnamese-English dictionary and pecking at a typewriter when Dan walked into the Chinese-French CORDS building.

"*Chao, Co* Monique. *Manh gioi?*"

"Good afternoon, Lieutenant!" she smiled. "I'm fine, how are you?"

"Toi manh gioi." She's pretty and cool and crisp, and damn, she has interesting eyes.

"Where did you learn to speak such Vietnamese, Lieutenant . . ." Those brown eyes focused on the green cloth name tag sewn on Dan's fatigue jacket. ". . . Lieutenant *Bridges*. You were not so fluent before."

"In Nuoc Trong. But my Vietnamese is still number ten . . . and please don't call me 'Lieutenant.' It's 'Dan,' remember?"

"*Of course.* May I help you, Lieutenant Dan?" Her *ao dai* was emerald-green, over black silk pants. She wore opentoed sandals, and her nails were painted cherry pink. That reminded Dan, for a second, of other pink nails. But he quickly erased the girl that VC mortars killed the night he arrived in Nuoc Trong. He'd learned how to do that.

"Just Dan . . . could you please make sure I'm on Air America to Can Tho this afternoon? That's Lt. *Dan Bridges*."

"Please sit down." Monique flowed from the chair and studied a chart.

"You are confirmed, Lieutenant . . . Dan." She sat back down as Dan reached to hold her chair. He felt silly. *Say something. Anything.*

"How long have you lived in Vi Thanh?"

"All of my life," she turned to stare out the window at the muddy Xa No Canal. "This was the village of *Mere*. But my father was from Paris."

"Paris is beautiful," Dan said.

"Paris, and San Francisco, and London, too . . . wonderful cities, and I will visit *all of them*. But I think Paris is best of all." She added "Paris is most lovely in the springtime."

"I thought you'd never been to France."

"Not *yet*. But *Papa* told me so much about Paris, and the flowers and monuments and the wine. I am so sorry that my father is gone. He would have loved so much to know you, a fellow officer who knows Paris."

What was Monique's father like? Dan wondered. A Frenchman who stayed behind with his mistress in this Godforsaken Delta village . . . yet telling his daughter about the grandeur of Paris. Was he another sorry-ass soldier who got hung up on the local women? Or maybe he was in the Foreign Legion, a man without a country.

"Your father was in the French Army?"

"Of course."

"Was he . . . a *Legionnaire*?"

"*Troi duc oi!*" Monique snapped. "Papa . . . a filthy *Legionnaire*? My father was a major of Airborne, he commanded a *bataillon*.

"He was a graduate of the *Ecole Inter Armes de St. Cyr*," she added with dignity.

"I'm sorry . . . of course." An officer from St. Cyr, the French West Point—*here*? Didn't Culver say that Monique's father was *a sergeant like Felipe and me*? I'd better change the subject.

"It's almost noon. Let's have lunch!" Dan said, impulsively.

"I do not know you, Lieutenant Dan."

"Monique, we were strangers the *first* time we met, but not now. This is the *second* time, so we're old friends. Besides, I want to talk . . . about *France*. And you can order."

Monique raised her eyes. "You are right. Shall we old friends go?"

It looked shabby from the outside, but a battered BIERE LARUE sign announced, in Vietnamese and Chinese, that this was a restaurant. They sat at a white metal table in a patio, under an arbor of saplings.

A teenaged waiter poured warm beer over ice for Dan. Why don't Vietnamese use the ice to chill beer? he thought. The boy then brought a menu and chopsticks, soy, *nuoc mam*, and a dish of sliced red peppers. Monique ordered.

"To us," Dan said.

Monique clicked her orange drink saucily against his glass.

A soup of mushrooms and onion slices arrived, then shrimps in sweet-and-sour sauce, and fried rice cooked with pork and green peppers.

Dan didn't know enough about France to really talk about it, so he told Monique about the arid Rio Grande Valley, where irrigated farms grew lush crops of cotton and vegetables. He talked about his family, and friends in college. His stories made this strange woman laugh. Then Dan thought: *Where are my friends now? Not in Vietnam.*

The two-hour lunch passed quickly. Dan tipped the waiter, and they walked back to CORDS. It was 2:15, and a Vietnamese driver was starting a white Scout, to meet the Air America flight.

"Can I see you the next time I'm in Vi Thanh?"

"Why not, *old friend*?"

Dan blew her a kiss as the Scout headed to the Vi Thanh airstrip.

The long, pointed fuselage of the six-passenger plane reminded Dan of the needle-nosed garbage fish in the Xa No Canal. A red-white-and-blue flag and black letters labeled it AIR AMERICA. Dan didn't know that the CIA ran the "Invisible Air Force." Nor that it was the world's largest airline, in aircraft and flying hours.

"Hang on, good buddy." Dan's stomach pushed at his throat as the pilot took off almost vertically.

"This is a Pilatus Porter. The Swiss designed it for short runways in the Alps," the pilot yelled over the roar. He wore a tan safari suit, a gold medallion, and a solid-gold Rolex. A leather holster slung from the pilot's seat held a CAR-15, or Colt Commando, a modified M-16 with a twelve-inch barrel and retractable stock.

"This sweet bird can take off from its tail, and land on its nose. It's great for these jerry-rigged Delta airstrips, where some VC son of a bitch is always waiting to AK you from the mangroves."

An Air America plane had been shot down, Dan knew, leaving Vi Thanh last year.

The plane's other passengers were a U.S. Army bird colonel, two ARVN majors, and a civilian wearing a sports shirt.

The Porter landed steeply at Ca Mau, the Delta's southernmost provincial capital, then at Rach Gia, along the Gulf of Siam. After forty-five minutes, its passengers unloaded in Can Tho.

"How do I get to Binh Thuy?" Dan asked a GI outside the two stucco rooms that served as Can Tho's air terminal.

"The shuttle bus left five minutes ago, but you can probably hitch a ride at the main gate."

"Thanks." Dan shouldered the duffel bag. The potholed road outside the airfield was packed with slow-moving, honking air force pickups, Vietnamese and U.S. Army trucks, Hondas, bicycles, a few French Citroens. An old man dodged a barreling Vietnamese armored personnel carrier, fell, and spilled his vegetable cart.

A jeep with an enlisted driver and an army major in crisp fatigues pulled over.

Nice of them to stop. Then Dan remembered he was in Can Tho, and gave the major a friendly salute. The return salute lashed.

"*Lieutenant!* Do you know the regulation for headwear in Can Tho?"

"Did I do something—"

"Read it, Lieutenant. *Why* are you wearing a jungle hat? All U.S. Army personnel *will* wear the baseball-style cap in this city. Am I understood?"

"Yes, sir." What's wrong with my jungle hat? The goddamn army issued it to me.

"Do you *have* a baseball cap?"

"Yes sir . . . but it's back at—"

"Where are you headed?"

"To Binh Thuy. My buddy's in the hospital there."

"Binh Thuy has a PX, Lieutenant. You *will* purchase a regulation army cap there. *Do you read me?*"

"Yes, *sir.*" The *sir* was flat. You Can Tho prick, in your starched fatigues and spit-shined boots.

"Are you angry at me, Lieutenant?"

"No, *sir.*"

"You *sound* like you're pissed off. I suggest you change that tone of voice. Now, do you want a ride to Binh Thuy?"

"I'll make it okay," he said, but thought: No way will I ride with a fucked-up bastard like you.

"Then good day, Lieutenant." The major waited.

Okay, I'll play your silly game. Dan's salute wasn't contemptuously sloppy—nor snappy enough to convey much respect. The major's return salute was knifelike. The jeep pulled back into the traffic.

That son of a bitch sure got his rocks off on that, Dan thought. What makes so many of those lifers that way?

Three airmen pulled up in a battered air force truck.

"Want a ride?"

"Thanks." Dan scrambled onto the truck bed.

Dan left the Binh Thuy PX wearing a stiff new baseball-style cap, with a black first lieutenant's bar pinned to its front. I'm playing your game, major, he thought as he rolled his jungle hat and stuck it into a fatigue pocket, then walked into the drizzle. *Asshole.*

Dan's lunchtime high with Monique had vaporized. No matter how good you feel, if you're in the army some bastard will fuck it up.

Now, where's the 76th Field Hospital?

Even asleep, he looked ten years older than the Alan of three weeks before. Dan set the duffel bag by the hospital bed and touched his former commander's shoulder.

"AOOGH!" Alan sprang, pushing Dan back, the other hand drawn to protect his face.

"Alan! Take it easy, pal. It's me, *Bridges."*

Alan looked confused, then fell back flat.

"Dan. I'm sorry. I sleep a lot, and when I wake I seem to have . . . *a problem with it, that's all."*

Alan's eyes were yellower than they were that last night in Nuoc Trong.

"I came to drag your ass back to MAT 96, hepatitis or not." Dan gripped Alan's hand. "You can't leave *me* with those two Stone-Age sergeants and that hippie radio operator."

"That team is *all yours*, baby!" Alan said. "For me it's two days and a wake-up, and bye-bye the Nam!"

"Lucky bastard."

Alan shrugged. "You think so? I'll go straight to an army hospital in Oakland for at least a month."

"And Laura?"

"She'll meet me in Oakland, but the doc says no strenuous activity."

"Does that mean . . . ?"

"I didn't have the balls to ask. I guess it depends on whether I have a private room, or go into a goddamn ward. I *still* have enough strength for one thing. My *second* plan, when I reach the World, is to set my duffel bag down!"

They laughed, and that broke the tension.

"At least you'll be out of the army."

"Right on, brother! I shit you not—all I want out of the army is—out of the army. *No mo' Mothah Green.*

"How're Joe, Enrique . . . Bob?"

Dan told Alan about the men, then about *that* operation.

"You can't change some things," Alan shook his head.
"Fuck it."

"But I had a rifle, I could have threatened the chief. I
didn't really *try* to stop him. I just stood there. It's almost
like *I* shot that prisoner."

"*Grow up*, Dan!" Alan's voice turned hard, and distant.
"Nuoc Trong isn't grad school, and you're not in the *real
world*. You're in Chuong Thien Province. Get that through
your thick, farmer skull.'"

"But—"

"You're headed for trouble, friend. Save the struggle with
your conscience for later. You can debate morality back in
Texas, maybe, after your third Coors. *But not here*."

Alan's fingers dug into Dan's arm.

"The war *sucks*, Dan, it's ugly. You think you haven't
killed lots of innocent men and women and goddamn kids—
for the Green Machine? Don't jive me, the H & I artillery
we called each night blew away dudes that deserved death
a hell of a lot less than *one motherfucking VC prisoner!*"

Alan held out his palms. "The blood gets on *your hands*,
too, Dan.

"Could you have *shot* the chief? Hell no, you'd have
backed down, and that prisoner would still be one dead son
of a bitch VC.

"Grow up!" It was an order, and a plea.

Alan turned his head into the pillow.

"Those motherfuckers. Those miserable dirty goddamn
rotten sorry motherfuckers."

Dan touched Alan's shoulder.

"I'm sorry, Dan. I'm so fucking, truly sorry for you."

I should be sorry for what happened to *you*, Dan thought.

"Good luck, Dan. Learn fast, you hear? That's all I can
say. Good-bye."

Alan's handshake seemed stronger than his body or his
psyche.

"I've never known a man like you, Alan."

Dan walked down the empty hospital corridor after the
painful visit. Why did Alan's *good-bye* sound like my death
sentence? The hallway was gloomy, but sunlight glared
through glass windows at its end.

Dan wasn't sure who those *sorry goddamn motherfuckers*
were. But he knew they had taken Alan's youth.

Transition 12

They that sow in tears shall reap in joy.
He that goeth forth and weepeth,/bearing precious seed,
shall doubtless/come again with rejoicing, bringing his/
sheaves with him.

—Psalms 126:5–6

As the sun sets on 22 February 1990, Susan and I walk through palm and banana trees to the IRRI guesthouse for "chicken on a stick."

That's what we call IRRI cocktail/buffets, because we're invariably served skewers of grilled chicken as hors d'oeuvres. This party is to meet scientists attending a conference on integrated pest management, or nonchemical pest control.

We mingle with entomologists, plant breeders, and economists from a dozen countries that IRRI has gathered in Los Baños. Like me, many wear *barong tagalogs*, the finely embroidered, open-tailed dress shirt that substitutes for a suit at any formal affair in the Philippines.

IRRI amazes me, even after seventeen years. Rice science bonds men and women who, otherwise, would never be under the same roof. Scientists from mainland China and Taiwan discuss, in their common language, a new strain of brown planthopper. A North Korean in a Mao-type jacket is avoiding a scientist from the University of Seoul. They'll be talking in a day or two.

Insects fly across the India-Pakistan border at will, but researchers cannot. Scientists from both countries, who work forty miles apart, have traveled five-thousand air miles to IRRI, to share data on pest control. A rice agronomist from the

300

University of Arkansas drinks San Miguel from a frosty mug with an Iranian entomologist who sips orange juice. The Iranian looks like he wants a beer too, but can't risk it. Other Iranian scientists might report him.

"Tom, I've been looking for you." I turn. It's Dr. Robert Rhoades, anthropologist with the International Potato Center, called CIP for its Spanish acronym.

CIP is one of thirteen International Agricultural Research Centers that have been established around the world in the past thirty years. All are patterned, basically, after IRRI, and have the same goal: to increase production of the crops and livestock that feed the developing countries.

CIP focuses on potato, the world's fourth most important food crop. Only rice, wheat, and corn (or maize) feed more of mankind than that lowly tuber. CIP is based in Peru, because the potato originated in the Andes Mountains. Thus, its greatest genetic diversity is found there. But Bob Rhoades works in Los Baños, on CIP's program to catalyze potato research and production in Southeast Asia.

"Would you go back to Vietnam for my next *National Geographic* article?"

"*What?*"

"I have a proposal. Let's talk—outside." We grab fresh beers and work through the crowd. I was a little jealous of Rhoades's latest *National Geographic* coup. In 1982, Rhoades had published "The Incredible Potato," a *Geographic* "commodity feature." It explained to 18 million subscribers, and 70 million readers, how important the potato is, and how scientists from CIP and cooperating research institutes are raising its yield and nutritional value.

Rhoades's next *National Geographic* feature would address another global issue: *genetic erosion*: How traditional plants of all crops disappear when farmers adopt high-yielding varieties.[1] How the natural habitats of wild species—the ancestors of the varieties that feed us today, and genetic building blocks for the plants that will feed our children—are disappearing, victims of roads, dams, housing developments.

The new Dallas–Fort Worth airport, for example, makes my return to Texas easier—but concrete runways and screaming

[1] Rhoades, Robert. "The World's Food Supply at Risk." *National Geographic*, April 1991.

jets now cover land where wild grapes once grew. A recent forest fire in Borneo destroyed wild rices found nowhere else.

When those plants vanish, so do their genes. We take for granted those packages of DNA, the material through which life reproduces itself. But genes control traits that may, in turn, control the destiny of future generations.

Take wild rices. They look like weeds, but they've withstood centuries of insect and disease attack in the swamps of Asia. *Survival of the fittest* has made each strain remarkably resistant to local pests.

When bred into farmers' seeds, that natural resistance can reduce—maybe eliminate—the need for costly pesticides that help destroy our environment.

The primitive deepwater rices that farmers grow along the mighty rivers of Asia—the Ganges, the Brahmaputra, the Mekong—are another example. Nature has given those rices genes that make their stems grow as long as eighteen feet, to protect their seeds from rising floodwater. That ability to elongate could be genetic insurance if global warming raises the sea level and pushes rivers back, expanding and deepening the world's deltas. Many scientists think that we're already suffering from the *greenhouse effect*.

Rice breeders have long wanted to combine the remarkable traits of wild and primitive rices with the high-yield potential of their distant, domesticated cousins. But they couldn't cross-breed the two types; they're too different. Biotechnology now makes that possible.

The urgency for genetic conservation would be the main theme of Rhoades's new *National Geographic* article. An example is how IRRI scientists traveled by jeep and sampan across Cambodia, despite a terrible civil war, in the early 1970s. Their mission: to save a handful of seeds of each threatened rice variety, while there was still time. Those seeds were preserved in cold storage at minus ten degrees Centigrade or fourteen degrees Fahrenheit in the IRRI gene bank, along with seeds of more than seventy thousand of the world's estimated one hundred and forty thousand wild and traditional rices. The seeds should germinate a century from now.

But IRRI plays it safe, because their genes mean so much to humanity. We monitor the living seeds and replant when their viability drops.

After 1975, the maniacal Pol Pot regime ordered Cambodian

farmers to quit planting their hardy deepwater varieties—
because deepwater rices weren't grown in the glory days of the
Khmer Empire. That insane command was the death knell for
deepwater rices that farmers had grown, always selecting seeds
with the best traits, for centuries.

Starving Cambodians ate the last seeds of hundreds of other
traditional rice varieties.

In the 1980s, IRRI returned duplicate sets of seeds of 524
Khmer varieties to their homeland. All of the seeds germi-
nated. Those rices grow, once more, on Cambodian farms.

But Cambodia, and the world, lost hundreds of irreplaceable
rice varieties—and their precious genes—forever. Those 524
rescued varieties would be gone, too, had there been no IRRI
gene bank.

Bob Rhoades and I stop under a giant mahogany tree, away
from the light and din of the guesthouse. Dr. Klaus Lampe,
IRRI's director general, is now introducing guests over our
sound system.

"*Go back to Vietnam?*" I ask Bob. "*What are you driving
at?*"

"*National Geographic* wants another photo for the article,"
Rhoades says. "How scientists saved seeds of a threatened
plant variety, preserved them in a gene bank, then later bred
that plant's key genes into an improved variety. Years later, the
genes return, through the new seeds, to the country where they
originated.

"The crop can be wheat, corn, potato, it doesn't matter—but
the story has to be *real*."

"I still don't follow you."

"Tom, I showed those articles about your 1988 return to that
awful place in the Mekong Delta to the *Geographic* editors,"
Rhoades says. "They want *Vietnam* to be the country and
Hargrove to be a vehicle to show how genes move, what they
mean to mankind.

"We want you, as a former soldier who learned about rice
through the war, then became an IRRI scientist, to return to
Vietnam . . . bringing new seeds that carry genes from a forgotten Vietnamese variety.

"Could you and scientists from the University of Can Tho
go back together, and give IRRI seeds to your old friend—that
farmer who grew the first IR8?"

"Ba Lien? He also planted the first IR20 in Vietnam. Joe

Ona and I gave him those seeds. One of Ona's friends stole them from an IRRI seed-multiplication plot . . . that was in the spring of 1970."

"You can pack the new seeds in a bag marked INTERNATIONAL RICE RESEARCH INSTITUTE," Bob adds.

This is getting wild, but I pick up on it.

"*Tetep* could be the source of the genes," I say. "It's an old Vietnamese variety that farmers quit planting in the sixties. But IRRI had stored seed samples in the gene bank. Tetep can withstand blast, the main rice disease in the Delta. IRRI has bred that resistance into new rices that yield five or six times more than Tetep.

"I could ask our plant breeders which new IRRI experimental lines—with Tetep genes—would grow well in the Ca Mau Peninsula."

But I know it won't happen. The idea is too far out.

"Perfect!" Bob says. "Lynn Johnson will capture the return of Tetep's genes to Vietnam on film."

I knew the *National Geographic* photographer, but not well. I had arranged Lynn's one-week visit to the Philippines, six months earlier. She shot a dozen rolls of film in the IRRI gene bank, then we helped her join seed collection expeditions to remote areas of India and Nepal.

"Let's talk to Xuan." I say.

Back in the IRRI guesthouse, I signal my old friend Dr. Vo Tong Xuan. I'm proud that Xuan is now the newest member of IRRI's fifteen-person Board of Trustees, which sets IRRI policy. I was one of three IRRI scientists who nominated him.

Rhoades starts to explain how important *National Geographic* coverage could be to Vietnam. He doesn't need to. Xuan knows. As the guesthouse crowd moves to the buffet table, we plan a strategy to convince Dr. Lampe that the trip will help both IRRI and Vietnam.

We never test our strategy. Thirty minutes later, Bob Rhoades pulls Xuan and me aside.

"I talked with Klaus in the buffet line," he says. "Lampe sees *National Geographic* coverage as a *great* opportunity to publicize IRRI's work.

"It's a go!"

CHAPTER XXI
Home His Footsteps

India, Iran, across Europe, and Texas, 1970. Nuoc Trong
Village, Chuong Thien Province, 1969

> This is the way the world ends
> Not with a bang but a whimper.
> —T. S. Eliot,
> "The Hollow Men"

> Breathes there the man, with soul so dead,
> Who never to himself hath said,
> This is my own, my native land!
> Whose heart hath ne'er within him burn'd,
> As home his footsteps he hath turn'd
> From wandering on a foreign strand!
> —Sir Walter Scott,
> "The Lay of the Last Minstrel"

A week after my discharge from the army, I came down
from the mountains of northern Thailand to Bangkok, to catch
that weekly U.S. embassy flight from Saigon to Karachi.

We had a layover in New Delhi, so I wandered through its
teeming streets the evening of 26 June 1970. India was so
crowded and poor. Thousands of families, on that thin line between poverty and starvation, cooked meager meals over sidewalk fires. Where does the wood come from? I thought. There
are no trees around Delhi.

Indians are right to call their country *Mother India*, I
thought. Most people were younger than fifteen. What happens
when *they* start breeding families of six or more?

The *doomsday prophets* are right. India is a hopeless case. There'll be famine here before the 1970s end.[1]

I got off the embassy flight in Karachi the next day. While waiting two days for an Air Iran flight to Tehran, I roamed that fascinating, but impoverished, city and hired dilapidated British taxis to tour the Pakistan countryside. My impressions were like those in India.

After ten days, I reached Susan in Iran. My in-laws, Charles and Marjorie Sheldon, lived in a large home with a swimming pool. Susan and I had a suite.

Marge Sheldon was born and raised in Rotan, Texas, so we had plenty to talk about.

Buck Sheldon was a generous man from Minnesota who saw the ocean at age eighteen, and vowed to see its other side. He'd played professional football for the Philadelphia Eagles, and loved the game. But in the Great Depression, pro ball was also a way to pick up a few extra bucks on weekends.

---

[1] By 1990, I'd returned to India twenty or thirty times, and prospects for the world's second-most populous country looked different on each trip. India could still be dismal, but I became fascinated with her vastness, the myriad of cultures, her temples and the sense of timelessness that her Buddhist and Hindu roots evoke. By the mid-1970s, the Green Revolution had filled India's grain bins, and bought her a few more years of time. In 1985, India donated 100,000 tons of grain, mostly rice and wheat, *as its own food aid* to drought-stricken countries of Africa.

But agricultural technology is only first aid for the problem—not a long-term solution. Farm production can't keep up with rampant population growth forever.

India's population, when IR8 was released in 1966, was 506 million and its rice production was 46 million metric tons a year. When I walked New Delhi's streets in 1970, the population had risen to 554 million, and rice production had already jumped to 63 million tons. By 1989, India had 835 million citizens, and grew 92.5 million tons of rice. By the year 2020, India will have at least 1.4 billion people, and rice production must double again—to 167 million tons.

How will India grow that much rice? It has no idle land to bring into production. The only interim measure, until India controls its numbers, is higher yields per crop, and more crops per year.

The same spectre threatens Bangladesh, Pakistan, the Philippines, Vietnam, Nepal . . .

If I'm really an idealist, I often think, my career should have been population control, not agricultural science.

During World War II, Sheldon worked on the Manhattan Project, the atomic bomb. His job in Oak Ridge was engineering, not nuclear physics. He led the team that packaged the bombs, designing how they'd fall after leaving army air force bays over Hiroshima and Nagasaki. Sheldon didn't know much about atom-splitting—but he knew that this was one hell of a big bomb, and had to drop right.

My father-in-law built airfields in the Aleutian Islands during the Korean War, then helped build the boom town of Kitimat in Canada. In the mid-1950s, he supervised construction of the dry docks and ship repair facility, the heart of the U.S. Naval Base at Subic Bay, Philippines.

Sheldon spent the next eight years building the port of Kuwait. Back then, the sheikdom shared a U.S. embassy with Saudi Arabia. Sheldon petitioned the State Department to open an American Embassy in Kuwait. Some high-ranking Kuwaitis wanted him to be their first U.S. ambassador—but Sheldon was a builder, not a diplomat.

Buck Sheldon died in 1983, but he's still remembered in that troubled region as a man of honesty and integrity, who loved the Arabs.

In 1970, Sheldon was vice-president of Santa Fe Construction Company in Iran. By then, he'd finished building the strategic port of Bandar-e-Abbas, which guards the Strait of Hormuz—the narrow waterway connecting the Gulf of Oman to the Persian Gulf. He was also building a railway bridge over a deep mountain gorge in a northwestern Iran, to bring the Orient Express from Turkey to Iran. Iran was America's staunchest ally in the Middle East back in those days of the shah. Remember?

"If you're around Buck Sheldon, there's always good food and good drink." I heard that a lot. Wherever Sheldon lived, his hospitality made him a local legend. I probably needed the food; people said that I was gaunt when I arrived in Tehran. I considered myself lean, but old photos made me think that the first description was more accurate.

Susan and I had been separated too long. Like in Hawaii, it was hard to get to know each other again. Most times were good, but some were bad.

The social life was busy for Tehran's international community. Susan and I were included in most of the Sheldons' invitations.

Elegance best describes a Tehran dinner party. Hors d'oeuvres were usually bowls of Iranian caviar, the same as Russian caviar only taken from sturgeon that *Iranian* ships caught in the Caspian Sea.

Vodka was often served straight from bottles frozen in blocks of ice. Caviar and vodka ... that reminded me how close, physically, Tehran is to the Soviet Union.

Vietnam veterans who processed out of the military in Oakland, California, often faced demonstrators who heckled and ridiculed, even threw stones at them. I missed that experience; Tehran had few liberals during those autumn days of the shah. What *I* came to dread was the *right wing* reaction to Vietnam.

An oil executive asked about my Vietnam tour at a seated dinner. I explained, briefly, that I was an army officer who mainly advised the Vietnamese about agriculture.

"Were you a *combat officer?*" the oilman asked.

"I didn't lead troops." That was the *wrong answer.*

"You're lucky, young man, to have never seen war firsthand. *I* led a platoon, then a company, and finally—after so many field-grade officers were killed—a *battalion* across Europe from June of 1944 until VE day in '45. We killed thousands of Krauts."

"Vietnam is *different.*"

"Bullshit. George Patton would have taken the *offensive!* U.S. tanks would have rolled across North Vietnam in two weeks. The only soldiers in Vietnam today would be our occupation troops in Hanoi."

What could I say?

"How do you *really* feel about the war?" an oil executive's wife asked at another party. "You're the only person I've known who's *been there.*"

I thought she was serious. Another mistake.

My answer wasn't what the socialite lady wanted to hear. I closed our conversation with. "Vietnam is tragic, but the war was never dull. Nam was the most interesting year of my life."

"I hope your wife—or your in-laws—never hear you say that!" She walked away.

I developed a theory in Tehran. Most men and women who've been to war *want* to tell what they've seen and done.

Except, maybe, those who suffered unimaginable horrors. Plenty did, but I wasn't one of them.

But I learned—quickly—*to keep my mouth shut about Nam*, around both doves and hawks. I didn't want to start a fight with a conservative who thought we should nuke Hanoi, any more than with an adamant peacenik.

Most people, of course, were in neither camp. They didn't care.

Having to purposely avoid talking about the past twelve months was frustrating . . . and hurt my pride. Disregard that I'd been in Vietnam, and think: Can you imagine returning from a dangerous year in an isolated Asian village ten thousand miles from America—to find the experience taboo to mention?

It was like pretending that the past year never happened. But *any* story, from Vietnam, reminded people of what they didn't want to know.

And Susan? To her, Vietnam was—and still is—a tragedy so immense, so terrible, it's best not to speak of it. She despises the war as a totally useless waste of lives, little short of murder on both sides. There was nothing fascinating about it.

I agree on all points but the last. I guess that's a big difference between men and women.

So I couldn't tell Susan about the war, either . . . or maybe I *wouldn't*, I really don't know.

To be fair, I had never even written to Susan about what Chuong Thien Province was like. She didn't want to know, and would have hated learning. Besides, I didn't really understand it, myself. My tour wasn't bad, I wrote in my diary (*although I didn't know I had written that until 1987*). I didn't dramatize Vietnam.[2]

The first time I told Susan personal things about Nam, and then not much, was after that black spring of 1977. We don't talk about it today, and never will.

I *thought* about the war, though . . . a lot.

---

[2] In 1990 Bill Smith, fellow editor and my best friend at IRRI, reviewed a draft of this book. Over beer on his porch, Bill said:

"Hargrove, you still haven't faced your ultimate problem from Vietnam."

"What do you mean?" I said.

"You feel that you never finished your tour of duty. You have a bizarre guilt trip—*so many of your friends died over there, but you're still alive.*"

But those Tehran days were mostly fun. Susan's nineteen-year-old brother came to Iran from college in the States for the summer. Miles was funny, charismatic, and brought a stream of young people to the Sheldon home.

The Gentry family was my favorite among the Tehran crowd. Charley Gentry was head of Texaco in Iran. The Gentry twins spent that summer with Charley and Christine in Tehran. Fred, a junior in college, was conservative, but opposed the war. His brother Marco had been crippled by polio, wore leg braces, walked with crutches, and smoked a lot of Iranian hash. Marco liked war stories, but was disappointed that I couldn't tell him more about that famous Grass of Nam.

The three Gentry men invited me for five days of fishing in the Elburz Mountains of northern Iran. We drove a Land Rover above the tree line to a rocky moonscape of stark boulders and wild streams of cold, rushing water. That fishing trip was a return to the camaraderie of men who liked one another, living a special outdoor life. It came at a good time.

We slept in tents and woke at dawn to fish. During midday, we read or climbed rocky escarpments. Late in the afternoon, we fished again. At night, we pan-fried trout and potatoes over an oil burner, then talked ourselves to sleep.

Persian goatherders laughed at our naive efforts to fool trout with spinners and hooks. Boys often left their herds, waded into the icy stream, reached under rocks, and threw trout onto the river bank.

How? I don't know. But those shepherds caught—by hand—a fourth of the trout dinner that the Gentrys and I gave when we returned to Tehran.

After six weeks, it was time to start back to Texas. The trip took another six weeks, and most of my Vietnam savings. We visited Susan's Arab friends in Kuwait and Lebanon, toured Istanbul and Greece, then found ourselves in Yugoslavia.

In the ancient port of Dubrovnik, Susan recognized her headmaster from high school in Switzerland, dining with another man in a rooftop restaurant. She left our table to introduce herself, but he had already recognized her.

"Who's your companion?" he asked. Susan explained.

"My friend and I noticed that young man around town earlier," the former headmaster said. "We were talking . . . something terrible must have happened to him. He looked . . . *haunted.*"

The next week, we were in Rome. I left Susan in our pension, and went to buy budget tickets to London. I'd fly military from the U.K. to the States, and Susan would take the cheapest charter.

I found a hole-in-the-wall travel agency that specialized in cut-rate tickets for students. While negotiating, I saw a hand-printed sign: WANTED: SOMEONE TO RETURN VOLKSWAGEN TO TRAVEL AGENCY IN COPENHAGEN. GAS AND TOLLS PAID.

Denmark is closer to Texas than Rome, I thought, and dialed the number. Half an hour later, I drove a yellow VW to our pension.

The five days of travel were good—and free. We drove across northern Italy, the Swiss Alps, and Germany, then delivered the VW to the travel agency in Copenhagen.

"Those damned Italians!" the travel agent swore. "This car should have gone to *Amsterdam*! Now I'll have to find someone to drive it to Holland."

I volunteered.

"Okay! We'll pay your expenses. Enjoy Copenhagen tomorrow, while we service the car."

We delivered the VW to an address in Amsterdam three nights later, and collected expense money. The city's streets were packed with long-haired youth, and throbbed with protest music. Amsterdam's tolerance of drugs made it the world mecca of the flower movement, that summer of 1970.

We were in England a few days later. I went to the London office of Santa Fe, where Buck Sheldon had arranged that I could cash checks. There, I mentioned our expense-paid trip across Europe in the VW.

"You did *what*! And you left the car in Copenhagen for a day, then drove it into Amsterdam *from the north? Are you crazy?*"

"I don't get it . . ."

"How do you think those drugs *reach* Copenhagen and Amsterdam? By special delivery?" Maybe the executive was paranoid. He'd spent a lot of time trying to get an employee out of jail over the past month, a nice fellow who had agreed to carry a young woman's suitcase from the plane in Beirut. The two kilos of hashish stashed in its false bottom were hard to explain to Lebanese customs officers.

Was the free trip a ploy to move drugs to northern Europe? I don't know. But if we'd been caught in a VW loaded with

North African hash, I doubt that my previous year in Nam would have helped establish my innocence.

Finally, we were back on the Hargrove farm in West Texas. That first evening, after the embraces, tears, the talk of all that had happened over the past fifteen months, Daddy said, "Tommy, I want to show you something."

I followed my father to the tractor shed. He was proud of the new John Deere 4420, and rightly so. The shiny green tractor was one of the first with a cab, plus air conditioning and heating, power steering, and an automatic transmission.

Daddy played a Loretta Lynn tape to demonstrate the fidelity of its radio and eight-track stereo tape deck.

I *had* to say it. "Daddy, do you remember the summer of 1960, when Mother had surgery in New Orleans, and you left a wetback and me to do all the farming?"

"Yeah you did a real good job for a kid of sixteen."

"I sure did. I drove that old Farmall-M tractor twelve hours a day, and it didn't have power steering and air-conditioning.

"Do you remember when I asked, that summer, to use *my own money* to put a radio on that Farmall tractor?"

"Not *really* . . ."

"Well *I* do. You hit the ceiling.

"You yelled, '*Tommy, that's the most damnfool idea you've ever had! Put a radio on that tractor, and you'll plow up our cotton, listening to that rock 'n' roll music. Farming is work, not fun!*' "

"But Tommy . . ."

"And now you show me *this*? My *car* doesn't have a stereo tape deck."

Then I asked: "Daddy . . . why wouldn't you let me put a radio on that damned tractor?"

Daddy thought a minute, then said, "I don't know . . . a tractor radio wouldn't have hurt anything."

I later wrote about another son's homecoming. My text was fiction, but I saw it happen in one of those awful villages in Chuong Thien Province:

Chapter 9

The monsoon rain lapsed and the sun scorched steam from the muddy streets. Dan, Khang, and the chief sat in the village office, studying a map of VC positions along the

Snake River. From the new outpost, local militia would provide security for a pontoon ferry to connect Nuoc Trong by road to Vi Thanh.

A bridge would be built across the Snake, the chief swore, to replace the one blown in 1945. But that would be after the Communists were defeated and *hoa binh* came. *Peace won't come to Chuong Thien soon,* Dan thought.

An excited voice rose outside. The chief stopped in midsentence, then sprang from his chair.

"What's wrong, Khang?" Dan sensed tension.

"I don' know, *Trung Uy*. Let's go see."

Three PF militia stood outside in black peasant trousers, camouflaged shirts, and sandals. They carried M-2 carbines, but a Chinese AK-47 assault rifle was slung, muzzle down, from one man's shoulder. Behind them, two other troops carried a stretcher.

A soldier talked carefully and quietly to the chief as he stepped into the black mud.

The litter bearers avoided the chief's eyes as they set the blood-stained stretcher before the village office, then stood aside.

Bare and muddy feet stuck ludicrously from under the poncho. Dan sensed what Cam would find.

The chief knelt by the stretcher and lifted the rubberized shroud. A stiffened arm was half-raised, in ghoulish salute. The corpse's pockets were turned inside out.

A blend of dried blood and mud caked the teenager's bare chest. A lieutenant at Fort Sill, just back from Vietnam, had told Dan that Vietnamese hardly bled, no matter where they were hit. He never saw *this* one, Dan thought.

One eye was glazed over, the other was a raw wound with a gray gel coagulated below. The boy's lips were curled, silently describing the brutality of his death. An ivory Buddha on a metal chain, like the one Dan now wore, rested across his throat.

Dead Vietnamese look so much bigger than live ones, Dan thought. And why do they turn that slate-gray?

The chief stared into the horrible face, then drew the poncho back over the body.

I should say something, but *what*? Dan felt that he shouldn't be witness to the chief's reunion with this last son who'd cast his lot with the Viet Cong.

Cam showed no emotion as he lifted the dead boy from the stretcher, turned silently, and carried him into his home next door. The poncho slid into the mud.

"Let's go back to the team hut, Khang."

How much can these people suffer, God, and for how long? What other cute tricks have you planned? But Dan knew there was no God—*not in Chuong Thien Province.*

Black clouds again blocked the sun, and heavy raindrops darkened Dan's fatigues as he walked through the mire.

We lived with my parents that fall, while I sent out resumes, made phone calls ... and thought about writing a novel. Agricultural science editors are scarce, so I had lots of job offers ... in the States. But I wanted to work in Asia, or Africa, or Latin America.

Meanwhile, food was free at the Hargrove farm, and I helped neighbors harvest cotton for $1.25 an hour.

But that couldn't last for long. I *had* to land overseas work soon, or take a boring conventional job like everyone else.

CHAPTER XXII
We Don't Go There Anymore

Ames, Iowa, the winter of 1970 and the spring of 1972 ... but really, Chuong Thien Province, 1969–70

In the fall the war was always there, but we did not go to it any more. . . . It was a cold fall and the wind came down from the mountains.
　　　　　　—Ernest Hemingway, *Men Without Women*

The winter of 1970–71 is gray in my memory. I've had worse times, before and since, but marked by strong passions of red or black, violence or anger, tragedy or despair. That winter of my life was as colorless and dismal as the cold gray skies of Iowa.

The war dragged on, but only on TV and in the papers. I didn't go there any more, but I knew that Khang and Frank and *Dai Uy* Hong and Monique and Norm were still there . . . if Chuong Thien Province hadn't killed them since I'd flown out on that ugly army Otter. It seemed so long ago, but had been only six months.

I should have been happy. I'd survived, and was now a well-paid professional. But that cold wind from the mountains—for me, it was knowing that I might spend years in Ames, Iowa—depressed me.

It was wrong, I knew, but I secretly missed Chuong Thien Province: her sunshine and intrigue, palm trees and rice fields, and danger. And, I guess, the rush of adrenalin, a hormone as intoxicating and addictive as opium, that came with the package. I thought of Chuong Thien like an illicit lover—an older, sinful, and passionate lady of the darkest night who once seduced a young man. I'd left her cold in June of 1970, but I was back with her in the early hours of each morning . . . feeling secret pain about what I'd seen happen there, combined with a worse secret—*guilt*—for wanting her back.

She was a bad place that hurt a lot of good people, but *I* came home with no physical scars. Nor emotional scars, I thought. Susan and my mother and a few friends weren't so sure.

My tour had been easy, and I felt a little guilty about that, too. I got irrationally angry when family or friends suggested that the experience had changed me. It would be another seven years before I'd recognize that something bad, indeed, had happened.

Coming back to Iowa State University, where I'd done my M.S. degree before the army, was a bad mistake. But what were my options?

After spending most of my army savings on three months of travel through the Middle East and Europe, Susan and I lived on the Hargrove farm in Texas for another three long months. I helped neighboring farmers harvest cotton for minimum wages, while trying to get work with CIMMYT—the International Maize and Wheat Improvement Center in Mexico—or with IRRI, or *any* agency that would send me back overseas to work in international agriculture.

Few veterans knew what to do with their lives after Vietnam. But I knew *exactly* what I wanted: to be part of the exciting new Green Revolution, spearheaded by the IRRI semidwarf rices and CIMMYT wheats. No farm technology, *anywhere*, had spread faster than those new cereal varieties, or had more positive effect on the lives of hundreds of millions of the world's poorest people.

There was no global system of International Agricultural Research Centers. Not yet. But I knew it would evolve.

President Abraham Lincoln changed U.S. agriculture, and in many ways, that of the world, when he signed the 1862 Morrill Act. That started the U.S. Land Grant system of agricultural universities and research stations in each state, and made American agriculture the world's most productive.

The International Centers would also change Third World agriculture. The movement had already begun, and I wanted to be part of it. The centers wouldn't make farming in Bangladesh like on our farm in Texas, I knew—but this fresh approach to agricultural development might hold off famine until mankind learns to control its numbers.

But international work is like money; if you have it, and you're good, it's easy to get more. The hard part is getting the first overseas experience.

But *damn it!* I *had* that experience. I'd played a key role in the spread of IRRI rice varieties in the Mekong Delta. Yet no developmental agency saw it that way. My army tour in Vietnam was a detriment, not a plus, to international work.

I got one overseas offer—as a civilian propagandist in the Land to the Tiller program. That was because my Land Reform cadre in Chuong Thien had led the Delta in redistributing old French and Chinese plantations to farmers.

But Mrs. Hargrove didn't raise a fool. I had better sense than to go back to Vietnam. Besides, that would mean moving Susan to a *safe haven* in Bangkok or Taipei or Manila to wait for visits, like Betsy Olsen and Urai Gillespie.

I finally *had* to take a job. A position at a respected agricultural university could lead to international work.

I sorted through the evening mail in my tiny office at Iowa State University at 5:00 P.M. in February 1971.

My parents had forwarded a letter from Mexico. Its return address was CIMMYT.

God, don't let this be the letter I've wanted for so long.

I'd never been to CIMMYT, but knew I wanted to work there. The wheat and maize center was becoming a lot better known since Norm Borlaug picked up that 1970 Nobel Peace Prize.

I stuffed the CIMMYT letter into a pocket and wrapped myself in woolen overcoat, gloves, and muffler. Those clouds are getting darker and . . . Lord, I hate Ames, Iowa, I thought. I'll read the letter when I get home, grab a quick dinner, then return to the campus for my 7:00 P.M. graduate class in research methodology for education.

No matter how dull we considered Iowa, its opportunity for graduate education was a compensation. An ISU Ph.D. would help me in a career in international agriculture, and I had a good start. I'd picked up extra credits when I'd done my M.S. from 1966 to 1968. As Iowa State faculty, I now could take one course per semester toward my doctorate degree during the work week. I always took another two courses at night. That made me, in reality, a half-time grad student, while working full-time.

I walked four freezing blocks through the 1971 blizzard to the nearest parking lot . . . at least, the nearest for *my* level of faculty.

Our 1964 Chevrolet was icy, but felt warm after the cutting wind. Two minutes of coaxing started the car, then I turned the heater to high.

Sleet was falling as I pulled into Safeway's asphalt parking lot. I dashed in, threw essentials from Susan's list into a grocery cart, then on impulse, tossed in a couple of avocados. Tropical fruits in Iowa in the worst winter since the 1870s. America is dull, but amazing.

Back in the freezing car, I couldn't wait any longer. I tore open that letter.

Dear Mr. Hargrove,

CIMMYT has opened a new position: English editor for the wheat program. We find your biodata, which you sent from Vietnam in May 1970, interesting. Your qualifications seem to fit those of the position.

The wheat editor must be willing to live in Mexico, and travel extensively to report on new wheat technology in Latin America, the Middle East, and Asia.

A job description is enclosed. If you wish to apply . . .

I swore, crumpled the letter, and threw it against the dashboard. I then guided the Chevy over icy streets to our new, three-bedroom condominium with its electric garage-door opener, garbage disposal, and hellacious payments.

I could kill for the CIMMYT job, and *knew* I'd be the best qualified candidate for it. But I couldn't apply.

Iowa State had offered me by far the best salary of any university, but with a gentlemen's agreement that I'd stay at least two years.

Now, two months after starting a job I hated, I stared at that letter from CIMMYT. Iowa State had no legal hold on me. But the red-dirt ethics my father had taught, did. A man *might* break legal contracts that lawyers wrote—but not his *personal word*, sealed with a handshake.

I began writing my novel that gray 1971 winter, wishing I'd kept a diary in Vietnam.

I wrote steadily each night after work, and through most weekends, for more than a year. Then the spring of 1972 brought a frightening experience. It was after my return from the Des Moines VA, or Veterans Administration, hospital where I'd been treated for an intestinal parasite that I'd picked up in Nam. The army doctor in Saigon, who identified the bug during the medical examination required for an army discharge, was proud of himself. He'd searched the medical journals and found that the parasite had never been reported outside North Vietnam. That didn't really surprise me. I'd shared meals in Chuong Thien with a lot of Catholics who'd fled the North after the 1954 Communist *liberation.*

The parasite wasn't giving me problems, but the army had classified me as 10 percent disabled. I guess I still am. I got the disability status so I'd qualify for VA treatment if the parasite caused complications later. But I've never received a monthly veteran's benefit check. That requires at least 15 percent disability.

I did nothing about that benign bug for almost two years after my discharge. But in April 1972, I felt that I'd better get rid of it, just to be safe. I made an appointment at the Des Moines VA hospital.

The VA doctor, who had retired from regular practice a dozen years earlier, prescribed a massive dose of a malaria treatment he'd doled out freely to soldiers in the Pacific during World War II. For five days, I took twenty-four Atabrine tablets a day—and didn't know that I was having a psychotic drug reaction. Going on a prolonged bad trip—but not knowing why you're freaking out—is scary.

I never slept during those frightening days and nights. I did flaky things at work, like leaving my car unlocked with ten thousand dollars worth of audiovisual equipment in the backseat. I said unreasonable things to Susan and to friends. And I talked about Chuong Thien Province—a lot—as I popped four Atabrine tablets every six hours. I got continuously worse, but didn't hallucinate until the fifth mind-altered night. That's when I decided to record my increasingly clear thoughts about the war . . . as another chapter of fiction for my novel.

Later, of course, I realized that the drug-induced text made no sense, and had no place in the book. Besides, my new text described Lt. Daniel Bridges as a civilian, after Vietnam, with a boring job at Kansas State University and bad memories of Chuong Thien. But I'd *already killed* Bridges, down by the Snake River.

Later, I filed the chapter and never saw it again until I cleaned old files in 1991. I read the 1972 text, and thought: This probably describes my inner self during that time better than any of my normal writing. It also hinted at how Hemingway's writing had influenced me, and how badly I wanted—*needed*—to write about Chuong Thien.

I'd drafted that chapter on the back sides of bright pink, but free, paper: throwaways of the Iowa State home economics press release series "The Homemaker's Helper: Those we love."

Chapter

Two barefoot men in black pajamas and cone hats pad silently through the green haze. They probe ahead with Chicom SKS's, held at waist level and tipped with gleaming steel bayonets. *My God, they've got me!*

No, goddamn you! Dan screamed the words silently and sprang up in bed, then stared numbly at Janice, sleeping beside him.

Jesus Christ, how long has it been since those little yellow men came after me? Why now, when I feel so goddamn lousy? Can't they see I'm not in Vinh Hoa or Kien Hung or anywhere in goddamn Chuong Thien Province? Besides, I'm not even the man they want. They want Lieutenant Calley or Audie Murphy, and that sure as hell wasn't me. I wasn't a war criminal or a hero, but I wasn't a Saigon warrior either. I was an average guy who did a not-so-dramatic job, and I'm not *there* anymore, I'm in Manhattan, Kansas, and it's April 1972, so *leave me the fuck alone, will you*?

Dan drained the ice water left in his glass on the bedside table. His knees were rubber and his mind felt free and hot, floating above as he stumbled downstairs, refilled the glass, and added ice cubes.

Why can't I sleep, and what's wrong with my body?

And why did I make a fool of myself last night? Or was it the night before, I can't remember. Maybe it was all inside and some of it *had* to come out. But why like that? Why did that bitch in the black cocktail dress *say* those things? And why didn't I ignore her? Everyone at the faculty cocktail party must think I'm fucking nuts. Psychologists say that talking helps, but I don't feel any better. Why did I rave that garbled nonsense when my mind is so clear now? And why does my head burn when the rest of me is so goddamned cold?

Could it be those little yellow pills you're taking, Dan? The ones to kill that Asian parasite that infiltrated your Caucasian gut? Those pills to cleanse your *war wound*?

War wound . . . *that's a good one.* If I ever have a kid and he asks if I were wounded in Nam, I'll point to my gut and tell the little bastard that I'm a disabled veteran, but I never got shot. No, the NVA got me with a sneakie little fucking Commie parasite bred in Hanoi. Won't that be a kick in the ass? And those pills aren't affecting me, I just can't sleep, that's all.

Well, maybe it wasn't those pills, Dan. Maybe you *had* to say those things last night, because it's always with you. If you lived in Vietnam as a young man, then wherever you go for the rest of your life, it stays with you, for Vietnam is a

movable fuck job. A movable, bloody, tragic, son of a bitch
fuck job.

That's not very original. And I haven't written much that
was original either . . . but that man did. I wonder what he'd
say about my book, my Commie parasite, the things I saw.
Probably that my writing's fucked up, and he'd be right. Because he's the only man who could write about war, truly,
like it was. *I* never saw his long winding corpse-strewn
trenches, or the horror and terror of a large army in full re-
treat. But that was Italy in 1917, not Asia in 1969. Yet look
how he wrote about the soldier's return to America after
he'd seen strange things and been to awful places and felt
strong emotions, but people didn't give a damn unless he
had some really *interesting* stories, like finding naked German women chained to machine guns. So he told the boys
at the pool hall just a few things that he didn't really do, but
that his buddies did. Then he despised himself, and didn't
talk about the war anymore, and soon he felt almost nothing.

You love to read him, Dan, because *he* knew the horrible
secret that every man who's been there hides in his soul, but
the blind fucking sheep who haven't, can't see. You share
the secret but hide it deeply, only sometimes a little gets
out because it's always there and it's a movable fuck job,
isn't it?

Putting it on paper for the few who might understand
made him a god, didn't it? Who else could live on, after
blowing his fucking brains out with a shotgun? Maybe *that
secret* made him do it—knowing that man is only a dirty,
despicable, cringing, cowardly, brutal animal, whose primary
instinct, whose ultimate thrill is to fuck, not love; to kill, not
save; to destroy, not build. But don't think I mean just you
fucking sheep out there. No, I've seen and felt what *I'm* really like, deep inside, and it's not pretty. You haven't. And
I'm only just now seeing the true depths.

Goddamn, why is this room so cold, and why does my
head hurt so much? Not this head, but my other head that's
floating in the dark across the room and saying this.

But I'll make those bastards read this, by God. They'll
think I'm out of my fucking mind and I hope they do—
because being crazy is part of the secret. Like that stale, sick
stench of flesh that's decaying on living bones, that horrify-

ing smell of death that, you know, is penetrating your own body.

I'll never think this clearly again and I must write it to drill some of this into your fucking heads. War is a bloody and humiliating dysentery that turns your guts into painful water. War is choppers coming in with corpses stacked three deep, and that's even more obscene. The bodies aren't just thrown in. No, the first and second layers of bloody ash-corpses are crisscrossed, and the living are stacked on top so a wounded man's head rests on a dead man's feet. And war's a yellow man on a blood-soaked stretcher, whose face twists with horrible pain. But you've seen it so many times, you don't feel anything. *Not one fucking thing.*

And war is when you finally return home, filled with those horrible and haunting—yet wonderful—secrets. Then a fat sheep asks how many of them yellow-bellied gooks did you kill over there and you say that you spent a lot of time trying *not* to kill or be killed, but when you killed, it was clean with jagged shrapnel but goddamnit, I was *really in the war.* But he's sure glad you weren't at the front like his nephew who was in Da Nang where it's *really* tough and where little gook kids put ground glass in bottles of Coke, or blow themselves up, along with any GI who's stupid enough to trust them, with hidden hand grenades. His nephew saw it dozens of times. And you want to shake the blind bastard and say I've heard that fucking story a hundred times, and I'm sure your nephew saw it, and I know it happened, but did you ever consider that *you* may have made him lie, because I was in a hundred villages at the slimy bottom of the Mekong Delta, and I never saw it. But no, you shake your head and say that must have been awful, and gooks have no respect for human life.

Yeah, and war is that pretty girl in the chic black dress at the cocktail party who asks where you've been, then says *How could you*? and walks away and you're embarrassed for her, even more than for yourself, because you know ... or *hope* ... that someday she'll know how cruel she was. But you said those things back, those things you shouldn't have said ... why?

I have another secret. There is no God. There never was, never will be. *Our nada who art in nada, nada be thy nada.* See? Hemingway knew that long before I did. If there's a

God, then what kind of son of a bitch is he? Don't tell me that it's man, not God, that causes innocent people to suffer so greatly. You say that God created man in his own image. If so, then God's gotta be a *real lousy bastard.*

But I know an even greater secret. It's in my head now, the head that's floating above me, and it's filling this room, and I'm going to tell you while it's so clear . . .

My *greater secret* was more babbling about God, the war, and Chuong Thien Province. As I worsened, the two yellow men returned, and the room got colder, and a huge scorpion snapped claws at me, then turned into a spider, and finally faded away . . .

I wrote dozens of pages, but nothing about how that fifth crazy night ended. My babbling woke Susan during an insane hallucination at dawn. My skin had turned a sick yellow, with bright red splotches. Susan rushed me to the Ames emergency clinic. There, a doctor took one look at my jaundiced skin and said: *"Hepatitis."*

We later learned that it was only a drug reaction to Atabrine. I'd soon be okay.

CHAPTER XXIII
A Return to the House

Ames, Iowa, Saigon, and Chuong Thien Province, 1972

> He shall return no more to his house,
> neither shall his place know him anymore.
> —Job, 7:10

After almost two years in Iowa, escape finally came through an unexpected phone call. But the job offer was in the only place outside the USA where I didn't want to go, that spring of 1972.

The phone rang as I was writing a bulletin on how agricultural research helps Iowa farmers and, in turn, urban consumers. The benefits were real, but the job was boring.

"Take line one," the office secretary said. "It's a Dr. Hank Stoddard of the vet college at the University of Minnesota."

Dr. Stoddard coordinated a preventive veterinary medicine program in Vietnam, on contract to USAID. Its purpose was to teach Vietnamese animal husbandry cadre how to *prevent*, rather than *treat*, livestock diseases. Vaccines were the key.

A veterinarian had returned to the States without finishing his contract—he'd had enough of Vietnam. The Minnesota project now had to spend, or lose, the money earmarked for his salary. They wanted to use those funds to publish two books, in Vietnamese, on prevention of livestock and poultry diseases. The veterinarians were already drafting the English text, but none had the time or expertise to arrange translation and publication.

Their solution: bring an agricultural journalist to Saigon to handle the job. But what professional would take a four-month consultancy in a war zone? My name appeared.

I hadn't been with Iowa State long enough to request leave, so I'd have to resign my university position, with no job lined up afterward, to take the contract.

Also, we'd just learned that Susan was pregnant with our first child. That complicated our lives.

Taking the consultancy made no sense—except that it *could* lead to a permanent overseas job. International agencies might consider an application from USAID/Vietnam more seriously than one from Iowa.

Susan surprised me. She agreed that I should return to Nam. My wife wanted out of Ames, too.

We had a fallback, if the plan didn't work. The consultancy paid good money—it *had* to. Savings could help send me back to graduate school, to finish my doctorate.

I had another, selfish reason. Returning to Vietnam might help me finish my novel.

In June of 1972, Susan and I were towing our Corvair behind an unairconditioned U-Haul rental truck, on the road from Ames to Rotan, Texas, where she'd live for the next four months.

At sundown, I drove off the freeway in Topeka, Kansas, where we had motel reservations. With my new Vietnam salary, we can dine on prime sixteen-ounce Kansas T-bones, I thought as I pulled under the Holiday Inn's thirteen-foot overhang—in our fourteen-foot truck.

Bricks crashed on the U-Haul's hood. *There goes my steak dinner.* To make it worse, we were at the wrong Holiday Inn. We ate hamburgers again that night.

In Rotan, we found Mother and Daddy shocked and angry. We're Texans, so going to war when your country calls was understandable, even if no one understands why. Vietnam, the first time, was for God and what America stood for . . . if you used enough imagination. But quitting a secure job and leaving a pregnant wife—to return to the war when I didn't *have* to—was *irrational.*

A week later, I had left Susan behind, for Vietnam once more. As planned, I got off the PanAm 747 in Manila, and rode a bus two hours south to Los Baños. There, I took a tricycle cyclo to Millar's Grocery.

I walked in as José Ona, my buddy from Vietnam two years before, was filling rice bins in his father-in-law's store. He was amazed to see me. Joe's USAID contract had expired, so he was back in the Philippines, waiting for the next one. With typical Filipino hospitality, he arranged a lavish lunch with his family.

Joe then borrowed a car from the family of his brother-in-law Yambao, an agronomist who was still in the Mekong Delta. We drove to the prestigious International Rice Research Institute, which had never answered my letters exploring for job possibilities.

The timing was good. IRRI had just opened a new position for a science editor, and there *couldn't* be many experienced agricultural journalists who knew rice. I left a biodata and samples of my work.

In Saigon, I moved into the Eden Roc Hotel. Each morning, I reported to a grimy office at the Ministry of Animal Science, where I wrote about swine and poultry diseases.

In the evenings, I'd stuff my pockets with pencils and chapters of my novel, and stroll down Tu Do Street.

Tu Do had been the smart Rue Catinat when Saigon was the proud gem of the French Empire. But she was garish and decadent that summer of 1972. Bars and hostesses were almost as numerous as two years before—but only thirty thousand potential dollar-paid customers remained in all of Vietnam.

A backbeat of rock 'n' roll pulsed onto the street as girls in miniskirts competed to lure the few GIs into garish dens. Buying a few rounds of *Saigon tea*, the bar girls promised, would lead to erotic thrills afterward. A soldier who refused to buy the inappropriately named *ladies' drinks* was a "Cheap Charley."

"Saigon Cowboys," long-haired Vietnamese draft-dodgers who wore Hollywood sunglasses and peace medallions, rode two on a Honda—so the cowboy on the back could snatch an unwary soldier's watch as the cowboy driver swerved back into traffic.

At dusk, I often stopped at the Continental Palace Hotel. A wooden French propeller hung over the veranda bar, where Graham Greene drafted *The Quiet American.* We called it the "Continental Shelf," for the flotsam of war that drifted there. A drink at the Shelf was a ticket to Saigon's theater of the absurd: soldiers and spooks, whores and money changers, and secretaries from the French Embassy. Air America pilots drank with transvestites, dope peddlers, and aid workers. Mercenaries and war correspondents bought beer for, and shared joints with, a few hippies on that dangerous and spaced-out road to Vientiane.

Artillery fire rumbled in the distance as overhead fans pushed air dripping with humidity and laced with enough marijuana smoke to stone the cyclo drivers and pimps who waited on the sidewalk.

I'd order gin and tonic, and watch the Shelf's crowd for an hour while editing chapters. Then I often met Fred Lippincott and Henry Green, air force majors stationed in Saigon. Fred was a gourmet who dictated where we'd dine. He often led us to Le Tour d'Argent by the Saigon River where our dinner started with shrimp paste grilled on peeled sugar cane. Then came *cha gio*, made by filling pockets of rice tortillas with bits of shrimp, crab, lettuce, and mint leaves, then dipping the rolls in *nuoc mam.* The meals were washed down with lots of *Ba Mui Ba* beer. We ended Chinese style, with plates of braised rice noodles, each made from a single, coiled strand, and fresh papaya with lime.

But we sometimes had lobster and cheap Algerian wine at the L'Amiral or Etoile, where haughty waiters embarrassed customers whose French wasn't perfect. Fred Lippincott's came close. We might go to the U.S. officers club on the roof of the Rex Hotel for sirloin steaks. We dined once at the Vietnamese Air Force officers club near the Tan Son Nhut air field. I'd never been in a combination officers club–massage parlor before.

August found me back in the Mekong Delta, drinking coffee in a French-style, streetside cafe in the old part of Can Tho, by the Bassac River. I was with six Vietnamese animal husbandry cadre and Dr. Steve Dille, the USAID veterinary adviser for the Delta. Steve was planning a new campaign to vaccinate water buffalo against hoof-and-mouth disease.

The cafe's front was open, except for steel-wire grills to block terrorist grenades. As we entered, I noticed two middle-aged construction men in dirty gray safari suits, drinking *Biere Larue* at the back of the cafe. That's odd, I thought. Americans usually drink in the red-light bars of Ben Xe Moi, not here in old Can Tho. I took a seat near the door, with my back to the street—a foolish move.

I practiced Vietnamese phrases as boiling water percolated through the tin basket of freshly ground coffee that sat on my cup.

"My jeep!" one of the construction men spilled our coffee, almost knocked our table over, dashing for the door. *"Get the fuck out of here! A kid on a bicycle stuck a package in my jeep!"*

I'd seen a lot of false panic in Vietnam. *Khang sau*, I thought. *No sweat.* We're in *Can Tho*, not Chuong Thien. But the construction man was scared. We'd better leave!

"Stay away from that goddamn vehicle!" The civilian meant the army-style jeep that he'd chained to a light post, to prevent its being stolen, ten feet from the cafe front.

"A kid shoved a yellow box under the seat, then pedaled away!"

I saw the box. That scared *me*, too. The Vietnamese ag cadre started waving the crowds off the packed street.

The construction man then did something very brave—or awfully stupid. Sometimes there's little difference.

He ran to the jeep, grabbed the yellow box, and hurled it. I hit the pavement.

The box broke open on the street. Three red flashlight batteries, lashed together, spilled out and landed a foot from the yellow package.

My God, it *was* a bomb! But it's okay now, the detonator has broken away. I eased up and walked toward the defused package.

About twenty feet away, I saw wires connecting the batteries to the yellow box. *The detonator—it's still hooked to the bomb!*

I dived back to the pavement and crawled, hugging asphalt. Oh, Hargrove, I thought. When that mother blows, it'll take out this whole block—including me!

From nowhere, a Vietnamese soldier darted into the street with wire cutters, snipped, and held up the package.

The kilo of *plastique* explosive was in a yellow cardboard box labeled Black Draught Laxative.

It hit me late that night. That bomb had *our number.* The kid set it to blow Steve and me and a U.S. jeep away as we sipped our French coffee. We were alive, but only because of a civilian construction man who shouldn't have been there . . .

Two decades later, I still don't sit with my back to an open door.

Something so strong, it was almost primeval, drew me back to Chuong Thien Province.

I arrived in Vi Thanh as Henry Kissinger and Le Duc Tho were talking peace in Paris, and the last U.S. ground combat unit, the 3d Battalion, 21st Infantry, was leaving Vietnam. America wanted to think the war was winding down, that an "honorable peace" was at hand. Never mind those hundreds of thousands of North Vietnamese troops who were tightening the noose on South Vietnam's destiny as we pulled out.

I was excited as a Vietnamese soldier drove me through mire from the air strip. Then a slim man flagged the jeep down by the Vi Thanh hospital. "Dr. Vinh," the deputy agricultural chief, had recognized me from two years before as we passed. He was crying. His four grandchildren had just detonated a VC mine while playing by the road. Three were dead. What could I say, I hope the fourth child lives?

The Vietnamese couldn't believe it . . . an American *returning* to Chuong Thien? For no reason but to *visit*? That had never happened.

My old mistress, I found, had been anointed in blood time

and again. The situation was far grimmer than when I'd left her.

I stayed in the CORDS compound, where I'd lived before. That night I drank a bitter mixture of cognac and beer from a brass trophy cup etched TEXAS STATE TRACK CHAMPIONSHIP: 1929 with Khang and Oahn and *Dai Uy* Hong and Dick Burke, who'd replaced Frank Gillespie. I'd stolen the cup, as a kid's prank, from a trophy case at Rotan High School. We'd drunk bootleg beer from the trophy—it held a quart—along dusty West Texas roads in more innocent, teenage days. I took the trophy cup to Texas A&M, then Pauline Fleming, an old friend from Rotan, sent it to me in Vietnam. Drinking from the Texas trophy soon became a Vi Thanh tradition, so I'd left it with my Vietnamese friends in 1970.

The night was black like only the lower Delta, deep in the monsoon season, can be. The cup passed from man to man in the soft glow of an oil lantern, augmented by ghostly flares fired around the perimeter.

The blast of outgoing 155mm shells interrupted our conversation. A desperate ARVN unit blared frantic and metallic radio calls for more artillery from an outpost surrounded by North Vietnamese troops in Kien Thien, twenty kilometers south.

But there wasn't much to say. The Americans were leaving, and we all knew the Vietnamese didn't stand a chance. Everyone in that room—except, maybe, Burke and me—would soon be a prisoner, or a refugee, or more likely, dead.

I asked about Monique, the model for the Monique in my novel, as we drank ourselves to numbness.

"I only know, Tom, that Monique went to Saigon to work at Maxim's in the fall of 1970," Khang said, taking a long pull from the Texas trophy cup.

The next morning I watched an agonizingly familiar sight. Men rushed stretchers into the Vi Thanh hospital from an insect-looking Huey, while its crew stacked corpses by the helipad. The wounded and dead were Vietnamese, like most were before, but in 1972, the chopper's pilot and crew were also Asian.

I flew out on an Air America Porter flown by a CIA-paid pilot, one of the last American cowboys. I was more despondent than angry, as we barreled almost vertically from the Vi

Thanh airstrip. This time, I was leaving Chuong Thien Province for good . . .

The next Saturday afternoon, I walked to Maxim's, down by the Saigon River. The heat inside the expensive night club was stifling, but the air-conditioning wouldn't come on until opening time, hours away. I explained my purpose to the *madame*, who took me to meet a hostess in her room.

"Yes, I remember Monique, the beautiful French girl. She was my special friend." The hostess was tall, but wore a shortie nightgown. It wasn't a see-through nightie, but she wore nothing underneath, and wasn't concerned about exposing flesh as she bent to face a cracked mirror above the sink. This *was* Saturday, and she had to be ready for tonight's customers—not so many as at the height of the war, but Maxim's always attracted Saigon's most affluent crowd.

"Monique was cashier—until she became girlfriend of General Chan, numba one important man," the girl said, rolling hair onto a curler. "She and the general went ever'where: Da Nang, Ban Me Thuot, Dalat, Hue."

"*But what happened to Monique?* Where is she now?"

"We don' hear nothing for mebbe one year," she shrugged. "Prob'ly she die . . . you wanna buy me a drink?"

I tipped the hostess and walked up Tu Do Street to Rosie's Bar. I ordered a black-market Budweiser and thought . . . Monique was pretty and different and a bit shallow. She wanted one thing desperately: out of Chuong Thien Province. To me, Monique symbolized the war, though God knows she didn't want to. Monique *was* Vietnam: a tragic hybrid, born from conflict of East and West.

I drank my Bud . . . really, Hargrove, Monique is no more a tragedy than each of the thousands of VC, ARVN, and NVA soldiers, and thirty or forty U.S. advisers, and God knows how many thousand civilians, slaughtered routinely and for nothing—over a dismal piece of swampy terrain.

No, it's just that I knew the *real* Monique . . . sad and French and now, I suppose, dead. Then I learned to love her, a little, by creating a new Monique for my novel. That's all . . .

That evening I wrote to Bud Shields, my Texas Aggie buddy, in West, a central Texas town about like Rotan. Bud had served as an army captain, and district senior adviser in Kien Hung, the Cambodian district where I'd spread IR8 and learned about Buddhism. Bud had promised to write when we last shook hands in Vi Thanh. But he didn't.

My only good news was about Major Phiep, Bud's close friend and counterpart:

After you left, Phiep was promoted to Lt. Col., transferred, and named district chief of Kien Thien. We both know that KT needed a strong leader who was honest, for a change.

But my other news was also about Chuong Thien, and Col. Phiep's fate, and anguish:

Chuong Thien has been by far the hardest-hit province in the Delta since the April offensive began. More than 3,000 GVN military casualties in May and June.

Phiep and the new DSA led reinforcements to besieged outposts regularly—*too regularly*, some say. They set a pattern. So . . . a remote Kien Thien outpost was hit in May. Phiep and the DSA brought relief troops in by sampan—they couldn't get choppers. Phiep laid flank security on both sides of the canal, but the VC set *that* trap just for him. The DSA died first. Then Phiep was killed, carrying his U.S. counterpart's body from the canal.

An ironic aftermath. A huge crowd of VN attended Col. Phiep's funeral in Vi Thanh. As the procession marched through town, an American sergeant, driving a garbage truck, cut through, crossing in front of the truck carrying Phiep's coffin. There was almost a riot, but the PSA got things quieted down. The sergeant was transferred out of Chuong Thien the next day, but the damage was done. One more example of why only a selected few intelligent and empathetic men should be allowed on any advisory team.

Sorcerers across Chuong Thien now claim contact with Col. Phiep's spirit. Dick Burke told me that VN commanders even plan operations on intelligence, like NPA and VC troop movements, that Phiep sends from the dead. Do I believe that? I don't know. Strange things happen in Southeast Asia. We both know that.

At least 5,000 enemy troops—mostly NVA—are now in Chuong Thien. They've cut the road from Vi Thanh to Kien Hung, probably permanently. The ferry across the Snake River was blown, again and again, until GVN finally gave it up. (In fact, *no* ferry is still in use in CT.)

The new hootches that farmers were building along that road while we were there—all are abandoned. Only NVA live on the Kien Hung side of the Snake River.

The Communists have overrun about 100 of the province's 250 outposts since April. GVN has retaken only eight. The NVA overran the U.S. district team hut at Kien Thien. The KT team killed six NVA inside the hut, retaking it.

The Cambodians have been fantastically loyal to GVN during the offensive. Saigon's offensive against the North Vietnamese in Cambodia probably united them.

Chuong Thien was always a damned bloody place, Bud, but it's far worse now. Sorry I don't have more pleasant news. One shouldn't make sentimental journeys back to a place like Vi Thanh, and expect to find satisfaction or happiness. I enjoyed meeting, eating, and drinking with my old VN friends—but I feel a deep sense of depression over it all.

I also wrote:

When this VN tour ends, I may move to South America. The International Center for Tropical Agriculture near Cali, Colombia—called CIAT for its Spanish acronym—has contacted me about a job. I could also do my Ph.D. research while working there.

Bud never answered that 1972 letter.

At dawn a week later, Dr. Gary Beck and I headed north to Nha Trang, a seaside town that was popular as a resort before the war, in a Ford truck with a purebred Duroc boar in the back. Beck was leader of the Minnesota veterinary team, but had served two previous tours in Vietnam as a Green Beret captain. He was stationed in Nha Trang during one of those tours, and now chose to live in a French villa there, rather than a USAID apartment in Saigon.

The Duroc boar and I shared a common bond. He, too, had escaped Iowa for the tropics. But the boar's mission was to leave strong Midwestern genes among Vietnamese stock. I came to escape a dull life.

We heard gunfire as we drove down a steep valley road north of Xuan Loc. Ahead, prone ARVN soldiers pumped a stream of automatic weapons fire across the road into the forest, and took return fire. Beck thought quickly. We couldn't stop, or turn around, so—

"Hang on!" Beck shifted down and gunned the motor. I dived to the floorboard, clutching a shotgun. We barreled and bounced through the firefight. Not a single bullet hit the truck. The Duroc boar slept through it all, dreaming whatever hogs dream about.

Nha Trang was lovely, but the scores of prostitutes on its streets weren't. Most were amateurs in that oldest of professions—refugees, driven from villages around Quang Tri, further north, by the newest NVA offensive.

A cyclo driver stopped me along a Nha Trang street. "You want girl? I take you special place. Vietnamese girl, Chinese, mountain girl . . . all, I have jus' for you. You want virgin?"

"No thanks. I'm not in the mood for virgins today."

"But sir! I have *ref'rence*." The cyclo driver proudly handed me a letter, printed crudely by ballpoint pen:

TO WHOM IT MAY CONCERN:
This is to certify that Mr. Huong is a dam good pimp. He always gets you good pussy and his girls don't hardly ever have the clap
Certified:

SSGT Curtis Hawkins
C CO 3BN 1ST INF DIV

"Good ref'rence?"

"A wonderful reference." I walked on.

I listened to the Armed Forces Vietnam Radio Network on 23 September 1972 in Saigon, while packing my suitcase.

My trip the next day was important. A cable from the International Rice Research Institute had arrived a few days before.

Steve Breth, head of IRRI communications, had reviewed my biodata, checked my references, and invited me to fly to the Philippines to interview for a new position: science editor.

I paid little attention to the radio news until I heard the word *Manila*:

We repeat, President Ferdinand Marcos has declared a state of national emergency and decreed martial law in the Philippines. All radio and television stations, and newspapers, have been shut down. Manila International Airport is closed to incoming and outgoing traffic. We will inform you of further developments . . .

It was two weeks before I got into the Philippines. I expected tanks, troops, and sandbagged bunkers to line Manila's streets, like in Saigon. But the only obvious change since my visit en route to Vietnam was a 10:00 P.M. curfew and removal of the sign CHECK WEAPONS AT THE DOOR from bars and restaurants.[1] President Marcos had declared the ownership of firearms illegal in a country reported to have more guns per capita than my native Texas.

IRRI offered the job. I accepted. I'd return to Texas when the Vietnam consultancy ended in early November. We'd move to the Philippines, after Susan had the baby.

But I didn't go straight from Saigon to Texas, I stayed in Asia for another week. The reason: because the baby was due late that same month.

If that sounds illogical or irresponsible, blame the Internal Revenue Service for my reasoning.

The IRS would slap income tax on my Vietnam earnings if I stayed in the States thirty-three days between overseas assignments.

I flew from Saigon to Phnom Penh, excited about finally visiting what I considered Asia's most exotic country. But the capital was all I saw of war-torn Cambodia. Foreign tourists— that's what I was, although I didn't *consider myself a tourist*— couldn't leave the city limits.

I checked into the old Royale Hotel, renamed Le Phnom

[1] Those signs were up again by the late 1980s, and firearms were about as common as before.

when General Lon Nol overthrew Prince Sihanouk in a military coup two years before. Then I set out to explore the city.

Phnom Penh was a lot like Saigon must have been, a decade before. A sleepy, French-colonial town with broad boulevards, red-tile roofs, French restaurants, saffron-robed Buddhist monks, and graceful wats with spiraling eaves. It didn't really seem like a city at war. Taxi drivers, waiters, anyone who dealt with the public spoke French, but most were then studying English.

A convoy of American deuce-and-a-half trucks barreled through Phnom Penh during my first afternoon there, carrying teenage Cambodian soldiers to the fighting a few miles away. I'd watched the same scene dozens of times, but with Vietnamese actors. The troops assumed I was American, and waved and cheered because, like almost everyone in that doomed city, they knew the United States would save them from the insane Khmer Rouge. But *I* knew those boys were riding to slaughter in U.S. 2.5-ton trucks. Cambodia was even more hopeless than Vietnam.

July, 1991. Thinking about Cambodia in those days reminds me of a new agricultural term. Rice scientists sometimes call Cambodia's main agricultural system today *widow farming*, because women head most rural households: widows . . . and 60 percent of the country's remaining labor force is younger than eighteen.

Cambodia planted 6 million acres of rice, and was an exporter in the late sixties. Pol Pot's brand of Khmer socialism reduced its rice land to less than 1 million acres. Land planted to rice has gradually increased to 4.5 million acres, but Cambodia still imports half a million metric tons of rice yearly.

Meanwhile, 1.5 million acres of rice land lie idle because the war decimated not only Cambodia's farmers but also water buffalo, its main source of farm power.

Mechanization is out of the question; it takes one tractor to bring each 125 acres into production. Cambodia has only twelve hundred tractors.

Almost all of Cambodia's agricultural specialists—few, and poorly equipped before the war—died or fled during the Pol Pot era. Rebuilding the infrastructure is difficult and expensive. Fanatic children soldiers of the Khmer Rouge destroyed all scientific equipment, plus buildings, labs, and irrigation systems.

Cambodian agriculture must start again from scratch.

But this gives the country a chance to intensify rice production while avoiding the mistakes of other countries, such as pesticide misuse.

IRRI mounted a crash program to help Cambodia in 1987, funded by the Australian Government. We had trained fifty-one Khmer agriculturists in basic rice technology by 1991. The IRRI-Cambodia project stresses rice varieties and technologies to raise yields and improve soil fertility, while avoiding chemical pesticides and minimizing use of fertilizers.

Transition 13

Ho Chi Minh City, 18 May 1990

The setting sun makes it hard to scan the landscape below as we descend. First, I see only rugged hills that change to rubber plantations and coconut groves, then rice fields cut by twisting rivers and muddy canals. A few water-filled bomb craters come into view as we approach Ho Chi Minh City, then a line of pockmarks ... from a B-52 stick.

I'm returning to Chuong Thien, a province that doesn't even exist, not on the new maps. It's my third return since leaving her in June 1970.

Why? For *National Geographic*? To promote rice science for IRRI? For Vietnam?

For all of those reasons. But I'm *really* coming back *for me*.

My 1972 return was macabre. The 1988 return was too short and too overwhelming to comprehend.

This time, I'll spend three days in Vi Thanh, find Vietnamese friends, explore the old places. Maybe I can drive that road to Kien Hung, cross the Snake River and visit *Sai* Ngoc at the

Cambodian monastery at Dinh Anh village again, sit under that giant Buddha while the monk practices English by explaining Buddhism . . .

The Ilyushin touches the runway at Tan Son Nhut, where our chartered Braniff DC-8 of scared GIs landed twenty-one years ago. The Soviet-made airliner taxis past dozens of domed concrete shelters built to protect U.S. aircraft from Soviet-made rockets.

Along this same runway in 1988, we passed a junkyard of broken war relics abandoned in 1975: Caribou C-7s, Huey UH-1s, DC-3s. Now, the ghostly planes and choppers are gone, melted down as scrap metal in Japan.

Getting into Vietnam, this time, was not easy. Susan and I had no trouble, I'm with IRRI. The problem was Lynn Johnson, the *National Geographic* photographer.

Lynn's entry visa would also go smoothly, I thought. Vietnam knows how influential *National Geographic* is. Lynn's photos would project a positive image, especially in the United States where Vietnam so desperately wants "normalization" of diplomatic relations.

I was wrong. I had applied for visas ten weeks before our scheduled 15 May entry. A month later, telexes from Hanoi confirmed that all three visas were approved and waiting at the Vietnamese Embassy in Manila. Lynn flew to the Philippines six days early so we'd have ample time to handle any unexpected red tape.

On 10 May, a Vietnamese Embassy official told Lynn there was a mistake. Hanoi had *not* cleared her visa. I sent a barrage of telexes, faxes, and phone calls to Hanoi and Ho Chi Minh City.

May 15 passed. Still no visa.

"Maybe there's political trouble in Vietnam," I phoned Lynn, who was waiting in Manila. "Could the Communist officials suddenly want to keep media out?"

"I read about a big celebration planned this month," Lynn said. "Something about Ho Chi Minh . . ."

That triggered it. "Lynn, hold for a minute."

I pulled my Vietnam diary onto the computer screen and entered "Ho Chi Minh" on *word search*. I had written his name five times. The fifth reference was in the last diary entry I made in Vietnam:

19 May 1970

In exactly one month I will be a civilian and leave VN.

Today is Buddha's birthday—more important, it's also Ho
Chi Minh's birthday—VC mortared Vi Thanh last night—
six or seven rounds hit 31st ARVN Regt. Also a plastic
mine on one—

Those cryptic notes from two decades ago told me what was
happening today.

That night, Susan pieced the situation together from newspapers and magazines. Word of the changes sweeping Eastern
Europe, China, the USSR had reached intelligentsia, clergy,
and labor leaders in Vietnam. A protest on 19 May—the one
hundredth anniversary of Ho Chi Minh's birth—would draw
world attention, and a professional, American photographer
like Lynn would *not* be welcome.

I sent more telexes, and pulled every string that my IRRI
position allowed. Hanoi finally faxed Lynn's visa on 17 May.
No other journalist, I later learned, had been allowed to enter
the country since early May. Only IRRI's prestige in Vietnam
got her the visa.

Meanwhile, I'd booked seats on every flight to Ho Chi
Minh City. We'd catch Air Vietnam the next day.

Our Manila departure was delayed two hours, but not by air
traffic or mechanical problems. An hour after takeoff time, Filipino airport workers told me that the Air Vietnam pilots and
crew weren't even in the terminal—they were shopping in Manila. The crew finally appeared, pulling carts of food, cigarettes, and clothes to use or sell in Vietnam. The two-hour
flight was spartan.

"What kind of plane were we on?" Lynn asks as we go
through immigration in stifling heat at Tan Son Nhut Airport in
the Ho Chi Minh City.

"The kind with bad food," Susan responds.

We're considered an IRRI delegation, even though not the
standard group of plant breeders, entomologists, and economists. Lynn is small and quiet, with round glasses and curly
red hair. Her backpack is stuffed with four Leica range finders,
six lenses, and one hundred and forty rolls of Kodachrome 64.

Susan doesn't like this trip, and I'm surprised she's here.

She's never been to Vietnam, but her personal memories of it may be worse then mine. Susan is hoping that we'll somehow be denied admission, sent back to the Philippines.

Workers finally push carts of luggage into the terminal. I'm relieved to see the most vital piece, a box marked INTERNATIONAL RICE RESEARCH INSTITUTE. It holds eight kilograms of seeds of two advanced IRRI rice strains. Their experimental line numbers tell part of their complex histories: IR41996-118-2-1-3 came from the 41,996th cross, or hybridization, made at IRRI. The other numbers tell which plant was selected from subsequent generations. The second line is IR50404-57-2-2-3.

Genes of the forgotten Vietnamese variety Tetep have been packaged into the seeds of both rices. So have genes of more than twenty other varieties that plant breeders from a dozen nations have crossbred over thirty years.

We clear customs easily, then we're met by Dr. To Phuc Tuong, an irrigation engineer with the University of Agriculture and Forestry near Ho Chi Minh City. Tuong completed his university education, from bachelor's degree to doctorate, in New Zealand. His English is excellent and his sense of humor better.

Bicycles and motorbikes crowd the streets of the city that will always be Saigon to me. "This feels like China," Susan says. Lynn agrees. I don't.

We check into the Majestic Hotel, where the old Tu Do Street meets the Saigon River. Like most places from the past, the French-era hotel now bears a new name: the Cuu Long, or Mekong Hotel. I had requested rooms there partly so Nguyen An Khang—now Nguyen An Huu—could find me easily, if he got my letters. Of course, I'd written that we'd arrive on 15 May—three days earlier.

I had good news for Khang. His role as a U.S. interpreter had been verified by three other Chuong Thien veterans: Frank Gillespie, Chauvin Wilkinson, and Dick Burke. Wilkinson, now an attorney in Baton Rouge, even sent a handwriting analysis on law-firm letterhead. He compared Khang's 1990 signature with one on a map of Chuong Thien that friends signed at his farewell party in 1971. The Orderly Departure Program in Bangkok had reopened Khang's case, and he now seemed eligible for U.S. immigration. But does Khang know that?

I check. There are no messages for me at the front desk.

Our room is spacious, and has a rattling window air conditioner.

"This room is the pits," Susan says and my stomach tightens. Susan's idea of roughing it is staying in a fat-towel hotel and ordering things by room service. What will Can Tho be like? . . . worse still, Vi Thanh?

But Susan perks up that evening as we stroll along Tu Do Street, where I lived for four months in 1972. The street has been renamed Dong Khoi, for the revolutionary resistance movement against former president Ngo Dinh Diem.

Tu do means "freedom." I soon learn a popular joke in Saigon: Tu Do Street was renamed when freedom fled in 1975.

There was little freedom in the old Republic of Vietnam either, of course, but jokes like that reflect how people feel. I learned *that* in black propaganda courses at Fort Bragg.

The street looks a lot like before . . . if you forget the bars and GIs and Saigon cowboys, and ignore the red banners and flags for tomorrow's celebration of what would have been Uncle Ho's one hundredth birthday. We pass a seedy side street that GIs called "Skag Alley." Dope was peddled freely here during the war. I wonder if it still is?

We pick a restaurant and I order: soup, spring rolls, a sliced beef dish, rice. Then we stroll further up Tu Do, passing the Caravelle Hotel, now renamed the Doc Lap, or "Independence." War correspondents must have written thousands of stories in its rooms.

Then . . . *there she stands*. The once grand Continental Palace Hotel.

It won't be the same, but we go in for a beer anyway. The Continental Shelf has turned respectable, and hopes to attract foreign businessmen. Its open-air veranda has been glassed in and air-conditioned, and houses a souvenir shop. I wonder what happened to the wooden French propeller over the bar? Gone, too, is the decadence and, I must admit, *romance* of wartime Saigon.

Walking back to the hotel, I'm surprised to see Maxim's, the pseudo-French nightclub where I searched for the half-French Monique in 1972. I stay behind while Susan and Lynn walk on to the Majestic. I *must* go in.

The front room is crammed with parked motorbikes and bicycles. I work my way through them and climb a stairway to the club's entrance. Teenage couples gyrate to a Vietnamese band blaring New Wave. Others nurse contraband Heineken or canned Coca-Cola at candlelit tables.

It's better this way. I don't enter Maxim's.

CHAPTER XXIV
A Grass Called Rice

IRRI, Los Baños, Philippines. January 1973 through November, 1991

> With coarse rice to eat, with water to drink, and my bended arm for a pillow—I have still joy in the midst of these things.
> —Confucius, *The Confucian Analects*

Miles was born on Thanksgiving Day, 1972 . . . ten days after I returned from my second, civilian tour in Vietnam. At age four days, my mother and I drove him thirty miles through a rare West Texas snowstorm to Snyder, the nearest town where a passport photo could be made.

At age six days, Susan and I drove Miles seventy miles to Abilene to apply for a passport. Miles had his own passport on his tenth birthday—in days, not years.

When Miles was twenty days old, we had sold the car, shipped our household goods to the International Rice Research Institute, and closed the house in Rotan, where Susan had lived the past four months. We were on a plane to England, then would spend Christmas in Iran with Susan's parents. I had been back in the USA exactly thirty days.

We followed that insane schedule for the same reason I had delayed my return to Texas: if I stayed in the States for thirty-three days, the Internal Revenue Service would take a lot of my earnings.

That may sound insensitive, even cruel, but Susan agreed. She didn't want to pay those annoying taxes either. Had there been complications, my plan was to fly to Mexico and hole up in a cheap hotel until I could return and escape ahead of the IRS.

We beat the IRS by three days.

Susan was exhausted when John and Marsha Lippincott met our flight in London, and took us by train to their Oxford flat.

We two couples had become friends when John was an army intelligence lieutenant, just back from Vietnam, at the JFK Center at Fort Bragg. John had been a MAC-V adviser in Vinh Long, a Mekong Delta province about like Chuong Thien, in 1968–69. It was a bad tour, especially when the VC overran Vinh Long during the 1968 Tet Offensive. After his discharge, John was accepted as a Ph.D. candidate at Oxford. The Lippincotts had moved to England soon after I shipped out to Nam.

John had a deep sense of history, and had written to me in Vietnam: "History permeates Oxford, but isn't being made here. History is being shaped in places like Vinh Long and Chuong Thien."

In Oxford, we talked about our present lives, and what we'd do in the future. But little about Vietnam, a bond that held us together.

John finally told me that he was writing a book about the Vietnam experience.

My friend was obviously torn by . . . something. Maybe I could have helped him, but how? I'd had an easy tour in Chuong Thien Province, and carried no ghosts of my own. That's what I thought, back then. Really.

Also, John and I had both learned that talking about Vietnam *embarrassed* people . . . including us. It made people uneasy, like discussing a death they could have prevented.

We stayed with the Lippincotts for three days, then flew to Tehran to spend Christmas with the Sheldons. I arrived in the Philippines on 14 January 1973. Susan and Miles followed a month later.

I was proud to join twenty-five scientists from ten countries, the elite, professional core of the International Rice Research Institute. But in many ways, I had joined IRRI back in 1969.

The Institute offered travel, excitement, prestige, and most important, a sense of satisfaction in meaningful work. Its future challenge awed me, because it seemed impossible—to ensure that Asia's farmland, which was shrinking yearly, would produce enough rice to feed a population that was increasing by almost 3 percent per year.

The origin of the remarkable grass that means life itself to Asia goes back 130 million years, to Gondwanaland. There, wild rice spread until the ancient supercontinent broke and drifted apart to become Asia, Africa, the Americas, Australia, and Antarctica.

The Bible doesn't mention rice, but it plays an important role in all the ancient Asian equivalents of Christianity.

About ten thousand years ago, humans gathered seeds of wild rice from the marshes of Asia. The first farmer—probably a woman, not a man—eventually learned to plant seeds near home, to ease her daily harvest. Taming the wild grass gradually settled the nomadic, hunting tribes of Asia. They became farmers.

Rice became Asia's lifeblood. Today, the cereal provides more than half the daily food for one of every three persons on earth.

Perhaps I should mention a few facts about rice that few Westerners know:

-More than 90 percent of the world's rice is grown and consumed in Asia, where 60 percent of the world's people live.

-Rice is planted on 11 percent of the world's farmland. Wheat covers slightly more land, but farmers feed a lot of wheat to livestock. Rice feeds humans, almost exclusively.

-*Honda* means "main rice field" and *Toyota* translates as "bountiful rice field."

-Health food advocates in western countries pay a premium for brown, or unpolished rice, but rice is polished wherever it is the staple food. Why? Brown rice can be stored for only a few months, then oils in its outer bran layer turn rancid. Two-pound packages of brown rice may sell in San Francisco gourmet shops, but brown rice could never feed Hanoi or Jakarta.

Brown rice may, in fact, be *less* nutritious than white rice—because humans cannot digest and absorb it as easily.

Brown rice has more B vitamins, however, and 1 percent more protein. The difference in fiber and minerals is insignificant. Rice is 7 to 8 percent protein; wheat is 12 to 13 percent.

-The price of rice bran has soared in North America since 1989 because of reports that it lowers cholesterol.

-The largest domestic consumer of U.S. rice is Anheuser-Busch. Michelob, Budweiser, and Coors are rice-based beers. Breweries use mostly broken grains.

-The "wild rice" that brings ten to thirty dollars per pound in gourmet shops in North America and Europe is *not* rice. It is *Zizania aquatica*, an aquatic grass that American Indians have harvested for centuries in Minnesota, Wisconsin, and southern Canada. Since the early 1970s, farmers have grown "wild rice" commercially in California and Minnesota.

Zizania is North America's only native cereal, and the first wild food crop that man has domesticated since the time of the pharaohs!

How did IRRI enter the picture?

Asia was desperate for food after World War II. Only massive shipments of North American grain averted famine.

Technicians tried to transfer Western farm technology to Asia, but failed. Large machinery and seeds that must be purchased yearly didn't work on small farms.

The Club of Rome became big news in the early 1960s by predicting that the world's population would outstrip food production within a decade.

A "doomsday date" was set in 1966 with publication of the U.S. Department of Agriculture *1984 Graph*—the year that food needs of the hungry nations would exceed America's capacity to respond.

In 1967, the Paddock brothers moved the doomsday date nine years closer—to 1975—and predicted that the 1970s would be a "Time of Famines."

But other forces were also in action. In 1943, U.S. vice-president Henry A. Wallace had visited Mexico and was shocked by its pitiful crops of corn, and the poverty of its countryside. Wallace knew the potential of agricultural research. In the late 1930s, the Iowan had established Pioneer

Hi-Bred—the first major company to sell hybrid corn seed. Hybrid seeds revolutionized U.S. agriculture.

Wallace sent a personal appeal to help Mexican agriculture to Dr. Raymond B. Fosdick, president of the Rockefeller Foundation. In 1943, RF assembled four American agricultural scientists near Mexico City to work with Mexico's wheat and corn improvement programs. Dr. Norman Borlaug, a young plant pathologist, was part of that team, later known as "The Four Horsemen of the Rockefeller Foundation."

Scientists had traditionally sought better ways to control pests through chemicals. But Borlaug saw that *genetic resistance* to diseases and insects was cheaper and safer. That was the main goal as he and Mexican scientists started crossbreeding wheats, to develop better varieties for Mexican farmers.

Meanwhile, in 1946 Dr. S. C. Salmon, a USDA geneticist serving as agricultural adviser to Gen. Douglas MacArthur's occupation army in Japan, was surprised to find wheat growing like little bushes, two feet tall, in northern Honshu. The dwarf wheat variety, Norin 10, seemed to compensate for its shortness by thrusting up more, and stronger, stems.

Salmon sent Norin 10 seeds to Dr. Orville A. Vogel at Washington State University. The wheat breeder crossed the dwarf with U.S. varieties to develop Gaines, a short-statured wheat variety that produced heavier grain heads but wouldn't lodge, or fall over.

Vogel sent a packet of seeds that carried the Norin 10 dwarfing gene to Norm Borlaug. By then, Mexico's wheat production was already rising because of Borlaug's new disease-resistant varieties.

By the late 1950s, Borlaug had crossed seeds with the Norin 10 genes with local varieties to develop the first *semidwarf* wheats, no more than knee-high. The most successful was 8156—given that name for Borlaug's 8,156th cross. This variety, 8156, yielded bountifully in Mexico, and its seeds soon spread to Pakistan where it was called "MexiPak," then to Turkey, Iran, India.

Mexico had imported half of its wheat in the 1940s, but became self-sufficient in 1957. The semidwarfs covered 95 percent of Mexico's wheat land by 1963. Production had tripled by 1967, and Mexico started *exporting* wheat—even though its population had doubled, and per capita food consumption had increased by 40 percent. That year, the RF Mexican wheat program was formally transformed into the International Center for Maize and Wheat Improvement, or CIMMYT.

Meanwhile, in the late 1950s, executives of the Ford and Rockefeller Foundations met monthly for lunch in New York. During the 18 August 1958 meeting, an unplanned but remarkable dialogue took place between Dr. Forest F. or "Frosty" Hill, director of agriculture for Ford Foundation, and Dr. George Harrar, one of the "Four RF Horsemen" who had since risen to be RF's agricultural science director.

"You know, George, someone should work with rice the way you Rockefeller Foundation people have with corn and wheat," Hill said. RF was also concerned about the rice problem, Harrar replied.

"We have some money," Hill said as the lunch ended. "You have experience in conducting agricultural research in developing countries. We're both interested in doing what we can to help solve the world's food problem. Why don't we get together and see what we can do?"[2]

That conversation, over lunch, ended with a handshake that led to the two foundations establishing the International Rice Research Institute two years later.

IRRI itself was an experiment. It was the first modern research facility placed in a developing country to focus science on food production.

To me, what did *not* happen is the greatest success story of IRRI and CIMMYT.

The increased yields from IR8 and other IRRI varieties averted the predicted "Time of Famines"—at least, for a few decades. No new farm technology ever spread more rapidly. By 1990, the increased production from the new rice technology kept 700 million people alive. Almost all are in developing countries.

The total fed by the Green Revolution easily exceeds 1 billion people, if you add those fed by the CIMMYT wheats, and improved strains of potato, beans, millet, cassava, vegetables, and sorghum developed by other International Agricultural Research Centers. All were patterned after IRRI and CIMMYT.

[2] From *An Adventure in Applied Science: A History of the International Rice Research Institute*, by Robert F. Chandler, IRRI's founding director. IRRI published the book in 1982.

Global rice production rose from a stagnant 280 million metric tons in the 1960s to 485 million tons in 1990.

China is the world's largest rice producer, growing about 175 million tons a year. Next are India, Indonesia, Bangladesh, and Thailand. The rice harvest in Vietnam, the world's sixth-largest producer, is about 16 million tons.

A terrible drought swept South and Southeast Asia in 1987. It would have meant famine two decades earlier, but Asian countries survived on stockpiled grain. India's buffer stock was 24 million metric tons.

But there's a thin line between rice self-sufficiency and hunger. In 1990, the world's cereal reserves had dropped to the lowest level since the *world food crisis* of 1973.

Population pressure is frightening in the largest rice-dependent countries. Most of the world's rice is consumed by the farmers who grow it, or by villagers a mile or two away.

Only 12 million tons of rice—2.5 percent of the world's yearly production—goes on the international market. In contrast, most wheat crosses an international border before consumption.

Thailand leads the export market, selling 4 to 6 million tons a year. America is the world's second-largest rice exporter, but ranks only eleventh in production. The USA grows 6 million tons of rice per year, and exports a third of it. Arkansas grows the most rice, followed by California, Texas, Louisiana, and Mississippi.

Vietnam is an enigma. She had imported rice since 1964, and appealed for rice to stave off famine in 1987.

But Vietnam surprised the world in 1989 by throwing 1.4 million tons of rice on the international market. Crops were good, but rejection of Communist economic policy played a stronger role.

The State had previously forced farmers to sell most of their harvests at a low price so it could resell subsidized rice to government workers and the military. But Vietnam shifted to an open-market policy in 1989, and sold rice it had warehoused. With capitalism and reasonable prices, Vietnamese farmers found—and sold—rice they had hoarded. That flooded the market.

But in 1990, Vietnam exported only half a million tons of rice. Will Vietnam become a major rice exporter? I doubt it. Not with its postwar baby boom. That nation of 67 million has a growth rate of 2.7 percent. More than 1 million new babies must be fed each year.

Rice consumption is increasing in North America and Europe, both for health reasons and because rice fits well in convenience foods. Still, the average U.S. citizen eats less than nine pounds of rice per year, while a Vietnamese consumes more than four hundred pounds.

Higher production has also increased rice consumption in most developing countries. But consumption has plateaued in China, Egypt, Indonesia, Japan, Pakistan, Taiwan, and Thailand.

By the year 2000, the world must increase rice production from today's 480 to 560 million tons. By 2020, we must grow almost 800 million tons—a 60 percent increase—to hold off the "Time of Famines." By then, the world will have 8 billion people, and 4.3 billion of them—almost equal to today's global population—will be rice consumers.

Those figures are conservative, assuming that population growth will level off by the year 2000, and stabilize by 2020. I doubt that will happen.

The 800 million tons of rice will only maintain today's nutrition levels. Hundreds of millions of rice consumers, mostly in Asia, now live perpetually at the edge of starvation.

Farmers must grow the additional 320 million tons of rice on less land, as cities, factories, housing developments, and squatter shacks sprawl onto prime rice land.

Is it possible to feed so many people on less land, without destroying our environment?

Yes—but only with more investments in rice research, more new varieties, technology, training, and communication.

IRRI's research center and experimental farm today cover fifty-five hundred acres on the campus of the University of the Philippines at Los Baños. About eighteen hundred scientific and support staff work at IRRI; 94 percent are Filipinos. Eighty internationally recruited scientists, from about twenty countries, are based at Los Baños. Another twenty IRRI liaison scientists work with national rice programs in Bangladesh, Cambodia, Colombia, Egypt, India, Indonesia, Madagascar, Myanmar (Burma), Nigeria, and Thailand.

An IRRI team worked in South Vietnam on a project sponsored by the U.S. Agency for International Development from the mid-1960s until 29 April, 1975. On that day, the last IRRI scientist left a Saigon rooftop on an Air American helicopter as Communist troops were preparing to enter the city. A few months later, the new Communist regime sent a delegation to reestablish ties with the Institute. IRRI stationed, in 1991, a new team of scientists in Vietnam.

More than six thousand Third World rice scientists and extension workers, including 223 Vietnamese, had been trained at IRRI by 1991. About two thousand scientists had received M.S. and Ph.D. degrees through IRRI. Twenty-three were from Vietnam, and another ten Vietnamese were enrolled in graduate courses. Most IRRI scientists, like me, serve on graduate faculties of universities in the Philippines, and abroad.

Six hundred staff of national agricultural programs participate in yearly short-term training courses at IRRI.

IRRI became the prototype for about twenty nonprofit International Agricultural Research Centers. In 1991, thirteen were supported by the Consultative Group on International Agricultural Research. The CGIAR is a consortium, established in 1971, through which funds for international agricultural research are allocated to the various International Centers. CGIAR members are about fifty donor countries, international organizations, and private foundations.

The United States has traditionally been the largest IRRI donor, followed by Japan. But since 1989, Japan's contributions have been higher, due largely to the strengthened *yen*.

IRRI's 1990 operating budget was $37.6 million. Compare that with Texas A&M's annual budget for agricultural research and extension: about $170 million.

One F-16—without ammunition—costs about the same as a year of worldwide support for IRRI. One unbuilt B-2 Stealth Bomber could support the world network of International Centers for a year.

Transition 14

Ho Chi Minh City, 19 May 1990

Susan and I have breakfast in the rooftop restaurant of the Majestic Hotel, and watch processions honoring Ho Chi Minh's one hundredth birthday roll by in the streets below.

We have the morning to kill while Dr. To Phuc Tuong takes Lynn Johnson to the Cambodian Embassy. After Vietnam, IRRI's team in Phnom Penh will help Lynn document how Cambodia's few remaining farmers now plant seeds of traditional Khmer rice varieties that IRRI saved from extinction. She'll also photograph wild rices growing in the ruins of Angkor Wat—if heavy fighting hasn't spread to the Siem Reap area of Cambodia.

I stroll, with Susan, along Tu Do Street. Chinese-run antique shops display hundreds of old, and fairly new, watches. Susan has never collected timepieces, but is soon checking these out.

"I've never seen so many watches," I say. *"Why?"*

"What's the first thing desperate people sell?" Susan responds.

The watches are bargains, but we don't buy any.

Other glass cases are packed with old fountain pens, eyeglasses, letter openers, plus U.S. Combat Infantryman's Badges and paratrooper wings, Zippo lighters, a paperweight with the seal of a French Army parachute regiment.

U.S. dog tags are also for sale. Some are crusted, and seem to have been buried for years. One dogtag is dented, like a bullet had struck it. They're fake, of course, but I didn't know that last year when that report of the dogtag and skeleton of

350

an MIA named Harold Dixon reached me from Chuong Thien Province . . .

A brass image of George Washington against a purple background catches my eye.

It's a U.S. Purple Heart, the medal awarded to American servicemen who are wounded in action.

There's something strange about the medal; then I realize. Its surface is worn almost smooth. I turn it over, and can barely read the embossed FOR MILITARY MERIT.

Soldiers never wear Purple Hearts except, maybe, at the award ceremony. A purple-and-white ribbon symbolizes the medal on a uniform.

Someone carried this medal for years, in a pocket or wallet. Why?

The medal has a story. If I could only follow it back in time . . . a GI gave it to a girl, who carried it for a decade of waiting. She finally sold the Purple Heart for a dollar or two . . . maybe that's a romantic, and tragic, interpretation of the medal's smoothness, but I can't think of a better reason. I ask its price. Five dollars. I offer four, and walk back onto Tu Do, the new owner of that worn Purple Heart.

It seems better, somehow, that *I* buy and keep the medal, rather than some souvenir hunter who wouldn't appreciate its history.

Lynn and I take our rented Japanese van and Vietnamese driver up the old Highway 1 that afternoon. French soldiers in the 1950s christened the stretch of that asphalt artery around Hue *la rue sans joie*, or "the street without joy."

Our destination is the tunnels of Cu Chi—two hundred miles that the Viet Cong dug by hand: storage depots, schools, munition plants, hospitals.

During the 1968 Tet Offensive, VC battalions moved like moles through the hard clay into Saigon, twenty-five miles southeast. Men and women lived, and fought, in the honeycomb for years.

In 1965, the U.S. 1st Infantry Division set up headquarters at Cu Chi—on top of part of the tunnel complex. For weeks, officers and troops of the Big Red One agonized over how the VC could penetrate their disciplined perimeter, blow a few choppers, and disappear. Then they learned: the guerrillas were infiltrating from below.

American *tunnel rats* hunted VC in their own subterranean

lairs, armed only with pistol, bayonet, and flashlight. But not in Chuong Thien Province, where the water table was higher than the ground's surface most of the year. We never worried about VC tunnels.

Entry was the most dangerous part of the tunnel rat's job. He first had to drop straight down a four-foot shaft, then squeeze into the opening. The VC designed that vulnerability into the tunnels—to make the tunnel rat an easy target.

The entrance was always booby-trapped, of course. After a few yards, the tunnel dipped down forty-five degrees into a water trap, built to seal off each section and block tear gas that American soldiers might pump in.

The tunnel rat swam through that black water, not knowing what surprises the VC had waiting on the other side. Then he set out to find and kill the enemy . . . if he lived through the water trap.

All tunnel rats were volunteers. Most were from the corps of engineers—because a tunnel could be destroyed only by detonating explosives laid precisely through its length. Engineers are trained to blow things up.

Parts of the Cu Chi complex are maintained as a war memorial. Some tunnels have been enlarged from their original two-by-two feet to about three-by-three feet, so westerners can explore them.

We crawl through a hundred claustrophobic yards of heat and blackness that Lynn's tiny flashlight barely penetrates. There are professions, like songwriter, that I just don't seem meant for. I'll add tunnel rat to that list.

I finally paraphrase President Kennedy with what must be a standard joke among the few Americans who've gone underground at Cu Chi:

"Look, Lynn! *There's a light at the end of the tunnel!*"

On the road back to Saigon, Lynn photographs flocks of thousands of disciplined "cross-country ducks." Peasant drivers have trained the ducks, uniform in size and pure white, to march in near-military precision from field to field, gleaning rice left after the harvest. The ducks march like unthinking soldiers with no idea that their final review will be to the kitchens of Ho Chi Minh City.

We spend an hour at sunset photographing a farmer as he fishes for frogs in a rice field planted to IR19960.

"What caption would you write for that photo?" I asked.

"Something about how these farmers eke a living from every resource offered by the rice land," Lynn said.

"I wouldn't. I'd show this as proof of how science can both increase rice production, and clean up the environment." IR8 required pesticides that killed frogs and fish, I explain. But IRRI scientists had packaged natural genes into the IR19960 seeds that enable the plants to resist pests without chemicals. That allows wildlife to grow, once again, in the rice fields.

By now I've picked up a good photography technique: stand aside until a *National Geographic* photographer starts to shoot, then rush in to get the same shots!

We dine that evening on mushroom soup, chateaubriand, and *pomme frites* on the rooftop of the Rex Hotel. I remember three dollar steaks, Filipino bands, and the nightly parachute flares twinkling across the Saigon River from this same rooftop, when it was the Rex Officers Club. The meal is gourmet for Ho Chi Minh City in 1990. It costs about seven dollars each, including a bottle of *Cotes du Rhône*—French *vin rouge*.

After dinner, we stare down at thousands of teenagers cruising Ho Chi Minh's streets on bicycles and motorbikes. It's a sense of Saturday night freedom, the closest to an act of defiance that we'll see in today's Vietnam.

We go to bed early. Tomorrow we start the one hundred-mile trip to Can Tho, then fifty more miles into the Ca Mau Peninsula and the old Chuong Thien Province.

CHAPTER XXV
The Pit and the Stone

Philippines, April 1975

> Whoso diggeth a pit shall fall therein: and he that rolleth
> a stone, it will return upon him.
>
> —*Proverbs*

It was an exotic world up in Banaue where, two thousand
years ago, Ifugao tribesmen began carving massive terraces,
like stairsteps for the gods, to grow rice.

We five rice scientists had driven a four-wheel-drive truck
for two days through the rugged mountains of northern Luzon
to reach that isolated valley, often called the "Eighth Wonder
of the World."

The Ifugao tribal culture was as much like three centuries
ago as you could find in 1975. Many men wore loincloths and
carried spears. Bare breasts, off the road, were not uncommon.
But jeans were coming in rapidly, and the transistor radio had
already brought rock 'n' roll.

Ifugao warriors had clung to their way of life by fighting off
Filipino invaders from the lowlands, plus colonists and soldiers
from Spain, America, and Japan. We felt privileged to have
been accepted in that ancient culture, and knew it couldn't survive long. The Philippine government was cutting a new road
across the mountains from the west. It would soon bring
hordes of unstoppable new invaders: tourists.

But Banaue's proud culture faced a threat more ominous
than tourism. Life and religion on the spectacular terraces revolve around rice, from the wine the farmers drink, to the gods

they worship. But Ifugao rice production could no longer support the society.

The traditional rice varieties yielded as much as ever. Population was the problem. Banaue's numbers had doubled in the past twenty-five years. Ifugao men were now forced to leave the terraces their ancestors had painfully sculptured . . . for dollar-a-day jobs in the factories and farms of the lowlands, to buy rice for their families.

Western scholars who've never sweated in the fields may lament how new technology changes the lives of farmers in traditional societies. But *this* mountain culture can survive *only* if science makes the terraces produce more rice.

We were testing, on the terraces, fast-growing, high-yielding rices into which IRRI scientists had bred cold tolerance . . . rices that would allow Banaue farmers to grow two crops a year, instead of one. That would buy the culture a little more time.

We'd worked hard the past five days, but the clean mountain air had been rejuvenating. So was the isolation: no rush jobs, no telex or phone, radio, TV, newspaper.

Now it was over, and we drove across central Luzon's flat plain, baking and dusty in the dry season. The rough travel back in time had made this one of those rare, almost magic trips that one can never repeat. Banaue had forged that special bond known only to skilled people who do a needed job well, in a fascinating but difficult environment.

We hit a traffic jam on Manila's outskirts. Kids were hawking papers with a dramatic headline:

SAIGON FALLS!

Oh, God! My guts wrenched. I knew it would happen, like when you know an old, sick friend will die, but it still shocks, and hurts like hell. But it shouldn't hurt this bad and . . . *why?* . . . what was it all for?

The end came fast. Chuong Thien was the first province in the Mekong Delta to fall . . . she lay back for the North Vietnamese like the slut she always was. Vi Thanh, that whore, didn't give a damn about the tens of thousands of men and women who'd died for her.

I thought about dead men, and families destroyed for that hopeless cause . . . Joe Bush and Sergeant Ard and Jimmy Hargrove, Michael Arnovitz, Clyde Aderhold, Lieutenants

Donoway, Young, and Carlile, Sergeant Walker, Gene Oates, Tom Lipscomb . . . so many more.

And the South Vietnamese we left behind. What will happen to Khang, Colonel Nguu, Captain Hong, Bac? Are they already dead? Maybe it's better if they are.

For what? There was no answer because it wasn't a question, only deep internal anger, loss, empty nausea. My friends had died for nothing.

The magic camaraderie that welded our group in the Banaue terraces faded, in my mind, that evening. The other men were close friends—but they'd never known a Chuong Thien.

We ate fried chicken at an imitation Colonel Sander's in Manila, then drove on to Los Baños. I slept, that night, with angry memories of a Big Woman who never existed.

Chapter XXVI
Fleeing to the Fall

Philippines and Vietnam, April 1975

> O! what a fall was there, my countrymen;
> Then I, and you, and all of us fell down,
> Whilst bloody treason flourish'd over us.
> —William Shakespeare, *Julius Caesar*

A U.S. Army sergeant returns to rescue his friend as Saigon burns in April 1975.

Far-out? Maybe. *The Deer Hunter* turned me off, but mainly because the sergeant wore a Green Beret, with a 101st Airborne patch on his left sleeve—badges of different units—and a white, not olive-drab, T-shirt. If the movie had a technical adviser, the producer should have listened to him.

But flying back to save or join friends and family, as Saigon was falling? Half a dozen of my friends did that. All were civilians. In fact, only one had ever served in *any* army.

Dr. Vo Tong Xuan, then an agronomist with the University of Can Tho, had worked closely with Americans, especially with the IRRI team in Vietnam. He was presenting a paper at IRRI's annual International Rice Research Conference when he realized that South Vietnam would fall in days—or hours. Xuan caught the last PanAm flight to Saigon as Soviet-made tanks of the North Vietnamese Army poised to break into that tragic city. Xuan wasn't a Communist, he was a nationalist who would cast his lot with his country, whoever ruled.

As the 747 approached Saigon, thousands of Xuan's desperate countrymen were fleeing by chopper, boat, sampan—any way out to sea for pickup by U.S. Navy ships. The frantic evacuation of the last 7,100 U.S. civilian and military personnel in Vietnam, and more than seventy thousand Vietnamese, on 29 and 30 April was called Operation FREQUENT WIND.

Also on that 747 was a Nebraska farmer who'd attended the same IRRI conference. Dr. Dwight Kanter was a patient man, ideal for his job as rice breeder with IRRI's team in Vietnam. VC mortar rounds had hit Dwight's experimental plots several times, blowing away any meaningful data from his tightly controlled research. But Dwight always replanted his rice plots and waited for the next crop to give the data that Vietnam needed—and Vietnamese had destroyed.

Dwight was flying into Saigon to bring Thuy, his fiancée, out.

The couple left the city from the rooftop of a twelve-story apartment building on 29 April, in the largest heliborne evacuation the world has ever known. Low on fuel, their Air America chopper barely made it to the USS *Oklahoma*. American sailors immediately pushed the helicopter into the South China Sea, to make room for more refugees.

Dwight and Thuy joined the eighty thousand other evacuees gathered around vessels of a U.S. Naval Task Force, including the aircraft carriers *Enterprise* and *Coral Sea*. The strange group included twenty-six South Vietnamese Navy and commercial ships, plus junks, sampans, and nine packed barges towed by American tugboats. That flotilla of displaced humanity set sail on 2 May for reception centers being set up in Guam and the Philippines.

The couple spent two horrible weeks at sea, transferring in midocean from one packed refugee ship to another. Their mattress was a flattened cardboard box on a hot steel deck, and empty C-ration cans became prized possessions: water glasses for thousands packed on ships designed for war, not passengers.

Dwight couldn't communicate with IRRI, so I worried during those two anxious weeks. Did Dwight find Thuy? Are they dead or alive, captives or refugees?

The U.S. embassy in Bangkok could not confirm that Kanter had gotten out.

In mid-May, IRRI received a cable:

ARRIVING FROM GUAM WITH NEW WIFE. PLS ASSIST WITH IMMIGRATION FORMALITIES.
KANTER

Dwight and Thuy had married the week before, in a Guam refugee camp.

"I met an army sergeant—named Poindexter—who served with you in Nam," Dwight told me when he reported back to IRRI. "He was working with the refugees."

"Poindexter? Yeah, he was from Louisiana and 'top'—our first sergeant—in Chuong Thien Province. But how would he associate *you* with *me*? I haven't seen, or heard from, Poindexter since 1970."

"Gosh, I don't know. I told him that I worked with rice, and he asked if I knew Tom Hargrove."

Dr. Richard Tinsley had served in Vietnam with a MAC-V naval unit in 1967–68, then returned as a civilian graduate student to conduct his Ph.D. research. In 1974, the agronomist joined IRRI's team in the Mekong Delta. By mid-April 1975, Dick knew the fall was coming and sent Loan, his Vietnamese wife, and their children to IRRI. A week later, Dick booked an evacuation flight, with Loan's family, to the Philippines. Before leaving Saigon, Dick cabled Dr. Nyle C. Brady, then IRRI director general:

ARRIVING CLARK AIR BASE WITH FAMILY. PLEASE SEND CAR AND LOAN.
TINSLEY

Brady sent ~~two~~ IRRI cars with drivers. He also sent, as Dick requested, a personal *loan* of 500 Philippine pesos, then about seventy dollars. Dick appreciated the loan, but missed Loan. He later joked that seventy dollars seemed to be the value that IRRI placed on a wife.

Harlan Grosz and I had worked closely when he monitored land reform progress in the Delta. He flew to Saigon from Seoul, where he was then head of Ralston-Purina, to rescue in-laws.

Harlan was at Pentagon East, MAC-V headquarters, when shrapnel from a Chicom B-40 rocket struck two young Marine corporals beside him: Charles McMahon and Darwin Judge were the last American soldiers killed in action in Vietnam. Harlan never located his wife's family, and joined the flotilla to Guam.

Mai Bertotti took Air Vietnam from Bangkok, probably the *last* commercial flight to Saigon—but it didn't land.

Tim and Mai had left Vietnam, and were assigned to USAID in Laos. The Bertottis were at a USAID meeting in Bangkok, and staying at the old Chao Phraya Hotel, when they learned that Saigon was falling. Tim had cleared all paperwork for Mai's family to leave, and had made plans to go back to Saigon to bring them out. The U.S. embassies in Vientiane and Bangkok then issued a last-minute order: no American employee could enter Vietnam. But Mai didn't work for the U.S. Government. *She* would return.

"We knew we might be separated for a long time," Tim told me in 1990. "So Mai asked the children 'Who goes to Saigon with me, and who stays in Bangkok with Dad?' Edwin, then five, stayed with me but Gia and Luisa went with their mother."

Mai and the two girls, three and four, checked in at Bangkok's Don Muong Airport. The flight was fully booked, mostly with French and Vietnamese who hoped to rescue wives, sweethearts, or families.

"You can't take children—especially kids that *look like Americans*—into Vietnam," Mai was told. A Vietnamese family that lived in Bangkok, but were seeing relatives off on that Saigon flight, offered to take Gia and Luisa—and raise them if Mai didn't come back. Mai left her children with countrymen she didn't know, and boarded Air Vietnam alone.

"Mai couldn't contact me, so I didn't know that the kids

were still in Bangkok," Tim said. "The experience left me emotionally unstrung . . . *I* should have been on that plane, not her."

The airliner circled Tan Son Nhut, but couldn't land. Communist artillery was pounding the runways.

The pilot flew on to Hong Kong. There, police impounded the 727, because it now belonged to a *new* Vietnamese government. The Air Vietnam crew fled, hoping to blend into that Chinese city rather than return to their newly liberated country.

Mai bought a new ticket to Bangkok. By then, the Vietnamese family had returned the girls to Tim. The reunited family drove back to Laos.

The Bertottis were still in Vientiane when Communist troops took over Laos two months later, but that's another story.

José Ona, who taught me about rice, spent his last, frantic days in Vietnam helping with Operation BABY LIFT, the U.S. airlift of Amerasian children from Saigon. He helped load infants onto a C5A that crashed in the rice fields after takeoff from Tan Son Nhut. A terrible scene—hundreds of charred babies—haunted Joe on the last commercial flight out of Saigon.

Transition 15

Can Tho, 20 May 1990

They shall beat their swords into plowshares, and their spears into pruning hooks: nation shall not lift up sword against nation, neither shall they learn war any more.

—*Isaiah*

We set out early on the one hundred-mile drive from Ho Chi Minh to Can Tho.

"These are good roads," I comment. "South Korean construction firms built them, on contract to the U.S. Government. The Vietnamese have maintained them well."

"Maybe, but the roads don't seem to carry much heavy traffic." Susan is the daughter of a construction man.

The six-hour trip takes nine hours. Lynn spends two hours filming farmers transplanting rice seedlings around their ancestors' graves. Then we see a farmer throwing IRRI seeds onto dry soil to sprout with the first monsoon rains. That takes four more rolls of Kodachrome 64.

"You can feel a rapport between Lynn and her camera," Susan says. "A relationship that's . . . beautiful."

We love to watch Lynn work. She's both artist and technician. Before shooting, Lynn walks around her subject several times, studying the scene from every angle through a viewfinder. She spends a lot of time positioning people—not to fake a scene, but to make people resume normal work.

"I like to blend into the landscape, capture people naturally," Lynn explains. "But that's not possible in Vietnam. When I leave that van, I change the environment."

It's true. We attract crowds of howling, laughing children, crowds that swell as we travel further south. It wasn't this bad twenty years ago . . . during the war, kids learned that flocking around Americans could be dangerous. Also, Vietnam's postwar baby boom is adding a million new babies a year.

The mobs of kids make *me* feel claustrophobic, but it's much worse for Susan . . . female Caucasians seem to be the ultimate novelty in the Mekong Delta. Susan loves children, far more than I do, but she's also a private person.

Hundreds of screaming kids now surround her in the heat, she can't breathe. They touch Susan, tug at her hair in a deafening roar. I wish they'd leave her alone, but they won't. I'm afraid my wife will get hysterical, start punching out six-year-olds . . .

We cross the Mekong River by ferry at Vinh Long. At sundown, we reach the mighty Bassac. Can Tho, a city I once knew well, lies across that mile of brown water dotted with sampans and clumps of water hyacinth. I remember the Mekong Delta cowboy song that Khang and I wrote about this ferry crossing one scared afternoon two decades ago: "Cross the Bassac by sundown ... we're safe when we reach old Can Tho ..."

We stand under kerosene lamps at the ferry's bow as it pushes through the muddy river. Hawkers surround us, selling pineapple slices, bananas, beer, candy.

"I'll bet he'd like a cigarette," Lynn says for no reason, nodding at a stocky man in his fifties. I hold out a pack of British 555s, probably the most popular brand of foreign cigarettes across Asia.

"Thank you," the stranger says.

"Do you speak English?"

"A little. Where do you go?"

"Vi Thanh. Do you know that place?"

"Yes. I was deputy chief of Duc Long District in the old Chuong Thien Province from 1967 to 1971."

I stare at the man in the flickering yellow light. Do I remember you? I'm not sure.

"What's your name? What was your rank?"

"Nguyen Pham. I was a *dai uy*, a captain in intelligence."

"Did you know Capt. Miles Bollick?" Miles was the senior army adviser in Duc Long District in 1970. I'd tried—but failed—to locate him.

"It has been so long ..."

He didn't really understand my question, but the ferry is now docking at the Can Tho side.

"What happened to *Dai Tau* Nguu," I ask. "The Chuong Thien province chief?"

"Colonel Nguu ... he's still in reeducation camp." He tells me where, but I don't catch it.

"But the war ended fifteen years ago."

"*I know ...*" Buses and trucks are starting up.

"Quick! Write your address."

The former captain scribbles in my notebook, then disappears into darkness. I jump into our van as we roll into Can Tho.

Damn! I think. I promised Harvey Weiner ...

We check into a fairly modern hotel in Can Tho, and call the elevator by pressing two naked wires together ... carefully.

In our room, I flip through the folder of letters from other American advisers I'd brought—in case I met someone like that captain. I finally find what Harvey Weiner wrote after my 1988 return to Vi Thanh:

I wouldn't have recognized you from your photo, but I remember the old MAC-V Orderly Room.

I often wonder about the fate of my counterpart, Ngo Van Kim, a schoolteacher by profession. And my interpreter, Truong Nam Trung, whom we called Gerald. I'm sure they met slow and painful deaths, and I suffer thinking about it. I recruited Gerald from Vinh Binh Province. His parting gifts, and *Ong* Kim's, are in my law office. So is the shrapnel that killed my other Vietnamese counterpart.

Would I, as Chuong Thien's Phoenix Coordinator, receive the warm welcome you did? You brought new rice seeds while I brought death and destruction, even though I prevented hundreds of violations of the Geneva Convention by both GVN and American troops. But I couldn't stop the VC atrocities.

That former ARVN captain seemed *programmed* to appear as we crossed the Bassac, I think. He was intelligence, he'd know what happened to Harvey's men. It's too late now. Maybe that question wasn't in the program . . .

After dinner that evening, Lynn and I search Can Tho's streets for scenes to capture on film. Returning to the hotel, we pass a woman selling cigarettes by the Bassac River.

"Are you from America?"

"Yes."

"I worked for the Americans for nine years." Her English is clear and strong.

"For who? Where?"

"I was a nurse—an RN—for the Special Forces."

"A *Green Beret nurse*? Selling cigarettes on the street?"

"That is all they let me do." An anonymous *they*, I now know, is the main fear of most Vietnamese who were once our allies.

"You are the first American I have met since the war. But two years ago, I spoke in English with a man from Scotland. He could not help me, and *they* questioned me for three hours the next day."

"Is it okay to talk?"

"*Yes.* I want to show you my papers tomorrow, prove that I worked for the Green Berets."

The woman, Luu My Thanh, waits in the hotel restaurant when I come down for breakfast the next morning. A beautiful girl is with her.

"My mother teaches English in Can Tho," the thirteen-year-old explains in English that tears at my heart. "She says I must learn your language perfectly, for when we go to America."

"When is that?"

"I don't know. We tried to escape last year, but they caught our boat and threw all my mother's identification papers into the sea. That makes it difficult."

Talking in the hotel makes Ms. Thanh nervous, so we follow about ten feet behind her to a tenement a few blocks away. We climb musty stairs to a dismal apartment. Along one wall, tintype photos of long-dead ancestors hang above a teak Buddhist altar.

"Were you a Green Beret?"

I start to explain how I was assigned to Special Forces at Fort Bragg. It's too complicated.

"No, but I knew them well."

"I burned most of my photos in 1975," she says. That sounds familiar. "But I hid this one."

She hands me a black-and-white photo. A stunning young woman, wearing tiger-striped fatigues and canvas-sided jungle boots, stood by a sign that read AID STATION. She wore no insignia, but a nurse's badge was pinned proudly above her right breast pocket.

"Keep the photo . . . please. It was taken at Special Forces Camp C-4, outside of Can Tho."

"Do you remember the Alamo Lounge at C-4?" I ask. That's where I bought my .38 revolver in 1969.

"Yes, the Green Berets took me there when we came in from the field. We had big grilled steaks, and drank so much whiskey . . ."

Ms. Thanh takes an album from the altar.

"These photos were made in happier times." It's ironic that the war could be called *happier times*, I think as I leaf through the album's pages.

I turn to a strange, stark page: Ms. Thanh's face with a dozen expressions, the background cut away. I can barely recognize a floppy hat—a jungle hat—in one photo.

"Operations. I'm sorry, but I cut out the Green Berets in 1975."

At the bottom of the page Ms. Thanh and a friend, in brilliant blue and yellow *ao dais*, sit by a pagoda at the shore of a lake. A bleak silhouette is cut between the two laughing girls.

"That was Captain Dunn," she says flatly.

"Maybe you can help me find him, or Sergeant Higgins? I served them well, and I'm sure they would help me leave this country." She hands me her papers. Tenth Infantry, Long Khanh, 1965–66: "Adviser: Sergeant Higgins"; Special Forces Camp C-3, Bien Hoa, 1966–67; SF Camp C-4 "My old boss: Cpt./Dr. Dunn."

Ms. Thanh then worked for the Public Health Division of CORDS in Can Tho until 1971. "Supervisor: Dr. M. M. Shutte, M.D., Ph.D."

I can't locate those men after all these years.

Then I notice that she spent 1973 to 1975 as a physical therapist for the Saigon Adventist Hospital. "My boss: Harry Rutical."

"Maybe I could locate Mr. Rutical," I say. "The Seventh-Day Adventist Church, in Vietnam, was a lot smaller than the U.S. Army."

"Do you *promise* to try?"

"Yes." I feel uneasy, saying that. Promises made in Vietnam are hard to keep.

Lynn photographs Ms. Thanh with her bizarre album of cut faces, then we return to the hotel. We have to start on the last forty-five miles to Vi Thanh.

We pack and drive to the market before leaving Can Tho. There, we buy a dozen liters of bottled French mineral water and a case of canned Coke, as a crowd of children gathers to stare at Susan and cut off her air supply.

The pavement ends at Can Tho's southern limit and we bounce along a terrible road for an hour. Then Dr. To Phuc Tuong suggests that we stop to visit Diep Van Tiep, the first farmer to grow IR8 in Tinh Hau Giang village.

Ong Tiep's wife sets out pots of green tea while the farmer chops open fresh coconuts with a machete and pours the water over glasses of ice. Amazing, how ice appears when guests visit, even in the most remote villages of the Mekong Delta. It was the same, two decades ago.

Mr. Tiep shows Lynn how he germinates rice seeds before planting, and I notice that many of his tools are crafted from local resources ... the refuse of war. The farmer stirs IRRI seeds with an aluminum canteen cup, scoops them into a sack with a U.S. Army helmet liner.

His wife makes rice noodles with a sieve converted from a 105mm artillery shell casing. An expended casing from a 40mm M-79 grenade launcher serves as an ash tray.

I'm not religious, but a West Texas farm boy can never escape that Protestant upbringing. Watching the Tiep family use their farm implements brings back a forgotten Bible verse I'd once memorized for Sunday School ... something about beating swords into plowshares ... and a line from an old Negro spiritual "Ain't gonna study war no more."

We drive on. We obviously won't make it to Vi Thanh in time for our scheduled lunch with the People's Committee. As the van bounces along that awful road, we dine on local French bread with sardines, peanut butter, and plum jam that Susan has packed all the way from Los Baños. It's a fun, happy meal.

CHAPTER XXVII
The Black Spring of 1977

Graduate college, Iowa State University, Ames, April and May, 1977

> We two kept house, the Past and I
> The Past and I;
> I tended while it hovered nigh,
> Leaving me never alone.
> —Thomas Hardy,
> *The Ghost of the Past*

Grow like savages,—as soldiers will,
That nothing do but meditate on
blood.

—William Shakespeare,
King Henry V

The fall of 1976 was the most positive time of my life. Maybe it was setting me up for the black spring that would follow.

The Hargrove family was back in Ames, Iowa, this time with Miles, our four-year-old, and Tom G, three. I was a fulltime graduate student at Iowa State University again, on leave from IRRI to finish my doctorate degree. I'd already completed most of the coursework; I'd taken more courses than were required for my M.S., then picked up a lot more credits through the night classes I took while working at the university from 1970 to 1972.

A Ph.D. is, essentially, a license to do research. That's why the heart of a doctoral program is conducting an original research project, writing your results by a strict scientific formula, and defending that dissertation before a graduate committee of established scientists.

In 1975, Iowa State accepted my proposal for an IRRI research project on the international movement of rice genes—those chemical units of heredity that determine a plant's traits—as suitable for a Ph.D. dissertation. Dr. Nyle C. Brady, IRRI director general, gave me carte blanche to travel anywhere in Asia to gather the data—in thirty-six days.

I left the Philippines with a plane ticket an inch thick and traveled through nine Asian nations. I stayed in thirty-two hotels and boarded twenty-nine airplanes. I made three long car trips, rode two trains, and one boat to reach twenty-eight far-flung rice breeding stations during those incredible thirty-six days. I don't count riding the camel in Pakistan. That was for fun.

After two weeks, it seemed I'd done nothing, all my life, but ride planes to the airport nearest a key rice research station, check into a seedy hotel, hire transport to the station, interview breeders and analyze their records, return to eat and crash, then rise to catch another dawn flight, often to another country. I crossed the Indian border seven times on that trip, traveling to and from Bangladesh, Nepal, Sri Lanka, and Pakistan.

Wearing clean clothes was my biggest problem. I was seldom in one hotel long enough to have laundry done. When I was, I usually threw damp clothes in my suitcase, hoping they'd dry there as I dashed off to catch the next plane.

I returned to IRRI with a suitcase of mildewed shirts, and data that documented how Asian rice breeders had adopted IR8 and other IRRI semidwarfs as parents—genetic building blocks—over the past fifteen years.

IRRI granted me nine months leave in 1976 to return to Iowa State, finish my remaining courses, analyze the data, and write my dissertation. The leave was without pay, but I had a $7,500 research grant from the Rockefeller Foundation. The GI Bill paid another $450 a month. We lived okay, for a graduate student with a wife and two children.

Statistics was the only academic course that gave me real problems; I'm weak in math. But I hired a private tutor, who was completing his Ph.D. in statistics, to pound it into my head six expensive hours a week. I passed the two required stat courses . . . barely.

I finished my classwork during the first two academic quarters. I'd devote the last quarter, February to May 1977, to writing and defense of my dissertation.

The Ph.D. hassle was almost over, so Susan and Miles returned to the Philippines in late March. Tom G, our three-year-old, was staying with Susan's parents, who'd moved from Iran to California. That left only Daphne, Susan's Siamese cat, and me in Ames to finish up those last few weeks.

The dissertation was going well and life was smooth . . . so smooth that I started writing my novel again. I'd never really be content until I finished that book.

I soon fell into an intense lifestyle that I found comfortable. It revolved around writing. I worked on the dissertation for seven or eight hours a day, then wrote about Chuong Thien Province—as fiction—for three or four more hours each night.

While finishing the dissertation, I took my written exams. They were mostly to determine if a Ph.D. candidate had absorbed the philosophy of essential courses, rather than to measure how well he remembered technical details.

I hoped the written exams would be approved quickly, because money from both my RF grant and the GI Bill would end in May.

The last step—the final oral exam and defense of my

research—would be, essentially, a formality. I had a good graduate committee, five agricultural scientists who understood IRRI's work. All had doctorate degrees, and wanted to help me get mine. Most had worked overseas with development programs. All had reviewed, and tacitly approved in advance, the key parts of my dissertation.

I expected a bit of academic hazing, of course. I knew that the committee would make me rewrite parts of the dissertation, no matter how solid the research, or how well I wrote. That's part of the game. I'll play by those unwritten academic rules that European dons established centuries ago. I'll accept the committee's criticisms, do a quick rewrite, and be back in the Philippines in two weeks.

That's what I thought, at 9:00 A.M. that sunny morning in late April.

It was a typical Ph.D. final oral exam. My committee was gathered around a long mahogany table, preparing to pretend to be tough.

I served coffee and donuts to the committee members—a tradition at a grad student's oral exam.

That's when a secretary from the statistics department came in and handed an envelope to my chairman. It was results of my *written* stat exam—the last of those exams to be returned. My chairman opened the envelope.

FAILED!

The word was printed in belligerent red ink across the first page.

What? I was stunned. I thought the final written exams were mostly protocol. My answers may not have reflected statistical brilliance but, damn! Dr. Blair, the statistics professor who reviewed that exam, had already passed me in two stat courses. What does this mean? Will Blair make me take a stat course over . . . after I've passed both? He could, of course.

Then I saw Blair's handwriting below **FAILED**: "Hargrove is going too *fast!*" Blair resented me, I felt, because I was different from the other grad students. I was an established professional, with a job at least equal to his. In my mind, Blair had targeted the failure to arrive at my final oral exam. *That fat little bastard did a number on me,* I thought. A *real* number, and he did it deliberately.

"I'm sorry Tom, but could you leave the room?" my chairman said. Being asked to stand outside the room while the committee deliberates your fate is standard practice at Ph.D. exams. It's part of scholarly hazing. But waiting outside *before the exam begins*, is not.

Finally, I was called in.

"The committee has no choice," the chairman said. "We have to cancel the exam. We'll reschedule after you straighten out the statistics problem."

I wonder what happened to the coffee and donuts. I remember nothing after that humiliation, for a long time, but a bottle of Johnny Walker Black Label and a dark, angry blur, as murky as the waters of the Xa No Canal.

Except that graduate school and Chuong Thien Province somehow merged there in Ames, Iowa . . . and that Big Woman I'd written about in my fiction soon pulled me into her bed. It was as evil and deadly as the U Minh, the forest of darkness.

There was no term *Vietnam stress syndrome* in 1977, but I knew something awful was happening. I spent days, then weeks without sleep, hating myself and Blair and graduate school.

I stared at Blair's red handwriting, at the unopened statistics book I should be studying. None of it made sense.

A doctorate, family and friends, those were shallow things, no longer real. Only one thing *was* real: Chuong Thien Province.

Chuong Thien and I went on an insane orgy that lasted two months. The time was so terrible, it's hard to write about fifteen years later.

The living room table was now cluttered with the only thing I cared about: my novel. I'd pick a chapter randomly at noon or 3:00 A.M. or—it didn't matter, time no longer existed.

Hours later, I'd snap to, staring at a stack of edited manuscript and empty beer cans, mute evidence of where I'd been.

Was Chuong Thien killing me, or was I trying to take my own life? There's probably not much difference, but I wouldn't use a gun, I'd kill myself with whisky and dope, by cutting all ties but Chuong Thien, by replacing love and pride and hope with what seemed more natural emotions: anger and bitterness and despair.

But in that haze, I knew there was something I *had* to do. I pulled myself together enough to face the statistics problem. I'd heard that Blair, when he failed me, had somehow thought that I was getting a doctorate in nine months ... thus "Hargrove is going too fast!" Since then, Blair had learned of the graduate credits I had earned in 1968 and in 1970 to 1972.

"Dr. Blair knows you're studying statistics real hard, so you may not have to take another written exam," his secretary said. "He wants to quiz you, orally, on what you've learned. Is Wednesday at 10:00 A.M. okay?"

I wore a tan suit and matching tie and trimmed the beard I started growing, by not caring enough to shave, after that final exam. I'd lost twenty pounds, my eyes were hollow, and I could give a big goddamn about the whole world.

Blair's scared of me, I sensed, when I sat in his office. He's heard I'm a real psycho, freaked out and God knows what I might do ... I can smell his fear.

And I know what the fat son of a bitch wants: to get Hargrove out of Ames, Iowa—fast, and as far from him as possible.

Blair asked a few nervous questions. I pretended to talk— seriously—about stat.

"You understand statistics a lot better than before," Blair said. *Bullshit*, I thought, loud enough for him to feel it. I haven't touched a stat book since the day you sent that exam paper in. And I may reach across this desk and break your worthless fucking neck.

I left Blair's office half an hour later. I'd passed stat.

My dissertation defense was rescheduled; I don't know how. Someone on my graduate committee, maybe Bob Kern or Al Kahler, arranged it. But it could have been Bill Gillette or Wes Buchele or Harold Crawford. Or Steven Fletcher; he was concerned about what was happening, what I was doing to myself.

It was probably a group effort—and I owe a lot to those men today.

I showed up for the rescheduled exam, again in suit and tie, but was embarrassed that I'd forgotten to bring coffee and donuts.

The defense ended quickly. All committee members—except Dr. Fletcher—approved the dissertation.

Fletcher insisted that I rewrite part of the dissertation before he'd sign. I guess he felt that I should go through the *normal* ritual of a Ph.D. exam. Maybe he was right.

I hadn't known the agronomist before returning to grad school. My chairman suggested that Fletcher serve on my committee because he'd taught soil science in Indonesia, sponsored by the Baptist Church. He was, deep inside, a missionary who felt he could serve God better by teaching how to care for the earth than by saving souls directly. I accepted that. The same commitment attracts a lot of scientists to IRRI—not just Christians, but also Buddhists, Muslims, Hindus, Sikhs.

Fletcher had been concerned about the aborted exam—and more so, about what happened afterward. He'd asked me to drop by his office and talk, sometime during that haze. I did, and Fletcher meant well. But he wanted to talk about the Holy Ghost, when ghosts of a different type filled my head.

Fletcher didn't demand much, just that I rewrite a few paragraphs. I could have done it in an hour, before. But the job took a week.

I finished rewriting on a Saturday, and needed Fletcher's approval as soon as possible. I knew I *had* to get out of Ames. Fletcher was out of town until that evening, then he'd leave on Monday for a couple more days. So the dissertation *must* reach his hands on Sunday.

Late Sunday morning, I put on my suit and drove to the First Baptist Church of Ames. The service began at 11:00 A.M., so I entered at 11:15. I sat on a back pew and scanned the congregation. Dr. Fletcher and his family, pillars of that church, sat on the second row.

The sermon focused on a centurion, a Roman soldier who was saved from bitterness and blackness. I wasn't expecting that . . .

A rousing "Bringing in the Sheaves" closed the service. I was first to leave the church and shake hands with the minister. Then I stood by an oak tree and watched the congregation file out.

Fletcher was among the last to leave. He said a few words to the minister, shook hands, and started to walk on. That's when I stepped up, by the minister.

"You're a hard man to find, Dr. Fletcher," I said, extending my right hand and handing him the rewritten part of my dissertation with the left. "But I *knew* where you'd be on Sunday morning."

The way I delivered the rewritten dissertation clearly shook and, I guess, angered Fletcher. He called me back to his office later that week. We talked, mostly about religion. God and the Holy Ghost. Then he signed my dissertation.

Looking back, I'm not proud of bringing the dissertation to Fletcher at his church. Was I arrogant? Did I mock the deep faith of a sincere man who was trying to help me?

Maybe. I wasn't rational back then. But whenever I think of that dark spring—and I try not to, because it was the worst time of my life—I remember words of a centurion who pulled himself from the blackest depths of despair.

A lot of Ames was relieved when Daphne, the Siamese cat, and I left town a few days later. I'd pick up Tom G, who was now staying with my parents in Texas, to return to the Philippines together.

The two-day drive to Rotan took five days. Because ... Chuong Thien not only followed me, she now rode in the front seat, telling me where to go, who to see. She became that terrible and fascinating Big Woman that I wrote about in the winter of 1971, who so many men had used, and whose wrath destroyed so many men.

I was never psychic, but mental hits had grown uncanny after the doctoral humiliation. I passed a bearded man at a fireworks stand in rural Missouri. A mile down the road, I wheeled around, then braked in front of his stand and bought a gross of cherry bombs that I didn't want.

"Who were you with, in Nam?" I asked as he packed my fireworks.

He looked puzzled, but said: "The 1st Marines up in I Corps in '67 and '68 ... but how did *you* know?"

"Maybe because you're selling cherry bombs on a farm-to-market road in Missouri. I just knew. That's why I turned around."

We may have shaken hands, but I doubt that we exchanged names. I only remember, in my rearview mirror, the ex-Marine staring as Daphne and I eased the Chevrolet back onto the road from Ames to Chuong Thien to Texas.

We got only to Kansas City that evening, where I checked into a cheap downtown motel. Five men sat around a table in the bar. I joined them, like I had an appointment. All were Vietnam veterans, and two had served together in Cambodia back when no U.S. troops were there. Crazies, but they thought I was crazier, so it balanced out.

Daphne and I got to Hannibal, Missouri, the next day, and I searched for Mark Twain like I'd tried, years before, to find Sinclair Lewis and John Steinbeck. I didn't find Sam Clemens at his museum or the Tom Sawyer House, but I think we drank together in those redneck bars along the Mississippi riverfront.

When I stopped for gas in Eureka Springs, Arkansas, late the next morning, that damned Daphne sprang from the Chevvy and disappeared down the street. I found the cat in a knotty pine bar, sitting at the feet of a bizarre couple. Their eyes hit me first.

She wore an Indian-print robe, and had wide-open eyes that never blinked. Those eyes penetrated the floppy hat that covered half her face.

The redneck's eyes were black and bloodshot, but burned like they'd melt the mirror behind the bar. His hatred scared me . . . even me, and I didn't care enough to scare easily. His face was battered, crisscrossed by angry red stitches. The sockets around his blackened eyes were locked to that mirror. His only movement was lifting a glass.

The woman sketched his face in ink on a bar napkin. Her artwork was superb but chilling, because she captured him as broken and scarred and hate-filled as he was.

Rain began to fall as he drank steadily, and I approached my cat.

She spoke. "I hope it rains for forty days and forty nights."

"Why?" I asked.

"So water will cover the earth, and kill all the goddamn people, and drown all the goddamn cars."

"Why do you want to kill the people?"

"Because people are no goddamn good."

I believed her, but said, "Some are good."

"Bullshit." She pointed to the redneck. "Look what they did to him. Two men held the poor bastard while the other two beat him almost to death."

The redneck continued to hate and drink, oblivious to our talk.

"But why do you hate cars?"

"Because *I freaked out in a car, on an acid trip in L.A. in 1967.*" Her eyes rolled. *"That's why I'm crazy."*

This woman, I knew, was a victim of the sixties—more than me.

"Where are you going?" she asked.

"West Texas."

"I'd love to see Texas."

I hesitated, then said, "Come along."

"You're going in a car?" I nodded.

"No! I can never ride in a goddamn car again!"

"How did you get here?"

"I don't know, but I won't leave Eureka Springs—*not in a goddamn car.*"

Her napkin-portrait of the redneck intrigued me.

"Would you do a sketch of me?" I don't know why I asked that.

"I'll have to ask Philip."

"Who's Philip?"

"He takes care of me. Philip handles my jobs, my money, he tells the restaurants and stores that he'll pay for what I eat, or drink, or clothes that I buy, from money that my art sells. Remember . . . *I'm crazy.*"

"I don't think you're crazy," I said. But I knew she was—we all were. "Let's see Philip."

We left the bar and climbed a stairway to a studio. Philip was an artist, about thirty, and I sensed that he was protecting, not exploiting, this insane woman. Philip showed me samples of her work. The art was superb, but outer-edge: psychedelic art, like *Heavy Metal* published in its early issues . . . intricate, swirly pen-and-ink work. Study it closely, and you find dozens more pictures, stories, and mysteries hidden within the original work. LSD art—she could never draw like this if drugs hadn't bent her mind.

Philip approved the job—for forty dollars. I was almost broke and didn't want a portrait, but I sat anyway.

"Remove your glasses," she said.

"But I *want* to be wearing my glasses in the drawing."

"Take them off." I did.

First, she drew my eyes. They were as angry and dangerous as those of the battered redneck. She then sketched my face around the eyes. Last, she put my glasses on, in ink. The portrait frightened me.

Later, Daphne and I partied with the artists and crazies of Eureka Springs. The night was as insane as the woman imagined herself.

Daphne and I landed somewhere in East Texas the next night, and checked into a Holiday Inn. In the bar, I met a bitter divorcée whose husband, an army major, had left because he couldn't take her, the kids, the pets, the boredom . . . after Vietnam. Another victim—did I find her, or did she find me? Ei-

ther way, *why*? And how? But I didn't sleep with the divorcée
that night, I slept with the Big Woman ...

The next morning I found a note she'd written on the back
of a chapter I was editing at the bar. It read:

Intelligence ....high
Language...filthy
Hair..dirty
Drinking..too much
Potential ....high

You *must* pull yourself together. Remember—I, too, lost
most of my life to that war. It's not worth dying for. Not
again.

That broken divorcée's note shook me more than the concern of those respectable and reasonable people in Ames,
Iowa, who'd helped me so much, even though I didn't appreciate it ... because they'd never known a Chuong Thien. Her
message somehow made me see: I have a lot: Susan and my
family, and ... *I don't really want to kill myself.*

I was straighter when I pulled the Chevrolet up at our dryland cotton farm west of Rotan. But Mother and Daddy were
confused and hurt. They couldn't accept that I'd changed. It
wasn't their fault, what could I expect? All I'd ever written or
told my parents about Nam was about my rice and land reform
and pig projects—and how mostly Vietnamese, only a few
Americans, got hurt, and Chuong Thien was an easy tour.

I tried to explain the *real* Chuong Thien for the first time,
but it didn't work. "I didn't know you were ever in combat,"
Mother said.

My folks might have listened in 1970 ... but I couldn't tell
them, because I didn't know myself. Now in 1977, they didn't
want to hear it. I understood that.

"You've got to forget Vietnam, Tommy," Mother said. "You
had a hard time in graduate school, and you're upset. But really, everything is like it always was."

Mother meant it, but I knew that nothing would ever be like
before ... Chuong Thien changed it all, and grad school made
me see it.

I drove, alone, to the windswept hill of red clay east of Rotan, where pioneer farmers and ranchers started a cemetery on land too poor to graze cattle or plant cotton.

It took half an hour to find Jimmy Hargrove's grave where, for me, Vietnam really started. I knew that the Hargrove family, at Aunt Maud's request, had the coffin opened, to be sure it was Jimmy—but what was left of the corpse's head was wrapped in bandages. It was okay, the morticians identified Jimmy by scars that a butane explosion on a farm tractor had left on his hands as a kid.

But the war didn't affect me. No, I'm okay! I screamed across that red-dirt cemetery, where only the dead ... and maybe a Big Woman ... could hear me.

Finally, Tom G and Daphne and I boarded a plane back to the Philippines. The flight was pretty bad. I got into a fist fight with a drunk Hawaiian in the Honolulu airport. I guess I won, I laughed and taunted while the Hawaiian swung wildly.

I returned home to a very concerned Susan. She thought I looked, and acted, scary.

Back in Asia, I threw myself into rice. Everything began with carnage and the IRRI rice varieties, so going back to rice seemed natural. It wasn't easy, but rice slowly helped straighten out my head.

That's when I put my novel and Chuong Thien Province back on a dark closet shelf, and closed its door. I knew I could never handle Vietnam again.

Transition 16

21 May 1990

> It's funny how we are fascinated by the places where we came near to losing our lives. It's something like visiting one's own tombstone.
>
> —Morley Safer, *Flashbacks on Returning to Vietnam*

The water along the road gets deeper, and the houses that we pass, poorer. We're now in the Old Chuong Thien Province. I sense it.

The road turns to jagged, foot-long rocks that peasants are crushing with sledgehammers. This will be the first all-weather road to Vi Thanh.

No stones are found naturally in the Ca Mau Peninsula. These were barged from north of Saigon, down two hundred miles of interlocking rivers and canals. We clutch the seats so our heads won't hit the roof as the van crawls over the rocks.

Five hours after leaving Can Tho, we're driving through the Vi Thanh market. She'd look more familiar if we'd entered by water, along the Xa No Canal. But the only change I can see, from my 1988 visit, is red flags with yellow stars, and banners eulogizing Uncle Ho's birthday.

We pass the old MAC-V compound. The five or six rotting buildings don't shock me this time, but they look lonely, haunted ... *shunned*? MAC-V is still the only place in Vi Thanh that doesn't teem with people.

Tran Van Rang, still vice-chairman of the Vi Thanh People's Committee, meets us at committee headquarters, the building that once housed my Vietnamese Land Reform teams. He welcomes us with tea and coconut water on the second floor, overlooking the concrete slabs of my former CORDS quarters.

I explain that I'm bringing seeds of two new IRRI rice lines to Ba Lien ... but really, to help *National Geographic* explain, through a photo, what improved seeds and their genes mean to mankind.

Those rice seeds are beginning to worry me. I know they're good, but so are hundreds of other IRRI experimental lines. Yet local farmers *must* think these seeds are really hot. Why else would a scientist from the International Rice Research Institute fly from the Philippines, then travel for five days to the tip of the Mekong Delta, to bring a few kilos? Even more incredible, a famous American journal flew Lynn Johnson all the way from America to photograph me giving the seeds to Ba Lien.

What if farmers assume that these seeds are super strains of a new *miracle rice*—not because they're better than other IRRI varieties, but because *I* brought them, with a special urgency? They haven't even been tested in this region. What if they sweep farmers' fields across the Ca Mau Peninsula, then a pest epidemic wipes them out?

The seeds are *symbolic*, I stress. They carry genes from Vietnam ... genes that disappeared from farmers' fields decades ago. Now I, as a Vietnam veteran, am bringing those genes home, repackaged into high-yielding rice strains with pest resistance. Like all new seeds, I warn, these must be tested carefully, and distributed to farmers only if they prove superior.

Tu Rang then asks if I brought extra seeds of the two rices, so the People's Committee can multiply them for other farmers. I give up. *Yes*, I brought four extra kilograms.

We discuss our agenda for the next two days. "Do you want to visit any special places?"

"Can I go to the Cambodian monastery in Dinh Anh village, in the old Kien Hung District? I want to visit an old monk, *Sai Ngoc*, if he's still alive."

"Dinh Anh is not in Vi Thanh District. We are sorry, you cannot go there."

"How about Kien Long or Kien Thien?"

"Not possible. Sorry."

Drop it, Hargrove, I thought. The Vietnamese aren't *about* to let you visit a Cambodian monk who speaks English, or even a Khmer region. Don't you remember the Vietnamese-Cambodian animosity? The Cambodes have obviously suffered under the new regime, and the Vietnamese are afraid of what you and Lynn might hear . . . and write.

"The People's Committee will honor you with a banquet tonight," Tu Rang says. "But now you must go to the hotel and rest."

Surely it won't be *that same hotel*, by the market. The Vi Thanh Hilton was mainly an ARVN whorehouse before . . .

But it is. We check in at the lobby, which doubles as a bicycle repair shop. We lug suitcases and seeds up narrow stairs to the second floor. A clerk follows, carrying only a key ring. He opens a padlock and swings apart rusty steel doors to Lynn's cubicle, then to our room next door.

Susan jumps as a mouse-size cockroach scurries beneath a stark bed, draped by mosquito net. It has a grimy mattress, but no sheets or covers.

A sink stands against one wall. Susan turns on the tap and muddy water runs into the basin, through the drain, and onto our grimy floor of green linoleum.

Standards of the Vi Thanh Hilton have obviously slipped since its days as a South Vietnamese Army brothel.

Lynn soon knocks on the shutters, and we stand on the balcony overlooking Vi Thanh.

"The streets, the market—they're mud and standing water," Susan says. "How can people *live* like this?"

"Susan . . ." I reply, feigning patience. "This is the *dry season*. Wait till it starts raining."

"Don't take your cameras past the toilet," Susan warns Lynn. It's a single hole-in-the-floor type, and serves the entire hotel.

"The fumes will melt your film."

"It's not that bad," I say. Susan shakes her head.

"I used to visit Rod Fernandez, my Filipino buddy, here in the evenings. Rod would drop a bucket from the balcony by rope, which signaled the lady downstairs to fill it with bottles of beer. We'd sit and talk, and watch the sun set over Vi Thanh."

"Your friend had zip for class if he lived here," Susan says. "Be honest, Tom—have you ever stayed in a filthier place?"

"Lots of times." Then I think hard. IRRI has sent me on

rough travel through the backwaters of India, Bangladesh, Zanzibar . . . what about that desert town in northern Ethiopia two years ago? Its best hotel was full, and so was the next, until I finally checked into the last, and fifth-best hotel. Room service was simple: which of the obviously venereal-diseased maids do you want?

No . . . the Vi Thanh Hilton is worse.

I'd wanted to show Susan a beautiful and peaceful Vi Thanh, something worth fighting for.

"Why would *anyone* be fool enough to die for a miserable place like this?" she says. I can't win.

But Susan's spirits pick up after we settle in. There's no escape, so she'll make the best of Vi Thanh . . . maybe.

We prepare for tomorrow by pouring two kilos each of the two new rice strains into white cotton sacks marked with a green IRRI seal and INTERNATIONAL RICE RESEARCH INSTITUTE in bold, black letters.

We arrive for our banquet at the People's Committee restaurant, by the Xa No Canal, at 6:00 P.M. It's a rustic and rowdy banquet, the best Vi Thanh can offer.

A long table is lined with cans of Heineken Beer, Coca-Cola, and bottles of *baxide*. I've often said that no innovation spread faster than IR8 in Vietnam, but I'm no longer sure. Heineken and Coke were sold only in Hanoi and Ho Chi Minh City two years ago, but now smugglers from Singapore bring boatloads to the nine mouths—that the Vietnamese call the "Nine Dragons"—of the Mekong River. The contraband drinks never see Ho Chi Minh City and its taxes, and are found everywhere. A can of either costs almost a dollar, black-market rate. No one here can afford to drink it . . . but they do.

Tran Van Rang moves Susan to the opposite end of the table. She's just a wife; Lynn and I are the important guests. Susan is fed up with the Communist officials who she now, privately, calls *cowboys*. I smile. Susan glares.

The main course is eight-inch crawfish that look like lobsters, but taste better. I decide not to mention how we once gorged on the delicacy at the Delta Lily . . . or how the corpses dumped into Chuong Thien's waters drove the crawfish price down.

The Vietnamese begin the traditional Asian banquet sport—drinking the foreigners under the table—with *baxide* and beer. The Communists play the game exactly like the corrupt, running-dog lackeys that we imperialist Americans once came to help.

"I propose a toast to friendship between 'Merica and Vietnam. One hun'red pre'cent!" That means both parties must chug their drinks straight—100 percent.

"We now drink to the new IRRI seeds you bring. One hun'red pre'cent!"

I set a liter bottle of Jack Daniel's Black Label on the table, and propose my own toasts. Vietnamese can't handle bourbon. That's why I brought the whiskey, all the way from Los Baños.

The next course is *con chut*, roasted rats from the rice fields. Lynn slips her rat onto my plate. I wonder how Susan's doing?

Down the table, Tu Rang sees that Susan doesn't care for rats . . . so he insists that she eat one. Susan refuses, but Tu Rang keeps shoving rats onto her plate.

Finally, Susan fills two water glasses from the Black Jack bottle—straight, without coke or ice—and offers one to the political officer. She smiles, clicks glasses, says, "One hundred percent"—and downs the whiskey neat.

Tu Rang can't lose face to a woman. He drinks his glass of whiskey straight, then shudders. The lighting is bad, but he looks green and sick. Tu Rang staggers from the table, then we hear a splashing in the canal.

I can't believe that my wife drank six ounces of straight bourbon—that *isn't* her style. But Susan is so mad, it doesn't affect her. The alcohol obviously volatilized before it hit her stomach.

Lynn and I know why Susan did it. So, I think, do the Vietnamese.

A pale Tu Rang returns fifteen minutes later, but doesn't propose any more toasts. The banquet finally ends, and we return to the Vi Thanh Hilton.

Susan is no fun to talk with, and certainly not romantic, so I go for a walk under the stars of Vi Thanh. I'm being followed, of course, but I don't care. Soon I'm in the old MAC-V compound, alone in my mind.

Moonlight has turned the olive-drab orderly room silver and ghostly. The roof is about to collapse, but that doesn't matter. MAC-V will be torn down next month, Tu Rang said, and replaced with government sheds. I wish this could be a war memorial . . . it's one of the few U.S. posts that survived April 1975. I'm the only American veteran who'll ever return to wander through this camp, and this is my second time. That's an eerie thought, deep in the night of the Mekong Delta. I'm a long way from West Texas . . . but I've returned, again, to an unhappy home.

I find myself in a decaying wooden shed, barracks for junior-grade officers. We once sat on bunks here, and talked about families, or football, or home in Wisconsin, Massachusetts, or New Mexico . . . whatever stories lonely men tell in a miserable place.

A few more steps and I find the concrete slab of my old CORDS quarters, then the light post. I think of mortars, dinners I cooked at the Delta Lily, rockets, Frank and Lloyd, China Doll, Norm, Bob, Willie . . . and hootches in Vi Thanh burn, as the VC kidnap Duc . . .

The Vi Thanh hospital shimmers white across the road. I walk to its gate. It looks like twenty years before, untouched by time or the war, and that brings more memories.

The hospital should be a symbol of peace, but its rooms are filled with spirits of the dead and dying . . . more ghosts than linger at MAC-V, and not so friendly.

Why am I waking ghosts at midnight? Somehow, this seems . . . *dangerous*? Like maybe you're *pushing it*, Hargrove.

I walk back to the hotel and reality . . . or was I there?

A terrible noise shakes Susan and me from our hardwood bed. It's . . . music—rousing, patriotic music, at a decibel that hurts our ears.

I can barely read my watch. It's 5:00 A.M. I stumble to the door as the sun's first rays reflect off the Xa No Canal. A harsh female voice blasts propaganda at a volume no one can sleep through—words to assure that Vi Thanh citizens rise early, and think properly.

I thought the Communists gave up loudspeakers two decades ago. I never woke to propaganda broadcasts during my four trips across China, starting in 1979. Nor did I hear public broadcasts in southern or northern Vietnam in 1988. But I didn't sleep in Vi Thanh, either.

The Vi Thanh Hilton was like an oven, and the bedbugs didn't help us sleep. Our room had no fan, but what the hell? We didn't have electricity, either.

I pop a can of warm Coca-Cola, dress, and go to meet Tran Van Rang and the People's Committee for breakfast.

This is an important day, the climax of a hard trip. We'll take the IRRI seeds to Ba Lien.

We're heading north by sampan at 9:00 A.M. Lynn sits at the bow as we pass children swimming and women washing clothes in the muddy Xa No Canal. She holds her Leica M-6 range finder as respectfully as soldiers once held M-16s on this stretch, and watches the shore and passing boats as closely. But Lynn is looking for photos, for *that shot*. One that combines rice with people, and memories of the war.

I had told Lynn about the wrecked South Vietnamese river patrol boat that naked children dived from in 1988. Rice fields were in the background, so it should make a good shot. But a Japanese firm salvaged the boat six months ago, Tu Rang says. By now, it's part of a Toyota.

Lynn spots a boat loaded with unhulled rice. Our sampan pulls alongside, and we see that the boat's cargo is actually blocks of ice, insulated by rice husks. But Lynn wants to capture *every* aspect of how life in the Mekong Delta revolves around rice. She jumps aboard the ice boat, frames scenes with a 21mm viewfinder, and shoots three rolls. That's not much film, for Lynn.

We pass another sampan, and I see long, dishwater-blond hair. That's *an American girl*, sitting at the stern! She isn't, of course.

"It's strange to see an Amerasian child *here*. I may have known her father . . ."

"She's only six or seven years old, Tom. You probably knew her *grandfather*." Susan can be awfully cynical when she's unhappy.

We dock, and I recognize the Thanh Binh Agricultural Cooperative, with its Viet Cong cemetery . . . the same cooperative that I visited in 1988.

Is Thanh Binh a showplace commune, like those that the Communists take you to in China and North Vietnam? Half a dozen travelers have told me of a typical commune outside of Hanoi, one that few Westerners have seen. I always ask if Jane Fonda once visited there. The answer is, invariably, yes. Either Jane commune hopped a lot in 1968, or Hanoi sends all foreigners to the same commune.

But Vi Thanh has no foreign visitors, and doesn't need a showplace commune.

We're briefed by Mr. Bien, the cooperative's manager and

the hamlet's former VC political officer. In 1988, I had asked Bien about the site of the 1969 ambush of Lieutenant Donoway and Sergeant Ard and their interpreter. He replied: *No, they died across the canal, by the cemetery.*

"Most of our farmers plant IR19960 now," Bien says. "The dry-season crop averaged six tons a hectare, and our better farmers harvest eight tons—with less fertilizer than we give other varieties." Those are *very* high yields, but I believe him. The crops are beautiful.

"In 1988, your farmers grew IR13240 and IR64," I remind him. "What will you be planting if I return two years from now?" Sociologists who claim that Asian peasants resist change should visit Mekong Delta farmers.

"We're testing IR32429 and IR74," Bien says. "Of course, most farmers will want seeds of the new rices *that you've brought* from the Philippines."

I wince, and explain again that these two sacks of seeds, marked with the IRRI seal, are for a *symbolic photo*. Only testing will tell if they're better than other high-yielding rices. Bien obviously doesn't believe me.

Lynn presents a *National Geographic* map of the world to the commune, and I turn over a set of IRRI books. The ceremony ends, and we reboard sampans to go farther north. We turn east onto a lateral canal and step to the shore, where Lynn photographs farmers weeding an excellent rice crop.

The area looks deserted, but flocks of children appear to surround and touch Susan.

"One Frenchman owned all of this land," Tu Rang says.

"I know . . . but Saigon confiscated the plantation. I was in charge of redistributing his land to local farmers—the rice fields we're now standing in."

That's not exactly true, I was *adviser* to the Land to the Tiller program. I was coming here to check on a Land Reform team that was issuing the titles, the day I didn't arrive but Donoway and Ard did.

Land reform was the closest Saigon ever came to socialism. It undercut the VC promise to redistribute the plantations owned by a few French and Chinese landlords. I wonder if the farmers who got titles from us still work this land? I'll ask . . . but later.

We return to Thanh Binh. Now we'll go to Ba Lien's farm? "No," Tu Rang says. "We'll have lunch first."

We get bored after thirty minutes of waiting. Lynn wants to see the Viet Cong cemetery across the canal. Susan doesn't—but it might be an escape from the hundreds of children staring and poking at her. She now calls them *air-suckers*, and that's *not* a term of affection. We pole the sampan across the canal.

The path to the cemetery cuts through a peasant's hut, but it must be okay because he's set up a bamboo stand to sell drinks. His stock includes three cans of Singapore Coke and two Heinekens.

We walk past the monument, topped by a yellow star against a red background, that marks the cemetery entrance. Thanh Binh village covers three hundred and fifty acres, mostly rice fields. That's far less than half the cotton land that the Hargrove family farms in West Texas. Yet 355 men and women from Thanh Binh—one per acre—died for the National Liberation Front.

But we considered Thanh Binh a *pacified* hamlet in 1969–70. That many more villagers, at least, surely died fighting for ARVN and the local militia. The Communists don't have records on deaths of *American lackeys* . . . but they're still dead.

I see only about thirty graves. But the VC recorded burial sites, and teams are now moving scattered remains to cemeteries like this.

Government stones mark most graves, but families have built a few concrete crypts.

I study the inscription on a white crypt, 1969.

"I could have called the artillery that killed this guy," I tell Lynn, matter-of-factly. Wild rice grows around the grave, so Lynn pulls out cameras.

An old woman in black pajamas appears. Dr. Tuong talks with her, then says "She's the mother of that soldier."

That shakes me a little, of course, but I bow and say *"Chao, Ba."* An old man then joins her, from nowhere. His eyes are bright, and a thick white beard flows from his chin. He wears black trousers and white tunic, and carries a bamboo cane, but stands erect. I'll always remember the couple's dignity.

"This is Nguyen Chi Nang," Tuong says, and we shake hands. "He's ninety-two years old . . . and the soldier's father."

Mr. Nang disappears in the confusion, then returns with a framed tray—brass medals, hanging from red-and-yellow ribbons, awarded to his sons. All three died as VC guerrillas.

The dignified old couple with an ex-U.S. officer who could have killed their VC son . . . at his tomb . . . a tray of red-ribboned medals, *against a green background of wild rice . . . all in one frame*. Lynn starts shooting, changing lenses.

Dozens of children and villagers now surround us. Susan uses the diversion to escape from the kids.

The sun beats down hard, and the air is thick with humidity and emotion. How can both parents of this soldier, killed two decades ago, appear as . . . but Susan and I met Michael Arnovitz's childhood doctor by his name at the Vietnam Memorial. *That* couldn't happen, either.

"Tom . . . *do something*," Lynn says. "Make a rubbing of the inscription on the tomb." She pulls out a green pentel pen, and someone hands me a sheet of paper.

I trace the Vietnamese epitaph, forgetting that I'm being photographed. Tuong translates the words I don't know:

> Nguyen Ngoc Hau
> Born: 1947, Thanh Binh
> Died: 24 June 1969
> Region: Mat Tran 8, near the U-Minh Forest

The old farmer speaks.

"He remembers you," Tuong says, "from about twenty years ago." My heart freezes.

"You once brought me a sign," Tuong translates the old farmer's words. "It read *Than Nong 8*, to put in my field of IR8.

"You also gave me vegetable seeds from America."

Vegetable seeds. My God.

No one has talked with Mr. Nang. Even if someone had, it would be about rice. Only two people could know about the vegetable seeds—him and me. Maybe three, Susan sent the stocking full of vegetable seeds for Christmas, 1969. But Susan doesn't speak a word of Vietnamese, and she's hiding from the children.

The farmer talks more as I kneel by that tomb, and Tuong translates:

"You joked a lot in those days . . . you had a wonderful . . ." Tuong pauses, then finds the right English phrase ". . . *sense of humor.*"

I sit on the crypt, knowing that's not disrespectful here in

Vietnam. I'm getting close to an edge, and the old couple feels it. They're close, too.

"Can you give Mr. Nang something to remember you by?" Tuong asks.

I'm numb. "You have those 'friendly insects' books," he reminds me.

Of course. I search my pack and find *Helpful Insects, Spiders, and Pathogens: Friends of the Rice Farmer.* Dr. Merle Shepard, my songwriting buddy, was senior author and took most of the 166 color photos of insects that, if protected, can control most rice pests without chemicals. It's already published in a dozen languages, and I brought a good stock of the Vietnamese edition.

"The Nang family will always honor this book," Tuong says. "You should write a dedication on the title page."

I try to think of the right words for these farmers I once knew, sitting on the tomb of their Viet Cong son.

My mind won't function, so I simply scribble the date, then "To Nguyen Chi Nang," and sign my name followed by "International Rice Research Institute."

"Tom . . . you wrote the wrong date."

I look down at my words. *My God!* I wrote: *22 May 1970. 1970?* Where have I been?

I *know* where, and it scares me.

Lynn captures it on film. It shakes her, almost like me. Susan, too, when we break through the ring of kids, and Lynn and Tuong tell the story.

We return for lunch at the Thanh Binh Cooperative.

"You send out an antenna down here, Tom," Lynn says over mudfish and IRRI rice. "An emotional field that radiates, searches. It connects to fields of others, and draws them. It started in Saigon, and I've watched it grow stronger as we go deeper into the Mekong Delta.

"This place," she waved at the rice fields and palm trees and mangroves that line the Xa No Canal, "is its source, where it began. The closer you get to Chuong Thien, the stronger the power."

"I know," I said. "But *closer* can be mental, too. Going back on a computer hard disc can trigger these things, can zoom the past forward like . . . physically returning to Chuong Thien.

"The power . . . some would call it a *talent* or a *gift* . . . was frightening—dangerous—in 1977." I had told Lynn about my *black spring*. Throw three Americans together on a strange trip like this, through time and the Mekong Delta, and you get to know each other fast.

"That talent . . . whatever it is, went away when my head straightened out. Forever, I thought. But it came back."

"Were you this way in 1969?"

"*No*, I never even thought about it. A few strange things happened, of course. I could easily have died, several times, but didn't because of coincidences. But everyone who was *there* had those experiences. A construction worker sees a bomb planted fifteen feet from Steve Dille and me, but we don't. A Land Reform team doesn't show up, so I cancel a trip north on the Xa No Canal . . ."

I felt it then, but couldn't tell Susan and Lynn. *The Thanh Binh cemetery*, where those strange things just happened at the crypt—*that was the ambush site that day in October of 1969.* If my Vietnamese team had shown up, *I'd* have sprung that ambush, and *I* would have died . . . not Donoway and Ard of MAT 54 . . . *there*.

How did we get to the grave of Mr. Nang's son . . . *there*? I didn't ask to go to Thanh Binh, in 1988 *or* 1990. And *Lynn*, not me, wanted to visit that VC cemetery.

Bien, our host, had pointed out the exact ambush site in 1988 because *he knew*.

And Bien knew because he was the VC political officer. *Bien*, not a military officer, authorized the ambush. He may not have pulled a trigger that day, but he ordered triggers pulled.

Lunch ends. We shake hands with Mr. Bien, thank the People's Committee, and board sampans to go back down the Xa No Canal. We'll finally take those new IRRI seeds to Ba Lien.

CHAPTER XXVIII
Sixties Progeny

Music Row, Nashville, 1986

> The poet's turmoil strikes again
> As once more words they fail me
> Another bomb has just supplied
> The cross on which to nail me.
> —Anne Clark, *Poet's Turmoil
> No. 364*

> Casca, Eternal Soldier
> He bears a soldier's pain
> Death a withheld blessing
> Till the Savior comes again
> Tho' damned to live a soldier
> And fight in wars through time
> Casca grows no older
> And Casca cannot die
> —Tom Hargrove, "Casca,
> the Eternal Mercenary"

I limped along 16th Avenue—Music Row—in stiff new Tony Lama boots under a blazing July sun in 1986. I'd come to Nashville to sell my songs.

Music City USA would love my ballads, I knew. Time had mellowed the American public, swelled its interest in the Vietnam War. New books and movies were in demand, music would *surely* follow the trend.

I'd considered riding into Nashville by Greyhound bus, carrying my guitar like Hank Williams did. But I don't own,

nor can I play, a guitar, and Greyhound probably didn't even
run to Nashville anymore. So I flew in on Delta, with a brief-
case of cassette tapes and computer-printed lyrics.

I soon learned how hard it is to get a Nashville publisher to
even *listen* to an amateur's songs. I spent three hours and
twelve dollars on twenty-five-cent phone calls to about fifty of
Nashville's four hundred music publishers before I had any
luck.[1] T. J. McMann of Honeycomb Studios finally agreed to
review a couple of cuts.

I checked Honeycomb's address. No need to waste money
on a cab, I thought. It's only four blocks away.

My feet were aching, forty-five minutes later. Each block
was half a mile long. How could I have thought that 16th Avenue was a few studio-packed streets?

"Sit down, boy," T. J. waved me to a black leather couch in
his office at Honeycomb. I sat, gladly.

T. J. McMann was tall and lean, had a Kristofferson-type
beard, and his short-sleeved cowboy shirt displayed proud tat-
toos.

"Tough, ain't it?"

"Yeah, it's tough." I couldn't let T. J. know he was the first
Nashville agent I'd met.

"I didn't know there *was* any country songwriters in them
Philippine Islands—that's the other side of Hawaya, ain't it?"
I assured T. J. that his geography was correct.

"You write both lyrics and music?"

"No, my partner writes our music." I told T. J. how Merle
Shepard was a good ol' boy from Georgia who'd worked his
way through Vanderbilt University picking guitar in Nashville
honkytonks. *Why, Charley Rich himself offered ol' Merle a job
on the road when he graduated.* But I skipped over how Merle
turned the country star down to study for his doctorate at Texas
A&M, and was now head of the IRRI Entomology Department. That didn't seem the way to impress T. J.

"Let's hear what you boys got."

[1] Publishers are the songwriter's link to the music industry. They seek new
songs for their catalogs, print sheet music, make professional demo tapes,
"pitch" the songs to top singers and recording studios, then try to help the
songs climb on the charts. The publisher usually receives fifty percent of all
royalties. Having a song published doesn't mean it will be recorded. But few
songs are recorded without first being published.

I handed T. J. a preset cassette tape and lyrics sheet. He turned the stereo to an ear-piercing decibel. That didn't help the sound of "Sixties Progeny," which Merle had recorded on his home stereo rig in Los Baños:

> Facing forty isn't easy
> For the children of the Sixties
> Time dictates that fate must happen
>   But what happened to our dream?
> The screaming of the hawk and dove
> Was louder than our dreams of love
> I was part of all that happened
>   I'm a Sixties Progeny
>
> We had heard a different drummer
> In those days of endless summer
> On the commune wine was sweet
>   And still sweeter love was free
> But the Establishment went mad
> We got angry, times turned bad
> And I joined up with the movement
>   To make all men truly free

T. J. concentrated on the lyrics. *This guy takes our song seriously,* I thought, and that meant a lot. "Sixties Progeny" was special . . . to me. I'd drafted the song sitting on the grass, staring at that black marble wall and surrounded by ghosts. I guess a lot of us feel that way, the first time we visit the Vietnam Memorial. Merle moved into the chorus:

> Though today it seems absurd
> We trusted no one over thirty
> We turn forty in the Eighties
> But we're Sixties Progeny
>
> We ignored their proclamations
> Faced their hate with demonstrations
> Only we could make it happen
>   Love would be our legacy
> But our prophecy of peace
> Died on cold Chicago streets

And we drifted, hell-borne, helpless
  To a time of lunacy

I was living with the flowers
But I feared the distant fires
Lord I knew it wouldn't happen
  But it did, The Notice came
Could have crossed the Northern Border
To evade the profane slaughter
But I had to see what happens
  'cross the Border of Insane

My friends had claimed that an amateur songwriter could never sell new music in Nashville. Wait till they hear about this . . .

I had barely turned nineteen
Drafted in the Green Machine
Turning on to smoke and dying
  In the First Air Cavalry
Saw men wasted for our flag
Others fragged, some lost to skag
And we sang to keep from crying
  To the choppers' hard-rock beat

We returned to bitter truth
Licking wounds that killed our youth
What had happened, never happened
  We would start all over now
But our nation was divided
By position in that fighting
I think back on all that happened
  Can we learn from it somehow?

Though today it seems absurd
We trusted no one over thirty
We turn forty in the Eighties
But we're Sixties Progeny
We were of that generation
Had a plan to change our nation
You can see it didn't happen
  But we left a legacy

Lord why did you let it happen
To the Sixties Progeny?

T. J. handed back my lyrics.

"It's good ... but not commercial." That was the first, but
not the last, time I'd hear that Nashville rejection.

"Why don't you use ord'nary folks' words? What the hell
does *frag* mean? And *skag*?"

"Why, *frag* is a verb ... for when an enlisted man killed an
officer or NCO. It comes from fragmentation grenade. And
skag was Vietnam slang for heroin." I thought everyone knew
that.

T. J. shook his head. "Honeycomb's not gonna publish
nothin' about dope.

"And that word *progeny*. I figgered out what it meant, by
followin' the rest of your lyrics. But I never heard that word
in my life, till now."

T. J. lit a Marlborough and continued. "Let me tell you
somethin', boy. *I'm* a ninth-grade dropout. And that's why *I'm*
sittin' on this side of the desk, and *you're* over there. 'Cause
I know what the *common* folk want to hear—and they don't
want to hear about *no damn progeny*!

"Common folk don't want to hear about that damn war, neither. It's over."

The common folks, I thought, fought in Vietnam. T. J.'s rejection hurt a little, but I wouldn't argue with the only agent in
Nashville who'd listen to our music.

"You got anything else on that tape?"

"The other cut is 'Burned-out Oilfield Cowboy.' "

"Oilfield cowboy," T. J. said. "That sounds like a song I
might *relate* to."

I don't think so, but I'll play it ...

He stared into the broken mirror
Of a dim-lit Bangkok bar
She couldn't tell he'd come from Texas
And that he'd gone way too far
   Like her, he'd gone too far

A flower child facing forty
Time stole the youth she knew,

Still searching for the Sixties
On the road from Kathmandu
Still searching for the truth ...

He's a burned-out oilfield cowboy
His life's been one dry hole
His body's scars are nothing
Like the scars that scar his soul

I'd known the ex-Marine, and the hippie who wanted the flowers to bloom forever, through lots of friends. They shared memories, through my verses, in that Bangkok bar:

She:

I was living in the Haight
While you were over there
We learned to love while you learned hate,
Picked flowers from the air
Peace was our only prayer

He:

Mother Green, the Death Machine
Taught me what's wrong was right
I sold my soul to the rock 'n' roll
Of a scorching Armalite
And it all comes back at night ...

The oilfield cowboy and the ex-hippie shared the same bed that night. After all, they were pretty much alike. The sixties shaped both of them. After a couple more verses, my song ended with:

Lost cowboy, faded flower child,
From each life took its toll
Their bodies' scars are camouflage
For the scars that scar their souls

"Boy ... you write good, and you can structure lyrics proper. So I'm gonna give you some advice.
"You got *too much ejucation* to write songs for Nashville.

"But maybe you can overcome it. Go back to them Philippine Islands and write a song that *common people* can relate to. A love song, maybe, or something about drinkin' or cheatin'."

My feet, and ego, were blistered as I trudged back up 16th Avenue. I finally pulled off those stiff new boots, and walked the scorching sidewalk in socks.

A tour bus passed as I reached the crest of the hill overlooking the Elvis Presley Auto Museum, Barbara Mandrell's 1-hour Photo Studio, Minnie Pearl's Country-Fried Chicken, and the Dolly Parton Record Shop.

The guide spoke into a microphone, and fifty tourists' heads turned toward me. I could sense his words:

"Look to your right, folks. There's a down-and-out songwriter, carrying his cowboy boots and walking away from Music Row. Probably thought he'd make it big in Nashville . . ."

That evening's agenda was set. I was staying at the Hall of Fame Motor Inn, next to the Country Music Hall of Fame, for two reasons. First, friends at the fringe of the music business said that country singers and publishers hung out at its Country Music Hall of Fame Bar.

It was also the favorite drinking spot of the man who wrote and sang the top hit of 1966, a song that made him the Vietnam War's most famous soldier. I wanted to meet him—partly because of his fame, but I had more selfish reasons.

"Is Barry Sadler in town?" I asked the barmaid that evening. She glared, and said nothing.

"I've heard that Barry does his drinking here." I paid for my $1.50 beer with a $5.00 bill, and left the change on the polished-oak bar.

"Barry don't hang around Nashville much these days, thank God."

"So I've heard."

Sgt. Barry Sadler hadn't recorded any hits since his "Ballad of the Green Berets." But Sadler's life, after leaving the Special Forces in 1967, had been colorful. He made half a million dollars off the song, but spent it fast. Sadler then drifted back to the town that made him famous . . . and rich, for a while.

In Nashville, Sadler worked as a songwriter and, briefly, a police detective. He wrote *Nashville With A Bullet*, an awful detective novel. The killer slit throats, snapped backs, and strangled enemies in the dark—obviously precision work by a skilled professional. He turned out, of course, to be an ex–Green Beret that America, and Nashville, had done wrong.

In 1982, Barry shot a Nashville songwriter between the eyes after a quarrel over a woman. The unfortunate Lee Bellamy couldn't have been too bright. He'd threatened to kill both the woman and Sadler—and called the Green Berets a bunch of pussies.

"Forty feet at night by a single light in a parking lot," Sadler bragged. His victim had a bad criminal record that convinced the judge to reduce Barry's ten-year sentence to thirty days. But the Nashville police let Sadler know that he was no longer welcome in the Home of Country Music.

"Who'd know how to contact Barry?" I asked the barmaid.

"That guy at the end of the bar might help," she said, quickly pocketing my change. "He's one of Barry's drinking buddies."

I changed bar stools. "I hear you know Barry Sadler."

The paunchy, middle-aged man looked at me, but said nothing. He wore a knit polo shirt and an army crew-cut.

"Can I buy you a drink?"

"Black Jack Daniels on the rocks," he told the barmaid. "Make it a double."

"Is Sadler in Nashville?" I asked.

"Barry was in town a few weeks ago, but he's back in Central America now."

"What's he doing?"

"Selling guns and ammo, running Contras into Nicaragua—that's what Barry claims. The Indian jungle-bunnies in Guatemala call him 'Papa Gringo.'

"But *that ol' boy* knows Barry better than me." He pointed to a tall man wearing ostrich-skin boots, a silver rodeo buckle, and a black felt Stetson garnished with a turkey feather. I approached him.

"Why you lookin' for Barry?" the cowboy asked. Be careful, Hargrove, I thought. Sadler has enemies. Make sure this crowd knows that you're not one of them.

"I hear that Barry's about to make a comeback," I said. "He's putting together a new album, sort of a twenty-year-later followup to his "Green Berets" album . . . songs about Vietnam, looking back at it. I've written stuff like that."

"Yeah, they plan to sell that album over cable TV," the cowboy said. "Dial 1-800 . . . but Barry'll never cut the album.

He's makin' too damn much money down there in Guatemala."

The cowboy must mean Sadler's gun-running and mercenary businesses, I thought, but . . .

"Barry gets fifty grand—up front—for ever' one of them *Casca* books he writes, then more money when they hit the market. He's churnin' out four or five books a year. Hollywood even wants to make a Casca movie."

I'd read a couple of the twenty-three paperbacks in Sadler's series *Casca: The Eternal Mercenary*. In the first book, God curses Cascius Longinus, the legendary Roman soldier who speared Jesus on the Cross at Golgotha. He's condemned to be an eternal soldier: a mercenary who'll fight in army after army but can neither age nor die . . . until the second coming of Christ.

Casca fights and survives through twenty centuries of war, waiting for the Return. He always joins armies that lose. First a gladiator, Casca then serves with the Persian army, invades the New World as a conquistador. Casca is a Hessian mercenary during the American Revolution, a Panzer soldier at Stalingrad and, of course, a French legionnaire at Dien Bien Phu.

Women cause Casca great pain. Time ages each lover, but Casca stays the same . . . then he moves on to another army, another torrid romance.

I pulled out lyrics of a song I'd written about Casca—for the Sadler album. That convinced the cowboy that I was a true Barry Sadler fan, not associated with pinkos, the law or the government.

"*That* fellow knows how to contact Barry." The cowboy nodded at a swarthy little man sipping a martini. He looked a lot like Frank Sinatra.

His dress style was 1930s Chicago gangster: white linen suit, white shoes, white hat, and a black shirt with white silk tie. The cowboy walked to his table. I followed.

"*Huh-uh! You* stay *right there!*" the cowboy ordered.

They talked for a few minutes, then the little man pulled out a fountain pen, the kind that uses real ink, not a ballpoint.

The cowboy returned with a business card. On its front were crossed U.S. and Confederate flags, with **Star-Spangled Music Co.** embossed in bold letters.

"That address and this bar's the main contacts when Barry's

in town," the cowboy said. "Sadler's permanent address is on the other side."

I turned the card over and read, in black ink: "c/o Bar Europa, Guatemala City."

Back in the Philippines, I sent a tape and lyrics to the Bar Europa, but Barry didn't respond.

Barry Sadler never made that comeback album. He shot himself in the head early one morning in 1988, while showing off his .380 Beretta pistol to a woman as they rode from a Guatemala City bar by taxi. At least, that's in the official Guatemalan police report.

Soldier of Fortune magazine chartered an ambulance plane to fly the brain-shot Sadler back to Nashville. There, he's said to have come out of a coma to claim that Ben Rossen, his drinking buddy and partner in the Central American arms business, shot him, according to an article published in *Gentlemen's Quarterly* (April, 1990). Rosson was an ex–Special Forces sniper who claimed more than two hundred and fifty kills in Vietnam.

The man who made the Green Berets a legend died in Nashville in early 1989. Maybe his death was accidental, but by his own hand. Or it could have been suicide. But maybe Sadler was murdered. Only one thing is certain. Barry Sadler lived a lot like the Casca he created, and died in an aura of mystery and violence.

A month after my 1986 Nashville trip, I had written "Wedding Pictures in the Trash" and "Honkytonk Wife"—mainly to show T. J. McMann that I could really lower my writing to Nashville's level. I wrote two dozen songs for the common folk, plus six or seven more about the Nam experience.

My third annual trip to Nashville, in 1988, was about like the first two—except I no longer pitched my Vietnam ballads. My newest composition was a sad country song: "I Didn't Want to Shoot Your Daddy." I didn't think my favorite new song could be *kept* off the charts, because it focused on something close to the common people—the Yellow Pages. But "Let My Fingers Do the Walking (and I'll walk all over you)" didn't make it either.

My future's not in Nashville, I finally decided. Maybe I should concentrate on the novel . . .

Transition 17

Chuong Thien Province, 22 May 1990

We dock in front of Ba Lien's house, and I step ashore first. A man in his forties, not the old farmer, welcomes me. This guy is scared, and wears a long-sleeved, blue-and-black striped shirt, white shorts, and sandals. That's strange dress, for a farm along the Xa No Canal.

Even stranger, he greets me in poor English. I don't catch his name, but he's in the Ba Lien family. This *must* be the man who sent me that bizarre report of U.S. dog tags and skeletons last year.

Swirly waves of heat dance off the papaya and banana trees as dozens of children spot Susan, rush to her, laughing, shouting.

In the confusion, the dog-tag man tries to talk, but the cowboys move me forward.

The man approaches Susan and asks how many children we have. Then the cowboys surround and block him off.

"They won't let us talk," he says.

"Why not?" Susan asks, her back turned.

"They won't let us . . ." Two cowboys take the man away, so I never hear his story, first hand, of finding the dogtag and skeleton of an MIA named Harold Dixon in today's Chuong Thien Province . . .

Chapter XXIX
Dogtags and Skeletons

Los Baños, Philippines. Summer and fall, 1989
A handwritten letter, in Vietnamese, caught my eye as I sorted through a foot-high stack of mail, memos, and problems on my desk on 21 August 1989.

This was my first working day at IRRI after a month in Texas. I couldn't call that time "vacation," because I wrote, eight to fourteen hours a day, seven days a week. Owen Lock wanted nonfiction, so that's what he'd get ... mostly. I sent Lock twenty-five thousand words—about a fifth of a book—as the Federal Express office in Granbury, Texas, closed at 5:00 P.M. on 19 August, and prayed he'd like it. I was back home in the Philippines forty hours later.

A page of English text, a translation by a Vietnamese scholar at IRRI, was stapled to the letter. Its return address, I saw, was "Vi Thanh." I began reading:

> I send my regard to Dr. Thomas R. Hargrove and Mrs. Hargrove. God bless you and family.

The next words froze my heart:

> Please send these news to family of the died man. Information on dogtag like this:

> **DIXON, HAROLD**
> **U.S. 67 094-610**
> **587: 54-B022**
> **Baptist**

Good God! *Dogtag?*

Please contact with this address to receive skeleton.

> From: Mr. Ngo Huynh Duong
>   Common name: Mr. Ba Lien
>   Vi Duc Village
>   Vi Thanh District
>   Hau Giang Province

Ba Lien is asking me to go back to Chuong Thien to pick up a *skeleton*? Could this mean ... *an MIA*, an American serviceman who was *missing in action*? I read more:

> My name: Phung Van Tra. I am son of Mr. Ba Lien.
> Please write with me at: Post Office Box 109, Vi Thanh.

Is this a trick, a hoax? I knew that thousands of Vietnamese wanted, desperately, to escape ...

No, the letter *must* be authentic. Ba Lien had his son write it. And he doesn't ask for money or favors ... but he wouldn't. Ba Lien is one of those proud Asian peasants. New rice seeds were the only favor he *ever* asked. And Ba Lien is surely content to be buried by his ancestors along the Xa No Canal, in rich soil that he's farmed for eighty years.

I never heard of MIAs in Chuong Thien Province. But the VC held a few U.S. POWs—prisoners of war—in the U Minh Forest, about twenty miles from Ba Lien's farm. That's where Nick Rowe killed his guard and escaped from a swampy VC prison camp in 1968. Rowe had been captured while a Special Forces lieutenant, an adviser in Ca Mau, south of Chuong Thien.

I had met Rowe when he came to Des Moines in 1971 to promote his book *Five Years to Freedom*. In 1989, he was a full colonel assigned to the Joint U.S. Military Advisory Group, Philippines. JUSMAG is somewhat like MAC-V was in Vietnam. Advisers.

Rowe might have known a Harold Dixon in those terrible U Minh camps, I thought. But I can't ask, because Nick Rowe was assassinated in Manila four months ago by the Communist New People's Army ... maybe. Some think it was a "black"

operation by right-wing elements of the Philippine armed
forces.

But didn't the VC capture an American adviser . . . I believe
he was black . . . in Chuong Thien during the 1968 Tet Offensive, a year before I arrived? Maybe *he* was Harold Dixon.
Still, how could a body have been found, fourteen years after
the war ended, on Ba Lien's seven acres of intensely farmed
rice land?

My thoughts turned cynical. Could the Vietnamese Government be using Ba Lien—and his relationship with me—to save
face while turning over MIA remains they deny holding?

My 1988 visit to Ba Lien's farm certainly drew attention.
One of Vietnam's most popular newspapers politicized the
visit. That's how Khang, my interpreter, located me after all
those years.

And Tran Van Rang, once a VC political officer . . . actually,
still one . . . is a nephew of Ba Lien's wife. Rang said that Ba
Lien was never a VC, but supported the Revolutionary Forces.
Maybe the Communists are behind this . . .

But what if Ba Lien is sending me this information at terrible risk? If *I'd* opened his letter, instead of my secretary, I'd
have recognized that the English text was copied from a
dogtag and asked Mai Bertotti, not an IRRI scholar, to translate
it. Has Ba Lien's message reached the Vietnamese police?

Then I read the last line of that letter from Vi Thanh: "P.S.
There are many more skeleton."

More skeletons . . . I went to see Tim Bertotti.

Tim and I shared a special bond. No American at IRRI—
except me—had ever served in Vietnam until our new Director
of Administration arrived in 1989. Tim had spent four years as
a USAID adviser in the pacification program in the Mekong
Delta. Tim had even stayed in Vi Thanh for a week, in 1968.
He called it a *bad place*. Tim was a personal friend of Frank
Gillespie and Norm Olsen. His wife Mai was the daughter of
a My Tho police chief.

The letter shook Tim, too, especially when Mai confirmed
that the translation, although in bad English, was accurate.

The U.S. Embassy in Bangkok monitors MIA reports, Tim
said. I placed an international call.

My story was hard to explain to Lt. Col. James A. Spurgeon
of the Liaison Office, Joint Casualty Resolution Center. Where
do I start? Ba Lien? My return the year before?

I finally blurted the essentials.

"There's a lot of fraud in the MIA business," Colonel Spurgeon responded. "Including fake dogtags."

"But I *know* Ba Lien. He wouldn't lie to me. Besides, what could he gain?"

"I ran a computer search while you were talking," the colonel said. "No Harold Dixon, or any serviceman with a similar name, is listed among the Indochina MIAs, KIAs, or POWs.

"A Harold Dixon probably fought in Vietnam—but he made it home."

I also mailed a copy of the Ba Lien letter to Susan, who was still in Texas.

Something strange was going on, and my wife is persistent. She phoned half a dozen veterans' groups, then someone in the Pentagon. She soon had the Defense Intelligence Agency on the line, then finally, MIA Intelligence, the Special Office for Prisoners of War and Missing in Action.

Their analysis was the same as Colonel Spurgeon's.

In October an army colonel in DIA's PW-MIA office wrote that no Harold Dixon was killed, captured, or missing in Indochina. He enclosed a DIA report dated 1 Sep 1989. It was titled, appropriately, Dogtag Reports:

. . . the first two were received in 1979. Since then over 4,000 such reports have been received, and they continue to arrive at a similar rate monthly.

In each dogtag report, a person or persons—many of them still residents of Southeast Asia—claim to possess the remains of one or more Americans. As proof they offer information copied from U.S. military identification tags, tracings of dogtags, photographs of dogtags, actual dogtags, or other identification documents.

More than 2,900 U.S. military personnel have been named in these reports; 89% served in Southeast Asia and returned to the U.S. alive. An additional 7% were killed, but their remains were recovered, identified, and returned to the U.S. for burial. . . . About 4% name a serviceman who is unaccounted for, suggesting that someone has recovered his remains or personal effects from battlefield or crash sites.

However, several factors make it unlikely that private citizens recovered these items.

One ... is the duplication of claims involving a single missing service member. In most cases, several different people claim to have the remains and/or personal effects of each of the named servicemen. Frequently, each source claims to have recovered the same items on a different date or at a different location. These inconsistencies indicate that the people do not obtain their information by recovering items from battlefield or crash sites.

... two of the servicemen, whose remains and dogtags several persons claim to have found, are former POWs who returned alive and whose dogtags were taken from them by their captors.

Another factor is the practice of identification of remains advocated by Communist forces. Throughout the war they enforced a policy to find and bury Americans killed in action, and to send to central authorities a report of the burial location and the personal effects and identification taken from the body. Captured documents continually stressed that this effort was important to the "political struggle." In instances where this was done, the Governments of Vietnam and Laos should have knowledge of many of the missing men whose names have appeared in the dogtag reports.

There are several tragic aspects to many of these dogtag reports. Most of the persons reporting this information ask for assistance in resettling in the U.S. because they have been led to believe that if they possess the remains of American servicemen, they and their families will be resettled. In some cases, sources indicated that they have paid for this information. To discourage this type of ... exploitation, the U.S. Government provides no rewards or assistance for information on unaccounted Americans.

In conclusion, the known policy and practices of the Indochinese governments to collect information concerning U.S. war dead, coupled with the patterns in the dogtag reporting, *lead to the belief that the majority of reports reflect information and personal effects recovered by Vietnamese forces, not private citizens.*

Further, it would appear that these dogtag reports are managed by elements within the Socialist Republic of Vietnam in an effort to influence or exploit the PW-MIA issue. [Author's emphasis.]

Nevertheless, each report is carefully analyzed to determine its validity.

So the Harold Dixon dogtag is almost certainly fake, I thought. But the DIA report implied something larger, orchestrated by the Vietnamese Government.

The U.S. obviously left files behind in 1975 ... I could imagine Vietnamese workers, who don't know a word of English, punching out dogtags from those records in a grimy machine shop in Cholon, the Chinese section of Saigon. That made me laugh, a little—even though there was nothing funny about it.

But if four thousand dogtag reports have reached DIA, why hasn't *Time* or *Newsweek*, NBC or CBS, reported it?

Maybe the media simply haven't heard. The "Dogtag Reports" indicated that persons still in Vietnam send most claims, usually to relatives who are now refugees or immigrants abroad. I doubt that many such reports have reached U.S. veterans. How many still have personal ties to Vietnam? My IRRI job has made me an exception.

But I *had* to consider another possibility. Spooks and soldiers on covert missions sometimes carried fake identities. Could Ba Lien have found a skeleton with a dogtag that backed an assumed name? *If so, Harold Dixon would never appear on a DIA list.*

I studied the Ba Lien letter carefully. Its return address bothered me ... P.O. Box 109. How much mail would the old farmer get? Would he rent a post office box in Vi Thanh?

The address of his granddaughter, Huyen Xuan Dep, the little girl I once carried on my shoulders, was simply Vi Duc Village, Vi Thanh District. Is someone using Ba Lien's name?

I can trust Ms. Dep, I felt, so I'd contact her first.

Was the enclosed letter from Vi Thanh, I wrote, indeed written on behalf of your grandfather?

My second letter was "straight"—like I suspected nothing—and addressed to Phung Van Tra, the "son of Ba Lien." I can't return to Vietnam right now, I explained, but could you send more information? A rubbing of Harold Dixon's dogtag, perhaps, or a photo of the "many more skeletons." Exactly where did you find them?

Responses to both letters came two months later. First, Ms. Dep wrote, in Vietnamese: "The story that my grandfather found skeletons and dogtags was made up, to take advantage of your friendship with our family . . ."

Next, Phung Van Tra wrote:

I hope that God is Blessing you always. My father, Ba Lien, and my mother are happy that you think of them.

Have you written to U.S. Government to check the list of Americans who fought and helped Vietnam, and left their bodies like Dixon, Harold? Because of our affection, we would like to help the relative find their loved one.

Also, I want to use this occasion to ask if you can help my nephew. He use to work for the Americans in Can Tho and Vi Thanh up to the day the Americans got out. But your employee is still here. His name is below:

Employee name: Nguyen An Dai
Position Title: Community Development Assistant

Agency: CORDS

Length of
employment: Aug 1971 to April 30, 1975

Name of American supervisor: I Richard T. Burke
                                   II Terry J. Barker

Reason for separation: April 30, 1975

I hope you can help my nephew immigrate to America to find his freedom.

* * *

He had enclosed photocopies of Nguyen An Dai's CORDS ID and U.S. Government health insurance cards. Also, a rubbing of the Harold Dixon dogtag.

So, it *was* a macabre plot to exploit an emotional and traumatic issue. *Isn't that what Vietnam was about?* Bruce McAllister once wrote. *Lies and tricks and reality?* Chuong Thien was that, yeah . . . and the years haven't changed her.

I knew Dick Burke, and had heard of Terry Barker. Frank Gillespie would have their addresses. I'll write to Nguyen An Dai's former American supervisors later, I thought. Now, I'm burned out on dogtags and skeletons.

I added the letters to my *own* "Dogtags & Skeletons" file, and shut the drawer. I had to spend more late-night writing on the Chuong Thien of 1969–70, not her lingering ghosts of 1989.

But *who was* Harold Dixon? Were you an adviser, an infantryman, a sailor, airman? Where are you now? I wish I could tell you how your forged dogtag and nonexistent skeleton were the key to a desperate and hopeless scheme to escape the Vietnam that we both helped shape.

Maybe I will. Maybe "Dixon, Harold" will read my book.

Transition 18

Chuong Thien Province, 22 May 1990

I remember him working in the rice fields, bare-chested with sinewy muscles, wearing shorts and a white pith helmet. He's so much older now, far older than when I visited two years ago. The Ho Chi Minh beard is gone, and he leans on a cane whose handle is carved into a water buffalo head.

"Ba Lien . . ." Children cheer as we embrace. This must be the biggest excitement since the day the Communists took—Tu Rang would say *liberated*—Chuong Thien Province in April of 1975.

We move to the teak table in that familiar thatch house, and sip green tea. It's hard to talk over the noise the children make.

Susan walks in like an unwilling circus act. Her circle of jumping, laughing children grows as more kids join the fun.

"If the Commies can control people's minds," she says, "why don't they control these damn kids? They're *wrecking* Ba Lien's home!"

"Where's our dogtag man?" I ask.

"The cowboys . . . they *took him away*." The kids, the noise, the heat and emotion are getting to Susan.

A shrill cry and Ba Lien's grandaughter, Huyen Xuan Dep, rushes in. She presses her nose against my cheek and sniffs, kissing me the way Vietnamese do. Her three children join Susan's crowd.

Someone hands me the two sacks of IRRI seeds. I explain again that these seeds aren't special, but it's hard to explain why Lynn came from America to photograph me bringing them.

Ms. Dep presses the sacks to her bosom, like babies. She knows these seeds are the most wonderful thing to hit the rice world since IR8. Those seeds had *damned well better* be good.

We came to give the rice seeds to Ba Lien, and talk is impossible—so let's do it.

Ba Lien and I sit on the concrete patio where rice is dried, and Lynn targets us with her viewfinder. A belt of lenses and film is strapped to her waist, in easy reach. Lynn works two Leicas like they're part of her body. She reminds me, amazingly, of a well-equipped soldier who handles his weapons and gear well.

"Cross your feet." Lynn wants my army boots in the photo. She had asked me to wear something that symbolizes Vietnam, but I'm not the type to wear an old fatigue jacket. Besides, Mother burned my uniforms years ago, when she cleaned house in Texas.

I pour a cone of seeds onto a flat rattan basket, the kind farmers use to winnow rice. Ba Lien and Ms. Dep and I sift the seeds as Lynn shoots a dozen rolls of Kodachrome, from every angle. She finally signals that we're through.

Now we'll inspect Ba Lien's rice. He leads us through banana and coconut trees, past a flock of noisy ducks in a muddy lateral canal. Like most farmers north of Vi Thanh, he grows three crops a year of IR19960. This time I remember to lift Ms. Dep's little girl to my shoulders, carry her through the farm like I took her mother two decades ago.

It should be more dramatic after this long, hard travel, through time more than miles. I almost expect something strange to happen; that's become part of the Vietnam scene. But nothing does. I guess my psychic energy burned out two hours ago at that cemetery . . .

CHAPTER XXX
Laughing Wolves, Wings of Harmless Doves

West Texas, September 1990

> Behold, I send you forth as sheep in the mist of wolves: be ye therefore wise as serpents, and harmless as doves.
> —Matthew

> Oh that I had wings like a dove! For then I would fly away, and be at rest.
> —Psalms

I was searching, I guess, for red-dirt roots as the summer of 1990 ended. This return to West Texas would be my last chance to see Mother and Daddy before going back to the Philippines for another year . . . my twentieth year in Southeast Asia. That's most of my adult life.

I'd also hunt mourning doves on the old Hargrove place with Kenny McKinney, my brother-in-law. The last time I'd been home for the September dove season was in 1970, after the army.

Kenny and I spent three one hundred-degree afternoons under mesquite trees around the same muddy stock tank where we became friends, through the bond of hunting, when he was courting Becky. We talked more than we shot, but talk was more important.

We brought a new hunter this time. David Outterson, a fresh Baylor University graduate from Houston, had never fired a gun, but loved the outdoors and wanted to learn. I envied Kenny the special bond of teaching his new son-in-law the craft and ethics of hunting and shooting—something that, really, can be passed only from man to man.

I'll never have that satisfaction. Miles and Tom G are their mother's children when it comes to hunting and fishing. They think killing harmless wild birds is senseless. I must accept that. But if my sons had been raised on a dryland cotton farm, they might see that a reasonable harvest of wildlife is Nature's bounty for caring for the land.

When shooting was slow, I circled the tank to stir up more doves. But too many of the birds I hit, as I walked through the pasture, tumbled into thick brush along the creek and were lost. To me, killing game and then not using it is immoral. Searching for lost birds could also be dangerous. The late-summer heat dulls the senses of rattlesnakes in the brush, and they strike blindly at whatever moves.

Loud, sudden noises still make me jump, but I found the blast of my 12-gauge, the one I'd shot with as a boy, peaceful as the beautiful doves soared by.

My parents knew what a shotgun meant to me at Christmas when I was twelve, and bought a fine one. I cared for that Winchester Model 59 automatic, and wouldn't trade it for the most expensive shotgun made today. Maybe that's why Susan and I dipped into savings to buy Tom G an IBM AT compatible with a forty-megabyte hard disk and VGA color monitor—a system that, we hoped, would last him through college.

But I must admit a sense of irony when I compare my sense of values, as a young man, with those of my sons. My shotgun is a fine tool for killing. The computer is for knowledge.

That sharp smell of cordite triggers memories, but some are pleasant. It took me back, for a few hours, to days so innocent that I thought I knew about life. So did the blood-smell of cleaning our game, and the special fried-dove dinner for the Hargrove family.

A haunting sound stirred me at midnight of the last day on the farm—the laughing coyotes of Comanche lore. That primeval song from the canyons to our north drew me outside, into the night. I was raised with the mournful cry and gleeful yip of solitary coyotes. But dozens of the wolves had gathered that night to laugh in harmony, maybe at us humans who think we own West Texas.

I walked across Hargrove land . . . cotton fields I had plowed and hoed as a boy, and listened to the coyotes' taunting symphony.

The end-of-summer days in Fisher County are over, I thought. So is the camaraderie of men sharing the serious business of hunting. Next week I'll be back at my *real* business— rice in Asia.

I'd accumulated an extra month of vacation over the past years, and had used or, I hoped, *invested* that time writing— trying to finish this book—in our second home in Granbury, south of Fort Worth.

It wasn't easy. Saddam Hussein's invasion of Kuwait threw our summer into turmoil.

Susan was terribly upset as we watched an Iraqi tank fire into a special house—her childhood home—over television news. Her brother, Miles Sheldon, had returned to Kuwait twelve years before, and was now vice-president of Santa Fe International there. Miles and his family left on home leave four days before the Iraqi Army's blitzkrieg through the oil-rich but defenseless sheikdom. At first he felt a complex emotional mix of guilt, for not being with his staff in Kuwait, and embarrassment—he should have known that Saddam was crazy enough to do it. By now, Miles also felt relief that his family wasn't held hostage, and anguish for the country.

Miles and Hilda had lost home, bank account, and a 1990 Mercedes purchased the day before leaving. They had brought only suitcases packed for a two-week vacation in Texas. Hilda's parents, two brothers, and a sister were trapped in Kuwait, and the Sheldons were suddenly refugees from a country where they'd lived most of their lives, but weren't citizens.

Miles was now commuting between the Santa Fe office in Los Angeles, and New York, London, and Texas, where Hilda and the kids were staying with my mother-in-law until their lives made sense again.

Miles had received one bit of good news: the Iraqi soldiers hadn't looted their home, nor found his new Mercedes . . . not yet.

His response, ironically, made sense, in this situation: "Smash the car's windshield, take its wheels off, smear it with mud," Miles said. "Make the car look cannibalized."

I'd brought a laptop computer and portable printer to West Texas, so I could write when I wasn't hunting, or with my family. Mother was reviewing and editing daily drafts of my final chapters, as she had done almost two decades ago with my novel.

When Kenny, David, and I returned from our last afternoon of hunting doves, Mother made the only major suggestion I'd reject. She asked me to take out my chapter The Black Spring of 1977.

"I can't do that," I said. *"It happened."*

"Has Susan read this?"

"No, but Susan hates the war so deeply, she won't read about it. To her, it was a senseless mass murder. She doesn't understand why I *have to* write about it.

"I've asked Susan to read parts of the book where I write about her—but not *that* chapter."

"Then do one thing . . . *for me. Make Susan read about your 'black spring' before you submit the manuscript."*

"I will. And I may change some things, but I can't take the chapter out. It wouldn't be honest."

Those coyotes seemed to laugh more tauntingly as I thought of how to handle that *black spring* chapter.

In Granbury, I had talked with Alicia Medrano, who runs a small dry-cleaning business. Her husband is a supermarket clerk. I'd never met their son Carlos, but wished I had. He's a 1988 Texas A&M graduate, with a degree in Petroleum Engineering. Carlos served in the Corps of Cadets, and was commissioned an infantry second lieutenant. That's a big step up for a poor Mexican-American family in Central Texas.

The lieutenant was now shipping out to Saudi Arabia with the 82d Airborne.

"Would you send Carlos some unsolicited advice?" I asked Alicia. "Tell him it's from an Old Ag who's been there." I'd been in Kuwait, but that's not what *there* meant.

I told Alicia how another Texas Aggie, Charley Scruggs, the editor of *Progressive Farmer* magazine, once sent me this same advice. I followed Charley's counsel, but didn't know it until almost twenty years later.

"Keep a diary, Tom," Charley wrote in that special 1969 letter. "Write it down. I knew I'd never forget what happened when I was a young infantry officer in Europe 20 years ago— but I have. You think *you'll* never forget—but you will. Whatever happens in Vietnam, write it."

"Tell Carlos I'm passing something on, third-generation advice that I inherited. *Write it down.* Whatever happens on that Saudi desert—even if *nothing* happens—write what you're doing, your thoughts, emotions. You think you'll always remember. But you won't . . ."

I quit my own writing for only one day during those seven weeks of vacation, when Lee and Linda Lanning visited us in Granbury. Lee had retired as a lieutenant colonel after twenty years of service, and the Lannings now live in Tempe, Arizona. They had returned for a Texas Aggie reunion—Lee's Spider-D Class of 1968.

We share a lot of bonds . . . growing up in Fisher County, then Texas A&M . . . neighbors at Fort Bragg . . . Susan and Linda living together as waiting wives for a year.

"How's the writing, Tom?" was Lee's first question after the Lannings settled in and we opened icy cans of Coors.

That's a new bond, writing a book. Only four years ago I reviewed and did a light edit on Lee's first book, *The Only War We Had.* Four Lanning books were now on the market, and Lee was finishing two more. How does he do it?

"I've hit a tough part, Lee. The experience was too emotional to write about."

"Bad times in the Delta in '69?"

"No . . . Nashville in '86.

"But none of it's been easy. I planned to stay glued to one screen this summer." I pointed to the computer. "But *that* damned screen keeps competing." The TV. The Hargroves had monitored CNN, the Cable News Network, continuously since Saddam invaded Kuwait.

"But I'm finally putting the book to bed."

"There's only one Vietnam story, you know," Lee said. "We just all tell it differently."

"I like that."

"Don't steal it, Hargrove!" Lee said. "That line's in my next book . . . and copyrighted."

"*You've* come a long way, for a cheerleader from Roby," I said to Linda. She's now director of University Development, opening new educational markets for the University of Phoenix.

"I was *never* a cheerleader," Linda bristled, "I was a twirler."

"Both wore short skirts."

"Here's a souvenir from today's Saigon." I tossed my purchased Purple Heart on Lee's lap. Lee saw the worn brass, and reacted like I had three months earlier on Tu Do Street:

"Some soldier gave this to a girl . . . along with a promise to come back."

When American troops returned from Grenada in 1983, Lee said, he arranged a special award ceremony for the half a dozen GIs who'd been wounded. But the army no longer stocked Purple Hearts.

"I borrowed Purple Hearts from Vietnam veterans, so the general could pin real medals on the wounded men's chests. I hated to take them back after the ceremony, but we ordered a fresh supply from . . . whoever makes war medals. The Grenada veterans finally got *their own* Purple Hearts."

"I hope we don't need Purple Hearts now," Susan said. We all knew she meant Saudi . . . Kuwait.

"I can't believe you went back to Nam again, Tom," Lee said. "Your *third* return?"

"No, the fourth. IRRI sent me to Vietnam for a week in 1974, six months before Saigon fell."

There was a cease-fire, I told Lee, but I watched ARVN soldiers load a C-130 with bodies in Ban Me Thuot, in the Central Highlands. We were in the Delta a few days later, inspecting IRRI varieties at the My Tho Rice Research Station. The VC ambushed a PF militia unit just outside the experimental plots. A firefight interrupted our research for an hour.

"But that's not in the book."

"Why not?"

"I didn't *really* feel like I'd gone back to Nam, because I never got to Vi Thanh. I tried, but no U.S. civilians, except those who answered to Langley, Virginia, were allowed there by late 1974." I managed to call Vi Thanh by land line from Can Tho. That was the last time I spoke with Khang. My former interpreter had two pieces of good news. Farmers in Chuong Thien were now growing IR26, IRRI's newest and best variety back then, on a large scale. And he was getting married. I sent Khang an expensive hand-printed tablecloth from Bangkok the next week, but my wedding gift was stolen in the mail.

"How did you feel about the Vietnam of 1990?"

I thought. "It was wonderful, Lee . . . and terrible. The best nationality you can be, to tour Vietnam today, is U.S. It's better than being French . . . and you remember the Vietnamese love-hate relationship with France. The government wants to normalize relations with America . . . badly.

"The people—farmers, waiters, shopkeepers—assume you're a *Lien Xo*, a Russian. They call Caucasians from the Soviet Bloc *Americans without money*.

"Then they're fascinated to learn you're *really* from America . . . and amazed if you're a Vietnam veteran. Incredibly, I never met anyone who seemed to have really bad memories of us."

"I'd love to have that experience," Lee said. "I *think*."

"But I saw the other side of today's Vietnam," I said. "The chilling side."

I described how the new regime had emptied the huge French and ARVN cemeteries outside of Saigon, and replaced bodies with those of Communist soldiers. Thousands of families excavated, cleaned, and moved the bones of ARVN kin to family plots.

The oppressive and frightening side of today's Vietnam came through more clearly in 1990, I explained, because we spent three days in Vi Thanh, and eight days in other villages and cities across the Delta. In 1988, I spent six nights in five Delta towns, and never slept in the old Chuong Thien Province.

"We traveled from Vi Thanh back to Can Tho by sampan along the old Xa No Canal," I told Lee. At the pier, a desperate woman dashed from the crowd. "I remember you . . . I've watched you for three days!" she handed me a scrap of paper with her name and address. "But I was afraid to speak to you."

I recognized her: a hootch maid at the CORDS compound, the one who spoke fair English. "Are you scared now?"

"*Yes!* But I had to let you know *who I am*." She disappeared back into the crowd as we boarded the sampan.

"Since leaving, I dread getting my mail. Three letters have arrived from men and women who recognized me—but were afraid to talk, because they'd served with ARVN or USAID, and *they*, the People's Committee, wouldn't give permission.

"I don't know how they get the courage to write, the police *must* read the mail of anyone who's suspect. But still, *they write*. Those people are desperate—and they all see *me* as their only hope of escape."

I told Lee about the Green Beret nurse in Can Tho, and the thirteen-year-old girl who spoke wonderful English. Her mother inevitably wrote, asking if I would take the beautiful child as my own, to raise outside Vietnam.

"I saw the hard-core Communists in a new light. Cadre of the People's Committee were always our hosts. In 1988 I was fascinated to learn they were all ex-VC. They're fun to drink with, and some tell good war stories.

"But now I realize that those men were all VC *political officers*. And that's *still* their job: to make sure people think, and act, properly. They're elected by the people—but the people know they'd *damned well better* elect them."

"Those men are such bullies," Susan said. "They *terrify* the people." My wife watches crowds, how people interact.

"It's their eyes. Lynn saw it too," Susan said. "The *cowboys* have hard, beady eyes that will never meet yours, not honestly. And those little hats . . ."

Yeah, the hats. I didn't notice, until Susan pointed it out. The People's Committee cadre, across the Delta, wear brown felt hats with three corners and a feather, like stereotype gangsters. Did they learn that from old American movies?

I described secret meetings in the night, scary reunions with old friends. I didn't plan, or want, those meetings, they just . . . happened. They could have been dangerous for me, and far worse for the Vietnamese.

"But I can't write *that* into my book."

"You have to write honest, Tom," Lee said. "Like you saw it. A writer's job is to tell the truth . . . that's what Hemingway wrote, in *Men at War*."

"Not if the truth sends Vietnamese friends—who helped us *men at war*—to prison, or *back* to one of those godawful reeducation camps."

I'd written to Owen Lock about my frustration. Our mutual editor had dealt with such conflicts of emotion, honesty, and loyalty before. Lock's advice was short and realistic: "Protect your friends. Save the hard stuff for your *next* book."

"What about your interpreter?" Lee asked. "The one who wrote after seeing your picture in a Saigon paper?"

"I didn't see Khang. The police intercepted my letter, and wouldn't let him come to Saigon. But I met with a mutual friend, and learned that Khang never got my earlier letter either. The one with the good news, that his family was declared eligible for the Orderly Departure Program."

Our friend took copies of my letters to Khang, along with a photo of us on a sampan on the Xa No Canal in 1969—more proof that he worked for the Americans.

"Khang wrote in July. His family now has passports, so maybe they'll get out in a year or two."

"How did *Susan* like Vietnam?" Linda asked.

That's a delicate subject, so I said, "Susan stood up well, even though the travel was rough and living conditions, bad. By *my* standards."

"Susan's standards are probably a bit higher than yours," Linda commented.

My wife rolled her eyes. "Vi Thanh is the most miserable place on earth. I'm writing my *own* Vietnam book. And it'll outsell any macho war stories these men write!"

"Call your book *Susan in the Mekong Delta*," Linda said.

"Vi Thanh was worse, of course, during the war," I said. "But Vietnamese who sided with us remember those times as better. They at least had *some* money, and those outside the VC zones had what *now* seems like freedom."

We were served rat three times on the trip, I told Lee. Banquet fare.

"I caught Susan at the docks by the Xa No Canal, after the first rat dinner," I said. "She was trying to hijack a sampan to the U Minh Forest, Cambodia, the Gulf of Siam—anywhere out of Vi Thanh."

"Do you order red wine, or white, with rat?"

"Neither. Rat is served with *rice* wine. Every Delta gourmet knows that."

"Don't these come in six-packs?" Lee said. I got more beer.

Our talk shifted to A&M days. I pulled a couple of old *Aggielands* from a bookshelf, and searched for the clipping of a 1963 Texas University editorial that called for the disbanding of A&M—just because we started another little brawl at a basketball game in Austin.

We didn't find the clipping, but we skimmed midsixties photos and articles I had stuck in the yearbooks because . . . where else would I put them? Like a clipping about Jim Lanning—Big Hoss, Lee's brother—getting his Combat Infantryman's Badge for leading troops under fire.

A 1967 Christmas card showed three tired soldiers holding M-16s and gazing in awe at three wise men on camels, riding toward a star over the jungle to the east . . . I opened the card and read **"Season's Greetings from the 25th Infantry Division."** Beneath the orange-and-yellow Tropical Lightning emblem was scrawled: "Gig 'em. Hoss."

"That card is worth forty dollars," Lee said.

"You're kidding. *Why?*"

"Vietnam trivia. People *collect* this stuff, today."

A 1966 *Abilene Reporter* article announced the posthumous medals awarded to my cousin, Jimmy Hargrove.

"Wasn't he the first man from Fisher County to die in the war?" Lee asked.

"Yeah, and *Saga* published an article in 1969 about how his chopper was shot down, flying out of My Tho. He was trying to rescue a company of trapped Nungs, Chinese mercenaries, and their Green Beret advisers," I said. "I visited My Tho in 1988, and asked several ex-VC if they remembered a battle like that. None did."

Looking through those *Aggielands* revived a bond that Lee and I swear we've outgrown: the Corps at Texas A&M.

"Why don't you drive over to Stephenville tomorrow, and surprise the Spiders of '68 at our reunion?" I was two years ahead of Lee in Company D-1, Spider-D.

"And risk being held hostage in central Texas by middle-aged Aggies with long memories? No thanks. Robison or Hoegemeyer or Boethel or Randy Thomas—they might still hold grudges."

"We've forgotten . . . no, *forgiven*, what you did when we were fish." I didn't believe him.

"No, the Class of '66 was the last *real* Aggies. The Class of '68 was new army . . . a bunch of pussies." That wasn't true, but I had to say it. *Old Army.*

I changed the subject . . . slightly. "The Aggies went to Vietnam. Do you resent men of our age who didn't?"

"No, but it pisses me off that Dan Quayle implied that he was a Vietnam vet," Lee said.

"Texas Aggies were about the only group of men who claim to be educated that went," I said. "But if I disliked men who avoided Vietnam, I wouldn't have any American friends at IRRI. Anyone who could become a scientist was bright enough to stay out of the military."

"What does that say about *us*?"

"We can write books about it, Lee. They can't."

I walked on beneath thousands of stars in a Texas sky that made you dizzy to look into it. The coyotes' laughter made me think about other men and women whose lives were ripped apart by that war.

Like Lee Sanders. It's hard to believe that he's now a real estate broker in San Antonio. Lee loved to fight when we were at A&M, and was good. But Lee fought enough for a lifetime as a lieutenant, then captain and company commander, with the 101st Airborne.

Lee's last big fight was on Hamburger Hill, in the A Shau Valley on the Laotian border, in May of 1969. The ten-day battle pitted the Screaming Eagles against hardened North Vietnamese regulars of the 29th Regiment who called themselves "The Pride of Ho Chi Minh." The NVA were dug in deeply on a hill marked 937, for its altitude in meters on U.S. maps. But the Vietnamese called the hill Dong Ap Bia, or Mountain of the Crouching Beast.

Four hundred U.S. soldiers were wounded, and forty-six killed, on Hamburger Hill. NVA casualties were estimated at one thousand eight hundred. A month later, U.S. forces left and the Communist troops moved back onto that crouching beast.

The senseless battle left the terrible question: *Why?* The carnage came into American living rooms on TV news, and made dramatic headlines. The real victor was the U.S. peace movement.

I learned Lee Sanders's story through a letter he'd written in 1986. It made me write a song, but I didn't show it to Lanning. Nashville said "The Ballad of Hamburger Hill" was "good, but not commercial." The coyotes laughed deeper as the lyrics rolled through my mind:

> An instinct drove me to that Wall
> The Vietnam Memorial

I came and touched some friends today
  the feeling was surreal
Those names engraved in cold black stone
Brought pain and rage I thought were gone
Remembering, at age nineteen
  we took Hamburger Hill

We never really gave a damn
About that war in Vietnam
But growing up did not take long
  when we saw buddies killed
Young and scared and scarred but strong
We went forward behind napalm
Can you tell me, Lord, what went wrong
  up on Hamburger Hill?

Sanders's company took 100 percent casualties . . . by losing
men, getting green replacements, commanding and watching
those men cut down by NVA who held the high ground . . .
then throwing more fresh troops into the slaughter.

I showed Lee Lanning the Sanders letter . . . on my computer screen. I had keyed it, to merge into my book:

My company, D-1 3/187 101st Abn, started the fight. The
men who fought there named it *Hamburger Hill*, because it
was a true meat grinder. To be on the Hill was to witness incredible personal heroics of the American soldier, and an
unyielding mindset of those in command. It was amazing,
and says a lot about military thinking.

I kept a diary of what happened to my men on Hamburger
Hill. I commanded a lot of draftees, black militants, anti-war
pacifists. Every man knew that soon he would be killed or
wounded on the Hill. We also knew that the assault made no
tactical sense. But we were Infantry, trained to charge and
kill the enemy. We stuck together and when it came to nut-
cutting, every man was there!

    The NVA dug in high ground
    Calibrated mortar rounds
    Shot four hundred young men down
      I know they died in vain

> Hamburger claimed an awful price
> In soldiers maimed or sacrificed
> Do we blame war or homicide
>   for those black marble names?

But Lee didn't reach the top of Hill 937:

I was hit twice, but the bad one was on the last day of the battle.

We had fought through a line of spider holes and bunkers to 75 meters from the crest. I was manuevering men, trying to get snipers who were shooting from the trees. The rain started again. That's when a Chinese machinegun burst hit me.

Nor did Lee's company, as a unit, reach the crest of Hamburger Hill. Without its commander, the decimated company ceased to exist. His remaining men were rationed to other units that, foot by foot, reached the top and set the Stars and Stripes in Vietnamese soil.

> We took that damned Hamburger Hill
> Then walked away and left our kill
> The NVA came back next day
>   our world had gone insane
> I never shed my angry tears
> I laughed instead to hide my fears
> I kept it hid until today
>   The Wall showed me those names

The army awarded Lee Sanders a Silver Star, and military surgeons put most of his arm back on. During a year of therapy at Fort Sam Houston in San Antonio, Lee became a "jailhouse lawyer" for the wounded . . . mostly enlisted men, high-school dropouts who were grateful that America would pay the price of a new Thunderbird in exchange for a lost arm, leg, or mind. The refrain for my song was:

> I toasted friends we left behind
> Drank to their health in bitter wine
> We packed them in green body bags

Returned them draped in U.S. flags
Good men that I remember well
Wasted to take Hamburger Hill

Sanders also pointed out, in his letter, a statistic that surprised Lee Lanning and me:

Looking back, it seems incredible that at least eight Silver Stars went to men from one little company at Texas A&M—Company D-1, Spider-D.

I had read, in a 1986 issue of *Esquire*, that RKO Studios planned a Hollywood spectacular about Hamburger Hill. I told Lee's story in letters to the film's producer, director, and scriptwriter.

I stressed that Sanders kept a *diary* of the battle. Surely RKO will recognize how valuable *that* could be to the film, and ask Lee to be a consultant. The idea excited me, because *Hamburger Hill* would be filmed in the Philippines.

Hollywood never contacted Lee Sanders—but should have. A lot of the film was *really* about him. In the movie, a lieutenant didn't quite reach the top of Hill 937 ... his arm was blown away just short of its crest. That was Lee. Stories spread that he'd lost his arm when really, it was only shot apart.

Susan and I often heard rifle, machine gun, and artillery fire in the night as RKO filmed parts of *Hamburger Hill* in the rain forest of Mount Makiling. I visited the movie set, above our home, and met a few actors and directors. Their two technical advisers, I heard later, hadn't spent more than twenty-four hours on Hamburger Hill.

Lee Sander's son enrolled at Texas A&M in the fall of 1987, along with sons and, yes, *daughters* of several other midsixties graduates of Spider-D. David Lee Sanders is a cadet in today's voluntary Corps. His birthday gift in 1990 was a pair of Aggie boots, with military spurs.

But David Lee Sanders never served in his dad's old company. The professional military cadre assigned to Texas A&M finally had enough of Spider D-1's macho pride in being first in the Corps in Old Army hell-raising and hazing, last in marching and grades. Its cadets returned from the 1969 Christmas holidays to find notices taped to their doors: Spider-D had been disbanded. The last of the Spiders, including Raford

Hargrove, threw a final, ceremonial beer bust, then reported to new companies.

"Would you do it all again?" I'd asked Lee Sanders by phone.

"Absolutely."

Lee Lanning gave the same answer. Most Vietnam veterans seem to feel that way. Those who suffered most, feel it strongest.

"How about *you*, Hargrove?" Lee Lanning had asked. "Would you do it again?"

"That's a hypothetical question. *It doesn't matter.* I'll never be in my early twenties again, with a war going on, over there in Southeast Asia. Besides, I had no more choice than you. West Texas and Texas A&M dictated that we'd go."

My answer wasn't exactly true. We both could have avoided Vietnam.

"That's a cop-out," Lee said. "You can't write how the rest of us feel about the experience without telling how *you* feel. You owe that to your readers . . . and to *us*."

I thought. "If I could travel back in time to the sixties, knowing what I know today . . . how the war would end . . .

"But I *did* know, I knew the war was lost, even when I reported to Fort Benning in '68."

I started again. "Despite all that happened, yes, I'd go again. But not for patriotism. I'd go because . . ."

I had to think. "Because Vietnam shaped our generation. I know it sounds naive, but I'd go for the same reasons I went then—*to be there*. I can't explain why. And I'd want to go as an officer. I can't really explain that, either."

"I went for the same reasons, of course," Lee said. "Would you go to Saudi today?"

"If I were twenty-five . . . yeah, and so would you. For the same reasons."

I walked on, serenaded by those laughing coyotes, wolves that seem to know things we humans don't. I won't like writing that, and Susan will hate it. Miles is almost eighteen and Tom G, nearly seventeen years old. I can't imagine those boys on Hamburger Hill, or in Chuong Thien Province. But the average age of American soldiers who fought in Vietnam was nineteen.

I have no choice about writing it, of course. A writer's job is to tell it honestly, as he sees it.

CHAPTER XXXI
The Past Became Our Fate *or*
The Last, Final Chapter

Texas, then flying back to Asia, then Los Baños, Philippines in September 1990

> The flowers died when gunfire ceased,
> The beautiful went straight
> I journeyed East for inner peace,
> You fled back to escape
> But the past became our fate.
> —Tom Hargrove and Merle Shepard,
>   "Burned-Out Oilfield Cowboy"

The difference between truth and fiction is that fiction has to make sense.
> —Mark Twain, *Giant Book of Laughter*
> Henry Rosten

I've met my goal for the summer, I thought on my last day in the States. I finally finished the book, with those laughing coyotes in West Texas. I'll give the manuscript a last, hard edit during that awful thirty-four-hour trip from Dallas to Manila. Then I only have to make a few minor revisions.

Like correcting the mistake that Lee Lanning caught in his review of chapter 15. I had written, from my 1969 diary: "1LT Clyde Aderhold was killed over here." Then I expanded, in 1989:

"He was a platoon leader with the 197th Infantry Bri-
gade." ... Michael Arnovitz, now Clyde Aderhold ...
That's 66 percent of the best friends I made at Infantry
School ...

Lee scribbled: "The 197th was never in VN. Maybe it was
the 199th."

I wrote about Clyde, so I'm obliged to correct the mistake.
I went back to the diary, to find out what outfit he was *really*
with. I found only:

17 Jan 70
1Lt Clyde Aderhold was killed over here ... I ran into Herb
Sennett in Can Tho and he told me. We were all lieutenants
and friends in Infantry Officers School at Ft. Benning. Clyde
was the son of the President of the University of Georgia at
Athens. A quiet, chubby guy, I liked him.

Clyde's father surely knows what outfit he died in, and
should be easy to locate. Real easy. Maybe that's why I still
feel bad about not writing to the Aderholds in 1970, or calling
them when I returned. Clyde would have contacted *my* folks,
if *I* had been killed.

That afternoon, I dialed 555-1212 and asked for Athens,
Georgia. A recording gave me the number of a Dr. O. C.
Aderhold. *Doctor,* I thought. That *must* be Clyde's father.

A woman with a gracious Southern accent answered the
phone.

"May I speak with Dr. Aderhold?" There was a pause.

"What is the nature of your call?"

"I'm trying to contact a Dr. Aderhold who was once president of the University of Georgia at Athens. Is this the right
number?"

"It is but ... don't you know that Dr. Aderhold passed away
in 1981?"

I should have thought about that. We *children of the sixties*
are now in our forties.

"I'm sorry ... are you Mrs. Aderhold?" Yes, she was.

"So you're the mother of Clyde Aderhold?"

"Did you know Clyde?"

"We were buddies at Fort Benning, a long time ago."

"Then ... you must know that Clyde is also deceased."

"Yes, that's why I'm calling. I've always regretted not sending you and Dr. Aderhold a condolence note."

"I understand. It was hard. Not only for family, but also for his friends."

"Do you mind if I ask a couple of questions about Clyde's death?"

"No, it's been long enough. I can talk about it now."

"I'm writing a book, it's about Vietnam. I mentioned how upset I was when Clyde was killed. I want to include what unit he was in. Do you remember?"

A long pause followed.

"*Vietnam* ... what do you mean?"

"I was there, too, when Clyde died."

"Why ... *Clyde never served in Vietnam*, he went to Korea, and came home all right."

"*What? Clyde wasn't ... but I wrote about his death in my diary. Twenty years ago.* I learned from another lieutenant, a friend who knew us both."

"My son died in 1982."

"My God, I'm sorry ..." But we've both gone this far, I thought. I *have* to ask.

"Would you mind telling me ... how?"

"It was on the Fourth of July, and Clyde was at Fort Benning. He stayed in the army reserve, you know." I didn't, but said nothing. This conversation was hurting Clyde's mother.

"A lot of the soldiers were on leave. Maybe that's why it was so long before they found him."

"*What happened?*"

"Clyde was depressed ... very upset and despondent. You see, his daddy had died on July the Fourth a year before ..."

"Oh." My God, Clyde was alive all those years. I'd have contacted him long ago, but ... he was *dead*. And now he really *is* dead, by his own hand, on the anniversary of his father's death ...

I said condolences again, feeling the words more deeply this time, then set the receiver down. So ... it was another of those rumors, like the story that my Aggie buddy, Roy May, was killed.

I had called Athens to straighten out chapter 15. *Now* what will I do? Change what I wrote? Edit Clyde from the book?

No . . . until five minutes ago, Clyde was killed in Vietnam. I'll leave it in . . . but I have to add what I learned in 1990.

That night I went through my *Aggielands*, and put half a dozen newspaper clippings and letters that A&M buddies had written from Vietnam into an envelope. I'll review these on the plane, I thought. Maybe I'll find a few more details to add to the final manuscript.

The next day I was on Northwest Flight 29 at thirty thousand feet, between Detroit and Seoul. I was tired of editing, and frustrated. I still didn't know how to work Aderhold's true story into the book.

I opened the envelope and skimmed a couple of crumpled 1967 letters that Big Hoss Lanning had written from the field. I then read, for the first time since 1966, the *Abilene Reporter* article "Rotan Hero's Widow Presented Medals."

Beneath the headline was a photo of CWO James W. Hargrove, wearing a garrison cap. My first cousin had those chiseled features of a Hargrove, I thought, and of a farmer. But Jimmy was the only Hargrove who'd ever become a professional soldier.

The clippings had some interesting details. I'd forgotten that Jimmy had an agronomy degree from Texas Tech. And that he had remarried only four months before his death. That must have been when he returned to Texas on compassionate leave from Nam after Uncle Rob, his father, died. I went to see him three times while he was in Rotan, but he was asleep the first two. Jimmy didn't talk much about the war, when we finally visited. Only how he hated to ferry eighteen-year-old men, who looked like children, in and out of combat.

Nor did I know, until now, about Jimmy's Distinguished Flying Cross, with Air Medals First through Fourteenth Oak Leaf Clusters. That's a lot of time in the sky.

Chief Warrant Officer Hargrove distinguished himself by exceptional valorous actions on October 18, 1966, while serving as aircraft commander of the platoon leader's UH-1 helicopter providing armed support for an airmobile operation near Vi Thanh . . .

I froze, then read again. *Vi Thanh? No. No . . . there were thousands of villages in Vietnam!*

It's impossible . . . I've seldom seen the word Vi Thanh *in print*, anywhere, except a few army or USAID or CIA documents. No, this is absurd, Jimmy *couldn't* have died near Vi Thanh.

But no matter how many times I read that yellowed newsprint, *Vi Thanh* was there.

I tried to piece together what I knew of Jimmy's death.

It was quite a bit. The June 1969 issue of *Saga* magazine had carried a true adventure story, that identified Jimmy by name, about his last operation. That's how I learned that my cousin was trying to rescue *Nungs*—ethnic Chinese mercenaries—and Green Beret advisers. But the article focused on how the helicopter platoon leader, a major, and two crewmen escaped through VC lines after the crash.

The gunship was flying out of My Tho, about fifty miles south of Saigon. *Saga* located the actual battle only as "in the Mekong Delta," but I had assumed it must have been near My Tho.

No wonder none of those ex-VC soldiers remembered the battle when I asked, in My Tho, in 1988.

I was asking in the wrong village.

Now, as I'm finishing the book about Chuong Thien Province . . . how I keep returning, how she keeps throwing herself at me . . . I learn that Jimmy Hargrove . . . whose death, I wrote, really started the war for me . . . was killed outside of *Vi Thanh*, three years before I arrived? This is crazy, as insane as Chuong Thien Province herself.

Thank God I didn't see this clipping in Ames, Iowa, during that terrible spring of 1977. Chuong Thien almost destroyed me. She would have, if she'd had *this* for a weapon.

A week after returning to Los Baños, I showed the article to Miles.

"Did you tell Mom?" Yes. Susan was still in Texas, but we'd talked by phone.

"How did *she* react?" Miles asked. "Mom is *so* cynical about the war, and Vi Thanh."

"She said, *'Tom, that makes my blood turn cold.'* "

"Aren't you afraid people will think you knew this all along, and saved it for your last chapter?"

"Maybe, but I didn't. The word *Vi Thanh* meant nothing to me in 1966, when I stuck that clipping into my A&M yearbook. People could also say I knew about the diary all those years, right?"

"Yeah, I'll never forget *that* night, Dad. You were in *total shock*."

"I'll write what happened. Like Lee Lanning said, a writer has to tell it honestly."

Saying that bothered me, because I hadn't written—or told—the entire truth. I'd held one part back.

"Something even stranger happened after I read about Jimmy Hargrove," I said. "But I *can't* put it in the book."

"Tell me, Dad." Amazing. Miles and Tom G had grown from smartass teenagers to . . . young men who would never be kids again. It happened so fast, over the past couple of months. Now they wanted to talk with me seriously, like I'd talk with Susan or other adults. I liked the new relationship with our boys, but the change was also a bit sad.

"Reading about Jimmy being killed near Vi Thanh shook me so much, I couldn't write," I said. "So I put the clipping, and manuscript, away. I had bought *this book* in Fort Worth to read on the plane."

I showed Miles *Touring Nam*, a Bantam collection of short stories. Vietnam had dominated my reading over the past year, because other veterans' experiences trigger my own memories. I'd sworn to quit reading about Nam, the day I finished the book, and start a stack of new books. But I still hadn't mailed that final manuscript to Owen Lock.

"I'd read the first five stories in Texas, so I started the sixth," I said, and opened the book to "The Raid," by David Reed.

The story had seemed vaguely familiar as I read, while Northwest 29 droned toward Korea . . . Maj. Raymond T. Nutter, the leader of a helicopter gunship platoon, was flying somewhere in the Mekong Delta on a rescue mission. Two Special Forces advisers and thirty *Nungs* . . . *Nungs?* . . . had been airlifted on a strange commando raid to free a black U.S. POW the VC supposedly held. Intelligence had reported that VC abuse had driven the man insane—being paraded naked through the villages, with a rope around his neck.

The VC seemed to have planted the POW story to lure a rescue mission. Two Communist battalions had trapped and pinned down the mercenaries and their U.S. advisers.

The Huey UH-1 gunship flew through withering ground fire to rescue the trapped men.

* * *

"Viking Lead!" a Green Beret shouted on the radio . . . "We're being torn to pieces. Are you going to get us out?"

"*Viking Lead* . . . that was Jimmy Hargrove's call sign in the *Saga* article," I told Miles. "And I remembered a vague story of a black POW being held in Chuong Thien, but I never believed it." I read on.

The VC blew out the windshield of Nutter's ship with machine gun fire. Mortar shells burst directly beneath it, tossing it about violently . . . The Green Beret was frantic now.

"Viking Lead, are you going to get us out?" he screamed . . .

Nutter turned to the copilot. "Do you think we can get in and out?"

"What difference does it make? You're going to go in anyway," the copilot said with a grin. And those were the last words he ever uttered—a few moments later he was dead.

"That sounded a lot like Jimmy Hargrove's last words in the *Saga* article . . ."
The gunship reached the trapped men, but all were dead. The Huey's guns fired madly as it lifted to forty feet. Then VC .50-calibers shot the chopper's controls out. The ship careened wildly, and crashed into a grove of mangrove trees.

Nutter . . . was in a daze . . . He was trying to pull the copilot from the wreckage. "Sir, he's dead . . . He's dead and the Charlies are closing in on us."

Major Nutter and two surviving crewmen escaped, and VC hunted them through mangrove swamps and rice fields. The UH-1 crew killed four men that night, three with knives.
The men finally reached South Vietnamese troops . . . the 21st ARVN Division . . . *the 31st Regiment of the 21st ARVN was based in Vi Thanh* . . .
"By then, I was sure," I told Miles. "This was a rewrite of the *Saga* article. The dead copilot was James W. Hargrove.
"But how could Nutter have thought Jimmy was still alive?

I heard that he didn't have a head . . . not when the Hargove family opened his coffin in Texas."

And *how eerie* that, after thousands of pages of Vietnam literature, I started reading this short story on the plane, minutes after learning that Jimmy died in Chuong Thien Province.

Nutter thought bitterly about the events of the day. His platoon of five gunships had been ordered to escort 17 slicks (troopships) that were to carry out a commando raid near the town of Vi Thanh in the Mekong Delta.

There it is again! I thought. *Vi Thanh . . . and Jimmy Hargrove . . .*

When Miles left, I went back to my computer. I'll write this *last* Final Chapter, finish the book . . . again. But it's not the story I started twenty years ago. That bothers me. Maybe, once I've put my own story of Vi Thanh and Chuong Thien Province on paper, I'll go back and finish that novel.

Because my fiction tells the *real* story of the war, deep in the Mekong Delta.

But maybe it doesn't.

Transition 19

Northwest Flight 29 over Pacific waters, 8 September 1990

> Ere systemed suns were globed and lit
> The slaughters of the race were writ.
> —Thomas Hardy,
> *The Dynasts*

* * *

I've reread the yellowed newspaper clipping and short story a dozen times, but those words won't go away: *Chief Warrant Officer Hargrove* and *Vi Thanh*.

My mind drifts, and I'm back at that awesome rendezvous with my past in the VC cemetery where I should have died, in the province that, I now know, *killed another Hargrove, before I knew her*.

Her. The terrible but fascinating *Big Woman* that I once wrote about. Men abused her, and she destroyed men with revenge. Was she a shallow literary tool? No, Chuong Thien Province was always female, to me. Did she really exist, did she force me to recognize her through my writing? Or did I create that woman, then lose control of her?

I don't know, but I can't deny her any longer. Nor a force that keeps bringing me back . . . or throwing her at me.

How else can I make sense of things that don't? The black propaganda that I once studied and taught at Fort Bragg was nothing compared with the lies and tricks of the lower Mekong Delta.

That Big Woman and I found each other in one of Vietnam's most tragic war zones—but no history mentions Chuong Thien Province. The army sent me there, but I was never a soldier, not really . . . yet I was. I later regretted, deeply, never putting words on paper to craft into a book that was, really, about that Asian woman. Then I found the diary I never wrote, and it killed my novel.

In my diary, I wrote of returning to Vi Thanh to find no more war, and a Vietnamese equivalent of prosperity. Those were naive dreams to exorcise, I guess, the demons I didn't know I carried. I returned, all right, too many times. But I didn't find the peace that I needed.

As the 747 flies toward Asia, I'm back at painful meetings in the night with frightened men and women. Their crime is having supported a brutal and corrupt government that stood against another brutal system that was destined to win, and equally sure to fail. Fifteen years after the fall of Saigon, the new system is as corrupt as the one it replaced, still punishes its former enemies, and has betrayed its disillusioned heroes. My crime—*our* crime—was helping prolong the human suffering that the lost cause brought.

The despair of those who fought for Saigon is so deep, most remember the war as *happy days*. That desperation drives a peasant farmer to fabricate ghastly dogtags and skeletons, and an anguished mother to offer her beautiful daughter to a foreign stranger—that's an act of love, in today's Vietnam.

Yet men and women in the lands that bore Communism are destroying the system with deep anger. It can't survive in Asia. Progressive Vietnamese leaders see that the philosophy has killed incentive, brought fear and economic ruin. A shift to the free market is rendering Communism meaningless as an economic system in Vietnam. But economics only *created* Communism . . . then its leaders saw that the artificial system couldn't work without mind control. The hard-core Vietnamese Communists will continue to control people's lives—and minds, they think—until they can no longer block the forces that now sweep the Soviet Union, Eastern Europe, and threaten China.

I put the clipping of Jimmy Hargrove away, but I can't shut it from my mind. Why did you come . . . only *now*? To show that my other story of Chuong Thien Province *belongs* on that dark closet shelf? My novel was just a realistic slice of twelve shallow months of war there. It made too much sense. The truth makes none.

Yet the truth isn't even a good war story. *New rice seeds*, not heroics or heavy artillery, are why I'm alive today. New rice seeds keep bringing me back to Vi Thanh, where it began.

But it *really* began, for me, with your death—*there*—didn't it, Jimmy?

It's an endless cycle, like the giant wheel of Buddhism that explains how life repeats itself until one reaches Nirvana, a state of peace beyond existence. For me, Chuong Thien Province is the hub, the spoke of something that began aeons ago . . . or has been there forever? But *forever* has no meaning in a place and state of mind where time doesn't go from the past to the future. Cycles of birth, war, rice, death, truth and fiction, precious seeds of grief, seeds of resurrection.

I was drawn into one of those timeless cycles. Now I'm a minute sentence that means nothing, a word in a story that repeats itself forever.

Will it always be this way?

No. When I've explained the story to myself, I'll make my own peace with the Big Woman, and it will end. For me. Those cycles will continue endlessly, but I won't go there anymore.

Maybe . . .

Chapter XXXII
A Dragon Lives Forever

September and October 1990, Los Baños, Philippines
Back in the Philippines, I printed two five-hundred-sheet reams
of words on my new laser printer in twenty-one nights of frustrated writing—but I couldn't finish the book, again. The
words wouldn't come.

After dozens of drafts, I decided to gamble. I'd write to
Bruce McAllister. Writing time was precious, so the decision
wasn't easy.

29 Sep 90
Los Baños

Dear Bruce:

How is *Dream Baby* doing? I hope the book sells a million copies, because I feel it's a bit *my* baby, too.

I'm trying to finish my own book, so it's hard to take
time to write to anyone. But this letter has a special purpose.
Maybe you'll read it, someday. But I may never mail the letter, because it's really *to me*.

Bruce, my brother Raford has faxed that Mother's condi-
tion has worsened. I used my one-time IRRI compassionate-
leave ticket to fly back to Texas in March, when we learned
that she had cancer of the bone marrow. Her spirits were
high when we returned for home leave this summer. She
would beat this disease. Her mind may have been sharper
than before, in reviewing my manuscript.

The cancer has now spread, suddenly and extensively, and
we all know the end is near. We've said goodbye, so I won't
return. The family understands that.

But Mother *must* see my last chapters before that happens, because the book means as much to her as it does to me. Maybe more. She's been the book's best and most critical reviewer—also, it's strongest supporter, since I came home a little crazy in 1970. I didn't see it, but she did, and encouraged me to write it out. Mother has read, edited, and commented on fiction and fact, off-and-on, for 20 years.

I hope I don't have to fax the last chapters to Raford, the reason would be so obvious.

Those chapters are mostly set in Texas in 1990, so they should be easy. But I'm having a terrible time finishing them—maybe because I'm not writing honestly. You see, I can't send Mother chapters that describe how this race against time is largely for *her* . . . and why.

Maybe that's not honest. It's not easy to tell right from wrong, as one gets older.

Tonight, I thought . . . an unexpected letter from a California novelist in 1987 made me resume work on the book, as fiction. My response to you triggered a return to Chuong Thien Province and a complicated process that will result in a different type of book. That letter also became the main text of what is now chapter 2.

Maybe writing to McAllister—again—can help me find the words to end the book. Like completing a complex circle.

Is that honest? Or is it using friends?

Have I ever written to you without a selfish reason? Only once, and then I edited out six of the twelve single-spaced pages and kept them for myself.

I explained to Bruce how Mother asked me to take out the chapter about my insane spring in Ames, Iowa, and our compromise: to have Susan read that chapter before publication.

. . . Susan read The Black Spring of 1977, and we discussed it for two painful hours. The chapter stays, but I'll add more about how what I did hurt others who cared, and how a few friends helped me finish that Ph.D.

Bruce, the book won't end for another reason. Things I should always have known, keep flashing forward from the past . . . things that are hard to explain, except in a scary way.

I believe, a little, in such phenomena—for others. I accept

that your *Dream Baby* characters were drawn from CIA research on soldiers with *talents*. That's easy . . . I'm not part of that story.

But a week after your 1987 letter threw me back into Chuong Thien Province, Miles found my diary. Fifteen days later, Susan led me to Michael Arnovitz, through his doctor, by his name at The Wall . . . when I was emotionally torn over whether to write about the *real* Arnovitz as a thinly disguised Richard Bernstein.

A frightening mental field started materializing . . . for the second time.

People and—ghosts, I guess that's an OK word, they're from my past—began to appear.

I can't explain those ghosts . . . only that they came once before. But the 1977 ghosts were bad, they led me to self-destruction. Today's ghosts only carry messages about bad times, long ago. Maybe writing about them, calls them.

I described how clearly Lynn Johnson saw the talent, then watched it grow, as we traveled deeper into the Mekong Delta. I think it peaked at the VC cemetery. I wrote how Lynn compared the sense to an antenna that searches until it connects to fields of others, then calls or takes me to them.

Bruce, I could be a character in *Dream Baby*, at times.

But with a talent that wasn't on your team that took the *plastique* explosives, in bags marked as IRRI rice seeds, to the Red Dikes. What is it? I don't see danger in blue, or leave my body. I seldom have strange dreams.

You once wrote how Jung would describe such a gift: "When you enter your own deepest soul, you enter the deepest souls of others collectively, and they know it." Does that explain it?

A young lady from the Mekong Delta, a Vietnamese Ph.D. scholar at IRRI, recently read my 1988 articles. She wrote: "Chuong Thien Province seems to have been your destination."

She meant *destiny*, of course. And that word comes closest to describing what happens when I go back to Chuong Thien. The past pushes back into the present . . . like it was always programmed for the future.

But why didn't I have that power 20 years ago, when I

needed it? Maybe I did, but it didn't have time to show itself off. It had to move fast.

The last, and strangest, hit was three weeks ago. It began, I guess, when Lee and Linda Lanning visited us in Texas, and we found a 1966 newspaper clipping announcing the posthumous medals awarded to Jimmy Hargrove . . .

The letter got longer each night, until I felt it was finished . . . at least, complete enough for *my* purpose . . . on 6 October. But I didn't mail it. Over the next three nights, I merged portions of that letter into my manuscript, and they became the last chapters. Then I finished the letter . . . again:

9 October 1990.

You did it, Bruce. *It worked!* I only hope the words read well.

Last night I printed out the last of my book and delivered an envelope, with U.S. stamps, to a friend who was leaving for the States. Those final chapters should reach Texas in a few days. Mother will know how the book ends.

But she won't, of course. Not really. Because she won't see how I'll close the book . . . with *this* chapter, about how those last chapters were written.

Is that dishonest?

You once wrote, Bruce: *Isn't that what Vietnam was about? Lies and tricks and reality?*

Not even mothers are exempt, I guess . . .

We've never met, and I wonder if we ever will? Maybe that's not in the program.

A bizarre fax from my brother arrived yesterday, but it wasn't the message I dreaded:

All Jimmy Hargrove's family knows for sure is that he was hit in the face with .50-caliber machinegun fire. He arrived home with his head swathed in bandages. He was identified at the Rotan funeral home from burn scars resulting from a butane fire on a tractor when he was a teenager.

Raford was answering my request for more details on how our cousin died. It'll make sense only when you read the final chapter—or what *Mother* thinks is the last chapter.

But Raford doesn't always use good judgment, or tact, when he writes fax messages. My faxes land in a central IRRI fax machine where secretaries sort, and read, them. The messengers are also curious, so they read, then discuss faxes that concern foreign scientists. That's frustrating, but a fact of life for expatriates in the Philippines.

Raford didn't mention that Jimmy was killed 24 years ago, in Vietnam. The story of my Hargrove relative in Texas being shot in the face by a .50 caliber is now common IRRI gossip. Jimmy must like that.

Bruce, when I mail that final manuscript to Random House, Vietnam and Chuong Thien Province won't be so heavy on my mind.

The talent . . . whatever it is . . . will no longer be needed, so it'll fade away, or go to sleep. I *know* that, through instinct, logic . . . and experience. Without a purpose, it'll slip back into a deep cave like Puff, the Magic Dragon, when the little boy grew up.

But Puff didn't disappear, did he? It was the *boy* who disappeared, when he no longer needed Puff. Dragons live forever.

Chapter XXXIII
Would You Do It Again? A Mekong Delta Epilogue

Los Baños, Philippines, Texas, Pittsburgh, Washington, D.C., New York, Los Baños, 1991

. . . for all of us who came of age in the late sixties and early seventies the war was a defining experience. You went or you didn't, but the fact of it and the decisions it forced us to make marked us for the rest of our lives, just as the depression and World War II had marked my parents.

—Linda Grant, *Blind Trust*

Spring, 1991. My photo, bringing the new IRRI rice seeds to Ba Lien, appeared in "The World's Food Supply At Risk" in the April 1991 issue of *National Geographic*. It was one of twenty-four photos selected to illustrate the feature from 336,000 frames—*yes, 336,000*—that Lynn Johnson shot.

National Geographic reaches the Philippines by sea, so I hadn't seen the photo at 5:20 P.M. on 10 May when Santy went to the IRRI mail room. The afternoon mail is delivered to IRRI staff the next morning, but if your secretary bugs the mail clerks, she can get letters as they're sorted.

Santy returned with only one handwritten letter, postmarked Spring, Texas:

Dear Tom,
You may not remember me, but I've always remembered you. I was a MAT team leader in Chuong Thien Province in 1969–70. You often told me about the new rice you were growing there. It seemed to be accomplishing a lot more good than anything the rest of us were doing.

I skipped to the signature. My God, *Rob Briggs, of MAT Team 54!*
Briggs made it? He survived a year on the *hard-luck team*?

I saw a Nat'l Geographic photo of you introducing a better rice variety to replace those you planted 22 years ago. I had wondered what happened to you, & thought how dedicated you must be to still be helping the Vietnamese who have suffered so much.

I thought of Khang, my interpreter; that was the first time that a photo of me in today's Chuong Thien reopened doors to the past. *It's happening again.*
It was getting late, so I stuffed Briggs's letter into a pocket

to answer when I got home . . . but I didn't touch my computer that night. A frantic call from IRRI came at 6:20 P.M.: "*Chandler Hall's on fire! A bad fire!*"

My communication department, that I'd largely built over eighteen years, might soon go up in flames, along with a dozen books on rice science that were being edited or laid out.

But my first concern was the IRRI library, which holds the world's largest collection of scientific literature on rice—10 million pages. Some of the ninety-three thousand books, in Chinese, Japanese, Hindi, even Latin, date from the 1500s. Loss of that irreplaceable literature would be a tragedy for mankind. Susan and I sped to the Institute.

Firefighters stopped the blazes as photos were burning off the library's outer wall. The rice literature was saved, but four offices were gutted. One was the mail room. Filipino staff rescued only one mail bag before fire and water destroyed the rest of our correspondence, incoming and outgoing.

Had Santy not saved that single letter before the fire, I probably would never have known that Briggs wrote.

I answered Rob Briggs's letter a few days later:

The *Geographic* photo was made on the farm of Ba Lien, just south of where Lt. Donoway and Sgt. Ard of MAT 54 were killed. You may recall that Lts. Carlile and Young then took command of MAT 54. A few weeks later, Young died, Carlile was shot in the head, and *you* took the team. I describe that series of deaths in my writing.

In my writing . . . I tried to explain my book to Briggs, how his MAT 54 had played such a key role, especially in the part that was fiction. I enclosed chapter 5, The Final Chapter, which was, really, about when MAT 54 landed in *the death trap.* I threw in chapter 1, that strange night when Miles showed me the diary, so Briggs could get a feel for the story.

Briggs wrote again in June:

I was surprised and happy to get your response. I didn't know if my letter would reach you.

About your chapters. I never knew that the ball-grabbing incident triggered MAT 54's move from Hoa Luu to Vi Duc—but the guy I kicked off the hood of my jeep wasn't a village chief, he was a VN soldier who guarded the bridge

on the road to Vi Thanh. He swore he'd kill me the next
time I drove by. My boss, Capt. Miles Bollick of the Duc
Long District Advisory Team, said to lay low and not drive
to Vi Thanh for a while.

I later got used to holding hands with my VN friends. It
felt strange at first, but soon became OK.

No, no one gave me flak about wearing the shiny silver
1LT bar, instead of the black jungle type. Col. Le Vasseur
looked at it long and hard one day, but said nothing. Sgt.
Heath advised me not to wear the bar on operations. I can't
remember if I did or not.

The inscription was: "May the Lord hold you in the palm
of His hand." He did. My fiancée was Irish, and that's an
old Irish proverb. She had it engraved on the bar when I
made 1LT.

My God, I had no idea—it was *Briggs* who wore that engraved silver bar, and kicked a Vietnamese soldier from his
jeep . . . in the first pages of my book. I remember Briggs, and
that lieutenant . . . but as two different men.

I still have the bar, but not the girl. I guess we both
changed while I was in Vietnam, so we parted after I came
home in August, 1970.

*Rob Briggs played a key role in my book . . . yet neither of
us had known it.*
Briggs met a WAC officer while stationed at Fort Bliss, near
El Paso. They were married, and he's now a pilot, captain of
a Boeing 727, with United Airlines. The Briggs's home is in
Texas, but Rob flies out of Chicago.

We have 4 boys, ages 18 to 12. I showed Bertha your
writing about the ball-grabbing incident, then I showed her
the silver bar, which I had stashed somewhere.

I've often wondered what happened to the people I
worked with in Vietnam, both U.S. and Vietnamese. I know
nothing about any of them. Reading your Chapter 1, I remember being angry when Sgt. Walker was killed. His
friendly VN troops took his boots, wedding ring, and watch.
I remember others, mostly VN, who were killed.

When I arrived in Chuong Thien, I was assigned to MAT

56, but Col. Le Vasseur sent me to MAT 54. That team was demoralized and Le Vasseur thought I had sort of a sunny disposition that would be good for the men. I didn't know that I was replacing two lieutenants who'd died before me. But our hootch maid, *Ba* Hai, said that she saw me as another young, dead American when I arrived.

About the Christmas truce '69. The VC sighting that MAT 54 reported to you on Christmas Eve could *only* have come from me. I clearly remember calling it in, but I didn't know you were on the other end of the radio. I remember the VC waving to us as they walked across a rice field. It might be nice to keep track of them, I reported. The truce was off the next day.

For Tet 1970 the VC sent a personal invitation by name, *Trung Uy* Briggs, for a High Noon showdown in the plaza of a village we were in. Hoa An, I think. Miles Bollick said not to attend. He didn't need to tell me that.

Someday, I want to go back and look around. I'll visit the villages where I lived to see if anyone remembers me, as I do them. I told Bertha, and she just said "When?" Someday I will. I wonder if the VN will feel that we Americans abandoned them, and be unfriendly?

Your writing also interests me because I've never read a single book about the VN war, or been to a VN movie. I haven't visited the Vietnam Memorial in D.C., nor the traveling memorial when it came to Houston. I have few bad memories of the Vietnamese, or of my experience. In fact, most of what I remember is warm and good. I'm not screwed up in the head (I don't think), but I've never wanted to read someone else's account of Vietnam. I don't need to. I did it.

July 1991. Back in Texas on home leave, I finally rallied the courage to call Owen Lock. "Remember the letters I sent you from Rob Briggs, a buddy from Chuong Thien days."

"Yeah. The lieutenant who wore a silver bar engraved with a prayer . . . the ball-grabbing incident. Incredible, how you got that letter."

"Owen, since finishing the manuscript, I've talked with half a dozen men from Advisory Team 73. I tracked most down . . . but Briggs and Khang *found me*."

Most of the men had been lieutenants and captains in those

days, civilians at heart like me who were serving obligatory military tours. Frank Gillespie and Norm Olsen, of course, were *real* civilians.

All seemed to live fairly normal lives today—married, kids in college. Maybe some had nasty divorces, but I didn't hear of them.

Those men had put Chuong Thien Province behind, the day they left. At least, they tried. No man kept contact with others who'd shared the experience. Mine was, invariably, the first voice from our past. It stunned each man.

But every veteran, after the shock, was glad to hear from me, and amazed to learn that I'd returned to Chuong Thien . . . three times. Each was pleased to learn that I was writing a book, and that he might be part of it. A couple of men claimed they'd meant to write their *own* books about Chuong Thien, but . . .

All seemed relieved to *talk* about those haunting memories; they'd seldom talked, because so few *understood*. Every man wanted to know what happened to old buddies, American and Vietnamese. I knew, too often—and a lot of my news was bad.

Those phone and letter reunions were also a relief to me, because now I knew that Chuong Thien Province *really happened* to us, and she was as bad as I remember. That's important. It helped bury that nagging fear that *my* Chuong Thien lived mainly in my mind.

Most men had suffered from post-Vietnam stress syndrome, but some never saw what had happened . . . what was *just now* happening, in a couple of cases.

Every man who served in Chuong Thien Province feels blood on his hands. I carry fewer stains than many . . . but washing that blood away is tough, for all of us.

"Owen, you've let me add three or four 'final chapters' to the book, and I've sworn . . . no more. But could I add a *very short* final chapter about Briggs and Weiner, Gillespie and Olsen and Khang—what happened to them? An epilogue?"

Lock's answer surprised me. "Sure! I *like* for a book to end with *Where are they now?*"

That's how this unplanned chapter came to close *A Dragon*, months after I finished the book.

I had already started writing this epilogue, of course, before clearing it with Owen Lock. I had sent Rob Briggs more text, about MAT 54, for comments. He responded:

MAT 54 was not bothered too much after Donoway, Ard, and Young were killed. We accompanied the VN on a lot of operations and got into a few firefights. A lot of VN were killed, but no Americans from my team. That was partly luck. Also, because I wouldn't let my men take macho, stupid chances. And partly because I never thought my mission was to kill people who would not be a threat to me had I not been in VN in the first place.

You see, I was acutely aware that *I* wouldn't live in a grass hootch with mud floors for the rest of my life. For me, the war had an end in sight—I'd leave in August of 1970. But *they* would not. They would always live in squalor and oppression and fear. So while I was there I tried to do things to make life a little more bearable for them for a while, things that they might remember in future years and maybe think "*Trung Uy* helped us a little."

I taught English in the elementary school in Hoa An. The kids thought I was funny because my Vietnamese wasn't so hot, but we had a good time.

We gave medical help, usually to mothers with children, although the VN medic tried to sell the medicines that he got free. We passed out lots of soap. We sent some children to the Vi Thanh hospital to fix harelips and straighten club feet. Once a lady came to me with an infant in her arms. He was lethargic and I saw that maggots and worms were crawling through a sore on the side of his head. I got mad at her for being so stupid—not keeping the sore clean. The child acted so dull because worms were going in and out of his brain. I could do nothing for him, and that upset me more. I cleaned the sore, but the child died. I remember crying for the mother, and the futility of it all.

I've wondered, especially since learning why the VC didn't kill you—did they not bother *my* MAT 54 team too much either, because we didn't pose much of a threat? Could they have appreciated some of the things we did? Like the time I kept the RFs from chopping two prisoners' heads off? Maybe. Did it count that I didn't shoot the VC bastard we caught with a certificate of merit for killing Americans?

Lord knows the VC could have wiped us out. We travelled too regularly along the roads by jeep, or up the canal every couple of days in our Boston Whaler to get mail and food. Who knows why they didn't? Not me.

About MAT team service. It was to be a 6-month stint because of the hostile exposure. But whenever I asked about rotation, I got the usual bureaucratic reply: We have no available replacement. We MATS soon resented advisers at Duc Long and Vi Thanh, and felt that they were out-of-touch and pampered wimps. We developed a camaraderie in the field and I decided that I'd rather stay where I was. I quit asking about a replacement. I wasn't alone in those feelings and it became sort of a badge of honor, a macho thing, to be on a MAT team in the field.

Rob Briggs called me in Texas during that summer of 1991. We didn't talk much about Vietnam, but as our conversation ended I *had* to ask him the question that Lee Lanning had made *me* answer:

"Would you do it again?"

"I don't regret Chuong Thien," Briggs said. "It was *a growing time*. I didn't volunteer, but I made the best of it. I learned to speak passable Vietnamese. I made friends. But most of all, at twenty-three years old, I saw a lot of life and death. I learned how fragile life is, and the strength and depth of human will. I think I'm a better person for having experienced it all."

Then I asked others . . .

Harvey Weiner, our former Phoenix adviser, never got the postcard I sent from Vi Thanh in 1988. The local postmaster probably steamed off and resold the stamps. That's not shocking, for a village so impoverished and desolate.

But the Boston attorney answered my follow-up letter immediately. One of Harvey's sentences intrigued me: "I regret not keeping a diary, but I wanted to repress those times and, as you well know, family and friends do not understand."

I sent Harvey my articles about finding the diary, and returning to Vi Thanh. In November 1988, he wrote "they awakened memories and ghosts," and:

I, like you, *did* keep a diary . . . that I didn't know about— the diary of my mind. But the correct key is necessary to open the diary because I always keep it locked. Your story has unlocked it.

Harvey wrote about the deaths of Donoway and Ard on 18 August 1969, although he didn't realize that *I*, not the MAT 54 lieutenant and medic, should have died that morning.

> Lt. Donoway was as fine a young man as you could meet. One of my duties was to ship bodies of dead Americans from Chuong Thien to Saigon, and inventory their personal effects. I remember, vividly, going through Donoway's belongings and finding a pin of the flag of Delaware, his home state. Donoway had planned to pin it up at the "club" where we placed mementos of our states. I first intended to put his Delaware pin there, so we would remember him. Instead, I sent that pin back to his family. I wanted nothing of Donoway to remain in the country that had wasted him so cruelly. Top asked me to write to his family. I remember those words today as clearly as when I wrote them, and they tasted bitter in my mouth. My words were lies, because I knew that Donoway's death was in vain.
>
> When my 14-year-old son visited the Vietnam Memorial last spring, I asked him to touch the names of Doc Ard and Lt. Donoway, among many others. He did, and they knew it.

Another Weiner letter reached me in Texas in July 1991. Harvey commented on the homecoming of the Gulf War veterans:

> It was so different from *our* homecoming . . . *We* changed into civilian clothes as fast as possible, turned up our collars and hunkered down for two decades. America's reception for the Gulf War veterans was correct but, as we know, *they* did not live with that year-long constant fear:
>
>> Late at night when you're sleeping
>> Charlie Cong comes a'creeping
>> around . . .

Then Harvey commented on the chapters I had sent him about our 1990 return to Vi Thanh:

Your account (and particularly your wife's) has dampened my ardor to return to Victor Tango. I'd rather have a reunion of Advisory Team 73. After your book is published, save the addresses of those who undoubtedly will write, and organize one. It will help exorcise the ghosts.

Harvey also wrote about the long day that MAT 54 was in the "death trap."

I remember Lt. Bugansky, the young FAC who flew all that evening to call artillery and direct the battle. As he was leaving, I asked if I could go up with him with my M-16 to provide some firepower, since he had none. Bugansky gave me a strange look and said "No."

His look said *I'll probably die—and I don't want you to die with me.*

But Harvey questioned my memory of the fate of 1st Lt. Richard Carlile:

Lt. Carlile was *not* in a coma months after being shot. He was conscious, and in good spirits when I visited him in Can Tho a few days later. The bullets that were taken from his heart and head were in a glass jar by his hospital bed.

Why don't you track him down? He was from Scottsboro, Alabama, and should be easy to trace.

Finally, I enclose a picture of someone you remember clearly. Is *she* a ghost as well, or only *your* ghost?

I opened the enclosed envelope and froze. Monique—the *real* Monique—smiled from behind a typewriter in Vi Thanh . . . a lot like I pictured her in chapter 1 of my fiction.

I phoned Harvey Weiner from a Pittsburgh hotel room on 16 August 1991 as I was traveling on my last IRRI business before returning to the Philippines. We talked, first, about our families. Linda and Harvey have two sons, twenty and seventeen. By then, Miles and Tom G were eighteen and seventeen.

Talk shifted to Vietnam days, and I asked *that* question:

"Would you do it again?"

"No."

"Why not?"

"They say that every dark cloud has a silver lining. But Chuong Thien . . .?

"I wouldn't do it again because the negative far outweighed the positive. It was a year of worry for my wife and parents, and a year of fear for me. I had bad experiences better left unsaid. I lost friends, both American and Vietnamese. The year was for nothing because the American people and government lacked the will to win, even though the cause was probably just. Yet I made many American and Vietnamese friends . . . and acquired a taste for dog, cat, rat, and duck fetus."

I had one last question.

"Harvey . . . you didn't keep a diary, and until my first letter, you hadn't heard from anyone from those days. *How could you remember that Richard Carlile was from Scottsboro, Alabama?*"

"Easy. A historic rape trial was held there. Seven blacks were convicted." Weiner was, obviously, a true trial lawyer. "The U.S. Supreme Court overruled the convictions in 1932, because the defendants, the Scottsboro Seven, didn't have assistance of counsel."

The Scottsboro Trial had nothing to do with Chuong Thien Province, but it led to my locating a *very* alive Richard Carlile.

I wasn't *really* sure I wanted to know Carlile's fate. But on 19 August 1991 I dialed 555-1212 from my Washington, D.C., hotel room, and asked for Scottsboro, Alabama. I reached two wrong Carliles before asking to speak with the owner of the Carlile Restaurant.

"My name is Tom Hargrove," I said. No response. "I'm looking for an old army buddy named Carlile. We served together in Vietnam in 1969."

"I was in Nam back then. Who were you with?"

"Advisory Team 73, down in the Delta."

He paused. "Chuong Thien Province . . ."

"You were shot bad—five or six times—in September of 1969?"

"That's for sure."

"Then *you're* the Richard Carlile I'm trying to find. I was with you the day before you got hit. It took a full day to get you out. I thought you were dead for years . . . but then I couldn't find your name on the Wall at the Vietnam Memorial."

"That was a long time ago. What's your name again?"

He still couldn't remember me, but that was okay. Carlile was almost dead when he left Chuong Thien.

"It was on the Snake River." Carlile's memory then became remarkably clear.

"Yeah, we were airlifted into a double horseshoe ambush with a stripped-down RF company of fifty Cambodians from Kien Hung. I'd never been on an operation with that company, but what the hell, we were only after twenty-five VC. Our artillery could take care of them, even if that company couldn't.

"But what we ran into was beyond my wildest nightmare. Later, I learned that we'd hit five hundred VC in reinforced bunkers—but that was in the hospital in Can Tho."

"The team in Vi Thanh monitored the radio all that day," I said.

"A sniper got me first. I sank underwater in a rice paddy for more than a minute before the Cambodes pulled me out. My American sergeant went bananas, and VC fire knocked out my Prick-25 radio. So I crawled over the paddy dike to reach our one remaining radio, and called an air strike within one hundred meters of our position. That saved us. But the VC started shooting at me . . . hit me five more times before they gave me up as dead."

"You used the radio as a shield, but one AK round went through it, and into your head—that's what I remember."

"That was the last hit I took. The bullet deflected off the radio and lodged behind my left ear. I was unconscious for about sixty seconds. That wound affected my balance, but not my reasoning."

Richard Carlile told me more about his life, then and now. He'd taken an ROTC commission upon graduation from the University of Alabama, and had won two Bronze Stars by the time he was wounded. Carlile now owns a restaurant, half-interest in the local radio station, and real estate in the northeastern Alabama town of fifteen thousand. His wife Susan teaches math at Scottsboro High School, his daughter Mary Love teaches elementary school in Tuscaloosa, and his son Rob is a junior at Auburn University.

Maybe Carlile can clear up something that bothers me, I thought.

"I wrote that both you and Lieutenant Stephen Young were on MAT 54. But I also wrote about being with you at Duc Long. Was MAT 54 stationed there?"

"I was *never* with MAT 54. Lieutenant Young was the MAT 54 leader and was advising a unit that was airlifted north of the Snake River. I was operations officer with the Duc Long district advisory team, and was with the Cambodian unit that landed to the south. Both units had the same objective: to eliminate the VC, and converge on the Snake River."

I shifted the topic. "Do you remember when Donoway, Ard, and their interpreter were ambushed?" I asked. "Three weeks before Snake River."

"Yeah, the district senior adviser had gone on R & R, and left me in command," Carlile said. "I was acting DSA and was at a village meeting when I got word that Donoway had radio'd—in the clear—that he was coming to headquarters by sampan.

"I had my operations sergeant radio him to stay put—and to send any further messages by code. But Donoway and Ard had already left . . . we found their bodies tied to a wall along the Xa No Canal."

That shook me. "A *wall* . . . was it around a *cemetery*?" I thought, of course, about the Thanh Binh cemetery.

"I don't remember. But if you had seen what the VC had started to do to their bodies on that wall, you'd understand what happened next. I couldn't let it go. My ten-man Vietnamese intel squad, that I'd trained myself, and I tracked down the VC that sprang that ambush. We confirmed they were *the ones* and at dusk, ran a simple operation. It left the VC ambushers dead. We left fast and returned to Duc Long. The team was debriefed and told to keep the operation quiet.

"For me, there were only two ways to survive Vietnam: go nuts with worry, which I wasn't going to do, or play by the same animal rules the VC used. I opted for the latter."

"Richard, you suffered a lot. Would you do it again? The army, I mean, and Chuong Thien Province?"

Carlile reflected. "It infuriates me that we didn't go there to *win*, that politics held us back . . . and too many writers have stereotyped the Vietnamese troops as cowards. Not the militia that *I* trained and advised. They were *good folks*.

". . . but yeah, I'd probably be dumb enough to do it again."
"Why?"

"Family tradition, partly. I was lucky. I was born into a fairly successful family, went to college . . ."

Carlile was searching for words, so I said, "Maybe I know

how you feel. Damned few of the guys who fought there, Americans *or* Vietnamese, had any breaks."

"That's true, but there was something else," Carlile continued. "It was a feeling . . . a desire to try to correct a wrong. Other than that, I simply can't find words to explain it."

Carlile and I talked again a few days before I returned to Asia.

"Hearing your voice, and your stories, Tom . . . I'm beginning to remember you. Weren't you from Texas? Didn't you wear civilian clothes a lot?"

"Yeah, and I've wondered about that. Frank Gillespie wrote me an authorization to wear civvies. But would the VC have respected that piece of paper?"

"No. Besides, an officer out of uniform in a combat zone was *definitely* against the Geneva Convention," Carlile said. "But you didn't need to worry—if those bastards had captured you, *we'd* have gone in and brought you out."

"*You* wouldn't have, Richard—not after Snake River."

Richard Carlile paused, then said: "*I guess that's right.*"

I was to meet Frank Gillespie the afternoon of 20 August 1991 in Washington, D.C. He and Norm Olsen were the only men from Chuong Thien Province days with whom I'd kept contact over the years.

Frank's a complex man. In 1990, he'd written:

Reading about your second return to Vi Thanh pushed me back into those days. I guess that now means telling war stories. But before, the past meant not being able to watch "M*A*S*H," and trouble controlling emotions. I must have repressed a lot. I can't remember the name of a single U.S. killed or wounded in VN, except for John Paul Vann.

Frank now heads a division of USAID's Food for Peace program that distributes U.S. food, mostly grain, in Asia, the Near East, Eastern Europe, and North Africa. But he runs the program from the comfort of America's capital. That's hard for Frank, after a decade of dangerous living in Vietnam and Laos, followed by ten more fairly exotic years in Thailand and Indonesia.

In a 1988 letter, Frank described the day he decided it was time to leave Chuong Thien:

I usually travelled the rivers and canals alone, or with *Dai Uy* Hong. *Dai Uy* sometimes wore a straw hat and shawl, like an old woman, while I lay on the bottom of a sampan.

An ARVN soldier at some outpost handed me a ragged piece of paper—a cable that finally caught up with me—on one of those trips, on 3 Dec 70.

> CONGRATULATIONS ON BIRTH OF DAUGHTER.
> MOTHER AND CHILD WELL. BROWN.
> BANGKOK

Goodbye war. Get me a chopper to Can Tho, lay on a Volpar to SGN. Buy me a ticket to BKK. I was *there*, next afternoon.

Roslyn's birth changed me. I became more cautious, and decided not to return to VN after that tour. My future career would be based 80 percent on family considerations, 20 percent on job satisfaction. I've done that, but it's been frustrating.

Later. You started me recalling the past, which I hadn't wanted to do. Too much pain. I had a bad time dealing with this in 1981–82, and again in 1984 . . .

In 1990, Frank had written: "I applied to run a narcotics education program in Laos, but State Department doesn't want *tainted* USAID types from the old days."

"Where are your kids?" I asked after Frank and I shook hands in Washington in 1991, then lied about how neither of us had changed. Kids are a good starter.

"They're all looking East. Lisa's in Bali, with a company that manufactures clothes for export, and Roslyn teaches English in Taiwan. Russell is still in college in Los Angeles . . . for now."

"Asia must run in the blood," I said. It was true.

We discussed families and jobs, ambitions and frustrations for a couple of hours. But our talk was flat, artificial. We both knew it.

After a couple of drinks in the lounge of the Lombardy Hotel, we went to dinner.

"When will we spring Khang?" I asked. Frank was one of five Chuong Thien veterans trying to get our former Vietnamese interpreter into the Orderly Departure Program. But Frank could pull strings better than me. *He* sent appeals on U.S. State Department letterhead.

"Soon, maybe. Khang's brother Tien got out last year."

"Yeah, that surprised me, because Tien was with Operation Phoenix. I changed his name to *Truong* in my book, to protect him. And I *never* mentioned Tien by name in my letters."

Getting Khang out would help relieve Frank and me of at least one guilt trip. We both knew that, but didn't say it.

Discussing Khang finally triggered a shift in our conversation. It became *real* as the evening went on, because we drifted back to *unreal* days along the muddy Xa No Canal—to Monique and Ba Lien and IR8, to Harvey Weiner and Chauvin Wilkinson and Sgt. Bobby Howell, to the Delta Lily, our little bar.

And to Norm Olsen, of course. After all those years in Asia, fate and USAID drew our former boss to Africa. He and Betsy, and their children Mark and Lisa, had lived in Botswana, Cameroon, and were now in Uganda.

In 1989, Norm had written:

After almost 20 years in Africa, I compare us to modern-day mountain men. But we don't live in the Rockies and go down to St. Louis every couple of years; we live in Africa, then go to Washington D.C.

Mark and I sometimes discuss VN, particularly why, even with our overwhelming military superiority, the U.S. was unsuccessful. Mark has learned a bit about our old team through those talks.

I remember my Chuong Thien experience differently than you've written of yours. It was exciting and fulfilling. I'm generally pleased with my performance, but re-entry into the U.S. was difficult because of the indifference, even hostility, that one encountered.

I felt emotionally used up when my Vietnam tours ended, but I had no regrets. Nor do I now. *My* regret is that we could have won, but didn't.

The VN War has so many parallels with modern Africa, like: What level of intervention is appropriate? How do you deal with corruption? How can America help make sensible policy for such a vastly different and little-understood society?

We didn't have the answers then; we don't have them now.

You're on dubious grounds, I think, saying that the VN war was ultimately fought over rice. If rice were the main issue, we'd have won easily; rice yields increased at least 5% per year from the introduction of IRRI varieties in the mid-60s until the war ended.

In 1990, I wrote to Norm about inner conflicts.

Should I write the truth, as I saw it, or protect Vietnamese friends? Can I write about the war and its aftermath along with rice science and its promise? As an IRRI spokesman, I've always avoided politics. But this is *my* book, not IRRI's. Where do you draw those lines?

Norm responded:

Many of us faced similar emotional conflicts in VN. We supported a corrupt government, largely because the alternative looked far worse. Was it justified? What about the way we used force, particularly bombing? Problems in Chuong Thien were often solved by bombing isolated areas with few, if any, people. It clearly wasn't effective—in fact, it was often countereffective. But the organization demanded the bombing. It kept the generals happy, and did little overt harm. Of course, *in reality* the harm was great because, organizationally, we deluded ourselves into thinking that we were making progress.

You imply a clear lesson: avoid war in the future. I don't think it's so simple. I would raise some questions that—if answered correctly—might teach important lessons:

-Why didn't the U.S. military change how it fought the war when it became clear that we were ineffective, and that there were better methods?

-Corruption of the U.S. Army, i.e. Why did we allow inflation of *body counts*—VC casualty rates? Why did we tolerate incompetence and inefficiency? George Marshall would have fired 25% of our generals.

About the fighting spirit of "our" Vietnamese:

-Why didn't ARVN fight better? I always had a feeling that many ARVN officers felt they *really didn't deserve* to win. Also, that many corrupt officers and government officials wanted to prolong the war, to make more money.

In general, I have no quarrel with those Vietnamese who served, but many who should have been the leaders—the educated, the upper classes—opted out. Many are now in the USA.

Look at the current staffing of USAID. Many Vietnamese-Americans work for USAID, but I've never met one who served in a combat role in VN. Several managed to spend the war in training in the USA or Europe. It's less a matter of courage than of vastly different attitudes toward responsibility and commitment.

To me, this failure was the largest single reason why GVN lost.

Was VN the first U.S. war in which God was on the other side? I don't think so, but I suspect S/He was a bit disgusted with the way we fought and, perhaps, took a neutral stand.

From the VC perspective, if they fought for ideals . . . what happened to those ideals?

You may be disappointed in terms of lessons learned for future generations. In 1989 I gave a talk on VN to Mark's class at Stony Brook, a liberal Christian boarding school on Long Island. The students clearly believed that we had not applied enough power. "Nuke 'em"—that was their dominant reaction.

Norm also wrote about the inevitable fall of Communism:

From a strategic point of view, VN may not have been a total failure, although it was when viewed alone. But look at recent events [the crumbling of Communism]. As part of an overall containment policy, VN may have been a lost battle—yet the Pearl Harbor of an eventually victorious Cold War.

Talking about Norm brought up Tim Bertotti, a Mekong Delta buddy of both Frank and Norm, then my friend at IRRI two decades later. Tim is the most idealistic man, who's been at war, that I've ever known. He left IRRI in mid-1991, and is now director of administration for USAID in Indonesia. Tim had written:

Vietnam obsessed me, dominated my life during that time. I witnessed, felt, and manipulated the extremes of humanity: love and hate, good and evil, survival and death, hope and despair. Vietnam left me shaken, and marked indelibly for life.

I was there, in those lush and bloody Mekong Delta provinces. But *why* and for *what*? What happens to a man who believed in America, then saw that dream killed by greed and despair and too much death and too many coffins? It was set against a backdrop of anguish . . . the national pride that I saw America losing, the decline of our spirit and hope.

But as long as there are people without personal or political freedom, without food, shelter, health care—and deprived of hope—there must be men and women who pass by, and stop. They don't have to help, or even be emotionally stirred. They must stop and think. Ultimately, some will act. I think I did that.

I feel that we won the war, but let it slip. Yet I'd do it again.

"Frank, we weren't *honest* this afternoon," I said over after-dinner beers. "We shared a hell of a lot, so why did we waste such precious time?"

"I don't know. We should have started the evening talking about those days in Chuong Thien. We *knew* we'd end it that way."

"It was like we *denied* something . . . like we're ashamed to admit we once lived dangerous lives in a terrible place. *Even to ourselves. Why?* To prove that our lives are okay now? That we don't live in the past, that we've grown, matured?"

"Have we, really?" Frank asked.

I couldn't know, that evening, that I'd receive an unusual letter from Frank barely two months later. It was postmarked Vientiane, Laos:

I've just returned from a long road tour to the south, into the Champassack rice bowl, assessing the need for emergency food relief after the latest floods. I thought a lot of your returns to Vi Thanh.

I went back to Kengkok, where we'd lived 23 years ago. Mine was the last of three vehicles to arrive where a farmer was being interviewed. He said, "Good morning, Mr. Frank" in Lao as I walked up. The group was duly impressed.

I visited our former house, where the Pathet Lao once tried to kill my family and me. I had known the owner as a Lao Army officer, so I addressed him as "Major." He asked about Russell, Lisa, and Urai.

Whenever we discussed insects or diseases, Mr. Lathsanivong pointed out the pests in a pocket-sized IRRI book in Lao. I told him that my friend had published the book. He'd like more IRRI publications.

The book, of course, was *Field Problems of Tropical Rice*, published in twenty-four languages by 1991.

New York, 21 August 1991. The red message light on my hotel phone was blinking when I returned from my last dinner in the States for maybe a year. I was to return a call from Bud Shields in San Antonio. That surprised me.

The former captain and I had been good friends; he was the only other Texas Aggie in Chuong Thien Province. But Bud had never answered the letter I'd written after that first, anguished return to Vi Thanh in 1972. In 1988, I went through a network of friends to find his current address. That letter also went unanswered. I tried again in 1990, asking Bud to check what I'd written about him. He didn't answer. *Leave him alone*, I thought. *Bud wants to forget those days, and that's okay.*

But I realized that New York in 1991 might be my last chance to contact Bud Shields before the book went to press. I had called before going to dinner, and left a message on his answering machine.

Bud's voice was gentle, when we finally talked. At first, he was embarrassed about not answering my letters. Then he spoke openly about his life, now and then.

Shields, a supply dealer for Western Auto, is studying to become a Catholic deacon. His wife died soon after Vietnam. That must have been tough. He remarried, and is father of four children. Bud explained, "I stayed in the army for nine years, and felt okay about Chuong Thien until I got out. Maybe I used the army as a support group.

"But it started hitting in civilian life, and I avoided anything that reminded me of Vietnam—the movies, the books. Then one day I went to see *Platoon* . . . I don't know why. It was a terrible experience, and I cried. I wanted counsel, but couldn't find it. But it's okay now . . . most of the time."

Bud didn't want—yet *wanted*—to talk about Chuong Thien. Like the day that Frank and Khang and I arrived by sampan at Kien Hung District headquarters, and were welcomed by Bud's shaken advisory team. Thirty minutes earlier, the VC had floated a sampan carrying a U.S. five hundred-pound bomb, timed to blow the team away, down the canal. But the sampan tilted, the bomb rolled into the canal, and exploded underwater. The blast threw a water column three hundred feet high. Coming down, that water knocked half of the sheet-iron roof off the team hut.

I told Bud about finding Richard Carlile. Like me, he'd assumed that Carlile was dead.

"I moved a company of Cambodian troops into position that day, to hit the VC from the rear and get those trapped men out . . . but the Colonel wouldn't order an attack. I don't know why."

"What do you remember best about that year in Chuong Thien?" I asked.

"Some incredible things . . . like the day I took a platoon of Cambodes from the 434th RF Company to salvage a U.S. Navy PBR—patrol boat, river—that a Skycrane chopper had dropped into a rice paddy. The Skycrane was taking the PBR up north for repair when, somehow, it slipped from the sling at about ten thousand feet. We went in by chopper, and found the motor driven through the boat's bottom, five or six feet deep in the mud. We wouldn't leave anything for the VC . . . not if we could help it. So I called an air strike on that U.S. Navy PBR. Who'd believe a story like that?"

"I would, Bud. *I* was on the TOC end of the radio in Vi Thanh that day. The Skycrane reported the boat swarming with black and blue uniforms. We called a Huey gunship, and it reported eight KBAs. *I* paralleled your request for the air strike. The Phantom pilot who bombed the PBR reported, 'U.S. Air Force reports sinking a U.S. Navy ship in a rice paddy.' "

I remember that day so well, and even wrote about it in my diary, I thought. So why didn't I write it into the book?

Before hanging up, I asked Bud *that question*:

"*Yes*, I'd do it again." Bud said. "I wouldn't trade the experience of trying to help the Vietnamese improve their lives, and preserve some form of dignity and democracy, for anything."

Back in Los Baños in September, I found a copy of the letter I'd written to Bud Shields from Saigon in 1972, the letter I'd described in chapter 23.

That letter drew back clear memories of Chuong Thien Province's horrible casualties, Colonel Phiep's death, and my black despair after leaving Vi Thanh again.

But one sentence intrigued me: "When this VN tour ends, we may move to South America. The International Center for Tropical Agriculture—called CIAT, its Spanish acronym—has contacted me about a job."

As a young man, I'd dreamed of living in South America, but fate and Vietnam drew me into Asia. I'd almost forgotten about my 1972 flirtation with CIAT.

You see, during the summer of 1991 I'd also flown from Texas to Colombia to interview . . . at CIAT.

CIAT is a sister International Agricultural Research Center, established in 1967 and one of eighteen Centers (five were added after I wrote earlier chapters of this book) funded through the Consultative Group on International Agricultural Research.

I found CIAT a lot like IRRI; her experiment farm and modern white laboratories are the same, but with a Spanish flavor. So is the staff's idealism and work ethic.

CIAT scientists seek to increase farm production of four crops that feed most of Latin America, and much of the developing world: beans, cassava, tropical forages for livestock, and rice in Latin America (IRRI works through CIAT in the Western Hemisphere).

CIAT is taking a brave course toward sustaining the environment while raising food production. She's redirecting programs, and research funds, to tailor sustainable agricultural systems for farmers in three ecosystems: at the edge of rain forests, to prevent further deforestation; on the deforested hillsides and mountains; and on the vast and unused grassy savannas that cover an area four times the size of France with their highly acid and infertile soils. All of CIAT's work is in cooperation with national scientists.

I'd been in Asia, and at IRRI, for most of my adult life. It was time for a change. Especially now that the book was, essentially, finished.

On 19 September 1991, I accepted CIAT's offer to head its communication program.

But leaving IRRI, after nineteen years, was hard. Rice saved my life twenty-two years before, then became my life. I'd led the world's finest science communication unit for a dozen years, and it focuses on rice.

The hardest part was telling my staff of forty-nine, almost all Filipinos. I'd hired forty-seven of them.

Someday, I'll probably boast to grandchildren. If so, my greatest pride may be of my role in the development and spread of the new rice technology that fed almost one of every seven persons on earth by 1991.

How many men or women can make such a claim? I'll always be grateful to IRRI, to rice . . . and in a strange way, to Vietnam . . . for giving me that.

And Susan? She said, a few years ago, that we'd leave Asia and start a new life—when I finish the book.

That made me think. After two decades of Chuong Thien's legacy, *Susan* is also a veteran, like Frank Gillespie and Joe Ona and Rob Briggs. I *must* ask how *she* feels, even though I dread her answer. So I edited, for my wife, the letter I sent to men like Richard Carlile.

She surprised me by handing over two sheets of computer paper at noon the next day. Susan's response seemed addressed to herself, more than to me:

Would I do it again? **No.** Women don't seem to need the experience of war—perhaps childbirth is our battle. Besides, I had already seen enough of war, or its aftermath, in the Philippines and the Middle East by the time Vietnam came around. Rubble, refugee camps, broken families, fatherless children . . . those weren't just something I had read about or watched on TV.

When I was a child in the Philippines, a country still devastated by World War II, a French sailor gave me his cap (highly coveted because of its pom-pom). He asked me to wish him luck because he was on his way to fight a war in Indo-China.

Years later, in the Philippines as an adult, I sat in a restaurant and heard government officials at the next table discuss what to do with the shiploads of Vietnamese refugees floating around Manila Bay. Suddenly the ancient Greeks' thirty year war seemed less bizarre.

But someone *should* write a book about the "waiting wives" of the Vietnam War. I'm only concerned that it might be a boring, whining litany of cruelty, loneliness, and benign neglect. Especially if the wife waited, like Linda Lanning, my very pregnant housemate, and me in the anti-war San Francisco of 1969–70.

Memories ... the San Francisco Red Cross not wanting us as USO or Army hospital volunteers. "Waiting wives often get personally involved—and that interferes with being good workers."

... not being allowed to dine at the Presidio Officers Club because "We don't want the problem of waiting wives hanging around the bar." Thoughts of an Army directive that we'd lose our housing allowance if we moved in with parents.

Memories ... Thanksgiving dinner at a friend's home in the country. Another guest asked Linda if her husband enjoyed killing Vietnamese children. That guest designed fireproof fabric for airliner seats. *I think of you every time I fly.*

Hargrove, then return unscathed to play waiting wife among my friends in San Francisco. Many friendships were lost. And yes, now I care because some were from childhood, and I miss the opportunities of reunion in my middle years. Too much was said, or unsaid, to be comfortable. But I think I'd still marry Tom, even knowing how Vietnam would affect our lives.

Memories ... of forcing myself to continue walking up the hill as I watched two Army officers leave an official Army car and wait at the door of our SF flat. *Two officers in dress green uniform. That means a death notice. Is it Tom ... or Lee?*

Neither. One of the officers had seen me on the sidewalk, and thought I was an old girlfriend. At work, I tried to explain what had happened. "You should expect that," my coworker said, "if you married a man who'd go to Vietnam." She was right, of course.

Memories of waiting and watching for that plane at the Ft. De Russey R&R Center in Honolulu. It was 12 hours late—but the Army would extend our five days of R&R only if the flight were delayed by *17* hours. The kindness and enthusiasm of those amazing people who ran the Aloha R&R Center never flagged as planeloads of soldiers arrived. Memories of wives, fiancées, mothers and fathers whose soldiers didn't get off those planes . . . being quickly patted into offices. "I'll bet he was buying you a gift, and missed the plane," they assured. "Don't worry, we'll track him down and he'll be here tomorrow." There will be a special place in my heart, forever, for you wonderful R&R people.

Susan was the most cynical of all, so her next thoughts really threw me.

Would I do it again? **Perhaps.** Had I not, what would Tom and I have argued about over the years? And I'd have missed those strange post-Vietnam *coincidences* that couldn't happen . . . yet I was there, and witnessed so many as my husband went deeper into Vietnam, finishing the book. It's true that Tom forgot writing those damned diaries. Finding Arnovitz's friends by his name at the Vietnam Memorial was almost too much . . . then that awful cemetery north of Vi Thanh . . . then later, learning that Jimmy Hargrove was killed outside that same miserable village.

There's no reasonable explanation, but those things happened.

Without Vietnam, I'd have missed reading those letters from men who served in Chuong Thien. I've never met Harvey Weiner, but he's my favorite. *His* memories are unfogged by sentiment.

I'd have missed that 1990 trip to Chuong Thien Province. No one can top *my* cocktail party story of "the worst place I've ever visited." I'd have missed the sick look on Tom's and Lynn's faces when the People's Committee asked how I rated Vi Thanh's tourist facilities. I let a long minute go by before simply asking why no females served on the People's Committee. "The people elect Committee members," was the answer. "Unfortunately, the people don't vote for women."

Would I do it again? **Yes.** But if I could go back in time, I'd *also* join the Army, and volunteer for logistics.

All veterans have horror stories about screwups: "They sent my shot records to Ethiopia, my pay records to

Cebu . . ." ". . . 10,000 pairs of snow shoes airfreighted to Da Nang."

But those men and women, in the infantile days of computers, moved men and material remarkably well. They'd have taught me a lot.

Perhaps with that experience, I could even organize our move from Asia to South America without the anguish I now feel.

I guess Susan's letter *really* closes the book. But it was one of my most unsettling experiences. For Susan to look at Vietnam rationally—that's almost like Chuong Thien Province mellowing. Maybe she has. Maybe we've *all* mellowed.

But *A dragon lives forever* . . .

Postscript

I was in Washington, D.C., on 29 October 1992, helping raise support for the International Agricultural Research Centers. But this time, I represented CIAT, the International Center for Tropical Agriculture, not IRRI. And I was working out of South America, not Asia.

When I returned to the Guest Quarters Hotel that evening, a receptionist handed me a fax from Columbia:

CIAT received a call from a Mr. Kenz (spelling?; no one could understand him). The man sounded Oriental, and had just arrived from somewhere. He wants you to call him in Boston. Number is . . .

It's probably some Asian journalist who wants to reestablish contact, I thought. The poor guy . . . he probably speaks terrible English, then he calls CIAT where most people speak only Spanish.

But when I called, I knew I'd reached a Vietnamese home.

It was Nguyen An Khang, my interpreter during Chuong Thien days, who had used the name Nguyen Huu An since April, 1975. *He was out!* Along with his wife and four children. The family had reached the home of Tien, Khang's brother in Boston who had escaped earlier. I'd referred to Tien as *Truong* in this book, for his own protection while he was still in Vietnam.

To Those Who Helped

An author is probably the last person who can write fitly of his own work. . . . Though authors are touchy about their productions and inclined to resent unfavourable criticism they are seldom self-satisfied. They are conscious of how far the work . . . comes short of their conception, and when they consider it are much more vexed with their failure to express this in its completeness than pleased with the passages . . . that they can regard with complacency. Their aim is perfection and they are wretchedly aware that they have not attained it.

—W. Somerset Maugham, Foreword, *Of Human Bondage*

This book is mostly factual, built from memory, letters, and a diary that I never wrote. Parts of the book are fiction, from a novel I didn't finish. Both fact and fiction stem from swamps and rice fields, canals, rivers, and villages of the former Chuong Thien Province of the Republic of South Vietnam.

And from the people who served in Chuong Thien. I invented the names of most fictional characters. A few events are entirely fiction.

In the *nonfiction*, I have changed the names of some men and women, especially Vietnamese who served in Chuong Thien. My reasons are obvious . . . to protect former allies who fought for South Vietnam, then were trapped in that tragic country.

I have edited portions of my Vietnam diary, and letters from Chuong Thien veterans, for clarity. But no events have been added, or changed.

466

I owe special thanks to many friends. First, to Owen Lock for offering to *help* me, through a contract to write this book—and insisting that it be nonfiction. It is. To me, even the fiction is, really, nonfiction—because that's how I first tried to explain, honestly, about Chuong Thien Province.

Lee Lanning introduced the book to Owen. He later offered sound advice when I didn't want to send out early drafts for review: "That doesn't make sense, Tom. You *write* so others will know your story. If your writing is screwed up, you should hope that thousands of readers will recognize it—by buying your book." I sent the first review copy to Lee. Incidentally, I was Lanning's first editor, two decades ago, on the Texas A&M *Agriculturist* (the student magazine of the College of Agriculture).

An unexpected query from Bruce McAllister on the role that rice played in the Vietnam War, to use in *Dream Baby*, triggered a complicated process of review, advice, and encouragement that, eventually, influenced both our books. We've still not met but we will, someday—*if it's programmed*.

Without the friendship and influence of Dr. Vo Tong Xuan, I could never have returned to Chuong Thien Province in 1988. That made it possible for Dr. To Phuc Tuong to take Lynn Johnson, Susan Hargrove, and me back to Vi Thanh for *National Geographic* in 1990. Both Xuan and Tuong are brave and nonpolitical patriots who stayed in Vietnam after 1975 to help rebuild their country. Nothing I have written about past or present political regimes reflects their opinions.

Susan Hargrove opposed and hated the war, yet stood by me when I went and—probably tougher—when I returned. She later lived with me in Asia for nineteen years, and tolerated my writing this book. Susan remains not only my wife, but also my best friend, even after I took her to Vi Thanh.

When I came home in 1970, only my mother knew, instinctively, that writing was a powerful catharsis. She believed in this book but died, after fighting cancer for almost four years, a few months before its publication. But over 20 years, she had read and edited almost all of its text, both fiction and nonfiction.

Friends who read, critiqued, and edited the manuscript include: Bill Smith, Tim Bertotti, Steve Banta, George Krajcsik, and Gloria Argosino, all of the International Rice Research Institute (IRRI); and Elizabeth McAdam de Páiz of the Interna-

tional Center for Tropical Agriculture (CIAT). Santy Culala of
IRRI kept my files and correspondence straight.

I owe a special debt of gratitude to pioneer scientists of the
International Rice Research Institute, and cooperating researchers in Vietnam. Without the improved rice seeds and technology that they developed, I might have died in Chuong Thien.
More important, millions across Asia, Africa, and Latin America would certainly have died during the projected "Time of
Famines" of the 1970s.

I thank other Chuong Thien veterans who shared their expe-
riences, and their feelings about it today: Rob Briggs, Richard
Carlile, Frank Gillespie, Bobby Howell, Norm Olsen, José
Ona, Bud Shields, Harvey Weiner, and Chauvin Wilkinson.

Should I also thank the tens of thousands of men and
women who fought and died for the *wrong* side—to me, that
means *both sides*—because they thought it was right, or had no
choice? They certainly never *wanted* to be in the book.

Yes, because there'd be no book without them.

So . . . to brave, misguided, and haunted men and women.
Together, Vietnamese and American, we made Chuong Thien
Province a killing field.

But maybe all who share the Vietnam experience can, someday, relate to the quote that gave Lee Lanning's *Battles of
Peace* its name:

> War after all's but a flash in the pan,
> It's the battles of peace that makes the man.
> —Harry de Halsalle

I thank you all, the living and, especially, the dead. Because
Dragons live forever.

Tom Hargrove
Cali, Colombia
July 1993

Glossary

Agent Orange	The code name for the herbicide used to defoliate land and deny the VC cover. Agent Orange was actually 2,4-D or 2,4,5-T. It was later found to carry traces of dioxin, a highly toxic by-product.
Ao dai	The traditional Vietnamese dress, high-necked but formfitted, with long sleeves. At the waist, two panels fall front and back over trousers.
ARVN	Army of the Republic of Vietnam.
AW	Automatic weapon, or machine gun.
Baxide	Homemade rice whiskey.
Bonze	A Cambodian monk.
BOQ	Bachelor officers quarters.
Charley	Viet Cong.
Chieu Hoi	The GVN program to persuade VC to defect.
CIA	Central Intelligence Agency.
CIMMYT	The International Maize and Wheat Improvement Center, based in Mexico.
CORDS	Civil Operations/Revolutionary Development Support, the joint U.S. military/civilian agency responsible for the pacification program.
DEROS	Date of expected rotation from overseas.
DIA	The U.S. Defense Intelligence Agency.
DMZ	The demilitarized zone that separated North and South Vietnam.
Dong	The official currency of Vietnam, North and South, since 1975.

DSA	District senior adviser, the senior U.S. adviser in a district. The DSA could be military or civilian, depending on security. All DSAs in Chuong Thien Province were U.S. Army officers.
Dustoff	The radio code for a medical evacuation by helicopter when the patient was an American (also see "Medevac").
EM	Enlisted man.
ETS	Estimated termination of service.
FAC	Forward air controller.
GVN	Government of Vietnam.
Hamlets, villages, districts, and provinces	From four to eight hamlets comprised a village; ten to twenty villages, a district. Five districts comprised Chuong Thien Province: Duc Long, Long My, Kien Hung, Kien Thien, and Kien Long (see map).
HES	Hamlet evaluation survey, a monthly security rating of each province, district, and village, compiled by the military, the CIA, and USAID.
H & I	Harassment and interdiction artillery fire.
Hoi chanh	A VC defector.
Huey	A UH-1, the "workhorse" helicopter in Vietnam, manufactured by Bell Aircraft.
IRRI	International Rice Research Institute, Philippines.
IVS	International Voluntary Services.
Jars	Slang for U.S. Marines.
KBA	Killed by air.
KIA	Killed in action.
Klick	Kilometer.
Land to the Tiller	GVN's land reform program to redistribute former French and Chinese plantations to peasant farmers.
Langley	CIA (based in Langley, Virginia).
LOH	Light observation helicopter.
LZ	Landing zone.
MAC-V	Military Assistance Command-Vietnam, the U.S. military advisory group.
MAT	U.S. Mobile Advisory Team.

Mat Trang	Vietnamese for "the Front," or the Communist National Liberation Front. Americans referred to it as the Viet Cong.
Medevac	A medical evacuation by helicopter. In radio transmissions, the code "Medevac" meant the patient was Vietnamese ("*Dustoff*" meant he was American).
MG	Machine gun.
MIA	Missing in action.
NLF	National Liberation Front, the official name of the Viet Cong.
Nungs	Ethnic Chinese mercenary soldiers who fought for South Vietnam. Most *Nungs* were, ultimately, on the CIA payroll and were more loyal to the USA than to GVN. *Nungs* sometimes accompanied U.S. Special Forces on clandestine missions, and guarded OSA compounds.
Nuoc mam	A Vietnamese sauce made from fermented fish.
NVA	North Vietnamese Army.
NVN	North Vietnam.
OCS	Officers Candidate School.
Ong	"Mr." in Vietnamese.
Operation RANCH HAND	The program through which the U.S. Air Force and Army defoliated contested areas with Agent Orange.
OSA	Office of the Special Assistant to the Ambassador, the term for CIA in Vietnam. The OSA headquarters in each province was often called *"The Embassy House."*
People's Self-Defense Force, or PSDF	Local, unpaid militia organized to defend hamlets and villages from the Viet Cong.
PF	Popular Forces, village-level militia.
Phoenix Program	The GVN program, with CIA backing, to neutralize the Viet Cong Infrastructure, preferably through defection but sometimes by assassination. Called *Phuong Hoang* in Vietnamese.
Pi	Piasters, the basic Vietnamese currency.
PIO	Public information officer, the military officers in charge of press relations.
POW	Prisoner of war.
PRUs	Provincial reconnaissance units, strike forces of Viet Cong defectors that targeted Viet Cong Infrastructure.

PSA, Deputy PSA	Province senior adviser, the U.S. "counterpart" to the Vietnamese province chief. If the PSA were military, the deputy PSA was civilian, or vice versa. In Chuong Thien, the PSA was always military.
PsyOps	Psychological operations, the U.S. or Vietnamese units responsible for propaganda; often called *"psywar."*
RD	Revolutionary Development cadre, a paramilitary force of Vietnamese organized to "pacify" contested villages.
RF	Regional Forces, or provincial militia.
Roger	"I understand," in radio communication.
Roger that	"That's for sure."
Rotcie	An officer who received his commission through ROTC, or the Reserve Officers Training Course, at a U.S. university.
SAM	Surface-to-air missile.
TOC	Tactical operations center.
Top	First sergeant.
USAID	U.S. Agency for International Development.
VC	Viet Cong, from the Vietnamese words for "Vietnamese Communist"
VCI	Viet Cong Infrastructure, the Communist political leaders.
Victor Charley	Radio abbreviation of VC.
WIA	Wounded in action.
XO	Executive officer, or second in command.